Dubai & Abu Dhabi

"All you've got to do is decide to go and the hardest part is over.

So go!"

TONY WHEELER, COFOUNDER – LONELY PLANET

Andrea Schulte-Peevers, Kevin Raub

Contents

Plan Your Trip 4

Explore Dubai & Abu Dhabi 46

Understand Dubai & Abu Dhabi 193

Survival Guide 215

Dubai Maps 241

(left) **Spice Souq, Deira p53** Local spices are on sale at this working souq.

(above) **Emirates Palace, Abu Dhabi p135** A cultural hub of the city.

(right) **Gold Souq, Deira p52** A dazzling display of gold.

Dubai Marina & Palm Jumeirah p111

Jumeirah p95

Downtown Dubai & Business Bay p79

Bur Dubai p64

Deira p50

Welcome to Dubai & Abu Dhabi

Dubai and Abu Dhabi are a stirring alchemy of profound traditions and ambitious futuristic vision wrapped into starkly evocative desert splendour.

Cultural Dynamism

With Emiratis making up only a fraction of the population, Dubai and Abu Dhabi are bustling microcosms peacefully shared by cultures from all corners of the world. This diversity expresses itself in the culinary landscape, fashion, music and performance. Although rooted in Islamic tradition, this is an open society where it's easy for newcomers and visitors to connect with myriad experiences, be it eating like a Bedouin, dancing on the beach, shopping for local art or riding a camel in the desert. Dubai and Abu Dhabi are both fertile environments conducive to breaking down cultural barriers and preconceptions.

Shopping Haven

Shopping is a leisure activity in both Dubai and Abu Dhabi and malls here are much more than just mere collections of shops. Some look like an Italian palazzo or a Persian palace and lure visitors with surreal attractions such as an indoor ski slope or a giant aquarium. Traditional souqs, too, are beehives of activity humming with timeless bargaining banter. Meanwhile, in Dubai a new crop of urban-style outdoor malls has expanded the shopping spectrum yet again.

Innovation

It's hard not to admire Dubai and Abu Dhabi for their indefatigable verve, ambition and ability to dream up and realise projects. Dubai especially is a superlative-craving society that has birthed audaciously high buildings and palm-shaped islands. Sci-fi concepts such as flying taxis, a lightning-fast hyperloop train and an army of robocops are all reflections of a mindset that fearlessly embraces the future. And with many more grand projects in the pipeline for World Expo 2020, it's clear that Dubai is a city firmly in charge of writing its own narrative.

Nocturnal Action

After dark, Dubai sometimes seems like a city filled with lotus eaters, forever on the lookout for a good time. Its shape-shifting party spectrum caters for just about every taste, budget and age group. From flashy dance temples, sleek rooftop terraces and sizzling beach clubs to fancy cocktail caverns and concerts under the stars, Dubai delivers hot-stepping odysseys. Most of the nightlife centres on the fancy hotels, but there's no shortage of more wholesome diversions either, including shisha lounges, community theatre, live-music venues and the sparkling new Dubai Opera.

GABLE DENIMS / 500PX ©

Why I Love Dubai & Abu Dhabi

By Andrea Schulte-Peevers, Writer

Ever since first setting foot in Dubai back in 2007, this tiny powerhouse emirate and its big brother Abu Dhabi have fascinated me with their energy, optimism and openness towards people from all over the world. I'm a die-hard foodie, so the staggering variety of authentic global fare is exhilarating, and even shopping – which I normally consider a chore – is actually a joy here. Dubai and Abu Dhabi are both constantly in flux and it's been exciting to see them grow and mature as cities and as a society. I can't wait to see what the future holds.

For more about our writers, see p264

Sheikh Zayed Grand Mosque (p127), Abu Dhabi

Dubai & Abu Dhabi's Top 10

1

Burj Khalifa *(p81)*

1 Slicing through the slipstream of the sky's superhighways, there is no more potent a symbol of Dubai's aspiration to position itself as a major global player than its phalanx of futuristic skyscrapers. Above them all looms the Burj Khalifa, shaped like a deep-space rocket and at 828m the world's tallest building. Clad in 28,000 glass panels, it also lays claim to several more superlatives, including the highest outdoor observation deck, the most floors, the highest occupied floor and a lift (elevator) with the longest travel distance.

Downtown Dubai & Business Bay

Sheikh Zayed Grand Mosque *(p127)*

2 Abu Dhabi's snow-white landmark mosque was conceived by Sheikh Zayed, the country's 'founding father'. It has truly impressive dimensions with 80 marble domes held aloft by 1000 pillars and space for 50,000 worshippers. Open to non-Muslims, the main prayer hall is a visual extravaganza drenched in gold leaf and boasting massive crystal chandeliers, the world's largest handwoven carpet and pillars adorned with intricate semiprecious stones and floral marble inlays.

Abu Dhabi

UMAR SHARIFF / SHUTTERSTOCK ©

2

SANCHAI KUMAR / SHUTTERSTOCK ©

4

5

Louvre Abu Dhabi *(p156)*

3 The much anticipated, Jean Nouvel–designed Louvre Abu Dhabi finally opened to great fanfare in late 2017. Sunlight filters through its huge perforated dome onto a cluster of 23 galleries sheltering 600 priceless works that illustrate our shared humanity across time, ethnicity and geography. Highlights include a Da Vinci painting, a Chinese Buddha and a bronze statue from Benin. The dome pays homage to desert-palm shading – its geometric openings represent the interlaced palm leaves used in traditional roofing – and creates a cinematic 'rain of light' as the sun's rays pass throughout the day.

Abu Dhabi

Shopping *(p37)*

4 Shopping malls represent an integral part of the culture and lifestyle in Dubai and Abu Dhabi. Not merely places for maxing out your credit cards on fashion, electronics or gourmet foods, malls are also where locals go to socialise in cafes and restaurants, to catch a movie in a state-of-the-art multiplex or to get adrenaline kicks in an indoor theme park or game arcade. The best and biggest of the bunch is Dubai Mall, which features not only 1200 shops but also a giant aquarium, an indoor ice rink and a genuine dinosaur skeleton. DUBAI MALL (P82)

Shopping

Exotic Souqs *(p52)*

5 For a dose of *Arabian Nights* flair, head to Dubai's historic core and plunge headlong into its charmingly chaotic warren of souqs. There are sections for spices and perfume, but the headliner is the dazzling Gold Souq. Even if you don't have a thing for bling, a walk through here will feel like you've entered a giant Aladdin's Cave. It's fun to just watch the action, especially in the evening. If you're buying, sharpen your haggling skills no matter whether shopping for teensy earrings, an engagement ring or a dowry-worthy necklace.
SPICE SOUK (P53)

Deira

Al Fahidi Historic District *(p67)*

6 Wandering around this restored heritage area in Bur Dubai provides a tangible sense of historic Middle Eastern architecture and culture. Low-lying traditional courtyard buildings flank this quiet labyrinth of lanes, many of them featuring arabesque windows, decorative gypsum screens and wind towers. Some contain craft shops, small heritage museums, art galleries, artsy guesthouses or cafes serving local fare, including Arabic breakfasts and camel milk smoothies. The Sheikh Mohammed Centre for Cultural Understanding leads guided tours of the quarter.

Bur Dubai

Burj Al Arab *(p97)*

7 This landmark luxe hotel, with its dramatic design that mimics the billowing sail of a ship, floats on its own artifical island and has become the iconic symbol of Dubai's boom years. The interior is all about impact, drama and unapologetic bling, with dancing fountains, gold fittings, shiny marble and whirlpool baths your butler can fill with champagne if you so wish. If a stay exceeds your budget, you can still partake in the opulence by making reservations for cocktails, afternoon tea or dinner in the underwater restaurant.

Jumeirah

6

Dubai Museum *(p66)*

8 Housed in Bur Dubai's Al Fahidi Fort, the city's oldest surviving structure, this museum provides a well-laid-out introduction to the history of Dubai. Marvel at the turbo-evolution of this city from simple desert settlement to futuristic metropolis in just a third of a century. Dioramas recreate traditional scenes in a souq, at home and in the mosque, while other galleries focus on life at sea and in the desert. An archaeological exhibition illustrates the ancient history of the region with a display of items unearthed during excavations at local digs.

Bur Dubai

IMG Worlds of Adventure *(p91)*

9 In 2016, Dubai added four theme parks to its stable of attractions, including IMG Worlds of Adventure, the world's largest indoor theme park. Daredevils can join the Avengers in battling the evil Ultron, get pummelled by Thor in a lunch-losing top-spin ride, pose for selfies with a walking dinosaur and feel like a cannonball when going from zero to 100 in 2.5 seconds on the Velociraptor coaster. Little kids, meanwhile, will be enchanted by Ben 10, Gumball and the Powerpuff Girls in the Cartoon Network wing.

Downtown Dubai & Business Bay

Emirates Palace *(p135)*

10 One of the most expensive hotels ever built, Emirates Palace allegedly came at a price tag of a cool US$3.5 billion. Surrounded by carefully manicured fountain-laden gardens, it has its own marina, helipad and 1.3km-long sandy beach. The interior is an opulent feast decked out in marble, gold and mother of pearl, hundreds of palm trees and 1000 Swarovski crystal chandeliers. The exterior looks especially magical when illuminated at night.

Abu Dhabi

What's New

Dubai Frame

Shaped like a giant picture frame, this new viewpoint puts Dubai's past, present and future into perspective. (p69)

Dubai Canal

November 2016 saw the completion of the Dubai Canal that links Dubai Creek with the Gulf. (p101)

Dubai Parks & Resorts

Halfway to Abu Dhabi, this complex comprises four theme parks: movie-themed Motiongate and Bollywood Parks, plus Legoland and the Legoland Water Park. (p124)

IMG Worlds of Adventure

The world's largest indoor theme park has everything from kid's rides to walking dinosaurs, epic motion rides and an ultra-fast roller coaster. (p91)

Etihad Museum

In a striking structure, this insightful museum tells the story of the founding of the UAE in 1971. (p99)

City Walk

This new residential and entertainment district also harbours a gaming amusement park and an indoor rainforest. (p107)

Dubai Design District

This hub for creatives lures visitors with edgy architecture, public art, galleries, shops, cafes and cultural events. (p92)

Street Art

Dubai goes urban with commissioned street art popping up all over. Look for the Dubai Street Museum on 2nd December St in Satwa and for Dubai Walls at City Walk. (p102, p100)

Saruq Al Hadid Archaeology Museum

Part of the Shindagha Historic District, which is undergoing refurbishment, this new museum showcases Iron Age findings excavated in the desert sands south of Dubai. (p69)

Dubai Opera

The city's newest cultural venue at the foot of the Burj Khalifa presents musicals, concerts, comedy nights and, of course, opera. (p93)

Value-Added Tax (VAT)

VAT of 5% went into effect in the UAE as of January 2018.

Louvre Abu Dhabi

This archipelago of galleries lidded by a parasol-shaped roof showcases blue-chip pieces from around the globe and through the millennia. (p156)

Wahat Al Karama

Translating as 'oasis of dignity', this memorial honors Emirati soldiers and other UAE citizens who died in the service of their country. (p153)

Umm Al Emarat Park

Updated community park brims with such attractions as an animal barn and a lavish greenhouse with views. (p152)

For more recommendations and reviews, see **lonelyplanet.com/united-arab-emirates**

Need to Know

For more information, see Survival Guide (p215)

Currency
Dirham (Dhs)

Language
Arabic, English, Urdu

Visas
Citizens of 49 countries, including all EU countries, the US, the UK, Canada and Australia, are eligible for free 30-day single-entry visas on arrival in Dubai and Abu Dhabi.

Money
ATMs are widely available. Credit cards are accepted in most hotels, restaurants and shops.

Mobile Phones
Mobile phones operate on GSM900/1800, the same as Europe, Asia and Australia. Local SIM cards are easy to find in electronics shops and many grocery stores.

Time
Dubai and Abu Dhabi are four hours ahead of GMT/UTC. The time does not change in summer.

Tourist Information
Dubai Department of Tourism & Commerce Marketing (☎call centre 600 555 559; www.visitdubai.com) Has a comprehensive website and a call centre

Abu Dhabi Tourism & Culture Authority (☎02 599 5135; www.visitabudhabi.ae) Information desks at the airport, Ferrari World and World Trade Center Souk.

Daily Costs

Budget: Less than Dhs600
- Budget hotel room: Dhs300–400
- Meal in a food court: Dhs20–50
- Public transport: Dhs1–8.50
- Happy-hour beer: Dhs20

Midrange: Dhs600–1200
- Double room in a hotel: Dhs400–700
- Two-course meal in a restaurant: from Dhs80 without alcohol
- Entry to top attractions and sights: Dhs100–200

Top end: More than Dhs1200
- Four-star hotel room: from Dhs800
- Three-course fine-dining meal with wine: from Dhs400
- Drinks in a high-end bar: from Dhs100

Advance Planning

Three months or more before Double-check visa regulations. Book tickets for high-profile sporting and entertainment events.

One month before Reserve a table at top restaurants, tickets for Burj Khalifa and golf tee-times. Check concert venue websites for what's on during your stay.

One week before Check average daytime temperatures and pack accordingly.

Useful Websites

Lonely Planet (www.lonelyplanet.com/dubai) Destination information, hotel bookings, traveller forum and more.

Dubai Tourism (www.visitdubai.com) Dubai's official tourism site.

Visit Abu Dhabi (www.visitabudhabi.ae) Excellent official visitor website for travel planning and tourism.

Time Out Dubai (www.timeoutdubai.com) Online version of weekly entertainment and lifestyle magazine.

FooDiva (www.foodiva.net) Great restaurant reviews by a local foodie.

RTA (www.rta.ae) Public transport information and trip planning for Dubai.

WHEN TO GO

The best period is November to March, when temperatures are in the low 30°Cs. From June to September, temperatures average 43°C, with 95% humidity.

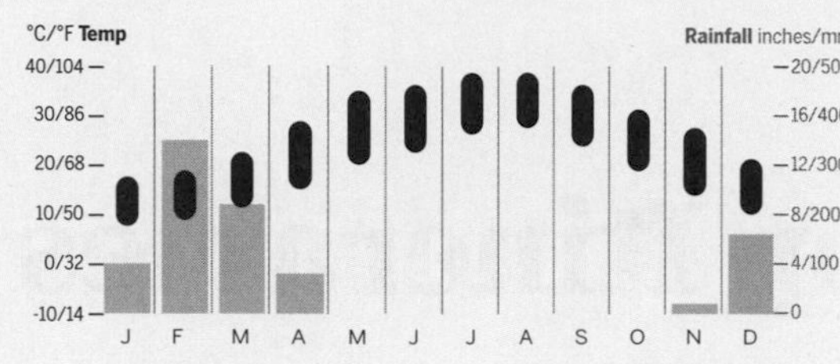

Arriving in Dubai & Abu Dhabi

Dubai International Airport The Dubai Metro's Red Line stops at terminals 1 and 3 and runs every few minutes between 6am and midnight. Buses take over in the interim. You need a Nol card before boarding. Taxis have a flag fall of Dhs25. Expect to pay about Dhs50 to Deira and Dhs80 to Downtown Dubai from the airport. Some hotels offer airport transfers.

Al Maktoum International Airport Bus F55 goes to Ibn Battuta metro station for onward service on the Dubai Metro Red Line. Taxis cost about Dhs70 to Dubai Marina and Dhs110 to Downtown Dubai.

Abu Dhabi International Airport An airport shuttle bus (Dhs4) links the airport with Al Zahiyah, stopping at the main bus terminal en route. Reasonably priced metered taxis are available for Yas Island and to all points of the city. Some four- and five-star hotels operate free shuttle buses from the airport. Car-hire desks are in the arrivals hall.

For much more on **arrival** see p216

Getting Around

Dubai

Before hopping aboard local transport, purchase a rechargeable pass (Nol card) from ticket offices or vending machines.

Metro Red and Green Lines link all major sights and neighbourhoods.

Bus Slower but useful for going places not served by the metro.

Tram Travels along King Salman Bin Abdul Aziz Al Saud St between Dubai Media City and Dubai Marina.

Boat Abras (traditional wooden boats) cross the Creek.

Taxi Convenient, metered, fairly inexpensive and fast except during rush hour.

Abu Dhabi

Getting around Abu Dhabi's main points of interest is easy. Most visitors use taxis as they are frequent, metered, usually clean and relatively inexpensive. Navigation is mostly by landmark or Satnav (GPS), not by street name, so come prepared. There is also a very good bus system.

For much more on **getting around** see p128 and p217

Sleeping

Butler service, Rolls Royce limousines, champagne baths – your imagination is the only limit when it comes to luxe lodging in Dubai and Abu Dhabi. Yet both emirates offer the entire gamut of places to unpack your suitcase, including boutique hotels, heritage B&Bs, quality midrange hotels and, of course, just about every international hospitality brand under the sun.

Useful Websites

Lonely Planet (www.lonelyplanet.com/united-arab-emirates/dubai/hotels) Recommendations and bookings.

Visit Dubai (www.visitdubai.com) The official tourist authority site also has accommodation booking function.

Abu Dhabi Bookings & City Guide (www.abudhabi.com) Covers a wide selection of capital hotels.

Visit Abu Dhabi (www.visitabudhabi.ae) The city's official tourism website gives useful information including places to stay.

For much more on **sleeping** see p180

Top Itineraries

Day One

Bur Dubai (p64)

Start with a Cultural Breakfast at the **Sheikh Mohammed Centre for Cultural Understanding** for a rare chance to meet locals and eat home-cooked Emirati food. Delve further into local culture and history with a spin around the **Al Fahidi Historic District**, dipping in and out of the various small museums and shops before finishing up at the nearby **Dubai Museum**.

Lunch Process impressions over lunch at the Arabian Tea House Cafe (p72).

Deira (p50)

Enjoy the short stroll to the breezy **Bur Dubai Souq** via the atmospheric **Hindi Lane** and then catch an abra (water taxi) across the Dubai Creek to forage for bargains in the bustling Deira souqs. Before plunging into the beehive of activity, take a walk along the waterfront to snap photographs of the colourful dhows (traditional wooden boats). Grab a juice from Jafer Binam Ali Cafeteria before sniffing exotic potions in the **Spice Souq** and squinting at dazzling jewellery in the **Gold Souq**.

Dinner Relax during a dinner cruise aboard Al Mansour Dhow (p58).

Deira (p50)

After dinner, take a taxi to **QDs** and wind down with a drink or a shisha while counting the twinkling lights of the Dubai skyline across the Creek.

Day Two

Jumeirah (p95)

Kick off day two with a guided tour of the stunning **Jumeirah Mosque** and then cab it down the coast towards the iconic Burj Al Arab and explore the charming **Madinat Jumeirah** village, perhaps stocking up on camel toys and pashminas at its faux souq or taking an abra ride around its network of canals past Arabian-style hotels and lush gardens.

Lunch Enjoy Burj Al Arab views and lunch at Souk Madinat Jumeirah (p107).

Downtown Dubai (p79)

It's the hottest part of the day so make a beeline for the **Dubai Mall** and visit the watery wonderland of the **Aquarium** before giving your credit cards a workout. Watch the sun set from the lofty observation terrace of the **Burj Khalifa** (book way ahead) and then see where you've just been during al fresco happy-hour drinks at **Treehouse**.

Dinner Marvel at the Dubai Fountain during a meal at Baker & Spice (p85).

Downtown Dubai (p79)

Wrap up the day with a nightcap at **Bridgewater Tavern** with views of the Dubai Canal, or get your freak on dancing up a storm at deliciously wacky **Cirque Le Soir**.

Day Three

Al Quoz (p84)

Pack your beach gear and then greet the day with strong coffee and a healthy breakfast at **Tom & Serg**, an ultra-hip industrial loft cafe, before perusing the latest in Middle Eastern art on a gallery hop around the **Alserkal Avenue** creative campus. Be sure to drop by Mirzam (p93) chocolate factory. Call an Uber and head to trendy Kite Beach (p100) for lunch.

Lunch See what the fuss about Salt's (p102) Wagyu burgers is all about.

Dubai Marina (p111)

Dedicate a couple of hours to sloth-dom by staking out a spot on the beach, swimming in the crystalline Gulf or getting in on the beach volleyball action. There are showers for rinsing off before showing off the day's glow during sun-downers at **360°** with front row seats of the ethereal Burj Al Arab. Afterwards cab down to **Dubai Marina** for dinner.

Dinner Take in glittering marina views over fusion bites at Asia Asia (p115).

Dubai Marina (p111)

Follow up with a digestive stroll along the Dubai Marina waterfront past bobbing yachts and glittering futuristic high-rises, perhaps stopping for a nightcap and more breathtaking views at the **Observatory** or **Atelier M**.

Day Four

Abu Dhabi (p126)

Begin this citywide tour of Abu Dhabi at magnificent **Sheikh Zayed Grand Mosque** (closed Friday mornings). Board the **Big Bus** here and enjoy the drive beside the Eastern Corniche mangroves. Alight at **Abu Dhabi Mall** and explore the regional craft shops at the **Khalifa Centre** opposite. Continue on the Big Bus to **Manarat Al Saadiyat**, a cinematic exhibition centre dedicated to local art and culture, and the stunning new **Louvre Abu Dhabi**.

Lunch Have lunch at Al Dhafra (p158), serving lavish Emirati buffets.

Abu Dhabi (p126)

Visit the neighbouring **Al Mina Fish Market** and then hire a bike from **Cyacle** at ADIA HQ and cycle part of the 8km to the public beach, enjoying the city's impressive skyscrapers en route. Ascend **Jumeirah's Etihad Tower** for the highest high tea in Abu Dhabi.

Dinner Eat a camel burger at Le Café (p142) in the opulent Emirates Palace.

Abu Dhabi (p126)

Enjoy post-dinner drinks in high-rise **Ray's Bar** in the Jumeirah at Etihad Towers across the street, before rejoining the real world with coffee and shisha at one of the late-night Breakwater cafes.

If You Like...

A Touch of Luxury

High Tea at the Burj Reserve a top table for tea with bubbly and heady views, 200m above sea level. (p106)

Gold Souq Prices are fair, the quality superb and the purchase a glittering investment. What are you waiting for? (p52)

Dinner at At.mosphere Dust off that platinum card for a window table at the world's highest restaurant. (p87)

Go for Gold Sprinkled with 24-carat gold flake, the capuccino at Le Café in Abu Dhabi's Emirates Palace is the ultimate in delicious decadence. (p142)

Art & History

Louvre Abu Dhabi A decade in the making, the Louvre Abu Dhabi was one of the world's most anticipated art museum openings. (p156)

Etihad Museum This new architectural marvel chronicles the founding of the United Arab Emirates in 1971. (p99)

Alserkal Avenue This cluster of warehouses has turned into a dynamic campus of galleries and creative outlets. (p84)

Dubai Museum Explore Dubai's history within the confines of the Al Fahidi Fort, the city's oldest building. (p66)

Al Fahidi Historic District Embark on a journey into Dubai's past on a wander around this atmospheric restored historic quarter. (p67)

Legoland Dubai (p124)

Gate Village Smock-and-beret types will love nosing around the contemporary galleries at this posh art hub. (p83)

Beaches

Kite Beach Kitesurfing is among the activities luring sporty types to this glorious band of sand. (p100)

JBR Beach A family-geared sandy strip; it has fun zones and glorious views of the Ain Dubai observatory wheel. (p113)

Sunset Beach With prime views of the Burj Al Arab, this is the beach where you shouldn't forget your camera. (p100)

Al Mamzar Beach Park This super-long, pristine and family-friendly beach comes with a pool, playgrounds and water sports. (p55)

Corniche Beach Sandy beaches, a generous promenade and grand views of the Abu Dhabi skyline give this ribbon of sand an edge. (p129)

Foodie Experiences

Frying Pan Adventures Fun and educational food tours explore the polyethnic culinary labyrinth of Bur Dubai and Deira. (p71)

Dubai & Abu Dhabi Food Festivals Savour new trends, celebrity chefs, cooking classes and fabulous fare at month-long foodie fairs. (p20)

Al Mansour Dhow dinner cruise Dhow cruises offer a romantic journey with a generous spread of Indian and Arabic food. (p58)

Friday Brunch Unleash your inner glutton at the buffets of what has become a Dubai and Abu Dhabi expat weekend ritual. (p117)

Mall Crawling

Dubai Mall The world's largest mall packs a serious retail punch along with family entertainment. (p82)

Ibn Battuta Mall This mall's stunning decor tracks the journey of a 14th-century Arab scholar from Spain to India. (p123)

Mall of the Emirates A dizzying number of shops and the dazzling alpine slopes of Ski Dubai feature here. (p107)

Souk Madinat Jumeirah Even if it's a bit 'Disney does Arabia', the look is sumptuous and the shops are filled with a tempting array of souvenirs. (p107)

Galleria at Maryah Island This luxury mall is at the retail heart of Abu Dhabi's new Central Business District. (p148)

Staying Out Late

Barasti Dance with sand between your toes or make new friends at this spirited beach-side hotspot. (p119)

Bliss Lounge This chic beach-front lounge has perfect views of the giant Ain Dubai Ferris wheel. (p120)

White Dubai Dazzling light shows and top DJs electrify this huge rooftop party den. (p89)

Bahri Bar There are daily drink deals in this Arabian-styled bar with Burj Al Arab views. (p105)

Ray's Bar A fancy bar on the 62nd floor of Abu Dhabi's sky-scraper offers dazzling cocktails and views. (p141)

Theme Parks

IMG Worlds of Adventure Experience thrill rides with dinos, superheroes and cartoon characters in the world's largest indoor amusement park. (p91)

Legoland Dubai This Lego wonderland comes with rides, live entertainment, a driving school and a huge Lego shop. (p124)

Motiongate This indoor-outdoor park counts rides inspired by *Ghostbusters*, *Shrek* and *The Hunger Games* among its attractions. (p124)

Bollywood Parks Dubai Plunge into the adventure and romance of India's huge movie industry crowned by a musical. (p124)

Urban Spaces

Alserkal Avenue This constantly evolving creative village has galleries, cafes, fringe theatre, offbeat stores and funky cafes in warehouses. (p84)

BoxPark A cool street mall built from shipping containers with concept stores and offbeat cafes. (p108)

City Walk Check out this fashionable outdoor mall with sleek architecture, stunning digital projections, street art and high-end boutiques. (p107)

Dubai Design District A cauldron of creativity, it has lots of public art, edgy buildings and a busy events schedule with international players. (p92)

Warehouse 421 This rusting steel-clad port area depot has been upcycled into a dynamic arts and cultural centre. (p157)

For more top spots, see the following:

- Eating (p27)
- Drinking & Nightlife (p31)
- Entertainment (p35)
- Shopping (p37)
- Sports & Activities (p42)

Month By Month

TOP EVENTS

Food Festivals in Dubai & Abu Dhabi, February

Art Dubai, March

Al Marmoum Heritage Festival, April

Abu Dhabi Grand Prix, November

Dubai International Film Festival, December

January

A blissful month here when much of the world is suffering post-holiday doldrums and icy conditions. Expect daytime temperatures averaging a pleasant 25°C.

Dubai Marathon

With mild weather and one of the flattest and fastest courses in the world, this full marathon (p43) attracts pounding participation from all over the world.

Dubai Shopping Festival

Held throughout January, this shopping festival (p78) lures bargain hunters from around the world. There are huge discounts in the souqs and malls, and the city is abuzz with activities, ranging from live concerts to fashion shows and fireworks.

February

Another warm and winning month, with sun-kissed weather and plenty going on, including many outdoor events. Pack a light jacket or pashmina for al fresco evenings.

Dubai Tennis Championships

Attracting the big serves of the world's top pros, the men's and women's tournaments are a firm fixture on the international tennis circuit (www.dubaidutyfree tennischampionships.com).

Dubai Food Festival & Abu Dhabi Food Festival

For several weeks, both Dubai (www.dubaifood festival.com) and Abu Dhabi (www.abudhabievents.ae) celebrate their gastronomic diversity with food-related events, entertainment, celebrity chef appearances, dining tours, food trucks and pop-up restaurants.

Dubai Jazz Festival

This popular festival (www. dubaijazzfest.com) sees top talent headliners, which in the past have included Sting, Carlos Santana and John Legend, but also gets the crowds toe-tapping with free jazz and blues concerts at various venues.

March

The weather might be heating up a fraction, but it is still near perfect in this action-packed month, with warm seas for swimming and plenty of space on the sand.

Art Dubai

Keep tabs on the rapidly evolving art scene in the Middle East and South Asia at this prestigious showcase (www.artdubai.ae) of nearly 100 galleries from the UAE and around the world exhibiting works at Madinat Jumeirah.

Burj Al Arab Swim

With proceeds benefiting a different charity every year, this event sees around 800 swimmers competing in an 800m or 1600m race around the iconic Burj Al Arab hotel.

Dubai World Cup

Dubai's racing season culminates in the world's

richest horse race (p88) and a big social event. With no betting allowed, attention also turns to the styles and hats of the attendees.

Festival of Literature

Sponsored by Emirates Airlines, this huge lit-fest (www.emirateslitfest.com) shines the spotlight on authors and poets from the Middle East as well as international best-selling writers.

Sikka Art Fair

Dozens of Emirati and Dubai-based artists create site-specific works spanning all media during this lively 10-day fair (www.dubaiculture.gov.ae) in Bur Dubai's Al Fahidi Historic District.

Taste of Dubai

A feast for foodies, this three-day festival (www.tasteofdubaifestival.com) offers not just delicious bites but also cooking classes, beverage tastings, concerts and all sorts of other entertainment for young and old.

April

It's still warm rather than blistering, but the school holidays mean you'll see more tourists during Easter break. This is a rollicking good month for beach fans and fashionistas.

Al Marmoum Heritage Festival

Held at the Al Marmoum Heritage Village some 40km south of Dubai, this four-week festival (p88) celebrates traditional Emirati culture with music, crafts, food, carnival rides; and camel races that see thousands of animals competing for prizes and prestige.

Fashion Forward

Models clad in the latest threads by the Middle East's top designers strut the catwalk at this twice annual fashion fair (also held in October) that also includes talks, seminars and panel discussions by industry insiders (www.fashionforward.ae).

May

Temperatures can nudge 35°C or more, so air-conditioned malls provide welcome relief.

Al Gaffal Dhow Race

This traditional dhow race follows the route once taken by pearl divers. It starts at the small uninhabited island of Sir Bu Nair and heads east for 23 nautical miles before finishing at the Burj Al Arab. All crew members must be Emirati.

July

It's hot! Most of life moves indoors and hotel rates drops significantly.

Dubai Summer Surprises

Despite the sizzling time of year, a combination of free kids' entertainment and major sales in shopping malls draws plenty of tourists for the more family-focused little sibling of the Dubai Shopping Festival. Runs July to mid-August.

October

Temperatures have started to cool nicely, although you can still expect humidity and toasty warm days early in the month. Nights are perfect for dining al fresco in shirtsleeves or for overnight desert trips.

Diwali

Lights, candles and firecrackers characterise this magical festival of light, which brings together the ever-growing community of Indian expats. Look for traditional sweets in supermarkets and lavishly lit balconies and windows, particularly in Deira and Bur Dubai.

Abu Dhabi Classics

This series of 12 classical concerts (http://abudhabievents.ae) brings international top talent to various venues around Abu Dhabi between October and May.

November

With the summer heat having subsided, visitors from colder climes are returning and much of life starts moving outdoors.

DP World Tour Championship

This golfing championship (www.europeantour.com) is the crowning tournament of the Race to Dubai that pits the PGA European Tour's top players against each other in 49 tournaments in 26 destinations over the course of one year.

Rugby Sevens

The first round of the 10-leg World Rugby Sevens Series is a three-day event (www.dubairugby7s.com) featuring 16 international squads, amateur teams and live entertainment. It's held at the Sevens Stadium, about 30 minutes south of Dubai.

Abu Dhabi Grand Prix

The F1 racing elite tests its mettle on this wicked track on Yas Island (www.yasmarinacircuit.com).

Abu Dhabi Art

Top regional and international galleries are joined by collectors, art aficionados and artists for four days of exhibitions, art talks, entertainment and children's programs at Manarat Al Saadiyat (www.abudhabiart.ae).

December

The end of the year marks peak tourist season for a reason: the sea is warm, the air is crisp and clear, and evenings are perfect for al fresco dining.

UAE National Day

The birth of a nation in 1971 is celebrated across the country on 2 December with a range of events, from boat parades to fireworks, concerts to horse shows and traditional dances to military parades.

Dubai International Film Festival

This star-studded non-competitive film festival (www.dubaifilmfest.com) is great for catching international indie flicks as well as new releases from around the Arab world, India and South Asia.

Top: Al Gaffal Dhow Race (p21)
Bottom: Fashion Forward (p21)

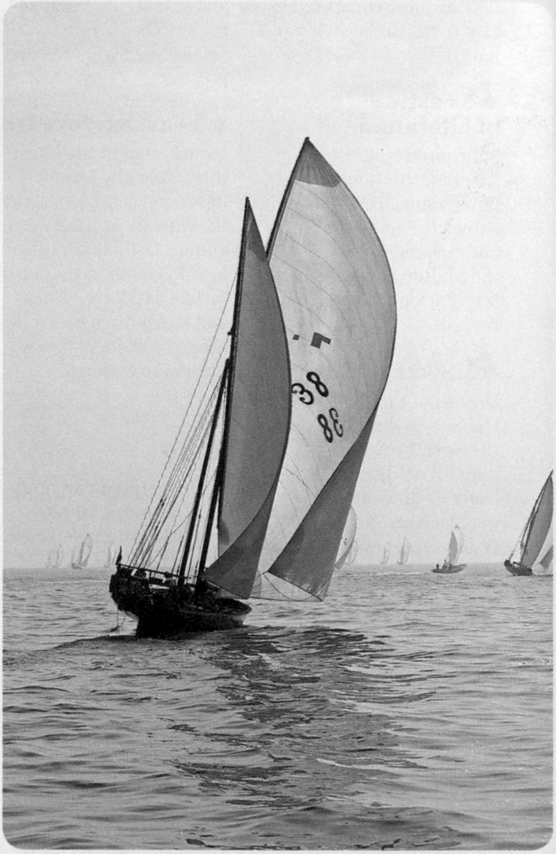

KARIM SAHIB / AFP / GETTY IMAGES ©

MAKSYM PORIECHKIN / SHUTTERSTOCK ©

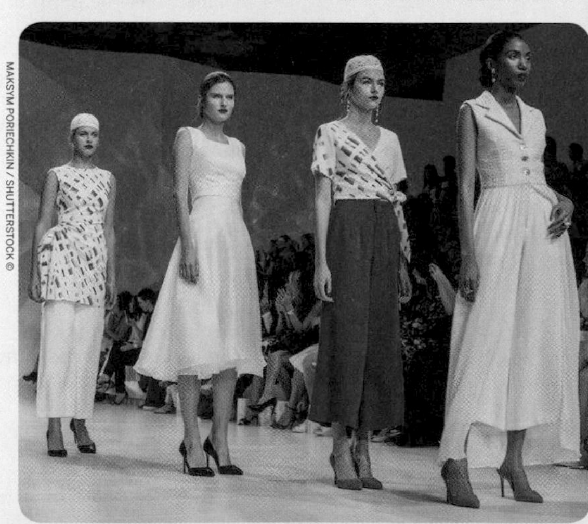

With Kids

Travelling to Dubai and Abu Dhabi with kids can be child's play, especially if you keep a light schedule and involve them in day-to-day planning. There's plenty to do from water parks and playgrounds to theme parks and activity centres. Most beach resorts operate kids' clubs.

VINEET VIRMANI / 500PX ©

Dubai Butterfly Garden

Animal Attraction

Aquariums

Kids fascinated by the underwater world will be enchanted by the Dubai Aquarium & Underwater Zoo (p82) at Dubai Mall or the labyrinth of underwater tanks and fish-filled tunnels at the Lost Chambers (p113) at Atlantis the Palm.

Green Planet

This indoor rainforest (p100) brings the tropics to the desert complete with birds, frogs, lizards, butterflies, turtles and other critters.

Meydan Horse Stable Tour

See championship thoroughbreds train and even swim in their own pool on behind-the-scenes tours (p88) of the famous stables.

Dubai Butterfly Garden

Pose with gorgeous winged creatures in this enchanting **indoor garden** (04 422 8902; www.dubaibutterflygarden.com; Sheikh Mohammed bin Zayed Rd (Hwy E311), Al Barsha South; Dhs50; 9am-6pm; P) with attached museum.

Falcon Hospital

Book ahead for a tour of this unique facility (p152) north of Abu Dhabi where you can to learn about falcons and meet them up close.

Keeping Cool

Public beaches

Al Mamzar (p55) in Deira, Kite Beach (p100) in Jumeirah and JBR Beach (p113) in Dubai Marina have the best family-friendly infrastructure.

Beach clubs

Most beachfront hotels have kids' care centres. Among the best are Sinbad's at the Jumeirah Beach Hotel (p189), Club Mina (p119) at the Le Meridien Mina Seyahi, and the Fairmont Falcons Kids' Club at the Fairmont Dubai (p187) on Palm Jumeirah.

Water parks

These are a hit with everyone from tots to teens. For spine-chilling slides,

NEED TO KNOW

Formula & disposable nappies (diapers) Sold at pharmacies and supermarkets.

Babysitting Ask for a referral at your hotel or try www.dubaimetromaids.com, www.maidszone.com or www.maid4uae.com.

Kids' clubs Many hotels have kids' clubs and activities.

Strollers & car seats Bring your own.

Transport Children under five years of age travel free on public transport.

Blogs See www.sassymamadubai.com, www.mommyindubai.com and http://dubaimoms.com

Aquaventure (p114) on Palm Jumeirah is a suitable launch pad, while the original family favourite, Wild Wadi Waterpark (p109), has both options for nervous nellies and adrenaline junkies. New player Legoland Water Park (p124) in Jebel Ali is geared more towards younger kids. In Abu Dhabi the go-to place for keeping tempers cool is Yas Waterworld (p164).

Dubai Mall ice rink

If liquid water isn't keeping your little ones cool enough, have them do pirouettes and disco dancing at the Olympic-sized ice rink (p94) at Dubai Mall.

Ski Dubai

Tackling the snow slopes and meeting penguins at Ski Dubai (p109) in the Mall of the Emirates. Now how cool is that?

Outdoor Adventures

Desert Explorations

For the ultimate holiday pic to impress their pals back home, consider sandboarding, camel riding, going on an overnight desert safari or even a trekking trip to the Hajar Mountains. A recommended company is Platinum Heritage Tours (p94).

Al Boom Diving

Young divers over 12 years of age are eligible for open-water dives with this well-respected outfit (p110).

Skimming the waves

Daredevils can also try their hand at kitesurfing with Dubai Kitesurfing School (p110) or Dukite (p110).

Playgrounds & Parks

KidZania

This interactive miniature **city for kids** (Map p258, D3; ☎04 448 5222; www.kidzania.ae; 2nd fl, Dubai Mall; tickets from Dhs150; ⏰10am-11pm; P 👪; M Burj Khalifa/Dubai Mall) in Dubai Mall offers the ultimate in role-play options.

Mattel Play! Town

At this relatively new contender (p110) tots get to interact with Barney & Co in 'edutaining' play.

Zabeel Park

This sprawling central park (p69) counts a lake with boating, an adventure playground and lots of shade among its assets.

Al Khalidiyah Public Park

There are good climbing frames and plenty of shade in this urban playground (p136) near downtown Abu Dhabi.

Theme Parks

There is lots of new stuff here as Dubai is working towards positioning itself as the theme park capital of the Middle East.

IMG Worlds of Adventure

Pose for selfies with 'real-life' dinos and go on adventures with Marvel and Cartoon Network characters in the world's largest indoor amusement park (p91).

Dubai Parks and Resorts

It's rides, thrills and shows galore at this trifecta of theme parks in Jebel Ali: movie-themed Motiongate (p124) and Bollywood Parks (p124) plus timeless kiddie fave Legoland (p124).

Ferrari World Abu Dhabi

Teens will cherish earning bragging rights to having 'done' the world's fastest roller coaster at this temple of torque (p162) on Abu Dhabi's Yas Island.

For Free

Dubai and Abu Dhabi have the reputation of being among the most luxurious and expensive destinations in the world. Fortunately, some of the best things in life are free (or almost free). Here's a handy primer on how you can stretch your budget.

IAIN MASTERTON / GETTY IMAGES ©

Ras Al Khor Wildlife Sanctuary (p84)

Freebie Attractions

A top free sight in Dubai is the choreographed dancing Dubai Fountain (p82) at Dubai Mall, with the lit-up drama of the Burj Khalifa as a soaring backdrop. Dubai Mall itself is filled with attractions, most famously the Dubai Aquarium (p82) (free peeks from the mall) and a giant dinosaur (p82) skeleton. The iconic Burj Al Arab (p97) cannot be entered without a reservation, but it looks better from the outside anyway – for instance from Sunset Beach or Madinat Jumeirah (p98), whose Arabian architecture and mock-souq are attractions in their own right. By contrast, access is free to all at Abu Dhabi's Emirates Palace (p135), another of the world's most expensive hotels. For close-ups of futuristic sustainable architecture, take a wander around Masdar City (p157).

Gallery Hopping

Shift into exploring mode and head to Alserkal Avenue (p84) in industrial Al Quoz or Gate Village at the Dubai International Finance Centre to keep tabs on what's happening in artists' studios around the Middle East. Abu Dhabi taps into the contemporary art scene at Warehouse 421 (p157) and the Etihad Modern Art Gallery (p135) and into old paintings and antiques at the adjacent Etihad Antiques Gallery (p135).

Great Outdoors

Some of Dubai's beaches may have been gobbled up by luxe resorts and beach clubs, but there's still miles of coastline where you can take a dip for free, including Al Mamzar (p55), Kite Beach (p100), Sunset Beach (p100) and JBR Beach (p113). The latter even offers free yoga (p125) several mornings a week. Of Dubai's parks, the most central is Zabeel Park (p69), which has lush flora, a lake and the new Dubai Frame observation tower. Bird lovers can spot flamingos and other winged critters at the Ras Al Khor Wildlife Sanctuary (p84). In Abu Dhabi, the Eastern Corniche offers miles of safe walking and running tracks with views across the mangrove forests.

NEED TO KNOW

Happy Hour & Ladies' Nights Offered by many bars throughout the week.

Wi-fi Most cafes, restaurants, spas, bars and malls offer free wi-fi for their customers. Free public wi-fi requires a local number for registration.

Transport The Dubai metro is fast, clean and inexpensive.

Mosque Mystique

Mosques in the UAE are generally closed to non-Muslims, which is why it's such a privilege to gain access to two of the country's most beautiful houses of worship. In Abu Dhabi, the vast Sheikh Zayed Grand Mosque (p127) is truly a stunner inside and out and can be seen entirely for free on your own or on guided tours. In Dubai, it's possible to admire the beauty of the Jumeirah Mosque (p100) on guided tours costing a mere Dhs20.

Museum Cheapies

Dubai has several free or low-cost museums where you can learn about the city's early days. The best of the bunch is the Dubai Museum (p66), which charts the city's turbo-evolution from Bedouin outpost to megalopolis. East of here, the Al Fahidi Historic District (p67) harbours a handful of free museums that focus on coffee, coins and art. For a trip into Abu Dhabi's past, swing by the exhibit at Qasr Al Hosn (p129), the city's oldest surviving structure; pay homage to the country's founding father, Sheikh Zayed, at the Zayed Centre (p135); or catch glimpses of daily life in the pre-oil era at the Abu Dhabi Heritage Village (p141).

Off to the Races

Admission is free and there is no betting, so the only dirhams you may have to spend are for the cab ride out to the Meydan Racecourse (p88) to watch some of the world's finest thoroughbreds and most famous jockeys sweat it out on the turf. The state-of-the art stadium is impressive in itself and the vibe can be electric. For a quintessential Arabian experience, there's nothing like attending a camel race. Seeing these ungainly beasts galumphing by the hundreds at top speeds makes for fantastic memories (not to mention photographs). Head to the Al Marmoum (p88) camel racing track south of Dubai or the Al Wathba (p164) track about 45km southeast of Abu Dhabi.

Souq Time

Wandering around the labyrinthine souqs in Bur Dubai and Deira or around the port Al Mina in Abu Dhabi is a fun and eye-opening plunge into local culture and, unless you succumb to the persuasive vendors, it will cost you no more than shoe leather. Browse the textile, perfume, spice and gold souqs, and don't forget to bring your camera. If you're interested in making a purchase, start off the bargaining process by offering half the quoted price.

Urban Art

Dubai has gotten more of an urban, arty edge thanks to the Dubai Street Museum (p102) project. Look for large-scale murals celebrating the UAE's history and heritage adorning entire house walls along 2nd December St in Satwa or the funky creations of the Dubai Walls (p100) initiative at City Walk in Jumeirah. Artful graffiti also hides among the historic nooks of the Al Fahidi Historic District (p67) in Bur Dubai.

Waterfront Ramblings

A stroll along Dubai Creek in Bur Dubai from the Al Ghubaiba metro station to the Al Fahidi Historic District (p67) offers a scenic and photogenic insight into the area's heritage. Study the architecture of the restored traditional courtyard houses once inhabited by the local ruling family. Watch the wooden abras (water taxis) criss-cross the Creek and brightly painted dhows (traditional wooden boat) bound for Iran and Sudan. Grab a coffee in a waterfront cafe and check out the offerings at the souq. In Abu Dhabi, the Corniche (p129) transports the rambler from the past to the present.

Eating

Filling your tummy in Dubai and Abu Dhabi is an extraordinarily multicultural experience with a virtual UN of cuisines to choose from. Arabic and Indian fare are most prevalent, but basically you can feast on anything from Afghan kebabs to fish and chips in the cities' myriad eateries. These run the gamut from simple street kitchens and fast-food franchises to family restaurants and luxe dining temples.

What's Trending Now?

ORGANIC, SEASONAL & FARM TO FORK

Taking global fare local is not a trend unique to Duba and Abu Dhabi, but it's arrived here with a vengeance. As awareness has grown, the demand for certified organic produce has increased right along with it. Locals farms have expanded their operations, and new farmers markets to stock up on the good stuff have been popping up everywhere. Even the big supermarkets have gotten in on the locavore trend – many now post the origin of their produce next to the price tag.

FARMERS MARKETS

From heirloom tomatoes to beetroot, it's amazing what will grow in the desert given the right techniques and microclimates. The organic trend extends to milk, cheese and other dairy products as well as to free-range eggs, local honey, dates and other goodies. A Dubai pioneer is Ripe Organic (www.ripeme.com), which launched in 2011 and operates a shop, a farming network and the community-oriented Ripe farmers markets, now with three locations. The city's weekly Farmers Market on the Terrace (p93) is another place for sourcing pesticide-free produce.

EMIRATI CUISINE

Restaurants serving Emirati food used to be rare, but thankfully this is changing. Modern Emiratis are accustomed to an international diet, but there are also a number of traditional plates rooted in the Bedouin tradition that have, over time, become infused with spices and ingredients from trading partners from India to Persia and Morocco. Typical dishes are one-pot stews featuring a combination of rice or some form of wheat, vegetables and/or meat or fish. Many are flavoured with cinnamon, saffron and turmeric and topped with nuts or dried fruit. During Ramadan, traditional dishes feature strongly in the *iftar,* the big feast served after sundown that breaks the fast.

Classic dishes include *harees,* a porridge-like stew made from cracked wheat and slow-cooked chicken or lamb. *Fareed* is a lamb stew layered with flat bread, while *machboos* is a casserole of meat or fish, rice and onions cooked in a spicy sauce. Fish features prominently on local menus and is usually served grilled, fried or baked. Look for *samak* (fish in gravy). The salt-cured variety is used in a local dish called *madrooba.*

CAMEL MILK

Bedouins have known it for centuries, but the health benefits of camel milk have started to make international headlines. Slightly pungent and salty in taste, it's lower in fat and has triple the amount of vitamin C and iron when compared to cow's milk. The number of cafes offering 'camelccinos' (camel milk cappuccino) or milkshakes or smoothies made with camel milk is growing at a steady clip. Camel cheese, chocolate and ice cream are also now a staple on supermarket shelves. Restaurants have also started to put camel dishes on their menus, although camel meat is not actually a staple in Emirati cuisine.

NEED TO KNOW

Opening Hours

As a guideline, figure on hotel restaurants being open from noon to 3pm and 6.30pm to 11pm daily. Many low-key indie eateries remain open throughout the day except on Friday when some don't open until the afternoon.

Price Ranges

The following price ranges refer to the average cost of a main course.

$ less than Dhs50

$$ Dhs50–100

$$$ more than Dhs100

Reservations

➡ Reservations are essential at top restaurants and recommended for mid-range eateries, especially for dinner. Be prepared to give your mobile number.

➡ For top tables, make weekend bookings – Thursday and Friday nights, and Friday brunch – at least a week ahead.

➡ Reserve through the restaurant (phone or online), www.opentable.com, www.reserveout.com or www.zomato.com.

Tipping

Many restaurants, particularly in hotels, automatically tack on a 10% service charge to the bill, which rarely gets passed down to the employees. Leave an additional 10% to 15% in cash, particularly at low-end restaurants. If service is perfunctory, a mere 5% is fine. If it's bad, leave nothing.

Vegetarians & Vegans

Duba and Abu Dhabii can be good for vegetarians, with lots of Asian and subcontinental cuisine on offer. Health-conscious cafes and restaurants have been sprouting faster than alfalfa and serve up inspired menus that leave veggie and tofu burgers in the dust.

Many of the Indian restaurants, particularly in Deira and Bur Dubai, have extensive vegetarian menus. Even those that are not dedicated vegetarian restaurants still do fantastic things with vegetables, *paneer* (cheese) and rice. You can also fill up fast at Lebanese restaurants with all-veg mezze, while Thai places have plenty of coconut and chilli-spiced veg curries and soups. Vegans may be more challenged, but certainly won't be limited to a few lettuce leaves and a carrot stick. Many fine dining restaurants have dedicated vegetarian menus as well.

Fast-Food Faves

Dubai and Abu Dhabi are fast-food havens, and we're not talking golden arches (although they're here as well). If there ever was a local snack food with cult status, it would have to be the shawarma: strips of marinated meat (usually chicken or lamb) and fat roasted on a rotating grill, slivered and stuffed into pita bread.

The selection of Middle Eastern mezze is simply stunning, ranging from humble hummus (chickpea dip) and creamy *moutabel* (eggplant dip) to *kibbeh* (meatballs) and tabbouleh (parsley, tomato and bulgar-wheat salad). India contributes not only its famous curries and biryanis (rice dishes) but also various *chaat* (street food snacks) like *bhaji* (fritters), *samosa* (savoury pastries), *puri* (deep-fried bread) and *dosa* (paper-thin lentil-flour pancakes). Kebabs are also a fast-food staple.

Self-Catering

Dubai and Abu Dhabi have big international supermarket chains with a bewildering selection of high-quality, international food items. Carrefour is probably the best stocked, but the quality tends to be better (and prices higher) at Spinneys and Waitrose. Both stock many products from the UK, North America and Australia and are predictably popular with Western expats. Some branches have separate 'pork rooms' that are off limits to Muslims. Choithrams is cheaper and caters more to the South Asian communities. In 2017 it became the first supermarket chain in the UAE to replace plastic bags with paper bags. Many markets are open until midnight; some never close.

A Question of Pork

Pork is available for non-Muslims in a special room at some larger supermarkets such as Spinneys. In many hotel restaurants, pork is a menu item and is clearly labelled as such. For those used to eating

Dubai: Eating by Neighbourhood

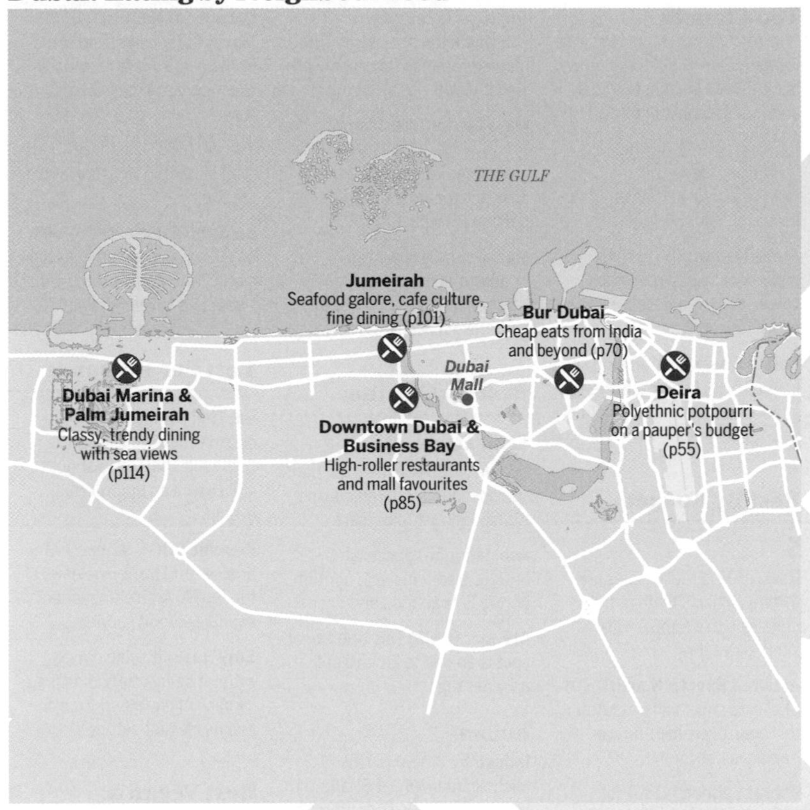

pork, the 'beef bacon' and 'turkey ham' alternatives that are commonly available are often nothing more than a reminder of how tasty the real thing is.

Food Bloggers

Dubai is a fast-changing city, so it's only natural that the gastronomic scene also develops at lightning speed. Fortunately, there are plenty of passionate food bloggers keeping an eye on great eats and new openings. Here are our top four, but there's plenty more you can link to via the portal www.fooderatiarabia.com.

Dubai Confidential (www.dubaiconfidential.ae) Lifestyle blog that also includes some savvy restaurant reviews and recipes.

FooDiva (www.foodiva.net) Greek–Cypriot–British expat Samantha Wood writes insightful and impartial reviews and even has her own free app.

I Live in a Frying Pan (www.iliveinafryingpan.com) Local Arva Ahmed is obsessed with ferreting out the best among Dubai's authentic hole-in-the-wall eateries and takes curious budget gourmets on food tours through her company Frying Pan Adventures (p71).

The Hedonista (www.thehedonista.com) Australian Sarah Walton has spent half a lifetime working around food and wine and now shares her extensive expertise on eating her way around Dubai and beyond in independent reviews.

Lonely Planet's Top Choices

Zuma (p88) This chic Japanese lair is one of the most buzzed about restaurants in town.

Pai Thai (p104) Thai morsels for the soul served in an ultra-romantic setting amid the canals of Madinat Jumeirah.

Aroos Damascus (p55) Seriously delicious Syrian staples served with a smile in a vast cafe to adoring crowds.

Bait El Khetyar (p130) Top spot in Abu Dhabi for Jordanian-style shawarma, hummus and labneh with garlic.

Best By Budget

$

Ravi (p102) Empty tables are as rare as hen's teeth at this unfussy curry temple with sidewalk seating.

Al Ustad Special Kabab (p70) Sheiks to shoe shiners clutter this cool, been-here-forever Iranian kebab joint.

Zahrat Lebnan (p130) Top player among the dozens of shawarma, grill and pastry shops near Abu Dhabi's Qasr Al Hosn.

$$

Leila (p86) Beirut import delights with updated Lebanese home-cooking in a nostalgic setting.

Baker & Spice (p85) Healthy and delicious salads and other cafe fare with a view of the Dubai Fountain.

Cafe Arabia (p153) Community hotspot that enlivens Abu Dhabi with artsy Arabian decor, tasty breakfast and other treats.

$$$

Tomo (p73) Eponymous gourmet kitchen of a tradition-minded Japanese star chef with stellar views.

Maya Modern Mexican Kitchen (p115) Richard Sandoval reinterprets time-honoured Mexican dishes in modern Michelin-decorated fashion.

Mezlai (p140) Feast like a prince amid decor inspired by a Bedouin tent at Abu Dhabi's Emirates Palace.

Best By Cuisine

Emirati

Logma (p103) Casual cafe that serves modern Emirati cuisine from breakfast to dessert.

Aseelah (p56) Successfully bridges traditional and contemporary Emirati food and decor.

Al Fanar (p103) This traditional spot is an ode to Emirati culinary heritage.

Indian

Indego by Vineet (p116) Michelin man Vineet Bhatia seduces diners with contemporary spins on Indian classics.

Eric's (p70) Unassuming neighbourhood charmer that delivers a taste-bud tingling culinary journey to Goa.

Tamba (p132) Next-gen Indian fare in a glamour spot atop Abu Dhabi's World Trade Center Mall.

Italian

BiCE (p116) Fabulous wine complements meals that have all the flavours of Italy locked inside.

Eataly (p87) Gourmet food hall and marketplace based at Dubai Mall.

Roberto's (p146) Rich pastas and risottos at Abu Dhabi's Galleria Mall.

Middle Eastern

Qwaider Al Nabulsi (p55) Makes fluffy falafel and some of the best *kunafa* (vermicelli-like pastry soaked in syrup) in town.

Zaroob (p85) Lebanese street food staples in an urban indoor setting.

Ka'ak Al Manara (p103) Mall-based outpost that makes delicious flat sesame breads with sweet and savoury fillings.

Best For Romance

Pai Thai (p104) If your date doesn't make you swoon, these top Thai treats should still ensure an unforgettable evening.

Pierchic (p104) Where Gulf breezes and front-row views of the Burj Al Arab complement soulful seafood goodness.

Stay (p118) It's fine dining without being stuffy thanks to Yannick Alleno's perky cuisine and its elegant setting.

Best Vegan & Vegetarian

Saravana Bhavan (p70) Don't let the unassuming decor put you off – the all-veg Indian is tops.

Govinda's (p70) Serves Sattvic food that not only eschews meat but also oil, onion and garlic.

XVA Café (p72) This charmer is tucked into a serene courtyard house in the Al Fahidi Historic District.

Comptoir 102 (p104) Health-conscious foodies flock to this Jumeirah cafe for inventive plant-based meals.

Drinking & Nightlife

Dubai may be famous for its glitzy clubs, but there's also a more low-key underground scene growing. The busiest nights are Thursday and Friday – weekend nights – when party animals let off steam in the bars and on the dance floor. Alcohol is served in hotels and some licensed venues only. Many locals prefer going out for shisha, mocktails or coffee. The party scene is considerably more subdued in Abu Dhabi.

Bars & Pubs

Snug pubs, beachside lounges, DJ bars, dive bars, cocktail temples, hotel lounges – there's such variety, finding a libation station to match your mood or budget is not exactly a tall order in Dubai. Generally, the emphasis is on style and atmosphere and proprietors have often gone to extraordinary lengths to come up with unique design concepts.

Venues in Downtown Dubai, Jumeirah, Dubai Marina and Palm Jumeirah tend to be on the fancy side and appeal mostly to well-heeled visitors and expats. Beachfront lounges and rooftop bars continue to be popular. Away from the five-star hotels, bars and pubs in Bur Dubai and Deira are more of a low-key, gritty affair. Note that prostitution, though officially illegal, is tolerated in many establishments in all parts of town.

Shisha & Mocktails

Most Emiratis and other Muslims don't drink alcohol, preferring to socialise over coffee, juice and mocktails. If you're not up for drinking, follow the locals to a mellow shisha cafe and play a game of backgammon. Even if you don't smoke, it's tempting to recline languorously and sample a puff of the sweet flavours. Shisha cafes are open until after midnight, and later during the winter months. The going rate is Dhs35 to Dhs125 per pipe for a session. Remember though: popular and atmospheric as the pastime is, smoking shisha isn't any better for your health than smoking cigarettes.

Clubbing

DJs spin every night of the week with the top names hitting the decks on Thursdays and Fridays. Partying is not restricted to night-time, with plenty of beach clubs like Blue Marlin Ibiza UAE kicking into gear midday on weekends in the cooler months. The sound repertoire is global – funk, soul, trip-hop, hip-hop, R&B, African, Arabic and Latino – although the emphasis is still clearly on house, tech and other EDM (electronic dance music).

LOCAL & INTERNATIONAL DJS

Globetrotting big-name DJs like Ellen Allien, Carl Craig, Steve Aoki, Russ Yallop, Roger Sanchez and Ben Klock occasionally jet in for the weekend to whip the crowd into a frenzy in the top venues and at megaparties like Groove on the Grass or Party in the Park. But there's plenty of resident spin talent as well. The roster is constantly in flux, of course, but names to keep on the radar include Jixo & Danz, KayteK, Siamak Amidi, Hoolz, Scott Forshaw, Ron E Jazz and Josephine De Retour.

PARTIES

Some top parties are put on by local record labels, promoters or event agencies such as Audio Tonic (progressive house), Plus Minus (deep house and techno), Analog Room (underground techno-electro), Stereo Club (electro), Globalfunk (drum & bass), Superheroes (house, drum & bass), Bassworx (drum & bass) and Bad House Party (indie-punk-eclectic).

NEED TO KNOW

Opening Hours

- Hotel bars are often open from morning to midnight or 1am.
- Clubs open at 10pm, get going around 11pm and close at 3am.
- Since 2016, Dubai bars are also open – and serve alcohol – during the day during Ramadan. Most clubs close during this period.

Costs

- A pint of draught beer will set you back Dhs25 to Dhs70, a glass of wine Dhs30 to Dhs75 and a cocktail Dhs40 to Dhs100.
- Clubs charge from Dhs50 to Dhs300 for big-name DJs. Women get free admission at many venues. Sometimes there is no cover but a minimum spend.

Music Bans

Dancing and loud music in public places is strictly forbidden. This includes beaches, parks and residential areas; dancing is restricted to licensed venues only.

Resources

The best source for the latest music and club world news, including an up-to-the-minute party schedule, is the free biweekly *Hype* magazine, available at bars, boutiques, gyms and spas around town and online at digital news stand Magster (www.magster.com; requires free registration). The booklet-sized *Infusion* magazine is another handy source, as are the Dubai pages of club-scene stalwart Resident Advisor (www.residentadvisor.net).

Dress Code & Door Policies

Doors are tough at many clubs, and anyone bouncers feel does not fit in with the crowd may be turned away. This goes especially for single men or men-only groups, since most venues only allow women, couples and mixed groups past the velvet rope. Some clubs require table reservations and minimum spends. The more upmarket ones also have a dress code (check Facebook or the website if unsure) that is strictly enforced, so make sure you've ironed that shirt and leave your jeans, sneakers and flats at home. Beachside venues are more relaxed, while indie and underground clubs tend not to have a door policy. Bring your ID, as they are sometimes checked.

Some clubs have been accused of racist policies, particularly against South Asians.

If a top DJ is at the decks, you can usually buy advance tickets online. For some club nights, you need to get on the guest list.

Happy Hour & Ladies' Nights

One way to stretch your drinking budget is by hitting the happy hours offered by a wide roster of bars, from dives to five-star lounges, either on specific days of the week or even daily. Discounts range from 50% off drinks to two-for-one deals or double measures on selected beverages. Most start early in the evening, usually around 5pm or 6pm and run for two or three hours. They're hugely popular with the after-work crowd and also a good way to ring in a night on the town. Some venues also have a second happy hour later at night.

Women have yet more options for liquoring up on the cheap during ladies' nights. Many bars and pubs go to extraordinary lengths to lure women with free cocktails, bubbly and nibbles. Of course, they don't do this out of the goodness of their hearts; after all, where there are tipsy women, men (who pay full price) follow. Some ladies' nights run all night; others only during certain hours. The most popular nights are Tuesdays and Wednesdays, with fewer deals on other nights and hardly any on the weekend. Check www.ladiesnightdubai.com for the latest news and a round-up of venues.

DESERT DRUM CIRCLE

Dubai Drums (www.dubaidrums.com) hosts regular full-moon drum circles (adult/child Dhs260/110) in desert camps. These sessions usually last several hours and occasionally until the early hours of the morning. Watch for the near-legendary all-nighter events. Drums and a barbecue dinner are provided.

Dubai: Drinking & Nightlife by Neighbourhood

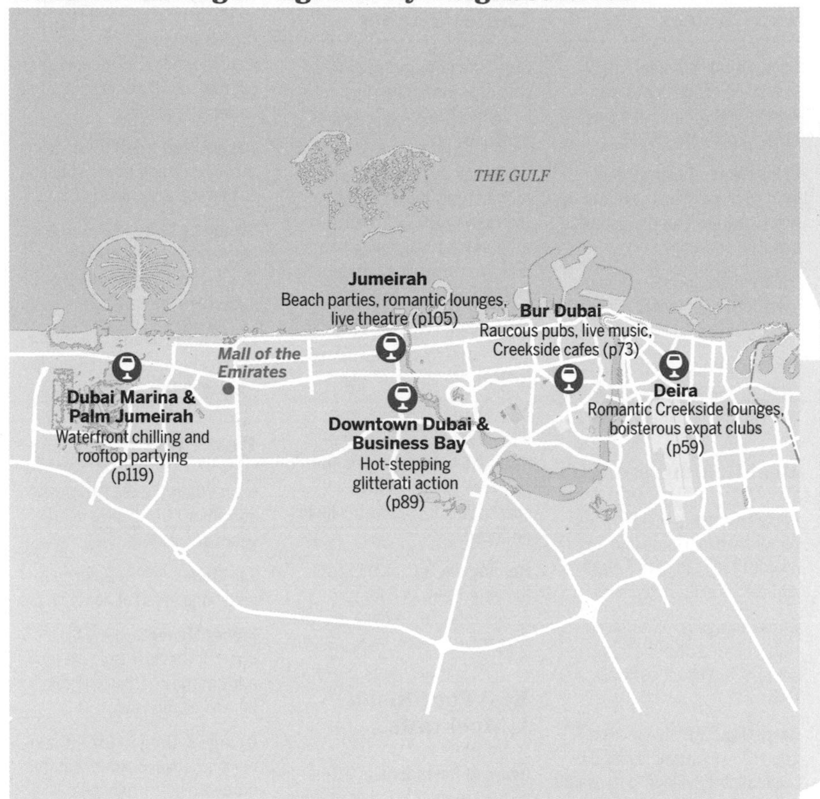

Buying Alcohol

One of the most common questions among first-time visitors is: 'Can I buy alcohol?' The answer is yes – in some places.

Tourists over 21 are allowed to drink alcohol in designated areas such as licensed bars and clubs attached to Western-style hotels. By law, drinking anywhere else does require being in possession of an alcohol licence; which is only issued to non-Muslim residents. The licence grants the right to purchase a fixed monthly limit of alcohol sold in special liquor stores such as African & Eastern and in some branches of Spinneys supermarket. Note that visitors are not officially permitted to purchase alcohol in these places, and staff are supposed to ask to see the licence.

When arriving by air, non-Muslim visitors over 18 may buy 4L of spirits, wine or beer in the airport duty-free shop. However, it is illegal to transport alcohol without a licence, whether in a taxi, rental car or the Dubai Metro. In practice, this is widely ignored.

Zero Tolerance

Dubai has zero tolerance when it comes to drinking and driving. And we mean zero: under no circumstances should you ever get behind the wheel of a car if you've had even one sip of alcohol. Getting caught could get you a one-month stint in jail, a fine and deportation. Even just being drunk in public is illegal and may also result in jail time and a fine of several thousand dirham. Also note that even if you are the victim of a crime (eg sexual assault or robbery), police protection may be limited if you are found to be under the influence.

Lonely Planet's Top Choices

Lock, Stock & Barrel (p119) Industrial-styled booze joint with unpretentious vibe and American comfort food.

Bridgewater Tavern (p89) Next-gen sports bar with trendy black-coloured food, shisha and canalside setting.

Irish Village (p59) A congenial Irish pub with blarney decor, a leafy setting and live music.

Iris (p163) High-tech meets rustic at this Yas Marina favourite with head-spinning cocktails.

Best Beachfront Bars

Jetty Lounge (p121) Sip artful potions while tucked into an overstuffed sofa at this classy and sensuously styled bar.

Bliss Lounge (p120) Chilled Dubai Marina dispensary of some of the finest cocktails in town.

Barasti (p119) Any time is a good time to stumble into the original party village in the sand.

Zero Gravity (p119) Bustling beach club with restaurant and bar.

Best Clubs

Blue Marlin Ibiza UAE (p121) Beachfront hotspot spins electronic sounds for party-hearty hard bodies.

Cirque Le Soir (p90) Flamboyant circus-themed club for uninhibited partying.

White Dubai (p89) Mega-club with dizzying light show on top of the Meydan Racecourse.

Base (p90) State-of-the-art partying in this giant club in Dubai Design District.

Best For Happy Hour Ladies' Nights

Pure Sky Lounge (p122) Sunsets over the Gulf go well with half-off drinks daily between 5pm and 7pm.

Observatory (p122) The home of the skinny ladies' night (Monday) with 150-calorie drinks and a happening happy hour from 5pm to 8pm daily except Friday.

Lucky Voice (p120) Buy one, get one free every day from 4pm to 8pm.

Barasti (p119) Beachfront institution offers 30% drink discounts daily between 4pm and 7pm, plus bottomless sparkly for Dhs50 for the ladies on Tuesdays.

Hemingway's (p143) Expat hangout well loved for pre-dinner lubrication daily except Thursday.

Best For Shisha & Mocktails

Reem Al Bawadi (p120) Spin tales of romance and adventure while kicking back in this Dubai Marina spot.

QDs (p59) Puff away languidly while looking out on the shimmering Creek and skyline.

Smoky Beach (p119) Hipsters mix it up with families at this chic but chill beachfront hangout.

Café Layali Zaman (p133) A regional crowd pleaser, this Abu Dhabi haunt is lively until the small hours.

Yacht Gourmet Restaurant (p142) With uninterrupted views of the capital skyline, this is a shisha classic.

Best Glam Factor

Club Boudoir (p188) Swish venue for beautiful people gyrating to a sound mix from hip-hop to *desi* (Bollywood).

Cavalli Club (p90) Strap on those heels and make a beeline to this sparkling dancing den.

Cirque Le Soir (p90) Acrobats, jugglers and clowns make this cabaret-style nightclub a superhot ticket.

Mad on Yas Island (p163) Biggest nightclub in Abu Dhabi for the see-and-be-seen crowd.

Best Pubs

Irish Village (p59) The classic is still going strong after nearly 20 years in business.

Tap House (p120) Gastropub with huge menu of beers on tap.

Fibber Magee's (p90) A bit down at the heel, but that just adds to the character of this perennial pub fave.

George & Dragon (p73) Channel your inner Bukowski at this hardcore barfly hangout.

Best Rooftop Bars

Siddharta Lounge (p121) Cocktails with a view of the glittering Dubai Marina at this ab-fab lounge by the pool.

40 Kong (p91) Power players and desk jockeys loosen their ties and inhibitions at this swanky outdoor bar.

Beach House Rooftop (p159) Sweeping Gulf views and sensuous lounge music.

Atelier M (p121) This stylish spot has a stellar perch atop the Pier 7 building in the Marina.

Treehouse (p90) Cocktails with views of Burj Khalifa in posh living-room-style cosiness.

Entertainment

Dubai and Abu Dhabi's cultural scenes are growing in leaps and bounds thanks to creative expat communities and the government investing in such ventures as the Dubai Opera to fuel the local performing arts scene. International A-list entertainers regularly make the city's state-of-the-art venues a stop on their concert tours.

Live Music

Alongside plenty of cover bands ranging from cheesy to fabulous, Dubai also has a growing pool of local talent performing at festivals and venues, including Barasti, The Fridge and the Irish Village. Rock and metal dominate, but sounds from punk to pop to hip-hop are also making appearances.

Homegrown bands to keep on the radar include rock groups The Boxtones, Bull Funk Zoo, Kicksound and Nikotin; the metal band Nervecell; the hip-hop collective The Recipe; electronic music mavens Hollaphonic and Arcade 82; singer-songwriter Ester Eden; acoustic fusion band Dahab; and alternative rock by Daisygrim. A major success story is Dubai-based Juliana Down, who became the first local artists to sign with a major label (Sony) in 2011.

One initiative nurturing local talent is Freshly Ground Sounds (www.freshlygroundsounds.com). Founded in 2013 by Ismat Abidi, the collective puts on acoustic and lo-fi sessions in small, indie community venues.

Classical music is not terribly prevalent, although has changed somewhat with the opening of the Dubai Opera whose extensive roster of events includes the occasional concert. Older venues to check out include Dubai Community Theatre and Arts Centre (DUCTAC) and the Madinat Theatre. The Dubai Concert Committee puts on the World Classical Music Series with concerts held at the One&Only Royal Mirage.

Abu Dhabi hosts top talent during the Abu Dhabi Classics concert series held at Emirates Palace and Manarat Al Saadiyat and at the historic Al Jahili Fort in Al Ain.

Festivals

Local and imported talent also rocks the many festivals, including mega-events such as Party in the Park, Groove on the Grass and Sensation. Major festival RedFestDXB has seen line-ups that include international hot shots such as Steve Aoki, Iggy Azalea and Rita Ora. Since 2015, the Wasla Music Festival has shone the spotlight on alternative Arabic music from such diverse genres as rock, soul and techno.

At the Movies

Catching a movie is a favourite local pastime, with most cinephiles flocking to mall-based high-tech multiplexes for the latest international blockbusters. Indie and art-house cinemas are slowly making inroads too, most notably Cinema Akil (p91) in the Alserkal Avenue campus. There's also a smattering of indie film clubs, most importantly the Scene Club (www.thesceneclub.com), founded by Emirati filmmaker Nayla Al Khaja. It screens international alternative flicks at the Roxy cinemas at The Beach in Dubai Marina and at City Walk. Loco'Motion (www.facebook.com/locomotionuae) hosts free screenings at various venues, including the JamJar at Alserkal Avenue.

A long-running outdoor cinema series is the free Movies under the Stars (p75) Sunday screenings at Pyramid Rooftop Gardens in Wafi City.

Theatre & Dance

Dubai's performing arts scene is slowly evolving with the best productions being put on at DUCTAC and the Madinat Theatre in Souk Madinat Jumeirah. Both present their own productions and visiting troupes, both in theatre and dance, especially ballet. Smaller performing arts spaces include the Courtyard Playhouse and The Junction, both in or near Alserkal Avenue arts campus in Al Quoz. The first play written in Dubai premiered at the latter in November 2016. Called *Howzat,* the dramatic comedy was written and directed by Australian playwright Alex Broun and tells the story of an Indian and a Pakistani family living on the Palm Jumeirah. In late 2017 the Vegas-style show *La Perle* by Dragone, created by a co-founder of Cirque du Soleil, became the hot ticket in town.

The most popular traditional dance in the region is the *ayyalah*. The UAE has its own variation, performed to a simple drumbeat, with anywhere between 25 and 200 men standing with their arms linked in two rows facing each other. They wave walking sticks or swords in front of themselves and sway back and forth, the two rows taking it in turn to sing. It's a war dance and the words expound the virtues of courage and bravery in battle. You can see the dance on video at the Dubai Museum or during festivals at heritage festivals around the UAE.

Lonely Planet's Top Choices

Dubai Opera (p93) Stunning new Downtown venue with a cultural roster ranging from opera to film screenings.

La Perle by Dragone (p91) Las Vegas–style show with acrobats performing on an 'aquatic' stage in a custom-built theatre.

Cinema Akil (p91) The pop-up indie film purveyor has found a permanent home at Alserkal Avenue.

Jazz@PizzaExpress (p123) Part casual restaurant, part live music joint, and always good fun.

Abu Dhabi Classics (p144) Top classical concerts with renowned orchestras held at the Emirates Palace and other venues.

Best Cinema

Cinema Akil (p91) Global art-house flicks amid the warehouses on Alserkal Avenue gallery campus.

Reel Cinemas (p92) Dubai Mall magnet features the latest in movie-going technology.

Movies under the Stars (p75) Free al fresco movies.

Vox Cinemas (p163) 3D and 4D films make for a sensory experience at Yas Mall.

Best Live-Music Venues

Blue Bar (p91) Long-running jazz and blues joint with wallet-friendly cocktails.

Fridge (p92) Alternative venue with weekly concert series featuring up-and-coming local artists.

MusicHall (p123) Weekend venue serving up world music in supper club surroundings.

Jazz Bar & Dining (p144) Jazz bands entertain a sage audience at this old Abu Dhabi favourite.

Du Arena (p164) Outdoor venue on Yas Island that's a prime stop for top international artists on tour.

Best Theatre

Dubai Community Theatre & Arts Centre (DUCTAC) (p107) Non-profit community theatre on top of the Mall of the Emirates hosts eclectic theatre for young and old.

Madinat Theatre (p107) Classic proscenium stage theatre with easily digestible cultural fare geared towards expats.

Courtyard Playhouse (p92) Beloved but tiny community theatre that presents improv, stand-up comedy and kids' theatre.

Dubai Mall (p82)

Shopping

Shopping is a favourite pastime here – especially in Dubai, which boasts not only the world's largest mall but also shopping centres that resemble ancient Egypt or an Italian village and feature ski slopes, ice rinks and giant aquariums. Souqs provide more traditional flair, and a growing crop of urban outdoor malls, indie boutiques and galleries beckon as well.

NEED TO KNOW

Opening Hours

- Malls are open from 10am to 10pm Saturday to Wednesday and until 11pm or midnight on Thursday and Friday (weekends).
- Malls get especially packed on Thursday night, Friday afternoon and on Saturdays.
- Souqs close from 1pm to 4pm for prayer, lunch and rest. Some supermarkets are open 24 hours.

Useful Websites

www.littlemajlis.com Specialises in handmade and artisanal items from around the region.

www.quickdubai.com Great for gifts, including last-minute needs such as cakes and flowers.

www.souq.com A local version of eBay, recently acquired by Amazon, with some top bargains and plenty of variety.

www.crazydeals.com From electronics to toys, it's bargains galore at this site.

Gold Souk (p52), Deira

Where to Shop

Dubai and Abu Dhabi have just about perfected the art of the mall, which is the de facto 'town plaza': the place to go with friends and family to hang out, eat and be entertained as well as shop. Most are air-conditioned mega-malls anchored by big department stores such as Bloomingdale's or Galeries Lafayette and filled with regional and international chains, from high-street retailers to couture fashion labels. Almost all have at least one large supermarket like Carrefour, Spinneys or Waitrose.

In Dubai, a recent fad has seen the arrival of urban outdoor malls like BoxPark in Jumeirah and City Walk near Downtown Dubai, with a smaller selection of shops calibrated to the needs and tastes of neighbourhood residents. There's also a growing number of indie designer boutiques, especially along Jumeirah Rd, as well as a bustling monthly flea market. Small Indian- or Asian-run department stores are great for picking up bargain basics.

If you're looking for local character, head to the souqs in Bur Dubai and Deira in Dubai or the Al Mina port area in Abu Dhabi. In these colourful, cacophonous warrens you can pick up everything from a gram of saffron to an ounce of gold, usually at good prices. It helps to sharpen your haggling skills. You may also be tempted by touts trying to sell knock-off designer perfumes and handbags – it's up to you to ignore them or accept their offer. Prices are usually fixed in modern souqs, such as Souk Madinat Jumeirah. Echoing an *Arabian Nights* set, they're filled with tourist-geared souvenirs of varying quality.

What To Buy

BEDOUIN JEWELLERY

Bedouin jewellery is a brilliant buy and, given the steady popularity of boho-ethnic chic, makes a great gift. Look for elaborate silver necklaces and pendants, chunky earrings and rings, and wedding belts, many of which incorporate coral, turquoise and semiprecious stones. Very little of the older Bedouin jewellery comes from the Emirates; most of it originates in Oman, Yemen and Afghanistan; cheaper stuff usually hails from India.

PASHMINAS

These feather-light shawls handmade by weavers in Kashmir from genuine pashmina (goat hair) or shahtoosh (the down hair of a Tibetan antelope) are a quality souvenir that you might actually use back home. They come in so many colours and styles – some beaded and embroidered, others with pompom edging – you'll have no trouble finding one you like. If you can't afford the genuine thing, don't fret: the machine-made ones are almost as pretty.

CARPETS

Fine Persian carpets, colourful Turkish and Kurdish *kilims* and rough-knotted Bedouin rugs are all widely available. Dubai has a reputation in the region for having the highest-quality carpets at the best prices. Bargaining is the norm. If you can't secure the price you want, head to another shop. When you buy a carpet, make sure you are given a Certificate of Authentication issued by the Dubai Chamber of Commerce & Industry.

ARABIAN HANDICRAFTS & SOUVENIRS

Arabian handicrafts are as popular with visitors as carpets, gold and perfume. The arabesque decor of top-end hotels and restaurants seems to inspire travellers to pack away little pieces of exotica to recreate their own little genie bottles back home. Head to the souqs for Moroccan coloured lanterns, Syrian rosewood furniture inlaid with mother-of-pearl, Arabian brass coffee pots, Turkish miniature paintings, and embroidered Indian wall hangings and cushion covers dotted with tiny mirrors.

PERFUME & INCENSE

Attars (Arabian perfumes) are spicy and strong. Historically, this was a necessity: with precious little water, washing was a sometimes-thing, so women smothered themselves in *attars* and incense. As you walk past Emirati women (and men), catch a whiff of their exotic perfume. You can find Arabian perfume shops in all Dubai's malls as well as in the Perfume Souq: a couple of Deira roads (Sikkat Al Khail and Al Soor) with a fairly high density of perfume stores.

Shopping for perfume can wear out your sense of smell. If you're in the market for Arabian scents, do what top perfumers do to neutralise their olfactory palate: close your mouth and make three forceful exhalations through your nose. Blast the air hard, in short bursts, using your diaphragm. Blowing your nose first is probably a wise idea... Some people incorrectly say to smell coffee grounds, but all this practice does is numb your sense of smell.

EXOTIC DELICACIES

Fragrant Iranian saffron costs far less here than it does back home. Buy it in the souqs or in supermarkets. Honey from Saudi Arabia, Yemen and Oman is scrumptious and can be found in speciality shops, the malls, the Spice Souq and in supermarkets. Its colour ranges from light gold to almost black.

FABRIC

Vendors at Bur Dubai Souq and adjacent lanes carry vibrant, colourful textiles from India and South Asia. They're fairly inexpensive, but quality varies. Silk, cotton and linen represent the best value. If you're no good at sewing, ask for a referral to a tailor. Dubai's tailors work quickly, and their rates are very reasonable.

ELECTRONICS

If it plugs into a wall, you can buy it in Dubai. Because of minimal duties, Dubai is the cheapest place in the region to buy electronics and digital technology. The selection is huge. For the lowest prices and no-name brands, head to Al Fahidi St in Bur Dubai and the area around Al Sabkha Rd and Al Maktoum Hospital Rd, near Baniyas Sq, known as the Electronics Souq. If you want an international warranty, shell out the extra money and head to a mall or Jumbo Electronics.

GOLD & GEMS

Calling itself the 'City of Gold', Dubai's glistening reputation grows from low prices and the sheer breadth of stock. There are a

PASHMINA: TELLING REAL FROM FAKE

Pashmina shawls come in all sorts of wonderful colours and patterns. Originally made from feather-light cashmere, there are now many cheaper machine-made synthetic versions around. Before forking over hundreds of dirham, how can you make sure you're buying the real thing? Here's the trick. Hold the fabric at its corner. Loop your index finger around it and squeeze hard. Now pull the fabric through. If it's polyester, it won't budge. If it's cashmere, it'll pull through – though the friction may give you a mild case of rope burn. Try it at home with a thin piece of polyester before you hit the shops and then try it with cashmere. You'll never be fooled again.

Dubai: Shopping by Neighbourhood

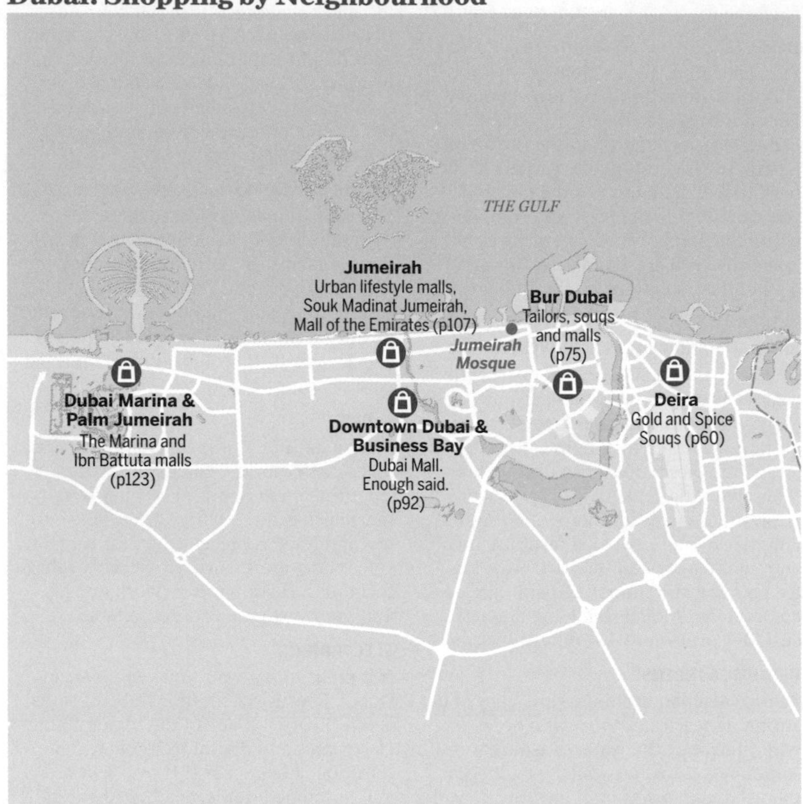

whopping 700 jewellery stores around town, including nearly 300 at the Gold Souq and about 90 at the Gold & Diamond Park.

ART

With new galleries springing up all the time and the scene becoming increasingly diverse, it's easier than ever to snap up a piece of original art created by a local or regional artist, especially since prices are still very reasonable. Nose around the cutting-edge spaces at Dubai's Alserkal Avenue or check out the more established players in Gate Village at the Dubai International Finance Centre (DIFC).

DATES

Dates are the ultimate luxury food of Arabia. The best ones come from Saudi Arabia, which has the ideal growing conditions: sandy, alkaline soil and extreme heat. Look for dates that are big and fat, with gooey-moist centres. Because they have a 70% sugar content, dates technically have a very long shelf life, but you'll find they taste best around the autumn harvest. A major purveyor of quality dates is Bateel, whose boutiques look like jewellery stores. For better prices, a huge range and good quality, head to the public produce market in Deira (next to the New Fish Market).

SOUVENIRS

The quintessential kitsch souvenir used to be a mosque clock with a call-to-prayer alarm. Now the souqs and souvenir shops overflow with wacky, kitsch gifts – glass Burj Al Arab paperweights, Russian nesting dolls in Emirati national dress, key rings strung with miniature towers, camel-crossing-sign fridge magnets, and coffee mugs and baseball caps with Sheikh Zayed or Sheikh Mohammed waving to the crowd.

Lonely Planet's Top Choices

Ajmal (p77) Exotic Arabian essential oils and perfumes sold in exquisitely beautiful bottles.

S*uce (p108) Sassy avant-garde fashions from a wide range of young international designers.

Gold Souq (p52) A pageant of glitter and craftsmanship that's fun to see even without buying.

Candylicious (p93) Willy Wonka would feel right at home in this super-sized sweets store with candy kitchen.

Wafi Gourmet (p143) Foodies salivate over the mother lode of Arabian edibles at this cafe-shop combo with outlets in both Dubai and Abu Dhabi.

Saturday Market (p164) On Yas Island in Abu Dhabi, this market showcases local crafts.

Best For Gifts

Camel Company (p107) Go camel-crazy at this multi-outlet boutique starring cuddly camels on everything from mugs to notepads.

Bateel (p76) Delicious dates presented like precious jewels in an elegant boutique setting.

Lata's (p107) Quality souvenirs from around North Africa and the Middle East.

Mirzam (p93) Dubai's own chocolate factory wraps its yummy single-origin bean bars in artistic designs.

Women's Handicraft Centre (p157) Run by the Abu Dhabi government, this centre supports local cottage industries.

Jalabiat Yasmine (p109) A fabulous assortment of quality pashminas, including precious hand-embroidered ones.

Miraj Islamic Centre (p143) High-quality – albeit pricey – souvenir and gift shopping.

Best For Indie Fashion

The cARTel (p93) Avant-garde fashions by local and international designers in the new design district.

S*uce (p108) Home-grown concept store that showcases regional designers in fashion, accessories and jewellery.

O Concept (p108) This edgy Jumeirah boutique has young things looking good at reasonable price tags.

O' de Rose (p108) Provides a platform for regional indie designers with a love for bold colour.

Fabindia (p77) His-and-hers fashion created by Indian villagers; perks up any outfit.

Best Markets

Ripe Market – Zabeel Park (p75) Happening market with quality local produce alongside artsy-crafty stuff and global snack stands.

Dubai Flea Market (p75) True bargains abound at this monthly market on the beautiful grounds of Zabeel Park.

New Fish Market (p56) Relocated to air-conditioned digs, but still a atmospheric (and odiferous) buying frenzy.

Carpet Souq (p159) Haggle hard for a hand-loomed kilim from the Baluchi traders at this Abu Dhabi market.

Best Modern Souqs

Souk Al Bahar (p93) Across from Dubai Mall, this richly decorated arabesque souq teems with restaurants and souvenir shops.

Souk Madinat Jumeirah (p107) This tourist-geared souk follows a harmonious rhythm of courtyards, alleyways and outdoor areas.

Souq Khan Murjan (p78) Part of Wafi Mall, this exotically styled labyrinthine souq takes its design cue from the bazaar in Baghdad.

World Trade Center Souk (p134) Norman Foster's interpretation of the Arabian souk sits on Abu Dhabi's old central market.

Souk Qaryat Al Beri (p154) An attractive warren of shops with views of Sheikh Zayed Grand Mosque across the Khor Al Maqta.

Best Shopping Malls

Dubai Mall (p82) A power-shopper's Shangri-La, Dubai Mall is the largest shopping mall in the world.

Mall of the Emirates (p107) Get lost amid the ample temptations of this mega-mall famous for its indoor ski slope.

BoxPark (p108) This urban strip brims with cool cafes and eclectic boutiques in shipping containers.

Ibn Battuta Mall (p123) Shopping goes exotic amid gorgeous decor in six country-themed courts, including Persia, India and Spain.

Yas Mall (p164) A handy pit stop after a spin around the adjacent Ferrari World Abu Dhabi theme park.

Galleria at Maryah Island (p148) Part of the 'wow' factor in the Sowwah Square complex on Al Maryah Island.

Sports & Activities

No matter what kind of activity gets you away from the pool, beach or shopping mall, you'll be able to pursue it in Dubai and Abu Dhabi, be it on or in the water, on the ice, in the desert, on the ski slopes or in the spa.

Water Sports

DIVING & SNORKELLING

Diving around Dubai means mostly nosing around shipwrecks on the sandy seabed of the Gulf at a depth of between 10m and 35m. The better sites are generally a long way offshore and more suited to experienced divers. Creatures you might encounter include clownfish, sea snakes, Arabian angelfish, rays and barracuda. For more exciting dives (or snorkelling trips), you need to head to the East Coast (Khor Fakkan and Dibba) or north to the rugged Musandam Peninsula, which is part of Oman. A well-established local company leading guided dives, snorkelling trips and certification courses is Al Boom Diving (p110).

SURFING & KITESURFING

Dubai ain't Hawaii (waves average 0.67m), but that's not stopping a growing community of surfers from hitting the waves at Sunset Beach next to the Jumeirah Beach Hotel. Prime months are from December to February, although October, March and April may also bring decent swells. If there are no waves, you can still hit the water on a stand-up paddleboard (SUP). Rent equipment or get lessons in either sport at Surf House Dubai (p110) whose website also features a surf cam and a daily updated surf report.

Kitesurfers congregate at northwest-facing Kite Beach, which also has two outfits – Dubai Kitesurfing School (p110) and Dukite (p110) – that offer lessons and courses. In Abu Dhabi, Eywoa (p165) on Yas Island offers the latest in equipment and on-the-water action.

MOTORISED WATER SPORTS

Practically all of the big beach resorts maintain state-of-the-art water-sports centres that offer both guests and non-guests a range of ways to get out on the water. The

BEACH FUN

Dubai residents love their beaches. Many who live in Jumeirah and the Dubai Marina, within splashing distance of the crystal-clear turquoise waters, make it a daily ritual to head down to the beach, while the rest of Dubai typically hits the sand on Fridays and Saturdays.

If you're not staying at a beachfront hotel fronted by its own sandy ribbon, you can either drop big dirham for a day guest pass, pay to chill at a snazzy beach club or go dipping for free at a public beach such as **Al Mamzar** (p55) near Sharjah or along **Kite Beach** (p100), **Sunset Beach** (p100) or **JBR Beach** (p113) in Jumeirah. All have undergone enormous infrastructure improvements in recent years and now come with changing rooms, toilets, showers, sunlounger and umbrella rentals, sports facilities, a jogging track, playgrounds and kiosks.

AL WATHBA CYCLING TRACK

Locals rave about the **Al Wathba Cycling Track** (Al Wathba; bike rental Dhs30-60; ⏲24hr), located 40 minutes by car from Abu Dhabi and near the camel racing track. You'll find five different scenic loops through the desert (8km, 16km, 20km, 22km and 30km), all of which are most cinematic at sunrise and sunset. The course is equipped with solar-powered lights as well, so you can ride into the cool night-time air. There's also a bar, a Besport bike shop and a changing room with lockers and showers. It's just off the E22 Abu Dhabi–Al Ain Rd.

menu may include waterskiing, jet-skiing, wakeboarding, parasailing and power boating. Priority is given to hotel guests; visitors can expect to pay higher rates or a beach access fee.

BOAT CHARTER

For a glorious perspective of Dubai from the water, rent your own skippered boat: try the Dubai Creek Golf & Yacht Club (p61). Options include a one-hour Creek cruise for Dhs450, but for the full experience book at least a four-hour trip that follows Dubai Canal out to the Gulf and from there to the World islands, Palm Jumeirah and the Burj Al Arab (Dhs1500). Rates are good for up to six passengers. Fishing trips cost Dhs2000 for four hours and Dhs375 per additional hour. In Abu Dhabi, one company offering sunset cruises and other watery adventures is **Belevari Catamarans** (Map p136; ☎02 643 1494; http://belevari.com; Corniche Rd (West), Hiltonia Beach Club, Fitness & Spa; child/adult sunset Dhs100/120, island Dhs199/349; ⏲sunset 5pm Tue-Thu, island 1pm Fri-Sat).

WATER PARKS

When the mercury climbs, a fun way to keep cool is with slides, thrill rides, lagoons, pools and beaches at a water park. Dubai fields four of these splash zones: the adventurous (Aquaventure; p114), the newest (Legoland; p124), the classic (Wild Wadi; p109) and the low-key (Splash 'n' Party; p110). In Abu Dhabi, meanwhile, Yas Waterworld (p164) is the biggest kid on the block with some 40 rides to plunge, zoom, catapult and pummel you.

Golf

Golf is huge in the Gulf, and nowhere more so than in Dubai, which has 10 major golf courses, including several at championship-level designed by big names such as Greg Norman, the man behind **Jumeirah Golf Estates** (☎04 818 2000; www.jumeirahgolfestates.com; off Sheikh Mohammed bin Zayed Hwy (Hwy E311), Sports City; Fire/Earth Dhs655/795 Sun-Thu, Dhs875/995 Fri & Sat; Ⓜ Jumeirah Lakes Towers). Other world-class courses include Majlis and Faldo, both at Emirates Golf Club (p125), and the sentimental favourite, Dubai Creek Golf & Yacht Club (p61). Overall, clubs don't require memberships, but green fees can soar to Dhs1100 for 18 holes during the peak winter season (November to March), although they drop the rest of the year, especially in summer. Proper attire is essential. If you're serious about golf, reserve your tee times in advance. Abu Dhabi also has its share of golf courses, include Yas Links Abu Dhabi (p165), which is partly set among mangroves.

Running

The winter months are cool enough for running nearly anytime during the day; in summer get up with the sun to avoid heatstroke. Running tracks have proliferated of late in Dubai. The classic is in Zabeel Park (p69), but newer ones parallel the beachfront in Jumeirah, Dubai Canal and the crescent of Palm Jumeirah (p125). A short but sweet run is through Al Ittihad Park on the Palm's trunk. Prefer running with company? Check out Desert Road Runners (www.desertroadrunners.club) or Dubai Creek Striders (www.dubaicreekstriders.org). If you're into the more social aspects of running (read: drinking afterwards), look into DH3, aka the Desert Hash House Harriers (www.deserthash.org). The **Dubai Marathon** (www.dubaimarathon.org; ⏲late Jan) takes over city streets in January. In Abu Dhabi, you can run (or cycle) along the Formula One track at the Yas Marina Circuit three times a week for free.

Desert Driving

Off-road driving in the desert (also disturbingly known as 'dune bashing') is hugely popular. At weekends (Fridays and Saturdays), the city's traffic-tired workers zip down the Dubai–Hatta road and unleash their pent-up energy on the sand dunes, such as the ruby-red heap of sand nicknamed 'Big Red'. All the major car hire companies provide 4WD vehicles. Expect to pay around Dhs500 for 24 hours for a Toyota Fortuner or a Honda CRV, plus insurance. If you have no experience in driving off-road, we strongly recommend first taking a desert driving course, such as those offered by **Desert Rangers** (☎04 456 9944; www.desertrangers.com).

Day Spas & Massage

Though you can get a good rub-down at most sports clubs, for the proper treatment make a booking at a spa. Avoid Friday and Saturday, which can get busy, and ask if the treatment includes use of the pool and grounds. If it does, make a day of it – arrive early and relax poolside.

Skiing

The largest indoor ski slope in the world, Ski Dubai (p109), at the Mall of the Emirates, is an incongruous but delightful stop for winter sports enthusiasts. You can also take lessons and learn how to snowboard.

Spectator Sports

HORSE RACING

Horse racing has a long and vaunted tradition in the Emirates. Racing season kicks off in November and culminates in March with the Dubai World Cup, the world's richest horse race. It's held at the superb Meydan Racecourse (p88), a futuristic stadium with a grandstand bigger than most airport terminals.

CAMEL RACING

Camel racing is deeply rooted in the Emirati soul and attending a race is hugely popular with locals and visitors alike. It's quite an exhilarating sight when hundreds of one-humped dromedaries fly out of their pens and onto the dirt track, jostling for position in a lumbering gallop with legs splayed out in all directions, scrambling towards the finish line at top speeds of 40km/h. Fastened to their backs are 'robot jockeys' with remote-controlled whips operated by the owners while driving their white SUVs on a separate track alongside the animals.

Racing season runs between November and April. The closest track to Dubai is Al Marmoum (p88), about 40km south of town en route to Al Ain. The other major track is Al Wathba (p164), about 45km southeast of Abu Dhabi. For the schedule, check www.dubaicalendar.ae (search for 'camel'). Admission is free.

MOTOR RACING

Motor sports are exceedingly popular in the UAE with the Abu Dhabi Grand Prix (p45), a Formula One race held in November at the Yas Marina Circuit on Yas Island, being the most prestigious event. One of the oldest races is the Abu Dhabi Desert Challenge (www.facebook.com/AbuDhabiDesertChallenge), held in March, an off-road rally that has brought top car and motorcycle drivers to the UAE since 1991. As for Dubai, the 24 Hour Race series (www.24hseries.com/24h-dubai) makes a stop in Dubai in January with the endurance race held at the Dubai Autodrome. Also look for events hosted by the Emirates Motor Sport Federation (www.facebook.com/emsfuae), which inaugurated the Emirates Desert Championship in 2003.

FUN FACTS ABOUT CAMELS

Camels...

- Can reach a top speed of 40km/h.
- Are pregnant for 13 to 15 months.
- Can go up to 15 days without drinking.
- Soak up water like a sponge when thirsty, guzzling up to 100L in 10 minutes.
- Don't store water in their humps.
- Have a life expectancy of 50 to 60 years.
- Have a three-part stomach.
- In Arabia are one-humped dromedaries.
- Can travel 160km without drinking.
- Move both legs on one side of the body at the same time.

TOP FIVE ABU DHABI SPORTING EVENTS

Abu Dhabi Grand Prix (02 659 9800; www.yasmarinacircuit.com; Yas Marina Circuit; Nov) The Formula 1 Abu Dhabi Grand Prix is a major event, attracting visitors from across the region as well as international racing fans. This annual day-night race has one of the most impressive circuits on the race calendar, including a marina setting and a section of track that passes through the Yas Viceroy Abu Dhabi hotel.

Red Bull Air Race (http://airrace.redbull.com; Corniche Breakwater; Feb) This spectacular, low-altitude air race virtually skims the water at 370km/h, flying only 20m above the water's surface. Pilots have to navigate a pylon obstacle course – thrilling viewing from the Corniche.

Mubadala World Tennis Championship (www.mubadalawtc.com; Sheikh Zayed Sports City) Featuring the world's best men's players, including Djokovic, Nadal, Wawrinka and Murray, this is a key event at the start of the tennis year.

World Triathlon (www.abudhabi.triathlon.org; Mar) If you thought you were fit, watch the world's best competitors swim, cycle and run, and you may feel it's time to get back in the gym. There's good viewing from the Corniche.

XCAT World Series Powerboat Race (www.xcatracing.com; Corniche; Dec) These 6000cc powerboats reach speeds of more than 190km/h along the breakwater in front of the Abu Dhabi Corniche, making for an exhilarating spectacle. Lots of street entertainment springs up along the beachfront as well, making for an enjoyable day out.

FOOTBALL (SOCCER)

Attending a local football match can be great fun as up to 10,000 spectators crowd into the stadiums to passionately cheer on their favourite team while a singer and a band of drummers lead song and dance routines to further inspire the players. Ten clubs compete in the country's league – called the Arabian Gulf League (www.agleague.ae) – which was founded in 1973 and went pro in 2008. The season runs from mid-September to mid-May. Check the league's website for the schedule and venues.

CRICKET

The enormous Indian and Pakistani communities in Dubai l-o-v-e cricket. You'll see them playing on sandy lots between buildings during their lunch breaks, in parks on their days off, and late at night in empty car parks. If you want to get under the skin of the game, talk to taxi drivers. But first ask where your driver is from – there's fierce competition between Pakistanis and Indians. Each will tell you that his country's team is the best and then explain at length why. (Some drivers need a bit of cajoling; show enthusiasm and you'll get the whole story.) Remember: these two nationalities account for about 45% of Dubai's population, far outnumbering Emiratis. Because most of them can't afford the price of satellite TV, they meet up outside their local eateries in Deira or Bur Dubai to watch the match. Throngs of riveted fans swarm the pavements beneath the crackling neon – it's a sight to behold.

Sports & Activities by Dubai Neighbourhood

- **Deira** (p61) Good boating, golfing, tennis and spas.
- **Bur Dubai** (p78) Running in Zabeel Park or Creek Park.
- **Downtown Dubai** (p94) Ice skating at Dubai Mall, fancy spas in the hotels, running along Dubai Canal.
- **Jumeirah** (p109) Swimming, boating, surfing, kitesurfing, SUP, water sports, Wild Wadi Waterpark, skiing, running.
- **Dubai Marina & Palm Jumeirah** (p124) Swimming, water sports, golfing, boating, diving, Aquaventure water park, sky diving, running.

Explore Dubai & Abu Dhabi

DUBAI'S **TOP SIGHTS**

Neighbourhoods at a Glance

❶ Deira p50

Deira feels like a cross between Cairo and Karachi. Dusty, crowded and chaotic, it's a world away from the slick and sanitised new districts that have mushroomed along Sheikh Zayed Rd. Along the Creek, colourful wooden dhows engage in the time-tested trading of goods destined for Iran, Sudan and other locales. Nearby, the bustling souqs are atmospheric ancestors of today's malls, where you can sip sugary tea and haggle for bargains with traders whose families have tended the same shop for generations.

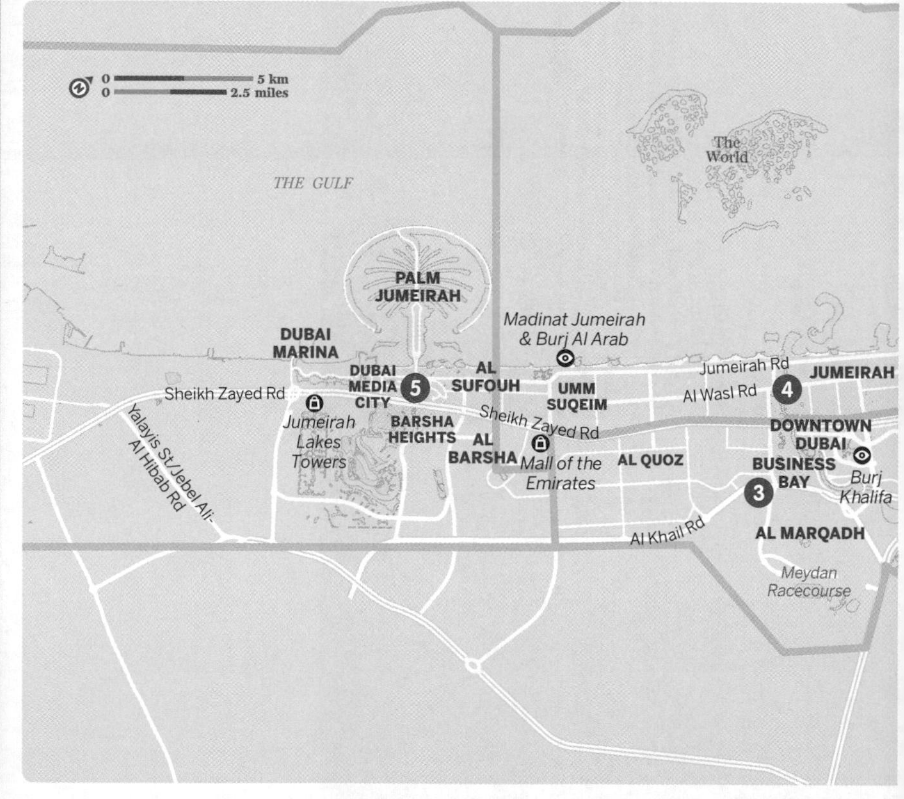

2 Bur Dubai p64

The site of the city's original settlement, Bur Dubai may not be as sleek and sophisticated as the newer townships, but it exudes a real community spirit rarely found elsewhere. Come here to soak up the city's past in the Dubai Museum and the restored Al Fahidi and Shindagha historic districts (the latter is getting a large-scale makeover). Stock up on fabrics and souvenirs in the souq and then watch the boat traffic on Dubai Creek from a waterfront cafe. The warren of lanes around the souq teems with wonderfully authentic ethnic eateries.

3 Downtown Dubai & Business Bay p79

Dubai's vibrant and urban centrepiece is anchored by the 828m-high Burj Khalifa, the world's tallest structure, and also brims with other distinctive and futuristic architecture, especially along Sheikh Zayed Rd and in the Dubai Design District. Downtown blockbuster sights include the Dubai Mall, the Dubai Fountain and the new Dubai Opera. Also new is the Dubai Canal that cuts through Business Bay before spilling into the Gulf. Further south, in Al Quoz, Alserkal Avenue has evolved into Dubai's main alternative arts and creative hub.

4 Jumeirah p95

Before there was the Palm Jumeirah and Dubai Marina, Jumeirah was the place where everybody went to realise their Dubai dreams. The emirate's answer to Bondi or Malibu stretches from the Etihad Museum to the Burj Al Arab. In between are excellent public beaches, urban lifestyle malls, boutique shopping and a mix of Mercedes and expensive 4WDs in villa driveways. The new Dubai Canal cuts right through and will reshape the district for years to come. New islands and peninsulas, meanwhile, continue to spring up offshore.

5 Dubai Marina & Palm Jumeirah p111

Dubai's southernmost districts are popular upmarket residential areas, but they also brim with luxurious beachfront resorts. Aside from tanning and swimming, diversions here include strolls along the Dubai Marina waterfront, The Walk at JBR and The Beach at JBR, and – soon – rides on the world's largest observation wheel. Jutting into the Gulf is the Palm Jumeirah, the smallest of three planned artificial islands, and home to fancy resorts and the Aquaventure water park. Meanwhile, further south near Jebel Ali, the theme parks of Dubai Parks & Resort beckon.

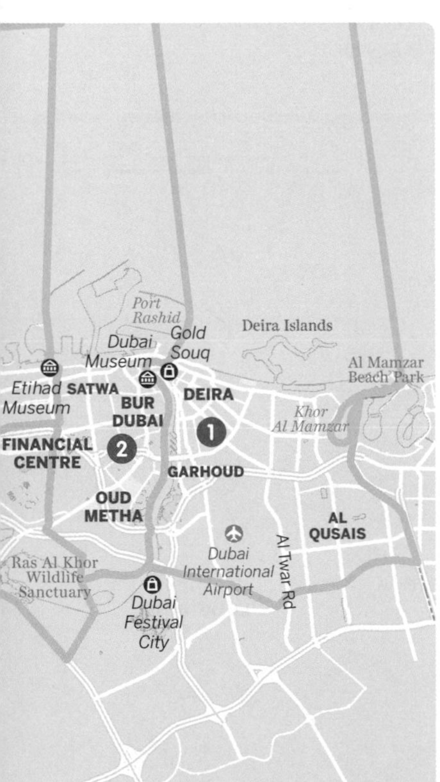

Deira

Neighbourhood Top Five

1 Spice Souq (p53) Plunging headlong into this colourful and pungent warren of lanes, a memorable feast for all the senses.

2 Gold Souq (p52) Wandering below the wooden arcades of this famous bazaar – like rummaging around a veritable treasure chest.

3 QDs (p59) Feeling mesmerised by the views across the glistening Creek while sipping cocktails and puffing on shisha at this al fresco lounge.

4 Dinner cruise (p58) Taking in Dubai Creek's skyline from the deck of a wooden dhow while grazing at the buffet and listening to an oud player.

5 Dubai Creek (p54) Crossing the Creek in a traditional abra (wooden ferry) in an atmospheric journey that has not changed for decades.

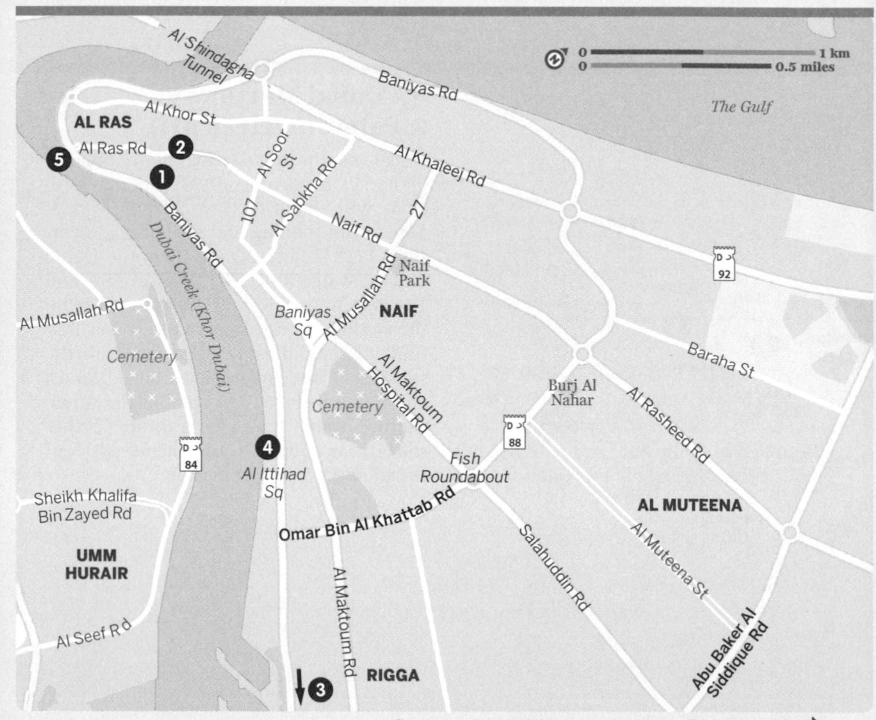

For more detail of this area see maps p244 and p246.

Explore Deira

Hugging the northern side of the Creek, Deira is one of Dubai's oldest and most charismatic neighbourhoods, a world apart from the sky-piercing towers of modern Dubai. The most historic area is Al Ras, near the mouth of the Creek, home to a century-old pearl trader's home (p54) and the city's first school (p54). Nearby, brightly painted dhows (traditional cargo boats) still dock along the waterfront as they have since the 1830s. But Deira's most seductive lure is its cluster of atmospheric souqs (spice, gold, perfume), a tangle of narrow lanes heaving with a cacophony of sounds and smells that bursts to life in the late afternoon.

Deira is also Dubai's most dazzlingly multicultural neighbourhood, a bustling cauldron peacefully shared by immigrants from around the globe. Many operate little restaurants perfect for soaking up the local colour and for sampling authentic fare from far-flung locales. For a more upmarket experience, book a dinner cruise aboard a dhow, festively decorated with twinkling lights, or head to a Creekside al fresco lounge in one of the high-end hotels. Deira also brims with nightclubs, usually found in budget or midrange hotels. They typically feature enthusiastic house bands, cheap beer and, yes, some illicit and seedy goings-on.

Further south along the Creek, Deira gets increasingly modern. There are big shopping malls like the Deira City Centre (p61) and architectural landmarks like the Etisalat Tower, easily recognised by the giant 'golf ball' at its top. Still further on, Dubai Festival City is not just another mall but, increasingly, an entertainment zone in this part of the city.

Local Life

➜ **Haggle** Enjoy bargaining in the souqs. It's a favourite local pastime and, as long as you're comfortable with a little light-hearted confrontation, it's good fun.

➜ **Traditional coffee** Kick-start your day by ducking into a tucked-away cafe for a shot of Arabic coffee or *karak chai* (spicy tea).

➜ **Exotic meals** Take a culinary journey to Yemen, Lebanon or wherever your nose leads you in the souqs and around Al Rigga and Salah Al Din metro stations.

➜ **People-watching** Watch wiry deckhands load and unload brightly hued dhows bound for Iran and India.

Getting There & Away

➜ **Metro** Deira is served by both the Red and Green Lines; they intersect at Union station. The Red Line travels to the airport.

➜ **Abra** Water taxis links the souqs in Deira and Bur Dubai.

Lonely Planet's Top Tip

A cheap and easy way to get a feel for the atmospheric Dubai Creek is by crossing it aboard an abra for a mere Dhs1. If you want a more in-depth experience, consider hiring a private abra to sail past various Creek communities with the wind in your hair and seagulls cheering you on. Boats can be hired at all abra stations; the going rate is Dhs120 per hour.

Best Places to Eat

➜ Al Tawasol (p55)
➜ Aroos Damascus (p55)
➜ Aseelah (p56)
➜ Qwaider Al Nabulsi (p55)
➜ Thai Kitchen (p56)

For reviews, see p55.

Best Places to Drink

➜ QDs (p59)
➜ Irish Village (p59)
➜ Juice World (p59)

For reviews, see p59.

Best Places to Shop

➜ Spice Souq (p53)
➜ Deira City Centre (p61)
➜ Gold Souq (p52)
➜ New Fish Market (p56)

For reviews, see p60.

KRITSANA LAROQUE / SHUTTERSTOCK ©

TOP SIGHT
GOLD SOUQ

'Dubai: City of Gold' screams the banner atop the rainbow-coloured LED display at the wooden entrance gate to Dubai's Gold Souq. Moments later you'll feel as though you've just plunged into a latter-day Aladdin's cave. Gold has been big business in Dubai since the 1940s. Today, the emirate is one of the world's largest gold markets, accounting for roughly 25% of the global trade.

Dozens of jewellery shops spilling over with gold, diamonds, pearls, silver and platinum line the souq's car-free, wooden-latticed central axis. From stud earrings to intricate wedding necklaces, it's a dazzling display and a must-see, even if you're not part of the bling brigade. Most shops are run by Indian merchants, while customers are mostly Indian or Arab, which helps explain the deep yellow tint of the gold and the often extremely elaborate designs, as is preferred in those parts of the world.

Simply watching the goings-on at the souq is another treat, especially during the bustling evenings. Settle down on a bench, buy a bottle of juice from one of the itinerant sellers and take in the colourful street theatre. With a little patience, you should see hard-working Afghan men dragging heavy carts of goods, African women in bright kaftans balancing their purchases on their heads and chattering local women out on a shopping spree.

Dubai being the capital of superlatives, the Gold Souq is naturally home to a record-breaking piece of jewellery. Stop at the Kanz shop just past the main souq entrance (off Old Baladiya St) to snap a selfie with the world's largest and heaviest gold ring, as certified by none other than Guinness World Records. Called the Najmat Taiba (Star of Taiba), the 21-carat beauty weighs in at nearly 64kg and is worth a hefty US$3 million.

DON'T MISS

- World's largest gold ring
- Strolling down the central arcade

PRACTICALITIES

- Map p244, B1
- Sikkat al Khail St
- 10am-1pm & 3-10pm
- Al Ras

SIGHTS

The main sights of Deira are all within easy walking distance of each other around the atmospheric mouth of Dubai Creek.

GOLD SOUQ — MARKET

See p52.

DHOW WHARFAGE — HARBOUR

Map p244 (along Baniyas Rd; MAl Ras) Stroll down the Creek for photogenic close-ups of dozens of brightly coloured dhows docked next to the Deira souqs to load and unload everything from air-conditioners and chewing gum to car tyres. This type of long flat wooden cargo boat has done trade across the Gulf and Indian Ocean for centuries, trading with such countries as Iran, Iraq, India, Somalia and Oman.

Most of the wares are re-exported after arriving by air or container ship from countries like China, South Korea and Singapore. In the morning and afternoon, you can watch the deckhands loading and offloading the wares. During the midday break, it's sometimes possible to chat with them – if you find one with whom you share a language. You then might learn that it takes a day to get to Iran by sea and seven days to Somalia, or what deckhands earn compared to the dhow captains. If your sailor friend is in a chatty mood, they may even regale you with real-life pirate stories. The pirates that work the waters off Yemen and Somalia sometimes make life very tough for Dubai's hard-working dhow sailors.

SPICE SOUQ — MARKET

Map p244 (btwn Baniyas Rd, Al Ras Rd & Al Abra St; roughly 9am-10pm Sat-Thu, 4-10pm Fri; MAl Ras) Steps from the Deira Old Souk abra station, the sound of Arabic chatter bounces around the lanes of this small covered market as vendors work hard to unload cardamom, saffron and other aromatic herbs photogenically stored in burlap sacks alongside dried fruit, nuts, incense burners, henna kits and shisha. Away from the tourist-oriented main thoroughfare, the tiny shops also sell groceries, plastics and other household goods to locals and sailors from the dhows.

MUSEUM OF THE POET AL OQAILI — MUSEUM

Map p244 (04 515 5000; www.dubaiculture.gov.ae/en; Sikka 21b, Spice Souq; 8am-2pm Sun-Thu; MAl Ras) FREE In 1923 this beautifully restored home tucked into the narrow lanes on the edge of the Spice Souq (p53) became the home of Saudi-born Mubarak bin Al Oqaili (1875–1954), one of the most important classical Arabic poets. A bilingual exhibit charts milestones in his life and work and also displays original manuscripts and personal belongings such as his desk, a gun and a pen.

With its richly carved teak doors, beamed ceilings, serene ambience and festive *majlis* (reception room), the private residence alone is worth a visit and makes for a nice respite from the bustling souqs.

PERFUME SOUQ — MARKET

Map p244 (Naif Rd & Al Soor St; 10am-1pm & 3-10pm; MPalm Deira) Several blocks with a preponderance of perfume shops hardly warrants the title 'souq', yet these stores sell a staggering range of Arabic *attars:* oil-based perfumes that are usually kept in large bulbous bottles and siphoned off into elegant flacons upon purchase. The most precious scents contain *oud,* from a resinous hardwood called agarwood, formed by the Southeast Asian aquilaria tree.

WOMEN'S MUSEUM — MUSEUM

Map p244 (Bait Al Banat; 04 234 2342; www.womenmuseumuae.com; Sikka 9 & 28; Dhs20; 10am-7pm Sat-Thu) Try on a *burka* (long, enveloping garment), find out about Ousha Bint Khalifa Al Suwaidi (the UAE's most celebrated female poet) and learn about the achievements of local women in the fields of science, trade, education, politics and literature at the region's first museum to train the spotlight on women.

The museum is tucked into the warren of lanes north of the Gold Souq and is a bit hard to find. Look for signs in the souq or on Al Khaleej Rd.

Conceived and financed by Emirati psychiatry professor Rafia Ghubash, the museum occupies three floors of a building called Bait Al Banat (House of the Girls), reportedly because it was the home of three unmarried sisters back in the 1950s.

COVERED SOUQ — MARKET

Map p244 (south of Naif Rd; 9am-10pm; MPalm Deira) Despite the name, this souq is not really covered at all; rather it's an amorphous warren of narrow lanes criss-crossing a few square blocks roughly bounded by Naif Rd, Al Soor St, 18th St and Al Sabkha Rd. Even if you're not keen on cheap textiles, faux Gucci, *kandouras* (long traditional robes), plastic toys and cheap trainers, you'll likely be entertained by the high-energy street scene.

NAIF MARKET MARKET

Map p244 (btwn Naif South, 9a & Deira Sts; ⌚8.30am-11.30pm; Ⓜ Baniyas Square) Although the historic Naif Souq burned down in 2008 and was replaced by this mall-style version, it's still an atmospheric place to shop and is especially popular with local women looking for bargain-priced *abeyyas* (full-length robes) and accessories such as hair extensions, costume jewellery and henna products.

For the liveliest ambience, visit in the evening and grab a shawarma and juice for sustenance.

NATIONAL BANK OF DUBAI ARCHITECTURE

Map p244 (Emirates NBD; Baniyas Rd; Ⓜ Union) In 2007 the National Bank of Dubai merged with Emirates Bank to form Emirates NBD, but its headquarters remains in this shimmering landmark overlooking the Creek. Designed by Carlos Ott and completed in 1997, it combines simple shapes to represent a dhow with a billowing sail, while the real-life dhows plying the Creek are reflected in its gold-coated glass facade. Best at sunset.

AL AHMADIYA SCHOOL MUSEUM

Map p244 (Al Ahmadiya St; Ⓜ Al Ras) Closed indefinitely for renovation, Dubai's first public primary school was founded by the pearl merchant Sheikh Ahmed bin Dalmouk and welcomed its first pupils (all boys) in 1912. Decades later Dubai's current ruler, Sheikh Mohammed, was among those who squeezed behind the wooden desks. The building itself is lovely with intricately carved courtyard arches, heavy ornamented doors and decorative gypsum panels. It remained in use as a school until the student body outgrew the premises in 1963.

No reopening date had been announced at the time of writing.

HERITAGE HOUSE MUSEUM

Map p244 (☎04 226 0286; www.dubaiculture.gov.ae/en; Al Ahmadiya St; Ⓜ Al Ras) Closed for renovation at the time of writing, this 1890 courtyard house once belonged to Sheikh Ahmed Bin Dalmouk, a wealthy pearl merchant and founder of the adjacent Al Ahmadiya School, Dubai's oldest learning pen. Built from coral and gypsum, it wraps around a central courtyard flanked by verandas to keep direct sunlight out, and

DUBAI CREEK

What the Tiber is to Rome and the Thames is to London, the Creek is to Dubai: a defining stretch of water at the heart of the city and a key building block in its economic development. Known as Al Khor in Arabic, the Creek was the base of the local fishing and pearling industries in the early 20th century and was dredged in 1961 to allow larger cargo vessels to dock. The first bridge, Al Maktoum Bridge, opened two years later.

The broad waterway used to end 15km inland at the Ras Al Khor Wildlife Sanctuary, but was extended 2.2km to the new Business Bay district in 2007. Thanks to another 3.2km extension – the Dubai Canal – the Creek has been linked to the Gulf since November 2016.

To this day, many people have a mental barrier when it comes to crossing the Creek over to Deira. It's a bit akin to some Londoners' aversion to going 'south of the river' or Manhattanites' reticence to head across to Queens. While it's true that traffic can be horrible during rush hour, congestion eased in 2007 with the opening of the 13-lane Business Bay Bridge near Dubai Festival City, and a six-lane Floating Bridge (open 6am to 10pm) near Creek Park. A fourth bridge, Al Garhoud Bridge, was widened to 13 lanes. There's also the Shindagha Tunnel near the mouth of the Creek, which is open for both vehicles and pedestrians, although it will soon be replaced by a bridge.

Using public transport, you have two options for crossing the Creek. The faster and easier is by Dubai metro; both the Red Line and the Green Line link the banks via underwater tunnels. The more atmospheric way to get across, though, is a Dhs1 ride aboard one of the motorised abras that connect the Bur Dubai and Deira souqs in a quick five minutes.

KEEPING COOL INDOORS – NATURALLY

The Al Ras neighbourhood in Deira and the Shindagha and Al Fahidi historic districts in Bur Dubai are great places to see and enter traditional houses, such as the **Sheikh Saeed Al Maktoum House** (p68) or the **Museum of the Poet Al Oqaili** (p53). Built from gypsum and coral, they typically wrap around a central courtyard flanked by verandas to keep direct sunlight out of the rooms. Another distinctive feature is the wind towers (*barjeel* in Arabic), a form of non-electrical air-conditioning unique to the region. Towers typically rise 5m or 6m above the building and are made of wood, stone or canvas. Open on all four sides, they can catch even the tiniest of breezes, which are then channelled down a central shaft and into the room below. In the process the air speeds up and is cooled. The cooler air already in the tower shaft pulls in and subsequently cools the hotter air outside through a simple process of convection.

sports lofty wind towers for cooling the air. If workers are on-site, ask nicely and you may be able to take a peek inside.

No reopening date had been set at the time of writing.

AL MAMZAR BEACH PARK — BEACH

(☎04 296 6201; Al Mamzar Creek, Deira; per person/car Dhs5/30, pool adult/child Dhs10/5; ⊙8am-10pm Sun-Wed, to 11pm Thu-Sat; P) This lushly landscaped beach park consists of a string of five lovely sandy sweeps and comes with plenty of infrastructure, including a swimming pool, playgrounds, picnic areas with barbecues, water sports and bicycle rentals, snack bars, lawns, Smart Palms for wi-fi access and air-conditioned cabanas (Dhs150 to Dhs200 per day, on Beach 4).

There are also sun loungers and umbrellas for rent, but food outlets are minimal so you might want to bring a picnic. No males over six on Mondays and Wednesdays ('Ladies Days'). The closest metro station is Al Qiyadah, about 6.5km away.

EATING

Deira has a fantastic street food scene with a United Nations of flavours and dishes at every corner. This is the realm of expat workers, from countries across the Middle East and South Asia, and they are hungry for the tastes of home. Expect authentic, traditional fare for just a few dirham. For more upmarket restaurants, head to the hotels.

★AROOS DAMASCUS — SYRIAN $

Map p244 (☎04 221 9825; cnr Al Muraqqabat & Al Jazeira Rd; sandwiches Dhs4-20, mezze Dhs14-35, mains Dhs15-50; ⊙7am-3am; M Salah Al Din) A Dubai restaurant serving Syrian food to adoring crowds since 1980 must be doing something right. A perfect meal would start with hummus and a *fattoush* salad before moving on to a plate of succulent grilled kebabs. Huge outdoor patio; cool flickering neon; busy until the wee hours.

SADAF IRANIAN SWEETS — DESSERTS $

Map p244 (☎04 229 7000; Rigga Al Buteen Plaza, Al Maktoum Rd; ⊙8am-midnight; M Al Rigga) Tucked into a small arcade, this little shop brims with spices, nuts, saffron, tea and other goodies from Iran, but insiders flock here for *faloodeh,* a mouth-watering dessert consisting of crunchy vermicelli-sized noodles drenched in a syrup made from rosewater, lemon and sugar and served with a scoop of saffron ice cream.

AL TAWASOL — YEMENI $

Map p246 (☎04 295 9797; Abu Bakar al Siddiq Rd, Al Rigga; mains Dhs25-75; ⊙11am-1am; M Al Rigga) Camp out on the carpet in the main dining room or in a private 'Bedouin-style tent' at this traditional Yemeni eatery. Staff will spread a flimsy plastic sheet to protect the rug from earthy dishes such as turmeric-laced rice topped with curried mutton or oven-roasted chicken *mandi* (rice topped with spicy stew). Ask for a spoon if eating with your hands doesn't appeal.

It's near the Clocktower Roundabout.

QWAIDER AL NABULSI — ARABIC $

Map p244 (☎04 227 7760; Al Muraqqabat St; snacks Dhs10-17, mains Dhs28-50; ⊙8am-2am; 👪; M Al Rigga, Salah Al Din) Behind the garish neon facade, this place at first looks like a sweets shop (the *kunafa,* a vermicelli-like pastry soaked in syrup, is great), but it also has a full menu of Arabic delicacies like scrumptious *musakhan* (chicken pie) and

WORTH A DETOUR

DEIRA'S NEW FISH MARKET

In sparkling new digs on the waterfront behind Dubai Hospital, Deira's **New Fish Market** (☎800 627 538; www.waterfront.ae; Al Khaleej Rd, near Abu Hail St; ⏰10am-10pm Sun-Wed, to 11pm Thu & Fri; 🚌17, C15, Ⓜ Abu Hail, Palm Deira) may have lost some of its character, but it's lost none of its bustle and bargains. Wriggling lobsters, shrimp the size of small bananas, metre-long kingfish and mountains of blue crab hauled in that morning are a photogenic feast even if you're not buying. The fish souq is part of the Waterfront Market development, which also includes sections selling local and imported produce, meat, dry goods and dates.

Much of the fish is caught right off the coast of the UAE, especially off Sharjah and Ras Al Khaimah, two emirates just north of Dubai. Shellfish usually comes from neighbouring Oman. It's fun to simply listen to the cacophonous din and to observe the wild haggling between the fishmongers and their customers. Come either early in the morning or in the evening (avoid the afternoon siesta hours), and wear sneakers or other waterproof shoes. If you're buying, be prepared to haggle, avoid overfished species like hammour and kingfish, and ask to have the fish cleaned.

sesame-seed-coated falafel *mahshi* (stuffed with chilli paste). The latter's fluffy filling is coloured green from the addition of parsley and other herbs. It's near Kings Park Hotel.

AFGHAN KHORASAN KABAB — AFGHANI $

Map p244 (☎04 359 0003; off Deira St; mains Dhs19-40; ⏰11.30am-1am; Ⓜ Baniyas Square) Big hunks of meat – mutton or chicken – charred on foot-long skewers are paired with Afghan *pulao* (rice pilaf), chewy bread and sauces. That's it. For added authenticity, eat with your hands and sit upstairs in the carpeted *majlis* (reception room). It's in an alley behind Al Ghurair Mosque.

ASHWAQ CAFETERIA — ARABIC $

Map p244 (☎04 226 1164; cnr Al Soor & Sikkat al Khail Sts; sandwiches Dhs4-7; ⏰8.30am-midnight; Ⓜ Palm Deira) In a prime people-watching spot near the Gold Souq, Ashwaq may be just a hole-in-the-wall with a few pavement tables, but their shawarma rocks the palate. Wash it down with a fresh juice.

YUM! — ASIAN $

Map p244 (☎04 205 7033; Baniyas Rd, 1st fl, Radisson Blu Hotel; mains Dhs32-49; ⏰noon-11.30pm; P 📶; Ⓜ Union, Baniyas Square) Though not as dynamic or sophisticated as some Asian restaurants, Yum! is a good pick for a quick bowl of noodles when you're wandering along the Creek – and you can be in and out in half an hour.

★ASEELAH — EMIRATI $$

Map p244 (☎04 205 7033; www.radissonblu.com; Baniyas Rd, 2nd fl, Radisson Blu Hotel, Al Rigga; mains Dhs45-195; ⏰12.30-4pm & 6.30-11.15pm; P 📶; Ⓜ Union, Baniyas Square) With its mix of traditional and modern Emirati cuisine, this stylish restaurant ticks all the right boxes. Many dishes feature a local spice mix called *bezar,* including the date-stuffed chicken leg and the camel stew. To go the whole, well, goat, order *ouzi,* an entire animal filled with legumes and nuts, slow-cooked for 24 hours. Nice terrace.

XIAO WEI YANG HOTPOT — CHINESE $$

Map p244 (Little Lamb Mongolian Hotpot; ☎04 221 5111; www.facebook.com/pg/xiaoweiyangdubai; Baniyas Rd; hotpots Dhs28-32, meats Dhs36-48, combos Dhs98-148; ⏰11am-1am; Ⓜ Baniyas Square) Next to Twin Towers, this authentic hotpot restaurant works like this: a bubbling broth inspired by Genghis Khan is placed on a hot plate on your table. Create a dipping sauce from a mix of satay, garlic, coriander, chilli and spices. Choose ingredients (fish balls, tofu, lotus root, beef slices) to cook in the cauldron. Dip and enjoy!

THAI KITCHEN — THAI $$

Map p246 (☎04 602 1234; www.dubai.park.hyatt.com; Dubai Creek Club St, Park Hyatt Dubai; small plates Dhs42-70, Fri brunch Dhs255-395; ⏰noon-11.45pm; P 📶 🍸; Ⓜ Deira City Centre) The decor is decidedly un-Thai, with black-lacquer tables, a swooping wave-form ceiling and not a branch of bamboo. Led by Supattra Boonsrang for more than a decade, the cooks here know their stuff: dishes are inspired by Bangkok street eats and served in sizes that are perfect for grazing and sharing. The Friday brunch is tops too.

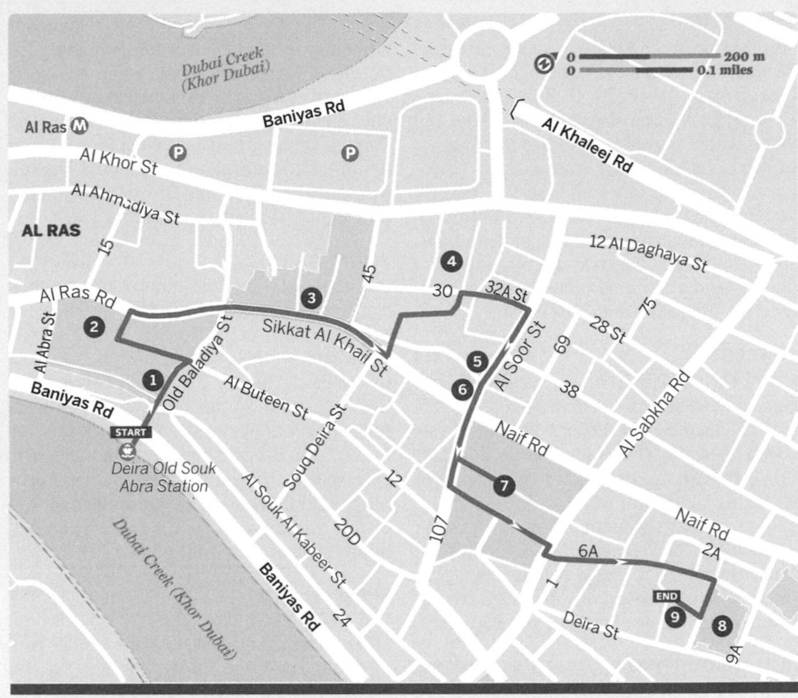

Neighbourhood Walk Deira Souq Stroll

START DEIRA OLD SOUQ ABRA STATION
END AFGHAN KHORASAN KEBAB
LENGTH 2KM; TWO TO THREE HOURS, INCLUDING MUSEUMS

As soon as you step off the abra at Deira Old Souq abra station, heady scents will lure you across to the ❶ **Spice Souq** (p53). Grab a fresh juice from the hole-in-the wall Jafer Binam Ali Cafeteria right by the entrance, then sniff around for saffron, turmeric and frankincense. To learn about one of Dubai's finest poets, pop into the ❷ **Museum of the Poet Al Oqaili** (p53), then find your way to Al Ras Rd and turn right. This takes you to Old Baladiya St and the wooden latticed entrance gate of the ❸ **Gold Souq** (p52), easily recognised by the lettering 'City of Gold'.

Take a selfie with the world's largest gold ring, then peruse the bling displayed in shop windows, from petite earrings to over-the-top gold pieces created for brides' dowries. Head north of the central arcade to suss out tiny teashops, simple cafeterias, busy tailors and barber shops lining narrow lanes. Look for signs pointing the way to the ❹ **Women's Museum** (p53) to learn about the important contributions made by Emirati women in such fields as art and science.

Head back south and turn left onto 32a St, then follow it to get to Al Soor St, one of the main drags of the ❺ **Perfume Souq** (p53). Turn right and pop into a shop or two to sniff out pungent Arabian *attars* (perfumes) and *oud* (fragrant wood). When you get to the corner with Sikkat al Khail Rd you can fortify yourself with a juice or a shawarma at ❻ **Ashwaq Cafeteria** (p56).

Cut diagonally across the intersection and plunge into the warren of tiny alleys of the ❼ **Covered Souq** (p53), where you'll find shops selling everything from textiles to shisha pipes. Find your way to Al Sabkha Rd and head down 6A St to get to the new ❽ **Naif Market** (p54), which has risen from the ashes of the historic Naif Souq. Wrap up with a carnivorous feast at ❾ **Afghan Khorasan Kebab** (p56), in an alley next to the Al Ghurair Mosque.

CHINA CLUB CHINESE $$

Map p244 (☎04 205 7033; www.radissonblu.com; Baniyas Rd, Radisson Blu Hotel; yum cha buffet Dhs139, mains Dhs40-170; ⏲12.30-3pm & 7.30-11pm; P 📶; M Union, Baniyas Square) The big draw at this handsome restaurant dressed in sensuous silks and embroidered tapestries is the yum cha buffet served nightly and at lunchtime on Friday and Saturday. Reliable à la carte choices include Sichuan spicy wok-fried lamb and crispy Peking duck carved and rolled tableside. The deep-fried ice cream is a delicious finish.

SHABESTAN IRANIAN $$$

Map p244 (☎04 222 7171; www.radissonblu.com; Baniyas Rd, Radisson Blu Hotel; mains Dhs105-185; ⏲12.15-3.15pm & 7.30-11.30pm; P 📶; M Union, Baniyas Square) This long-standing traditional Persian lair has a lovely panorama of glittering lights unfolding over the Creek. Take your time as you tuck into classics such as *fesenjan* (chicken in walnut-pomegranate sauce) or *ghormeh sabzi* (lamb stew) and finish up with a scoop of saffron ice cream. Live Persian music nightly except Saturday.

AL MANSOUR DHOW INTERNATIONAL $$$

Map p244 (☎04 205 7033; www.radissonblu.com; Baniyas Rd, Radisson Blu Hotel; 2hr dinner cruise adult/child Dhs185/100; ⏲8pm; P 📶; M Union, Baniyas Square) Take in the skyline on this moving feast aboard a trad wooden dhow decorated with bands of twinkling lights. Soulful Arabic song accompanies the lavish buffet spread that's heavy on Arabic and Indian choices. There's a full bar and an upper-deck shisha lounge for chilling. Board outside the Radisson Blu Hotel (p184), which operates this dinner cruise.

SUMIBIYA KOREAN $$$

Map p244 (☎04 205 7033; www.radissonblu.com; Baniyas Rd, Radisson Blu Hotel; set menus Dhs125; ⏲7-11pm Wed-Sat; P 📶; M Union, Baniyas Square) At Dubai's first *yakiniku*-style restaurant is interactive foodie fun for families and groups. Every stone table has a recessed gas grill where you cook your own meat, then pair it with sauces and condiments. The set menus featuring beef, chicken, fish or lamb, along with salad, rice, soup, kimchi and dessert, are good value.

TABLE 9 INTERNATIONAL $$$

Map p244 (☎04 227 1111; Baniyas Rd, Hilton Dubai Creek; 4-course dinner Dhs225, mains Dhs85-125; ⏲6.30-11pm; 📶 🍷; M Al Rigga, Union) The former fine dining restaurant launched in 2011 by Gordon Ramsay protégés Nick Alvis and Scott Price has been rebooted as a more casual bistro by Chilean chef Esteban Gomez. He's kept some of the Table 9 signature dishes, such as veal tenderloin with smoked pumpkin purée, while introducing grilled meats, Latin influences and a good-value four-course menu.

AL DAWAAR INTERNATIONAL $$$

Map p244 (☎04 317 2222; https://dubai.regency.hyatt.com; Hyatt Regency Dubai, Al Khaleej Rd; buffet lunch/dinner Dhs185/235; ⏲12.30-3pm & 7-11.30pm; M Palm Deira) In a city that likes to teeter on the cutting edge, this revolving restaurant on the 25th floor is endearingly old school. Fresh from a makeover in 2017, the decor is light and modern, the vibe serene, the buffet a bounty of European, Middle Eastern, Asian and Japanese dishes, and the views of the city predictably impressive, especially at night.

SPICE ISLAND INTERNATIONAL $$$

Map p244 (☎04 608 8085; Salahuddin Rd, Crowne Plaza Dubai Hotel; dinner buffet with soft/house/premium drinks Dhs219/279/349; ⏲6am-11.30pm; P 📶 👪; M Salah Al Din, Abu Baker Al Siddique) With dishes from China, Japan, India, Italy, Mexico and Mongolia, plus seafood and loads of desserts, this been-here-forever buffet restaurant delivers good value and a visual feast. It's popular with families.

ASHIANA INDIAN $$$

Map p244 (☎04 207 1733; www.ashianadubai.com; Baniyas Rd, ground fl, Sheraton Dubai Creek Hotel & Towers; mains Dhs58-148; ⏲noon-3pm & 7-11pm; 📶 🍷; M Union) This oldie but goodie serves modernised Indian fare in an elegant, dimly lit dining room that radiates the intimacy of an old private villa. The menu spans the arc from richly nuanced curries and succulent kebabs to fluffy biryanis and inspired shareable mains such as *raan lucknowi* (slow-cooked, 48-hour marinated lamb), all beautifully presented.

YALUMBA INTERNATIONAL $$$

Map p246 (☎04 217 0000; www.yalumbadubai.com; Airport Rd, Le Meridien Dubai; buffet with/without alcohol from Dhs219/159; ⏲5.30-10.30am, 12.30-3pm & 7.30-11pm; P 📶; M GGICO, Airport Terminal 1) In fast-moving Dubai, this restaurant has defied the odds and stayed popular even after more than

LOCAL KNOWLEDGE

GETTING LOST IN DEIRA

Sometimes it pays to rip up the script and improvise. Some of the most fascinating parts of town aren't home to a single tourist attraction worth recommending, but are brimming with the soul Dubai is so frequently accused of lacking. Dubai is considered a safe city – there aren't any no-go areas and even the scariest-looking alleyways will usually be quite harmless. Be adventurous and spontaneous. Put away the maps and follow your instinct. The following are some of the best areas in Deira in which to get hopelessly, joyously lost.

Naif The area between Naif Rd and Al Khaleej Rd is a labyrinthine muddle of slim, cluttered streets and one of the best places in town for urban photography. Walk past old men smoking shisha and playing backgammon on the pavements, pockets of Ethiopia and Somalia, hilariously awful fake Rolexes and games consoles, heady perfumes, blindingly bright shop facades, and the occasional goat walking nonchalantly down the centre of the street. You just don't get this on the Palm Jumeirah.

Al Muteena Easily reached by metro (get off at Salah Al Din), Al Muteena St is one of the most enticing walking streets in town, with wide pavements, palm trees and a park-like strip running along its centre. In the Iraqi restaurants and cafes you'll see *masgouf* – a whole fish sliced in half, spicily seasoned and barbecued over an open flame. And the shisha cafes have to be seen to be believed: check out the rock gardens, dangling fronds and artificial lakes. Nearby Al Muraqqabat Rd brims with superb Syrian, Lebanese and Palestinian eateries. A bit south of here, Al Rigga Rd is also packed with promising eateries and also boasts a lively street scene.

10 years in business. That's largely because of its legendary Friday champagne brunch (Dhs499), but on other days it also pulls in the faithful and the hungry with seafood extravaganzas, Sunday roast and other all-you-can-eat promotions.

MIYAKO JAPANESE **$$$**

Map p244 (☎04 209 6914; www.dubai.regency.hyatt.com; Al Khaleej Rd, ground fl, Hyatt Regency Dubai; nigiri Dhs35-85, teppanyaki sets Dhs280-370; ⏰12.30-11.30pm; P 📶; M Palm Deira) One of Dubai's oldest Japanese restaurants (since 1987), Miyako now flaunts a post-facelift contempo look while retaining its three-way split into teppanyaki room, sushi bar and tatami room. The menu is just as eclectic as it hopscotches from sushi to tempura, yakitori to ramen, and hotpots to rice bowls. Not the trendiest, but dependably authentic Japanese.

DRINKING & NIGHTLIFE

Given Deira's rich tapestry of ethnicities, the nightlife is just as diverse, ranging from Filipino nightclubs and chic Creekside outdoor lounges to Russian cabaret and a landmark Irish pub.

★IRISH VILLAGE IRISH PUB

Map p246 (☎04 282 4750; www.theirishvillage.com; 31A St, Garhoud; ⏰11am-1am Sat-Wed, to 2am Thu & Fri; 📶; M GGICO) This always-buzzing pub, with its Irish-main-street facade made with materials imported straight from the Emerald Isle, has been a Dubai institution since 1996. There's Guinness and Kilkenny on tap, lovely gardens around a petite lake, the occasional live band and plenty of pub grub to keep your tummy in a state of contentment.

★QDS BAR

Map p246 (☎04 295 6000; www.dubaigolf.com; Dubai Creek Club St, Dubai Creek Golf & Yacht Club, Garhoud; shisha Dhs65; ⏰5pm-2am Sun-Wed, to 3am Thu & Sat, 1pm-3am Fri; 📶; M Deira City Centre) Watch the ballet of lighted dhows floating by while sipping cocktails at this always-fun outdoor Creek-side lounge deck where carpets and cushions set an inviting mood. In summer, keep cool in an air-conditioned tent. Great for shisha-holics too.

JUICE WORLD JUICE BAR

Map p244 (☎04 299 9465; www.juiceworld.ae; Al Rigga St; ⏰1pm-2am Sat-Wed, to 3am Thu & Fri; M Al Rigga) Need some A.S.S., Man Kiwi or Viagra? Then head down to this actually very wholesome Saudi juice bar famous not only for its 150 fantastically creative liquid potions but also for its outrageous fruit sculptures. There's an entire room of them: it must be seen to be believed. The big outdoor terrace offers primo people-watching.

CIELO SKY LOUNGE BAR

Map p246 (☎04 416 1800; www.cielodubai.com; Dubai Creek Club St, Dubai Creek Golf & Yacht Club; ⏲4pm-2am Sep-May; 📶; Ⓜ Deira City Centre) Looking very much like a futuristic James Bond-worthy yacht, Cielo flaunts a sultry, romantic vibe helped by the bobbing yachts below and the cool views of the Dubai skyline across the Creek. One of the chicest spots on this side of town to ring in the night with sundowners and global bar bites.

KU-BU CLUB

Map p244 (☎04 222 7171; Baniyas Rd, ground fl, Radisson Blu Hotel; ⏲7pm-3am; Ⓜ Union, Baniyas Square) A resident DJ spins funky tunes at this windowless, tattoo-themed pick-up joint with secluded nooks that are made even more private with plush draperies. A good choice for drinks before or after dinner at one of the Radisson Blu's restaurants.

TERRACE BAR

Map p246 (☎04 602 1814; http://dubai.park.hyatt.com; Dubai Creek Club St, Park Hyatt Dubai; ⏲6pm-2am; 📶; Ⓜ Deira City Centre) With its sleek design, floor-to-ceiling windows and canopy-covered deck, the Terrace provides plenty of eye candy before you've even taken in the chic crowd or the dreamy sunset views across the Creek.

DUBLINER'S IRISH PUB

Map p246 (☎04 702 2455; www.dubliners-dubai.com; Airport Rd, Le Meridien Dubai Hotel, Garhoud; ⏲noon-2am; 📶; Ⓜ Airport Terminal 1, GGICO) This airport-adjacent Irish pub staple has eight beers on tap, above-average pub grub and a crowd that's chatty and friendly. On game nights and during the Friday brunch (1pm to 4pm, Dhs179 per person, including five house drinks) the place is usually elbow-to-elbow.

ISSIMO SPORTS BAR

Map p244 (☎04 227 1111; Baniyas Rd, Hilton Dubai Creek; ⏲3pm-1am; 📶; Ⓜ Al Rigga, Union) Illuminated blue flooring, black-leather sofas and sleek chrome finishing lend an edgy look to this sports-and-martini bar. If you're not into sports – or TV – you may find the giant screens distracting.

SHOPPING

It's the siren song of the souqs that lures shoppers to Deira. Stock up on spices, gold, perfume and souvenirs of all sorts, all sold at bargain prices (provided you bargain). Deira City Centre (p61) is the main shopping mall.

DEIRA CITY CENTRE MALL

Map p246 (☎04 295 1010; www.deiracitycentre.com; Baniyas Rd; ⏲10am-10pm Sun-Wed, to midnight Thu-Sat; 📶; Ⓜ Deira City Centre) Though other malls are bigger and flashier, Deira City Centre remains a stalwart for its logical layout and wide selection of shops, from big-name chains like H&M and Zara to locally owned stores carrying quality carpets, souvenirs and handicrafts.

There's also a huge branch of the Carrefour supermarket, food courts, a cinema and a Magic Planet indoor theme park.

WHAT TO LOOK FOR WHEN BUYING GOLD

There's no need to worry about fakes at the Gold Souq (unless you're in the market for a knock-off Rolex watch or Prada bag from one of the touts trying to tempt you). The quality of gold is regulated by the Dubai government, so you can be fairly confident that the piece of jewellery you've got your eye on is genuine.

Price is determined by two factors: weight based on the official daily international rate and the artistry of the item. The latest gold rates are posted throughout the souq and online (for instance at http://gulfnews.com/business/gold-rate). Most pieces for sale here are 14 or 18 carat.

Haggling is expected and vendors build in price buffers accordingly. Since the price of gold itself is fixed, focus on the intricacy of the artisanship as a point of discussion. Buying more than one item should also net you a discount, as does paying in cash. Sharp bargaining skills usually make merchants drop the initial asking price by 20% to 30%.

GIFT VILLAGE DEPARTMENT STORE

Map p244 (☎04 294 6858; www.gift-village.com; 14th St, Baniyas Sq; ⌚9am-1am Sun-Thu, 9am-noon & 2pm-2am Fri; Ⓜ Baniyas Square) If you've spent all your money on Jimmy Choo shoes and bling at the Gold Souq and need a new inflight bag, this cut-price place has a great range. It also stocks imported cosmetics, shoes, clothing, toys, sports goods, jewellery and amiably kitsch souvenirs.

AL GHURAIR CENTRE MALL

Map p244 (☎800 24227; www.alghuraircentre.com; cnr Al Rigga & Omar bin al Khattab Rds; ⌚10am-10pm Sun-Wed, to midnight Thu-Sat; Ⓜ Union, Salah Al Din, Al Rigga) Dubai's oldest shopping mall opened in 1980 and is a lot less flashy than its newer cousins despite an expansion that doubled its number of shops to 300. Aside from the expected Western labels, there are speciality stores selling national dress and Arabic fragrances. There's also a food court with 70 outlets and an eight-screen multiplex.

MIKYAJY COSMETICS

Map p246 (☎04 295 7844; www.mikyajy.com; Baniyas Rd, 2nd fl, Deira City Centre; ⌚10am-10pm Sun-Wed, to midnight Thu-Sat; 📶; Ⓜ Deira City Centre) You feel like you're walking into a chocolate gift-box at tiny Mikyajy, the region's home-grown make-up brand. Although calibrated to Middle Eastern tastes and complexions, the vivid colours will brighten up any face.

DAMAS JEWELLERY

Map p246 (☎04 295 3848; Baniyas Rd, Deira City Centre; ⌚10am-10pm Sun-Wed, to midnight Thu-Sat; 📶; Ⓜ Deira City Centre) Damas may not be the most innovative jeweller in Dubai, but with more than 50 shops, it's essentially omnipresent. Among the diamonds and gold, look for elaborate bridal jewellery as well as classic pieces and big-designer names such as Fabergé and Tiffany.

WOMEN'S SECRET CLOTHING

Map p246 (☎04 295 9665; Baniyas Rd, 1st fl, Deira City Centre; ⌚10am-10pm Sun-Wed, to midnight Thu-Sat; Ⓜ Deira City Centre) This sassy Spanish label is popular for its global-pop-art-inspired underwear, swimwear and nightwear. Expect anything from cute Mexican cross-stitched bra-and-pants sets to Moroccan-style kaftanlike nightdresses.

SPORTS & ACTIVITIES

DUBAI CREEK GOLF & YACHT CLUB GOLF

Map p246 (☎04 295 6000; www.dubaigolf.com; green fees Sun-Thu Dhs770, Fri & Sat Dhs875; Ⓜ Deira City Centre) In a scenic Creekside location since 1993, this par-71 championship course measures 6371m and is set amid beautiful landscaping with water hazards and coconut and date palm-lined fairways. Beginners can test their skills on the nine-hole par-three course, open daily from 7pm to 10pm.

Rates drop significantly from June to mid-September. The architecture of the clubhouse was inspired by the sail of a dhow (traditional shipping vessel) but is often likened to a miniature Sydney Opera House.

AMARA SPA SPA

Map p246 (☎04 602 1234; https://dubai.park.hyatt.com; Dubai Creek Club St, Park Hyatt Dubai; day passes weekdays/weekends Dhs300/350; ⌚9am-10pm Sun-Thu, 7.30am-10pm Fri & Sat; Ⓜ Deira City Centre) One of Dubai's top spas, Amara puts a premium on privacy with eight treatment suites, including three for couples, all with their own walled garden and outdoor rain shower. Each treatment – from 'cryo-therapy facials' to 'chiro-golf massages' – is calibrated to individual needs and carried out using prime products.

A popular package is 'Spirit of Arabia' (Dhs950), a two-hour ceremony involving a scrub down with Aleppo soap, followed by a peeling with a kese mitt (a Turkish exfoliating glove) and crowned by a full-body massage using the spa's signature oil of frankincense, amber, myrrh and sandalwood. Afterwards you can relax in the steam bath, in the sauna or by the palm-tree-shaded pool.

POLYGLOT LANGUAGE INSTITUTE LANGUAGE

Map p244 (☎04 222 3429; www.polyglot.ae; Al-Masaeed Bldg, Al Maktoum Rd; ⌚10am-9pm Sat-Wed; Ⓜ Union) Established in 1969, this school offers beginner courses and conversation classes in Arabic.

1

GLEN_PEARSON / GETTY IMAGES ©

2

4

FRANCESCO BONINO / SHUTTERSTOCK ©

1. Al Ahmadiya School (p54)
Though the museum is closed indefinitely for renovations, this school, founded in 1912, has lovely traditional architecture.

2. Abras
Motorised traditional wooden boats called abras run along Dubai Creek. View towards Bur Dubai from Deira.

3. Deira Souqs
Shop for a variety of goods at Deira's marketplaces, including carpets (see p76).

4. Spice Souq (p53)
Loose spices, dried fruit and nuts are just some of the goods on sale at this small covered market.

Bur Dubai

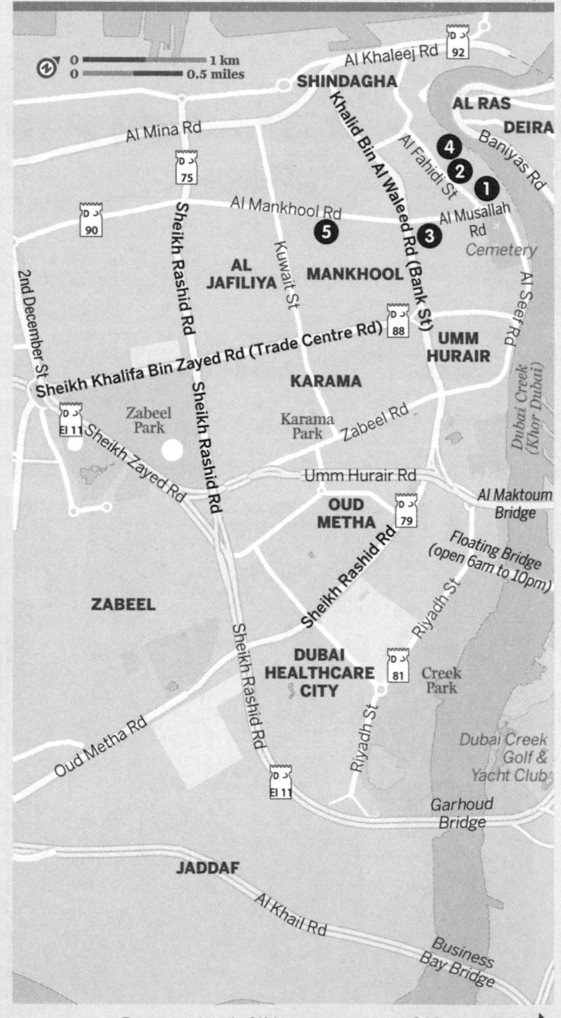

For more detail of this area see maps p248 and p252.

Neighbourhood Top Five

1 Al Fahidi Historic District (p67) Stepping into the past among these beautifully restored buildings filled with shops, galleries, cafes and heritage hotels.

2 Dubai Museum (p66) Getting an entertaining introduction to the city's turbo evolution through multimedia exhibits set up inside an historic fort.

3 Al Ustad Special Kabab (p70) Discovering tasty insights into Dubai's polyethnic fabric by chowing down with expat workers at Meena Bazaar eateries such as this Persian gem.

4 Bur Dubai Souq (p67) Haggling for textiles and souvenirs at this lively market covered by an ornate wooden arcade.

5 Frying Pan Adventures (p71) Delving into the city's melting pot of cuisines on a food crawl through old Dubai.

Explore Bur Dubai

Modern Dubai so dominates the city's image that it's easy to forget that there was life here before the petrodollar era. Thankfully, there's Bur Dubai to provide an eye-opening journey into the city's past. It was on the western bank of the Creek that the 800 members of the Al Bu Fasalah tribe from Abu Dhabi first settled in 1833. Their leader, Maktoum Bin Butti, was the founder of the Al Maktoum dynasty that rules Dubai to this day.

Although Bur Dubai stretches from the Creek to the World Trade Centre, the neighbourhood's most intriguing area is a compact section hugging the Creek. Peek into the city's past on a wander around the restored historic districts of Al Fahidi (p67) and Shindagha (p68) – the latter is partly closed for restoration – passing through the atmospheric Bur Dubai Souq (p67). The tangle of narrow lanes in this area brims with local eateries feeding expats from Nepal, India and Pakistan with authentic fare from their homelands.

Away from the Creek, Bur Dubai becomes rather nondescript, though not without its highlights. The Mankhool district is stacked with inexpensive hotel apartments, quirky nightlife, good restaurants and the upmarket BurJuman Centre mall (p76). Densely populated Karama has a strong community feel due to its mostly Filipino and Indian population. It's great for bargain shopping and bustling eateries serving princely meals at paupers' prices. East of Zabeel Rd, sprawling Oud Metha is easily recognised by the eye-catching Egyptian-themed Wafi Mall (p78) and pyramid-shaped Raffles hotel. Zabeel Park (p69) is one of the city's largest patches of green and home to the new Dubai Frame (p69).

Local Life

- **Creekside views** Settle down with a creamy avocado smoothie or a shisha at one of the waterfront cafes.
- **Meat-free munching** The lanes of Meena Bazaar have Dubai's highest concentration of Indian vegetarian restaurants, many of which are a beehive of activity.
- **Shopping adventures** Try on the traditional Punjabi dress of long tunics and baggy trousers in brightly coloured silk or cotton at the local clothing shops.

Getting There & Away

- **Metro** The Red and Green Lines intersect at BurJuman, with the latter continuing into historic Bur Dubai before crossing the Creek.
- **Abra** Water taxis link Bur Dubai to Deira from two stations near the Bur Dubai Souq.
- **Ferry** Dubai Canal ferries dock at Al Jaddaf Marine Station, and ferries to and from Dubai Marina at Al Ghubaiba Marine Station.

Lonely Planet's Top Tip

For an astonishing immersion in Bur Dubai's multiethnic food and culture, book a guided walking tour with local blogger and foodie extraordinaire Arva Ahmad, founder of Dubai's first culinary tour company, **Frying Pan Adventures** (p71). Enjoy exotic nibbles as she takes you through the bewildering tangle of Bur Dubai's narrow lanes.

Best Places to Eat

- Al Ustad Special Kabab (p70)
- Sind Punjab (p70)
- Kabul Darbar (p70)
- Arabian Tea House (p72)

For reviews, see p70.

Best Places to Shop

- BurJuman (p76)
- Fabindia (p77)
- Dubai Flea Market (p75)

For reviews, see p75.

Best Museums

- Dubai Museum (p66)
- Sheikh Saeed Al Maktoum House (p68)
- Crossroads of Civilizations Museum (p69)
- Saruq Al Hadid Archaeology Museum (p69)

For reviews, see p66.

TOP SIGHT
DUBAI MUSEUM

Unless some mad scientist invents a time-travel machine, this museum is your ticket to learning about Dubai's turbo-evolution from fishing and pearling village to global centre of commerce, finance and tourism. It has an atmospheric setting in the compact Al Fahidi Fort, built around 1800 and considered the oldest surviving structure in town. It is depicted on the 100 dirham note.

The fort is entered via a sturdy teak door studded with brass spikes that leads to the central courtyard dotted with bronze cannons, traditional wooden fishing boats and traditional dwellings, including an *areesha* (a hut made of mud and palm fronds that was the kind of traditional summer home most locals lived in until the middle of the 20th century). Pop behind the heavy carved wooden doors flanking the courtyard to check out modest displays of instruments and handcrafted weapons before heading down a spiralling ramp to the main galleries.

Cross the deck of a dhow to enter a mock souq with life-size dioramas depicting shopkeepers and craftspeople at work, enhanced by light and sound effects, historical photos and grainy documentary footage. Beyond are scenes showing pupils gathered around a Quran teacher and pearl merchants weighing the precious loot. This is followed by a section on life in the desert that includes photo-ops with a stuffed camel, a scene showing Bedouins drinking tea under a starry sky and an astronomy exhibit that reveals how the desert dwellers used the stars to navigate.

A section of the maritime gallery is dedicated to the fascinating pearl-diving exhibition, where you get to marvel at the fact that divers wore merely nose clips and leather gloves while descending to extraordinary depths. What really brings this part of the museum to life is the historical footage of the pearl divers at work.

The final section showcases finds from ancient settlements at Jumeirah, Al Qusais and other local archaeological sites. Most are believed to have been established here between 2000 and 1000 BC. Don't miss the large well-lit gallery opposite the gift shop, with its displays of unearthed artefacts from the numerous tombs in the area.

DON'T MISS

- Souq dioramas
- Pearl-diving exhibit
- Archaeology exhibit

PRACTICALITIES

- Map p248, G4
- ☎04 353 1862
- Al Fahidi St
- adult/child Dhs3/1
- 8.30am-8.30pm Sat-Thu, 2.30-8.30pm Fri
- Ⓜ Al Fahidi

SIGHTS

Bur Dubai is perfect for delving into Dubai's pre-oil past at the main city museum in an old fort and in two heritage areas flanking Dubai Creek.

DUBAI MUSEUM — MUSEUM

See p66.

★AL FAHIDI HISTORIC DISTRICT — AREA

Map p248 (Al Fahidi St; M Al Fahidi) FREE Traffic fades to a quiet hum in the labyrinthine lanes of this nicely restored heritage area formerly known as the Bastakia Quarter. Its narrow walking lanes are flanked by sand-coloured houses topped with wind towers, which provide natural air-conditioning. Today there are about 50 buildings containing museums, craft shops, cultural exhibits, courtyard cafes, art galleries and two boutique hotels.

★ALSERKAL CULTURAL FOUNDATION — GALLERY

Map p248 (04 353 5922; www.alserkalculturalfoundation.com; Heritage House No 13, off Al Fahidi St; 9am-7pm; M Al Fahidi) FREE This nonprofit runs the most dynamic cultural space in the Al Fahidi Historic District (p67). Galleries showcasing traditional and cutting-edge works by local and international artists orbit a central courtyard anchored by an arty urban-style cafe. Most of the art is for sale, a small shop stocks nifty gifties, and there's a contemporary Arab fashion boutique, a reading room and a workshop space upstairs.

COFFEE MUSEUM — MUSEUM

Map p248 (04 353 8777; www.coffeemuseum.ae; Al Fahidi Historical District, off Al Fahidi St; 9am-5pm Sat-Thu; M Al Fahidi) FREE This cute private museum in a historic Emirati home offers an aromatic bean-based journey around the world and back in time. Learn about the importance of coffee in different cultures, examine a rotating roster of old grinders, pots, roasters and related implements, and sample freshly brewed Ethiopian coffee (Dhs10) prepared by costumed staff.

Upstairs is a reading room, a children's corner and a modern cafe.

COIN MUSEUM — MUSEUM

Map p248 (04 392 0093; www.dubaiculture.gov.ae/en; Al Fahidi Historical District; 8am-2pm Sun-Thu; M Al Fahidi) FREE Near the Diwan Mosque in Al Fahidi Historic District (p67), this small eight-room museum presents nearly 500 rare coins from throughout the Middle East, including Egypt, Turkey and Morocco. The oldest were minted during the Arab-Sasanian era in the 7th century.

MAJLIS GALLERY — GALLERY

Map p248 (04 353 6233; www.themajlisgallery.com; Al Fahidi St; 10am-6pm Sat-Thu; M Al Fahidi) FREE Dubai's oldest fine art gallery was founded in 1989 by British expat Allison Collins and presents mainly paintings and sculpture by international artists inspired by the region, as well as high-quality pottery, glass and other crafts. It's located in an old wind-tower house on the edge of Al Fahidi Historic District (p67). The central courtyard surrounds a magnificent henna tree.

DIWAN MOSQUE — MOSQUE

Map p248 (Al Mussalah St; M Al Fahidi) FREE The distinctive ornate flat dome and slender minaret of this snowy white mosque watch over the Al Fahidi Historic District. Non-Muslims may only visit the interior on guided tours offered by the Sheikh Mohammed Centre for Cultural Understanding (p68).

BUR DUBAI SOUQ — MARKET

Map p248 (btwn Bur Dubai waterfront & Ali bin Abi Talib St; 8am-1pm & 4-10pm Sat-Thu, 4-10pm Fri; M Al Ghubaiba) Dubai's oldest souq flanks a central arcade canopied by an ornately carved wooden roof. Friday evenings here are especially lively, as it turns into a virtual crawling carnival with expat workers loading up on socks, pashminas, T-shirts and knock-off Calvins on their day off. In a section known as the Textile Souq you can stock up on fabrics – silk, cotton, satin and velvet – at very reasonable prices.

GRAND MOSQUE — MOSQUE

Map p248 (Ali Bin Abi Talib St; M Al Fahidi, Al Ghubaiba) Dubai's tallest minaret (70m high) lords over the more than 50 small and large domes that give the city's largest mosque its distinctive silhouette. Today's building was only completed in 1998 but is, in fact, a replica of the historic house of worship from 1900. As with all Dubai mosques except Jumeirah Mosque, it's off limits to non-Muslims.

As well as being the centre of Dubai's religious and cultural life, the original structure also housed a *kuttab* (Quranic school), where children learned to recite the Quran from memory. It's opposite the Dubai Museum.

HINDI LANE STREET

Map p248 (off Ali Bin Abi Talib St; Ⓜ Al Fahidi, Al Ghubaiba) Until the completion of a new temple in Abu Dhabi, only a tiny and ageing double-shrine, tucked behind the Grand Mosque since 1958, serves the UAE's nearly three million Hindus. Dedicated to Shiva and Krishna, it is entered via a narrow and colourful alleyway colloquially known as Hindi Lane and lined with vendors selling religious paraphernalia and offerings, including baskets of fruit, flower garlands, gold-embossed holy images, sacred ash and sandalwood paste.

Non-Hindus are allowed inside the temples but must first take off their shoes.

SHINDAGHA HISTORIC DISTRICT AREA

Map p248 (Shindagha Waterfront; Ⓜ Al Ghubaiba) Strategically located at the mouth of Dubai Creek, Shindagha was where the ruling sheikhs and the city elite lived until the 1950s. While some homes have been reconstructed and recast as museums, most of the area is fenced off at the time of writing, while it is being turned into a heritage district. Once the dust has settled, there will be a new Shindagha Museum as well as additional exhibits, heritage hotels and restaurants.

The redevelopment is part of a master plan to create a cohesive historical district on both banks of Dubai Creek in hopes of qualifying for Unesco World Heritage status.

SHEIKH SAEED AL MAKTOUM HOUSE MUSEUM

Map p248 (☎04 393 7139; Shindagha Waterfront, Shindagha Historic District; adult/child Dhs3/1; ⏰8am-8.30pm Sat-Thu, 3-9.30pm Fri; Ⓜ Al Ghubaiba) This grand courtyard house served as the residence of Sheikh Saeed, the grandfather of current Dubai ruler Sheikh Mohammed bin Rashid, from 1912 until his death in 1958. Today, the architectural marvel houses an excellent collection of pre-oil boom photographs of Dubai taken in the souqs, on the Creek and at traditional celebrations. There are also some insightful private images of the ruling Al

EMIRATI CULTURE DEMYSTIFIED

Anyone keen on delving deeper into Emirati culture and history should take advantage of the activities, Emirati meals and tours offered through this nonprofit **Sheikh Mohammed Centre for Cultural Understanding** (Map p248; ☎04 353 6666; www.cultures.ae; House 26, Al Musallah Rd; heritage/Creekside tours Dhs80/275, meals Dhs90-120; ⏰9am-5pm Sun-Thu, to 1pm Sat; Ⓜ Al Fahidi), based on the edge of **Al Fahidi Historic District** (p67). Guided by the motto 'Open Doors, Open Minds', this unique institution was founded in 1995 by Dubai's current ruler, Sheikh Mohammed bin Rashid, to build bridges between cultures and to help visitors and expats understand the traditions and customs of the UAE.

From mid-September to mid-July, the centre runs highly informative 90-minute guided heritage tours of Al Fahidi Historic District several times weekly. For groups of 10 or more, staff can also organise more comprehensive 2½-hour 'Creekside' tours that include a peek inside a mosque, an abra ride and a spin around the textile, spice and gold souqs in Bur Dubai and Deira. All tours conclude with a Q&A session and Arabic coffee, tea and dates.

To experience the culinary side of Emirati life, join one of the centre's traditional Bedouin-style meals. Depending on whether you come for breakfast, brunch, lunch or dinner, you'll get to taste such local dishes as *balaleet* (sweetened crunchy vermicelli), *chabab* (cardamom-spiced pancakes), *saloona* (a stew) or *machboos* (a rice and meat/fish dish).

The centre also runs hugely popular tours of **Jumeirah Mosque** (p100).

All tours and meals must be booked in advance. Check the website for the latest schedule.

Maktoum clan. Other rooms feature coins, stamps and documents dating back as far as 1791.

The original building dates back to 1896 and was enlarged and modernised several times. Sheikh Mohammed was born here in 1949 and spent the first 10 years of his life romping around the three inner courtyards flanked by 30 rooms behind richly ornamented teak doors and lorded over by four wind towers. Head upstairs to the *majlis* (reception room) to enjoy nice views of Dubai Creek.

SARUQ AL HADID ARCHAEOLOGY MUSEUM — MUSEUM

Map p248 (☎04 359 5612 ext 203; www.saruqalhadid.ae; Shindagha Waterfront; adult/child Dhs20/10; ⊙8am-8pm Sun-Wed, to 2pm Thu & Sat; Ⓜ Al Ghubaiba) Only discovered in 2002, Saruq Al Hadid sits deep in the desert sands of the southern reaches of the Dubai emirate and is believed to have been an iron-age metal 'factory' in operation between 1300 and 800 BC. Excavations have thus far yielded mostly swords, axe heads, daggers and other weapons, some of which are on display in this modern museum. Videos documenting the site's discovery and featuring interviews with archaeologists about their latest findings and theories provide further depth.

CROSSROADS OF CIVILIZATIONS MUSEUM — MUSEUM

Map p248 (☎04 393 4440; www.themuseum.ae; Al Khaleej Rd; Dhs30; ⊙9am-5pm Sat-Thu; Ⓜ Al Ghubaiba) This private museum in the Shindagha Historic District (p68) illustrates Dubai's historic role as a trading link between East and West. On display are hundreds of artefacts from the Ubaids, Greeks, Romans, Babylonians and other civilisations that passed through the region.

Highlights include a 7500-year-old bull-shaped vase and a 16th-century Kaaba curtain, as well as a 1st edition of the 1590 book that first mentions 'Dubai'. Other galleries display swords, daggers and other historical weaponry used across the region.

ZABEEL PARK — PARK

Map p252 (☎04 398 6888; Gate 1, off Sheikh Khalifa bin Zayed Rd; Dhs5; ⊙8am-11pm Sat-Wed, to 11.30pm Thu-Fri; 👪; Ⓜ Al Jafiliya) This sprawling park, where lots of palms and other greenery provide plenty of shade, is a weekend family favourite. It brims with activity zones, including a pretty lake with boat rides, an adventure playground, covered barbecue areas, a jogging track and a miniature train.

The park hosts a farmers market every Friday and a flea market on the first Saturday of the month (October to May). There's plenty of parking near Gate 1.

MINI-CRUISES

Dubai Ferry Cruises (Map p248; ☎800 9090; www.rta.ae; Shindagha Waterfront; adult/child Dhs50/25) runs 90-minute mini-cruises between Al Ghubaiba station in Bur Dubai and **Dubai Marina** (p111), passing by Madinat Jumeirah, the Burj Al Arab and Port Rashid. Trips depart at 11am, 1pm and 6.30pm.

Other options include an afternoon-tea trip up Dubai Creek at 3pm and a sunset cruise to Jumeirah Beach at 5pm. Ferries connect with the Dubai Canal route at Dubai Canal station.

DUBAI FRAME — VIEWPOINT

Map p252 (www.thedubaiframe.com; Gate 3, Zabeel Park; adult/child Dhs50/20; ⊙9am-9pm; Ⓜ Al Jafiliya) Opened on 1 January 2018, this 150m rectangular 'picture frame' sits in Zabeel Park (p69), right between historic and modern Dubai, and provides grand views of both parts of the city. Galleries on the ground floor tell the story of Dubai (the past) before visitors are whisked up to a viewing platform at roof level (the present). The final stop is another gallery depicting a vision of Dubai 50 years from now (the future).

Dubai Frame's opening was originally scheduled for 2015, but it was delayed by a copyright infringement lawsuit over its design and the need to replace the exterior cladding.

WAFI CITY — AREA

Map p252 (☎04 324 4555; www.wafi.com; Oud Metha & Sheikh Rashid Rds; Ⓟ; Ⓜ Dubai Healthcare City) Ancient Egypt gets a Dubai-style makeover at this lavishly designed hotel, residential, restaurant and shopping complex, complete with pyramids, hieroglyphs and statues of Ramses and Anubis.

The best time to visit is during the light and sound show that kicks off nightly at 9.30pm (September to May). In the cooler months, free outdoor movie screenings take over the Rooftop Gardens on Sunday nights at 8.30pm.

Wafi City was created in the 1990s and was one of the emirate's first new modern districts that combined entertainment, leisure, shopping and living.

CREEK PARK PARK

Map p252 (04 336 7633; off Riyadh St; Dhs5; 8am-10pm Sun-Wed, to 11pm Thu-Sat; P; M Oud Metha, Dubai Healthcare City) One of the emirate's oldest and largest parks stretches for 2.6km along Dubai Creek and is mostly popular with Bur Dubai expats who arrive on weekends to give the barbecue pits a workout. The gardens are quite nice, but many of the family-geared attractions like playgrounds, minigolf and a **children's museum** (Map p252; 04 334 0808; www.childrencity.ae; adult/child 2-15yr/family Dhs15/10/40, plus Creek Park entry Dhs5; 9am-7pm Sun-Thu, 2-8pm Fri & Sat;) are getting long in the tooth.

EATING

Bur Dubai is nirvana for ethnic eats, with oodles of tiny, low-frills cafes catering to homesick expats from Kerala to Kathmandu with superb and authentic street food. The narrow lanes around the souq and the backstreets of Karama near BurJuman mall are filled with hidden gems where you can soak up the local colour while filling up for under Dhs20.

KABUL DARBAR AFGHANI $

Map p248 (04 325 0900; Khalid bin al Waleed Rd; mains Dhs20-40; noon-midnight Sat-Thu, 1pm-midnight Fri; M Al Fahidi) Follow Afghan tradition: find a spot on the carpet, order lots of food and eat with your hands. All dishes are served with a soup, bread and salad, making for a filling and delicious meal.

AL USTAD SPECIAL KABAB IRANIAN $

Map p248 (04 397 1933; Al Musallah Rd; mains Dhs25-42; noon-4pm & 6.30pm-1am Sat-Thu, 6.30pm-1am Fri; M Al Fahidi) Sheikhs to shoe shiners clutter this funky, been-here-forever (since 1978, to be precise) kebab joint formerly known as Special Ostadi. Amid walls plastered with photographs of happy guests, a fleet of swift and quirky servers brings heaped plates of rice and yoghurt-marinated chicken into a dining room humming with chatter and laughter.

SARAVANA BHAVAN INDIAN $

Map p248 (04 353 9988; Khalifa bin Saeed Bldg, 3A St; mains Dhs15-17; 7am-11pm Sat-Wed, to 11.30pm Thu & Fri; ; M Al Ghubaiba) Head a block back from the Bur Dubai Abra Station to find this superb no-frills place, one of the best South Indian vegetarian restaurants in town. The vast menu includes wonderfully buttery *palak paneer,* creamy rogan josh, fragrant biryanis and other staples. Oddly, it also has a reputation for having excellent filter coffee!

ERIC'S INDIAN $

Map p252 (04 396 5080; 10b St, Sheikh Hamdan Colony, Karama; mains Dhs20-40; 11.30am-3.30pm & 6.30pm-midnight; ; M BurJuman, ADCB) Prints by Goan cartoonist Mario Miranda decorate the simple, buzzing dining room of this purveyor of magically spiced dishes from the tropical Indian state of Goa. The menu has few false notes, but popular items include the chicken 'lollipops' (drumsticks), the Bombay duck (actually a fish!) and the chicken *xacuti,* a mouth-watering curry with poppy seeds.

GOVINDA'S VEGETARIAN $

Map p252 (04 396 0088; http://mygovindas.com; 4A St, Karama; mains Dhs30-42; noon-3.30pm & 7pm-midnight; ; M BurJuman) Jains run this super-friendly, super-healthy, vegetarian Indian restaurant serving 'body-harmonising' sattvic food that uses only fresh, seasonal and organic produce and shuns oil, onion and garlic. Dishes to try include the velvety *paneer makhanwala* (Indian cheese in creamy tomato gravy) and the rich *dal makhani* (a rich black-lentil and kidney-bean stew).

Do save room for homemade Tru Frut natural ice cream from the attached parlour. Also tops for mocktails. It's behind Regent Palace Hotel in Karama.

SIND PUNJAB INDIAN $

Map p248 (04 352 5058; cnr Al Esbij & 29A Sts; mains Dhs15-38; 8.30am-2am; ; M Al Fahidi,

LOCAL KNOWLEDGE

HITTING THE 'OLD DUBAI' FOOD TRAIL

The narrow lanes of Bur Dubai and Deira are a feast for foodies: a beehive of shoebox-size restaurants where global expats cook up comfort food from home. With **Frying Pan Adventures** (www.fryingpanadventures.com; tours Dhs442) Arva and Farida Ahmed open the doors to the most exciting eateries to introduce you to delicious fare, from Moroccan to Nepalese to Indian, on their small-group walking tours.

Arva had already made a name for herself as a well-respected food blogger when she came up with the concept of Frying Pan Adventures, the first food tours in Dubai. Pick your favourite from her expanding roster, which includes the 'Middle Eastern Food Pilgrimage' and 'Little India on a Plate'. On each tour you'll enjoy nibbles at five or six hidden gems while Arva or her sister Farida shower you with often amusing musings about the food, the restaurant and local life.

Tours run for three to five hours and involve walking distances from 1.5km to 3km. Check the website for the schedule and to book a tour.

Al Ghubaiba) Like a fine wine, some restaurants only get better over time and such is the case with Sind Punjab, the first family eatery to open in Meena Bazaar in 1977. It still has a feverish local following for its finger-lickin' northern Indian specialities like butter chicken and *dal makhani*.

VAIBHAV — INDIAN $

Map p248 (☎04 353 8130; www.vaibhav.ae; Al Fahidi St; snacks Dhs2-20; ⌚7.30am-11pm; ✍; Ⓜ Al Gubaibha) This all-veg street-food haven does a roaring trade in *dosas* (savoury wraps), stuffed *parathas* (pan-fried flatbread) and other southern Indian soul food, all prepared in a Bollywood-worthy spectacle. Try it with a cup of spicy masala chai (tea). Busiest at night. It hides out in a nondescript lane off Al Fahidi St opposite the Elegant Corner nuts shop.

NEPALIKO SAGARMATHA — NEPALI $

Map p248 (☎04 352 2124; Al Fahidi & 11th St; mains Dhs10-22; ⌚9am-midnight; Ⓜ Al Ghubaiba) At this small and basic joint, Nepali expats soothe their homesickness with platters of tasty *momos* (dumplings), including a version filled with 'buff' (buffalo), as well as steaming bowls of *thukpa* (noodle soup). It's a bit set back from the street overlooking a car park.

LEBANESE VILLAGE RESTAURANT — LEBANESE $

Map p248 (☎04 352 2522; Al Mankhool Rd; mains Dhs20-70; ⌚noon-2am; Ⓜ Al Fahidi) At this tried-and-true eatery the best seats are under a shady umbrella on the pavement terrace (more appealing than the bright diner-style interior). The menu has few surprises, but does staples like grills, hummus and tabbouleh dependably well. Also handy for takeaway if you're staying in a nearby hotel apartment.

KARACHI DARBAR — PAKISTANI $

Map p252 (☎04 334 7272; 33B St, Karama Market; mains Dhs10-30; ⌚5am-2am; ✍; Ⓜ ADCB) A favourite pit stop of expats and Karama Market shoppers with an eye for a biryani bargain, this local chain puts tummies into a state of contentment with a huge menu of Pakistani, Indian and Chinese dishes. Reliable picks include shrimp masala, mutton *kadai* and butter chicken. The chef can be a bit too generous with the ghee (clarified butter). It's near Lulu Supermarket.

LEMONGRASS — THAI $

Map p252 (☎04 334 2325; www.lemongrassrestaurants.com; ground fl, Bu Haleeba Bldg, Oud Metha; mains Dhs24-65; ⌚noon-11.30pm; 📶; Ⓜ Oud Metha) Lemongrass' soothing mango-and-lime-coloured dining room is an ideal backdrop for brightly flavoured cooking that spans the arc from pad thai (nicely presented in an omelette wrapper) to curries with a marvellous depth of flavour. If you like spicy, say so; the kitchen can be shy with the heat. Located next to Lamcy Plaza.

JAFFER BHAI'S — INDIAN $

Map p252 (☎04 342 6467; Zabeel Rd, Karama; mains Dhs25-42; ⌚noon-4pm & 7pm-12.30am; ✍; Ⓜ ADCB) Jaffer Bhai, the self-crowned 'biryani king of Mumbai', now feeds his soulful fare to adoring crowds in this modern Karama eatery decorated with a timeline of his career. The chicken biryani gets tops marks and the mutton *nihari* (the house speciality) is quite good as well, although perhaps a bit oily. Finish up with *maharani rabdi,* the Indian spin on crème brûlée.

★ARABIAN TEA HOUSE CAFE $$

Map p248 (☎04 353 5071; www.arabianteahouse.co; Al Fahidi St; breakfast Dhs30-65, mains Dhs48-65; ⏰7.30am-10pm; Ⓜ Al Fahidi) A grand old tree, white wicker chairs, turquoise benches and billowing flowers create a sun-dappled refuge in the courtyard of an old pearl merchant's house. The menu includes lots of Emirati specialities, including *raqaq* (traditional bread), chicken *machboos* (spicy casserole with rice) and *saloona* chicken (in a tomato-based stew).

A lovely pit stop on a tour of the Al Fahidi Historic District (p67).

XVA CAFÉ CAFE $$

Map p248 (☎04 353 5383; www.xvahotel.com/cafe; Al Fahidi Historic District, off Al Fahidi St; dishes Dhs25-55; ⏰7am-9.30pm Nov-Apr; 📶🌿; Ⓜ Al Fahidi) Escape Dubai's bustle at this arty courtyard cafe where the menu eschews meat in favour of eggplant burgers, bulgar salad and *mojardara* (rice topped with sautéed veggies and yoghurt). The mint lemonade is perfect on a hot day. Breakfast is served any time.

KHAZANA INDIAN $$

Map p252 (☎04 336 0061; www.khanakhazanadubai.net; 12A St, Al Nasr Leisureland; mains Dhs50-175; ⏰12.30-3pm & 7pm-midnight; 📶; Ⓜ Oud Metha) Celebrity chef Sanjeer Kapoor's first signature joint is still one of the best Indian restaurants in town, if the loyal following of regulars is any indication. Everything from curries to tandoor dishes tastes genuine and fresh, and is inflected with an authentic medley of spices. Ample bamboo and rattan create a relaxed feel-good ambience. Full bar.

ASHA'S INDIAN $$

Map p252 (☎04 324 4100; www.ashasrestaurants.com/dubai; 1st fl, Pyramids, Wafi City; set lunch Dhs75, mains Dhs55-225; ⏰12.30-3pm & 7pm-midnight; Ⓟ📶🌿; Ⓜ Dubai Healthcare City) Namesake of legendary Bollywood singer Asha Bhosle, this sensuously lit dining room shines the spotlight on contemporary northwest Indian fare. The extensive menu ranges from tandoori kebabs (try the 'Kerala Chilly Garlic Prawn') to sinus-teasing curries and vegetarian options that don't sacrifice a lick to the taste gods.

Dine in or on the terrace overlooking the Wafi City courtyard. Full bar.

ANTIQUE BAZAAR INDIAN $$

Map p248 (☎04 397 7444; www.antiquebazaar-dubai.com; Khalid bin al Waleed Rd, Four Points by Sheraton Bur Dubai, Mankhool; mains Dhs46-130; ⏰12.30am-3pm & 7.30pm-midnight; Ⓟ📶; Ⓜ Al Fahidi) Resembling an exotic Mogul palace, Antique Bazaar's decor is sumptuously ornate with carved-wood seats, ivory-inset tables and richly patterned fabrics. Thumbs up to the *machli mirch ka salan* (fish with coconut, tamarind and curry) and the *gosht awadhi* biryani (rice with lamb, saffron and nuts). At dinnertime, a music and dance show competes with the food for your attention.

CREEKSIDE CAFE BREAKFAST $$

Map p248 (☎04 359 9220; http://creeksidedubai.me; Waterfront, Bur Dubai Souq; breakfast Dhs25-45, mains Dhs70-80; ⏰9am-8pm; 📶; Ⓜ Al Fahidi) This hip cultural space and cafe is especially beloved for its soulful coffee and Western-style breakfast, including homemade granola, French toast and eggs Benedict, but it's really a welcoming spot to sit any time of day thanks to its waterfront locale. If you're feeling adventurous, try the cardamom-and-date crème brûlée.

BAIT AL WAKEEL ARABIC $$

Map p248 (☎04 353 0530; Waterfront, Bur Dubai Souq, Meena Bazaar; mezze Dhs16-50, mains Dhs25-80; ⏰11am-midnight; Ⓜ Al Ghubaiba) Teeming with tourists lured by the romantic Creekside setting, this restaurant occupies one of Dubai's oldest buildings (from 1935) and has a great wooden dining deck that used to be a boat landing. Come for coffee, juice or mezze and enjoy the view.

CHUTNEYS INDIAN $$

Map p252 (☎04 310 4340; 19 St, Mövenpick Hotel Bur Dubai, Oud Mehta; mains Dhs50-115; ⏰noon-3pm & 7-11.45pm; Ⓟ📶; Ⓜ Dubai Healthcare City, Oud Metha) Chutneys provides a richly nuanced culinary journey to northern India. There's lots of familiar feel-good fare including juicy kebabs and fluffy biryanis as well as the signature

LOCAL KNOWLEDGE

TIME FOR A CUPPA?

Meena Bazaar is ideal for a pick-me-up in the form of a steaming cup of masala chai (also called karak or kadak chai). It's a blend of black tea boiled with milk, sugar and spices (typically cardamom, cloves, peppercorns and cinnamon, or a combination thereof) that was brought to the Gulf by expats from India and Pakistan and is popular even at the height of summer. Pop into any of the local cafes around here and treat yourself to a cup. They cost just a dirham or two.

dish *tawa murgh* – boneless chicken cooked on a *tawa* (griddle) in a thick tomato-onion sauce. The lunchtime *thali* (Dhs80) is great value.

HOT FISH SEAFOOD **$$**

Map p252 (☎04 357 8889, 055 839 8058; www.facebook.com/hotfish.restaurant; 6C & 39th St, Karama; meals from Dhs30; ⌚noon-midnight; Ⓜ ADCB) The sister restaurant of the fabled Bu Qtair (p103) sits on the corner of a lone gentrified block in working-class Karama, with plastic chairs and tables spread across the pavement beneath an awning. It serves the same simple food: prawns and fish marinated in red masala paste, then fried and served with coconut fish curry, rice and flaky paratha.

There's no menu (and certainly no booze); just opt for the catch of the day (usually sheri, pomfret or kingfish; avoid overfished hammour).

AWTAR LEBANESE **$$**

Map p252 (☎04 317 2222; Al Qataiyat Rd, Grand Hyatt Dubai; mezze Dhs35-70, mains Dhs65-150; ⌚7.30pm-3am Mon-Sat; Ⓟ📶; Ⓜ Dubai Healthcare City) Locals love the opulent Bedouin tent-style ceiling of this formal Lebanese restaurant, complete with belly dancer and live band. The menu presents a veritable lexicon of mezze perfect for grazing and sharing, while carnivores lust after succulent grilled lamb and other meats. The scene gets rockin' after 10pm. Shisha and full bar.

TOMO JAPANESE **$$$**

Map p252 (☎04 357 7888; www.tomo.ae; 13th St, 17th fl, Raffles Hotel, Wafi City; mains Dhs70-550; ⌚12.30-3.30pm & 6.30pm-1am; Ⓜ Dubai Healthcare City) The name of this gorgeously formal restaurant translates as 'long-time friend', which is quite apropos given its league of loyal followers. No gimmicky fusion here, just Japanese cuisine at its best: super-fresh sushi and sashimi, delectable Wagyu beef, feathery tempura and other treasured morsels. Plus dazzling views from the 360-degree terrace on the 17th floor of the Raffles Hotel.

PEPPERCRAB SINGAPOREAN **$$$**

Map p252 (☎04 317 2221; Al Qataiyat Rd, Grand Hyatt Dubai; dishes Dhs40-175, crab per 100g Dhs45; ⌚7-11.30pm Sat-Wed, to midnight Thu & Fri; Ⓟ📶; Ⓜ Dubai Healthcare City) If you've never had Singaporean food, Peppercrab is perfect for surrendering your culinary virginity. Prepare your palate with wasabi shrimp and seafood salad, then don an apron and get ready to do battle with the main event, the eponymous 'peppercrab' – a succulent, tender mud crab prepared in your choice of half a dozen ways.

DRINKING & NIGHTLIFE

Bur Dubai is not classic going-out turf, but there are some lovably divey pubs, as well as nightclubs popular with local Asian expats in the older hotels around the souq. Rock Bottom Café (p75) is popular with both Western expats and tourists.

GEORGE & DRAGON PUB

Map p248 (☎04 393 9444; www.astamb.com; Al Falah Rd, ground fl, Ambassador Hotel, Meena Bazaar; ⌚noon-3am; Ⓜ Al Ghubaiba) Keeping barflies boozy for a generation, this quintessential British dive comes with the requisite dartboard, pool table, greasy fish and chips, cheap beer and a painted window of St George jousting with the dragon. In the Ambassador, Dubai's oldest hotel (since 1971), it's fun, full of character(s) and a good place to wind down with a pint.

ROCK BOTTOM CAFÉ PUB

Map p248 (☎04 396 3888; Sheikh Khalifa bin Zayed Rd, ground fl, Regent Palace Hotel, Karama; ⌚noon-3am; Ⓜ BurJuman) This been-here-forever Western expat fave has

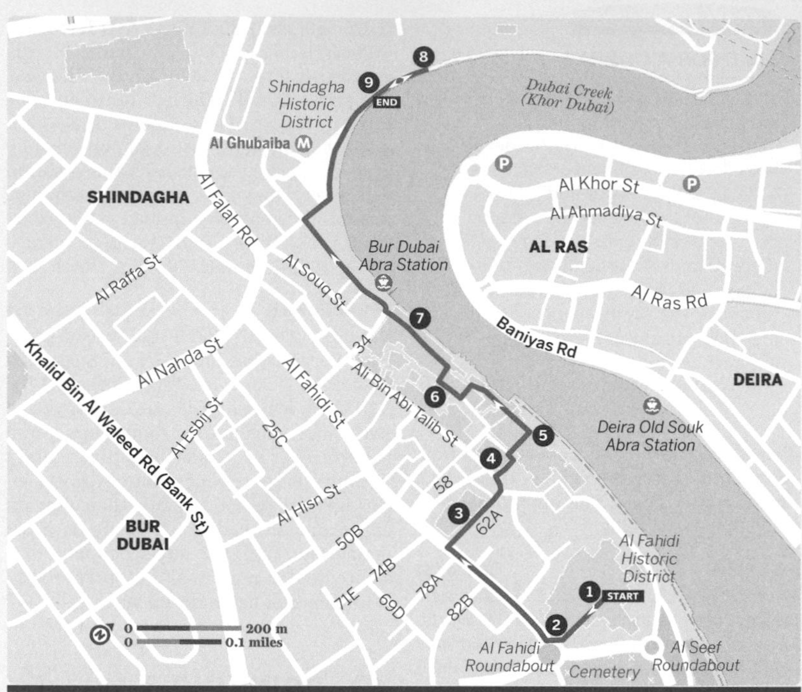

Neighbourhood Walk
Bur Dubai Waterside Walk

START AL FAHIDI HISTORIC DISTRICT
END BARJEEL HERITAGE GUEST HOUSE
LENGTH 3KM; TWO HOURS

Kick off your tour with a wander along the charismatic lanes of 1 **Al Fahidi Historic District** (p67), one of Dubai's oldest neighbourhoods. Check out the traditional wind-tower architecture and keep an eye out for small museums like the cute **Coin Museum** (p67) and **Coffee Museum** (p67). Look for street art as you make your way to the **Alserkal Cultural Foundation** (p67), whose galleries always display some intriguing works. Stop for refreshments in its courtyard cafe or relax in the enchanting walled garden of the **Arabian Tea House** (p72).

Thus fortified, check out the 2 **Majlis Gallery** (p67), the oldest art space in Dubai, before continuing west along bustling Al Fahidi St to the 3 **Dubai Museum** (p66), which introduces the history and development of this burgeoning city. Steer towards Dubai's tallest minaret, atop the 4 **Grand Mosque** (p67), and then follow the lane to the mosque's right-hand side before ducking into teensy 5 **Hindi Lane** (p68), a vibrant alley lined with pint-sized shops selling religious paraphernalia. This street is home to Dubai's only Hindu temple.

Exiting Hindi Lane takes you to the wooden arcades of the 6 **Bur Dubai Souq** (p67) and its colourful textile and trinket shops. Lug your loot to the waterfront and snap pictures of the abras at the Dubai Old Souk abra station before enjoying a juice on the deck of the 7 **Bait Al Wakeel cafe** (p72).

Follow the Creek north to the Shindagha Historic District, which is lined with the residences of Dubai's ruling family and is currently undergoing extensive redevelopment. Ignore the dust and make your way to the splendid 8 **Sheikh Saeed Al Maktoum House** (p68), which displays an intriguing collection of old photographs of Dubai.

Wrap up with a snack at the 9 **Barjeel Heritage Guest House** (p184) while watching the timeless ballet of boat traffic from your terrace table.

a '70s-era American roadhouse feel, with a cover band blaring out Top 40 hits and a DJ filling in the breaks with gusto. By day it's a regular cafe serving international soul food, but with a mob of friends and a bottle of tequila gone, it's the quintessential ending to a rollickin' night on the town.

COOZ BAR

Map p252 (04 317 2221; www.dubai.grand.hyatt.com; Al Qataiyat Rd, ground fl, Grand Hyatt Dubai, Umm Hurair; 9am-3am; ; Dubai Healthcare City) Sip a martini at this dimly lit, stylish cocktail bar and enjoy some smooth live jazz by the resident singer and pianist every night except Sunday, from 9.30pm to 2am.

ENTERTAINMENT

MOVIES UNDER THE STARS OUTDOOR CINEMA

Map p252 (04 324 4100; www.pyramidsrestaurantsatwafi.com; Pyramids Rooftop Gardens, Wafi City; 8.30pm Sun Feb-Apr; ; Dubai Healthcare City) FREE Every Sunday night during the cooler months, clued-in cinephiles invade the rooftop of the Pyramids Building, next to the Wafi Mall, to drop into a giant beanbag and enjoy a free classic flick. Food and nonalcoholic drinks are available.

SHOPPING

Bur Dubai offers wallet-friendly shopping for souvenirs, textiles and knock-off handbags, mostly in the souq and in the backstreets of Karama. Don't expect top quality, though, except in the high-end BurJuman mall (p76). Wafi Mall (p78) is more notable for its architecture than its shops.

DUBAI FLEA MARKET MARKET

Map p252 (055 886 8939; www.dubai-fleamarket.com; Gates 1 & 2, Zabeel Park; Dhs5; 8am-3pm every 1st Sat Oct-May; Al Jafiliya) Trade malls for stalls and look for bargains amid the piles of preloved stuff that's spilled out of local closets at Dubai's cherished flea markets, which take place every weekend in a different spot around town, including at this great location inside the vast Zabeel Park. Check the website for upcoming markets.

RIPE MARKET MARKET

Map p252 (04 315 7000; http://ripeme.com/the-ripe-markets; Gate 2, Zabeel Park; 9am-2pm Fri late Oct-Mar; ; Al Jafiliya) Held every Friday in beautiful Zabeel Park, this market features not only fruit and veg from local growers but also local honey, nuts, spices and eggs, plus arts and crafts, food stations and locally roasted gourmet coffee – pretty much all you need for a picnic under the palms.

THE ART OF BARGAINING

- Compare prices at a few shops or stalls so you get an idea of what things cost and how much you're willing to pay.
- When you're interested in buying an item, don't show too much enthusiasm or you'll never get the price down.
- Don't pay the first price quoted. This is actually considered arrogant.
- Start below the price you wish to pay so you have room to compromise – but don't quote too low or the vendor may feel insulted. A good rule of thumb is to cut the first suggested price in half and go from there. Expect to finish up with a discount of 20% to 30%.
- If you intend to buy more than one item, use this as a bargaining chip – the more you buy, the better the discount.
- Take your time and stay relaxed. You can come away with an enjoyable experience whether you end up with a bargain or not.
- If negotiations aren't going to plan, simply smile and say goodbye – often the vendor will follow and suggest a compromise price.

The popular market has expanded to a second location with the **Ripe Night Market** held from 10am to 8pm every Saturday at Al Barsha Pond Park. From late April to mid-October, the stallholders move indoors to Times Square Center (9am to 3pm on Saturdays).

BURJUMAN MALL

Map p248 (☎04 352 0222; www.burjuman.com; Sheikh Khalifa bin Zayed Rd; ⊙10am-10pm Sat-Wed, to 11pm Thu & Fri; 📶; Ⓜ BurJuman) Rather than rest on its laurels, Dubai's oldest high-end mall (open since 1992) just keeps reinventing itself. A recent remodel added some 200 shops (including luxury brands like Dior and Versace), a vast Carrefour supermarket and a 14-screen multiplex cinema. The upstairs food court, Pavilion Gardens, is an attractively designed, fountain-anchored space lidded by a soaring glass ceiling.

BATEEL FOOD

Map p248 (☎04 355 2853; www.bateel.com; Sheikh Khalifa bin Zayed Rd, 1st fl, BurJuman Mall; ⊙10am-10pm Sun-Wed, to 11pm Thu & Fri; 📶; Ⓜ BurJuman) Old-style traditional Arabian hospitality meant dates and camel milk. Now Emiratis offer their guests Bateel's scrumptious date chocolates and truffles, made using European chocolate-making techniques. Staff are happy to give you a sample before you buy. Most other Dubai malls have their own Bateel branches; check the website for details.

A PRIMER ON CARPET BUYING

Due diligence is essential for prospective carpet buyers. Though you may only want a piece to match your curtains, you'll save a lot of time and money if you do a little homework. Your first order of business: read *Oriental Rugs Today* by Emmett Eiland, an excellent primer on buying new Oriental rugs.

A rug's quality depends entirely on how the wool was processed. It doesn't matter if the rug was hand-knotted if the wool is lousy. The best comes from sheep at high altitudes, which produce impenetrably thick, long-staple fleece, heavy with lanolin. No acids should ever be applied; otherwise the lanolin washes away. Lanolin yields naturally stain-resistant, lustrous fibre that doesn't shed. The dye should be vegetable-based pigment. This guarantees saturated, rich colour tones with a depth and vibrancy unattainable with chemicals.

The dyed wool is hand-spun into thread, which by nature has occasional lumps and challenges the craftsmanship of the weavers, forcing them to compensate for the lumps by occasionally changing the shape, size or position of a knot. These subtle variations in a finished carpet's pattern – visible only upon close inspection – give the carpet its character, and actually make the rug more valuable.

Dealers will hype knot density, weave quality and country of origin, but really, they don't matter. The crucial thing to find out is how the wool was treated. A rug made with acid-treated wool will never look as good as it did the day you bought it. Conversely, a properly made rug will grow more lustrous in colour over time and will last centuries. Here's a quick test. Stand on top of the rug with rubber-soled shoes and do the twist. Grind the fibres underfoot. If they shed, it's lousy wool.

If you want a gorgeous pattern that will look great in your living room, pack a few fabric swatches from your sofa and curtains. Patterns range from simple four-colour tribal designs in wool to wildly ornate, lustrous, multicoloured silk carpets that shimmer under the light. Look through books before you leave home to get a sense of what you like. Once in the stores, plan to linger a long time with dealers, slowly sipping tea while they unfurl dozens of carpets. The process is great fun. Just don't get too enthusiastic or the dealer won't bargain as readily.

If you're serious about becoming a collector, read Emmett Eiland's book; also Google 'DOBAG', a Turkish-rug-making cultural-survival project, and check out www.yayla.com for other reliable background info. Follow links to non-profit organisations that not only help reconstruct rug-making cultures threatened by modernisation, but also help to educate, house and feed the people of these cultures, giving them a voice in an age of industrial domination.

THE ONE HOMEWARES

Map p252 (☎600 541 007; www.theone.com; 1st fl, Wafi Mall; ⏰10am-10pm Sat-Wed, to midnight Thu & Fri; Ⓜ Dubai Healthcare City) Nirvana for design-minded home decorators, this airy showroom unites funky, innovative and top-quality items from dozens of international manufacturers. Even everyday items get a zany twist here, like pearl-beaded pillows, tiger-print wing-back chairs and vintage-style pendant lamps.

AJMAL PERFUME

Map p248 (☎04 351 5505; www.ajmalperfume.com; Sheikh Khalifa bin Zayed Rd, BurJuman mall; ⏰10am-10pm Sat-Wed, to 11pm Thu & Fri; Ⓜ BurJuman) The place for traditional Arabian *attars* (perfumes), Ajmal custom blends its earthy scents and pours them into fancy gold or jewel-encrusted bottles. These aren't frilly French colognes – they're woody and pungent perfumes. Ask for the signature scent 'Ajmal', based on white musk and jasmine.

Other branches are in Deira City Centre (p60), Mall of the Emirates (p107) and Dubai Mall (p82).

FABINDIA FASHION & ACCESSORIES

Map p248 (☎04 398 9633; www.fabindia.com; Nashwan Bldg, Al Mankhool Rd; ⏰10am-10pm Sat-Thu, 2-10pm Fri; Ⓜ ADCB) In business since 1950, Fabindia is one of India's biggest retail chains and mostly sells products handmade by more than 50,000 Indian villagers using traditional skills and techniques. There's a huge selection of fashion, furnishings and handicrafts, including colourful *kurtis* (tunics), elegant shawls, patterned silk cushions and organic teas and chutneys, all at very reasonable prices.

It's opposite the Emarat petrol station.

DREAM GIRL TAILORS CLOTHING

Map p248 (☎04 388 0070; www.dreamgirltailors.com; Al Futtaim Bldg, 37D St, Meena Bazaar; ⏰10am-1pm & 4-10pm Sat-Thu, 6-9pm Fri; Ⓜ Al Fahidi) Kamal Makhija and his army of tailors have had women looking good since 1971. They can create original designs, copy a beloved dress or even sew you an outfit from a magazine photo.

HOLLYWOOD TAILORS CLOTHING

Map p248 (☎04 352 8551; http://hollywooduae.com; 37D St, Meena Bazaar; ⏰9.30am-1.30pm & 4-10pm Sat-Thu, 6-9pm Fri; Ⓜ Al Fahidi) In business since 1976, this outfit specialises in men's suits and has lots of fabrics to choose from. Turn-around time ranges from three days to one week.

LOCAL KNOWLEDGE

TAILOR-MADE FASHION

Labyrinthine Meena Bazaar teems with talented tailors (mostly from India) who will run up a dress or suit for you in two to five days. Some also sell material, although you could also pay a visit to the nearby Textile Souq (within the main Bur Dubai Souq), where you can ponder over endless swatches of wonderful fabrics. Reliable scissor-meisters include the poetically named **Dream Girl Tailors** and **Hollywood Tailors**, both on 37D St behind the Dolphin Hotel.

COMPUTER PLAZA ELECTRONICS

Map p248 (☎600 560 609, 055 335 5533; www.computerplaza-me.com; Al Mankhool Rd, Al Ain Center; ⏰10am-10pm Sat-Thu, 2-10pm Fri; Ⓜ Al Fahidi) This jam-packed computer and electronics mall has more than 80 outlets selling every kind of computer hardware and accessory, including printers and scanners, plus software, mobile phones and cameras. On the ground floor, a handful of fast-food outlets and an ice-cream counter keep tummy rumblings in check.

KARAMA MARKET MARKET

Map p252 (Karama Shopping Complex; www.facebook.com/karamaMarketDubai; 18B St; ⏰10am-10pm; Ⓜ ADCB) A visually unappealing concrete souq, Karama's bustling backstreet shopping area is crammed with shops selling handicrafts and souvenirs. Vendors may offer to take you to 'secret rooms' in the back of the building, which are crammed with knock-off designer bags and watches.

Quality varies, so it pays to have a keen eye and to know what the originals look like. Prices are low, but bargaining lowers them further.

ROYAL SAFFRON SPICES

Map p248 (☎050 282 9565; Al Fahidi Historic District, Al Fahidi St; ⏰9am-9pm; Ⓜ Al Fahidi) This tiny shop tucked into the quiet lanes of Al Fahidi Historic District (p67) is a

DUBAI'S SHOPPING FESTIVALS

Every year in January, the month-long **Dubai Shopping Festival** (DSF; www.mydsf.ae) draws hordes of bargain-hunting tourists from around the world. This is a good time to visit Dubai: in addition to the huge discounts in the souqs and malls, the weather is usually gorgeous and the city is abuzz. Outdoor souqs, amusement rides and food stalls are set up in many neighbourhoods. There are traditional performances and displays at the Heritage and Diving Villages, family entertainment across the city, concerts, fireworks and events in the parks. **Dubai Shopping Surprises**, a related event, is held during the unbearably hot months of July and August; it mainly attracts visitors from other Gulf countries. Insider tip: for the best bargains at either festival, come during the last week, when retailers slash prices even further to clear out their inventory.

photogenic find. It's crammed full of spices like cloves, cardamom and cinnamon, plus fragrant oils, dried fruits and nuts, frankincense from Somalia and Oman, henna hair dye – and quirky salt and pepper sheikh and sheikhas.

CITY CENTRE AL SHINDAGHA MALL

Map p248 (☎04 209 3536; www.citycentreshindagha.com; Al Ghubaiba Rd; ⏰10am-10pm Sun-Wed, to midnight Thu-Sat; 📶; Ⓜ Al Ghubaiba) With only 75 outlets, this mall, which opened in 2016, is small by Dubai standards and caters mostly to the needs of expat residents. Highlights include a large Carrefour supermarket and a seven-screen cinema.

WAFI MALL MALL

Map p252 (☎04 324 4555; www.wafi.com; Oud Metha Rd; ⏰10am-10pm Sat-Wed, to midnight Thu & Fri; 📶; Ⓜ Dubai Healthcare City) At the heart of Egyptian-style Wafi City (p69) district, one of Dubai's most architecturally striking malls is built around three stained-glass pyramids and guarded by two giant statues of Ramses II. Stock up on gifts from around the Arabian world in the basement's **Souq Khan Murjan**, which was modelled after the namesake Baghdad bazaar.

Alas, it's been eclipsed by bigger, newer and more central shopping centres, and is often sadly deserted these days.

SPORTS & ACTIVITIES

PHARAOHS' CLUB GYM

Map p252 (☎04 324 0000; www.cleopatrasspaandwellness.com; Wafi Mall, Sheikh Rashid Rd; day passes Dhs160; ⏰6.30am-10pm Sat-Thu, 9am-9pm Fri; 👪; Ⓜ Dubai Healthcare City) Pump it up at this fitness club, which has mixed and women-only gyms, a huge free weights area, an indoor climbing wall, and squash and tennis courts. Not only kids love the free-form 'lazy-river' rooftop swimming pool.

Downtown Dubai & Business Bay

DOWNTOWN & BUSINESS BAY | FINANCIAL DISTRICT | AL QUOZ

Neighbourhood Top Five

❶ **Burj Khalifa** (p81) Craning your neck to take in the entire height of this elegantly tapered skyscraper, which pierces the sky at 828m, making it the world's tallest building.

❷ **Dubai Mall** (p82) Shopping at the mother of all malls with a record-breaking 1200 shops.

❸ **Alserkal Avenue** (p84) Dipping into Dubai-style urban cool while keeping on the pulse of the latest in Middle Eastern art at this cluster of warehouses turned art-and-cultural campus.

❹ **Dubai Fountain** (p82) Feeling hypnotised by the beautifully choreographed singing and dancing fountain at the foot of the Burj Khalifa.

❺ **Dubai Design District** (p92) Mingling with top creative minds amid edgy architecture, hip cafes, fashion-forward stores and public art.

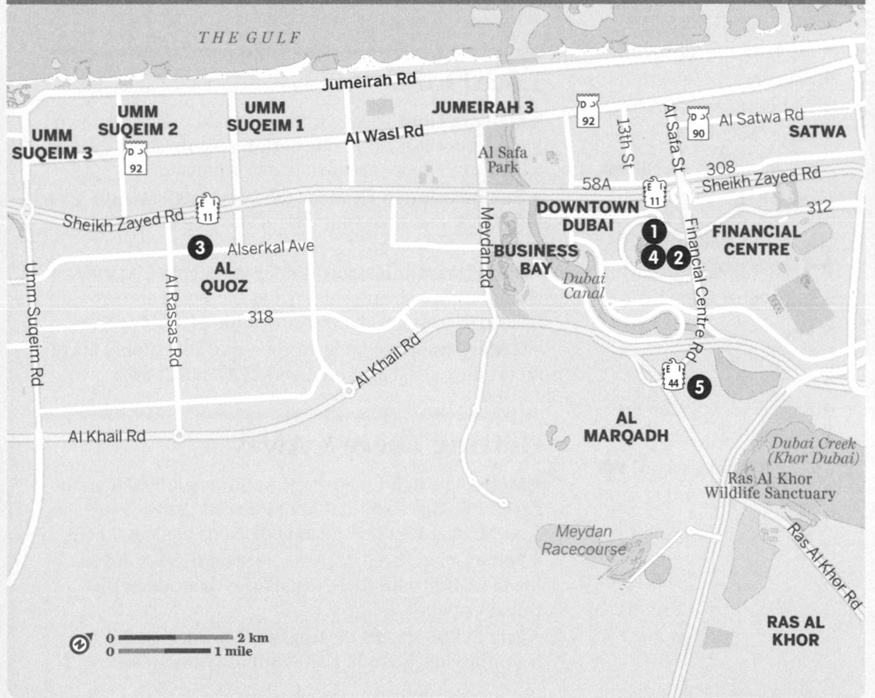

For more detail of this area see map p258.

Lonely Planet's Top Tip

A trip to the world's highest observation platform in the world's tallest building – the **Burj Khalifa** (p81) – is one of the hottest tickets in town. Book online as early as possible to secure a spot during your preferred time slot, especially if you're in Dubai on a short stay.

Best Places to Eat

- Zuma (p88)
- Zaroob (p85)
- Baker & Spice (p85)
- Tom & Serg (p89)
- Carnival by Tresind (p89)

For reviews, see p85.

Best Places to Drink

- Cirque Le Soir (p90)
- White Dubai (p89)
- Bridgewater Tavern (p89)
- Fibber Magee's (p90)
- Base (p90)

For reviews, see p89.

Best Places to Shop

- Dubai Mall (p82)
- Mirzam Chocolate Makers (p92)
- Candylicious (p93)
- Farmers Market on the Terrace (p93)

For reviews, see p92.

Explore Downtown Dubai

Downtown Dubai is the city's vibrant urban hub and a key destination for visitors. Its literal pinnacle is the Burj Khalifa – the world's tallest building – which overlooks the Dubai Mall. The world's biggest shopping temple, it also teems with crowd-pleasing attractions, including a massive aquarium, an ice rink and a complete dinosaur skeleton. The mall flanks the Burj Lake where the mesmerising Dubai Fountain erupts in choreographed dance, music and light shows nightly.

Dubai's financial heart, meanwhile, beats north of downtown along Sheikh Zayed Rd, the city's main artery. Banks, investment companies and the stock exchange make their home at the Dubai International Financial Centre (DIFC). There's little reason to visit unless you're interested in architecture, in which case the Gate Building and the Jumeirah Emirates Towers (where Dubai's ruler Sheikh Mohammed keeps his offices) make appealing photo ops. Art fans can scan the prestigious galleries at DIFC's Gate Village for the latest in Middle Eastern art.

To tap into Dubai's underground art and creative scene, urban adventurers should follow Sheikh Zayed Rd south to Alserkal Avenue. Right in the gritty, industrial district of Al Quoz, a cluster of warehouses has morphed into an innovative art campus, with cutting-edge galleries alongside an eclectic mix of design and photography studios, hipster cafes, community theatre, a chocolate factory, an art-house cinema and other creative enterprises.

Local Life

- **Mall crawling** To locals, the mall is the de facto town plaza, especially on Friday nights. Join in: shop, relax in a cafe, grab an ice cream or catch a movie.
- **Business lunch** Head for the DIFC (p83) around lunchtime and take your pick of several excellent restaurants.
- **Showtime** Grab a post-dinner juice, coffee or ice cream and stake out your spot at the Burj Lake for front-row views of the Dubai Fountain (p82).
- **Gallery hopping** Look for the finest in regional art on an evening stroll around Alserkal Avenue (p84).

Getting There & Away

- **Metro** The Red Line runs the entire length of Sheikh Zayed Rd. Major stations are Financial Centre, Emirates Towers, Burj Khalifa/Dubai Mall, Noor Bank and FGB.
- **Ferry** Dubai Ferry stops below Sheikh Zayed Rd in Business Bay, with three departures daily along the Dubai Canal.
- **Bus** Bus 95 travels the length of Sheikh Zayed Rd, from the Gold Souq in Deira to Ibn Battuta Mall.

TOP SIGHT

BURJ KHALIFA

The Burj Khalifa is a ground-breaking feat of architecture and engineering, with two observation decks on the 124th and 148th floors and a restaurant-bar on the 122nd. The world's tallest building (828m) opened in 2010, only six years after excavations began. Up to 13,000 workers toiled day and night, putting up a new floor in as little as three days.

Taking in the views from the world's tallest building is a deservedly crave-worthy experience and a trip to the 'At the Top' observation deck on the 124th floor (452m) is the most popular way to do it. Once you get to the platform, you can seek out high-powered 'viewfinders' that help bring even distant developments into focus (at least on clear days) and cleverly simulate the same view at night and in the 1980s. There are also six digital telescopes that use HD cameras with a high zoom to zero in on places outside the cityscape. Getting to the deck means passing various multimedia exhibits until a double-decker lift zips you up at 10m per second.

To truly be on the world's highest observation platform, though, you need to buy tickets to 'At the Top Sky' on the 148th floor (555m). A visit here is set up like a hosted VIP experience with refreshments, a guided tour and an interactive screen where you 'fly' to different city landmarks by hovering your hands over high-tech sensors. Afterwards, you're escorted to the 125th floor to be showered with Burj trivia and to take in another attraction called 'A Falcon's Eye View' that lets you take a virtual flight over the emirate by soaring over key attractions like a bird.

Note that prices go up during prime hours (around sunset) and that closing times may vary depending on demand and the season.

DON'T MISS

- Buying tickets in advance!
- Views, views, views
- Multimedia exhibits

PRACTICALITIES

- Map p258, D3
- 800 2884 3867
- www.atthetop.ae
- 1 Mohammed bin Rashid Blvd, entry lower ground fl, Dubai Mall
- At the Top adult/child 4-12yr Dhs125/95 non-prime hours, Dhs200/160 prime hours, At the Top Sky non-prime/prime hours Dhs350/500, audio guide Dhs25
- At the Top 8.30am-11pm, At the Top Sky 11am-10pm, last entry 45min before closing
-
- Burj Khalifa/Dubai Mall

SIGHTS

Downtown Dubai proper has most of the must-see sights, including the Burj Khalifa, Dubai Mall and the Dubai Fountain. Art lovers need to head to the gallery quarters in the Financial District and Alserkal Avenue in Al Quoz.

Downtown & Business Bay

BURJ KHALIFA — LANDMARK

See p81.

★DUBAI MALL — MALL

Map p258 (800 382 246 255; www.thedubaimall.com; Sheikh Mohammed bin Rashid Blvd; 10am-midnight; ; M Burj Khalifa/Dubai Mall) With around 1200 shops, this isn't merely the world's largest shopping mall – it's a small city, with a giant ice rink and aquarium, a dinosaur skeleton, indoor theme parks and 150 food outlets. There's a strong European-label presence, along with branches of the French Galeries Lafayette department store, the British toy store Hamley's and the first Bloomingdale's outside the US.

DUBAI AQUARIUM & UNDERWATER ZOO — AQUARIUM

Map p258 (04 448 5200; www.thedubaiaquarium.com; ground fl, Dubai Mall, Sheikh Mohammed bin Rashid Blvd; packages Dhs100-300; 10am-11pm Sun-Wed, to midnight Thu-Sat; P ; M Burj Khalifa/Dubai Mall) Dubai Mall's most mesmerising sight is this gargantuan aquarium where thousands of beasties flit and dart amid artificial coral. Sharks and rays are top attractions, along with sumo-sized groupers and massive schools of pelagic fish. You can see quite a lot for free from outside or pay for access to the walk-through tunnel. The basic package also includes access to the Underwater Zoo upstairs, whose undisputed star is a 5.1m-long Australian saltwater crocodile named King Croc.

The giant reptile is 40 years old and weighs in at an impressive 750kg. He's joined by his female companion (Queen Croc) and a menagerie of rare and unusual critters, including air-breathing African lungfish, cheeky archerfish that catch insects by shooting water, spooky giant spider crabs and otherworldly sea dragons. A new exhibit introduces night-active desert denizens of the UAE such as the Arabian toad and veiled chameleons.

For an extra kick, time your visit with one of three animal feedings: rays at 10am, sharks at 2pm and King Croc at 4pm.

Various add-on aquatic experiences, including a shark dive, cage snorkelling and a rad-looking trip on a miniature submarine called 'SharkScooter', deliver close-ups of many of these animals.

TOP TIPS FOR VISITING THE BURJ KHALIFA

- Timed tickets are available at the ticket counter and often sell out quickly. It's better to book online up to 30 days in advance.
- Book especially early if you want to go up at sunset.
- On hazy days, it's better to visit at night.
- Budget at least two hours for your visit.
- For a more in-depth experience, you can rent audio guides for Dhs25.
- No refunds or rain checks are given if the outdoor viewing terrace is closed for bad weather.
- Prices go up during prime hours (around sunset) and closing times may vary depending on demand and the season.

DUBAI DINO — PUBLIC ART

Map p258 (04 362-7500; www.thedubaimall.com; Dubai Mall, Financial Centre Rd; 10am-11pm Sun-Wed, to midnight Thu-Sat; M Burj Khalifa/Dubai Mall) FREE The Jurassic era meets the future in Dubai Mall's Souk Dome, the new home of *Amphicoelias brontodiplodocus,* an almost complete 155-million-year-old dinosaur skeleton unearthed in Wyoming in 2008. The long-necked lizard stands 7.6m tall and measures 24.4m long – including its whip-like tail – thus filling up the better part of the exotic arched and dramatically lit atrium.

DUBAI FOUNTAIN — FOUNTAIN

Map p258 (04 362 7500; https://thedubaimall.com/en/entertain-detail/the-dubai-fountain-1; Burj Lake; shows 1pm & 1.30pm Sat-Thu, 1.30pm & 2pm Fri, every 30min 6-11pm daily;

Ⓜ Burj Khalifa/Dubai Mall) FREE This dancing fountain is spectacularly set in the middle of a giant lake against the backdrop of the glittering Burj Khalifa. Water undulates as gracefully as a belly dancer, arcs like a dolphin and surges as high as 140m, all synced to stirring classical, Arabic and world music soundtracks played on speakers. There are plenty of great vantage points, including a new 272m-long floating boardwalk (Dhs20), which takes you just 9m away from the fountain.

Other good viewing spots are some of the restaurants at Souk Al Bahar, the bridge linking Souk Al Bahar with Dubai Mall, the Dubai Mall waterfront terrace or aboard a 25-minute **cruise** (Map p258; Burj Lake; per person Dhs65; ⏲5.45-11.30pm; Ⓜ Burj Khalifa/Dubai Mall) on a wooden abra.

SHEIKH ZAYED BRIDGE WATERFALL WATERFALL

Map p258 (Dubai Canal, Sheikh Zayed Bridge; ⏲7-10pm; Ⓜ Business Bay) FREE This illuminated and motion-operated waterfall cascades down both sides of Sheikh Zayed Bridge, stopping only for passing vessels.

Financial District

Anchored by the iconic twin Jumeirah Emirates Towers, the Financial District is the domain of the business brigade. At its heart is the **Dubai International Financial Centre** (DIFC; Map p258; www.difc.ae; Sheikh Zayed Rd; Ⓟ; Ⓜ Financial Centre), easily recognised by a minimalist triumphal arch called The Gate.

GATE VILLAGE AREA

Map p258 (Happiness St; Ⓟ; Ⓜ Emirates Towers) FREE Two wooden bridges link the massive Dubai International Finance Centre to Gate Village, a modernist cluster of 10 midrise stone-clad towers built around walkways and small piazzas. This is where many of Dubai's high-end Middle Eastern art galleries, including Ayyam (p83) and Cuadro (p84), have set up shop, alongside posh eateries like Zuma (p88). Note that the place is all but dead on Fridays and Saturdays.

AYYAM GALLERY GALLERY

Map p258 (☎04 439 2395; www.ayyamgallery.com; Bldg 3, Gate Village, DIFC; ⏲10am-10pm Sun-Wed, 2-10pm Thu & Sat; Ⓜ Emirates Towers) With branches at Gate Village and on the Alserkal Avenue gallery campus in Al Quoz, this top gallery's main mission is to promote emerging Middle Eastern (especially Syrian) artists and to introduce their often provocative, political and feminist work and voices to a wider audience outside the region itself.

EMPTY QUARTER GALLERY

Map p258 (☎04 323 1210; www.theemptyquarter.com; Bldg 2, Gate Village, DIFC; ⏲10am-7pm Sun-Thu; Ⓟ; Ⓜ Emirates Towers) It's always worth stopping by this top-notch gallery, which is the only one in the UAE focused entirely on fine-art photography.

BURJ KHALIFA FACTS & FIGURES

The Burj Khalifa is not only the world's tallest building (for now) but also flaunts other records and impressive figures, including the following:

- tallest free-standing structure
- highest outdoor observation deck (555m)
- highest occupied floor (160th floor, at 585.5m)
- longest lift (504m)
- highest number of floors (211)
- highest restaurant (122nd floor, at 452m)
- weight of concrete used is equivalent to 100,000 elephants
- the service lift has a carrying capacity of 5500kg
- the facade is made of 28,261 glass panels
- it takes three to four months to clean the facade
- in 2011 French climber Alain Robert scaled the Burj in just over six hours
- in April 2014 two other Frenchmen (Vincent Reffet and Frédéric Fugen) set the world record base jump from the Burj

WORTH A DETOUR

URBAN BIRDING AT RAS AL KHOR

Within earshot of construction sites and framed by highways, **Ras Al Khor Wildlife Sanctuary** (RAKWS; 04 606 6822; http://wildlife-ae.herokuapp.com; Oud Metha Rd & Ras Al Khor St; 9am-4pm Sat-Thu; Dubai Healthcare City, Al Jadaf) FREE on Dubai Creek is an important stopover for migratory waterbirds on the east Africa–west Asian flyway. Gracious pink flamingos steal the show in winter, but avid birdwatchers can spot more than 170 species in this pastiche of salt flats, mudflats, mangroves and lagoons spread over an area of around 6.2 sq km (2.4 sq miles).

There are currently two accessible hides (platforms) with fantastically sharp binoculars: the Flamingo Hide on the sanctuary's western edge near the flamingo roost off the junction of Al Wasl and Oud Metha Rds, and the Mangrove Hide overlooking the mangrove forest off Ras Al Khor Rd on the southern edge. There are common sightings of broadbilled sandpipers and Pacific golden plovers; in winter, great spotted eagles and other raptors may be patrolling the skies.

RAWKS' importance was internationally recognised in 2007 by the Ramsar Convention, the global treaty for the conservation of wetlands signed in 1971 in the Iranian city of Ramsar. In 2016 a Ramsar delegation visited Dubai to assess the impact of encroaching construction and find ways to minimise it in order to preserve the integrity of the site, which has increasingly become a tourist attraction.

While providing a platform for emerging talent, curators also put on shows featuring top international shutterbugs like Steve McCurry, Bruno Barbey, Marc Riboud and Al Moutasim Al Maskery. Many capture the zeitgeist with evocative, provocative or political themes.

It's part of the Gate Village gallery district at DIFC.

CUADRO GALLERY

Map p258 (04 425 0400; www.cuadroart.com; Bldg 10, Gate Village; 10am-8pm Sun-Thu, noon-6pm Sat; Emirates Towers) In a fabulous space taking up the entire ground floor of Gate Village's Building 10, this highly regarded gallery shines the spotlight on midcareer and established contemporary artists and sculptors, mostly from the Middle East. Some exhibits are based on work produced by artists participating in Cuadro's residency program. Lectures, workshops and panel discussions are also part of the gallery's schedule.

WORLD TRADE CENTRE LANDMARK

Map p258 (Sheikh Zayed Rd; World Trade Centre) Compared to its cloud-touching cousins, the 149m-high World Trade Centre seems small today, but when completed in 1979 was actually Dubai's first skyscraper on Sheikh Zayed Rd. The building is depicted on the 100-dirham note.

Al Quoz

★ALSERKAL AVENUE ARTS CENTRE

Map p260 (050 556 9797; www.alserkalavenue.ae; 17th St, Al Quoz 1; Noor Bank, FGB) Edgy contemporary art from the Middle East and beyond has found a home in Dubai thanks to the vision of Abdelmonem bin Eisa Alserkal. The local developer and arts patron has turned a sprawling warehouse complex in dusty Al Quoz into a buzzing gallery and cultural campus that also features a theatre, an indie cinema, cafes and a chocolate factory.

THE THIRD LINE GALLERY

Map p260 (04 341 1367; www.thethirdline.com; Warehouse 78/80, Alserkal Avenue, Al Quoz 1; 10am-7pm Sat-Thu; Noor Bank, FGB) A pioneer on Dubai's gallery scene and one of the city's most exciting spaces for contemporary Middle Eastern art, the Third Line represents around 30 artists, including Emirati Lamya Gargash and Lebanese photographer Fouad Elkoury. It also publishes books, hosts lectures and participates in such major international art fairs as Art Cologne and Art Basel.

LEILA HELLER GALLERY GALLERY

Map p260 (056 829 8026; www.leilahellergallery.com; Warehouse 87, Alserkal Avenue, Al Quoz 1; 10am-7pm Sat-Thu) This prestigious

New York import presents cutting-edge art from emerging and mid-career artists from the Middle East, Central Asia, Southeast Asia and Turkey.

GALLERY ISABELLE VAN DEN EYNDE GALLERY

Map p260 (☎04 323 5052; www.ivde.net; Warehouse 17, Alserkal Avenue, Al Quoz 1; ⏲10am-7pm Sat-Thu; Ⓜ Noor Bank, FGB) This edgy gallery has developed relationships with artists from Europe, Latin America and Africa whose work has some connection to the Middle East. Part of Alserkal since 2010, it has lifted some of the most innovative and promising talent from obscurity into the spotlight, including Beirut-based Raed Yassin and Iranian-born photographer Ramin Haerizadeh.

CARBON 12 GALLERY

Map p260 (☎04 340 6016; www.carbon12dubai.com; Warehouse 37, Alserkal Avenue, Al Quoz 1; ⏲11.30am-7pm Sat-Thu; Ⓜ Noor Bank, FGB) This minimalist white-cube space serves as a gateway to the UAE art scene for accomplished artists from around the world, and vice-versa. Some of them have roots in the Middle East, such as Tehran-born New York resident Sara Rahbar, whose textile art has made it into the British Museum.

GREEN ART GALLERY GALLERY

Map p260 (☎04 346 9305; www.gagallery.com; Warehouse 28, Alserkal Avenue, Al Quoz 1; ⏲10am-7pm Sat-Thu; P; Ⓜ Noor Bank, FGB) Green Art has been around for over four decades and played a key role in championing modern Middle Eastern art, including such masters as Fateh Moudarres, Louay Kayyali, Ismail Fattah and Dia al Azzawi. Its expanded multi-generational roster now also includes artists from North Africa and South Asia.

SALSALI PRIVATE MUSEUM GALLERY

Map p260 (SPM; ☎04 380 9600; www.salsalipm.com; Warehouse 14, Alserkal Avenue, Al Quoz 1; ⏲11am-4pm Sun-Thu; Ⓜ Noor Bank, FGB) Founded by prominent Iranian collector Ramin Salsali, SPM is the first private museum for contemporary Middle Eastern art in the region and has made it part of its mission to instil a love for art in new generations. Exhibits are drawn from Salsali's own collection of nearly 1000 paintings, sculptures, video art and installations.

CARTOON ART GALLERY GALLERY

Map p260 (☎04 346 6467; www.cartoonartgallery.org; 4B St, Al Quoz 1; ⏲10am-5pm Sat-Thu; Ⓜ Noor Bank, FGB) This bi-level space is the first gallery in the Middle East dedicated to cartoon and animation art from across the entire spectrum of media, from paint to video and print. Exhibitions might feature artwork and posters illustrating the world of Tintin or present animated cartoons by such famous names as Japanese artist Hayao Miyazaki. It's steps away from Alserkal Avenue.

EATING

Downtown Dubai is the purview of high-roller restaurants, with most of them located in the five-star hotels and the Dubai International Financial Centre (DIFC). To take less of a bite out of your budget, head to the Dubai Mall food court or the funky cafes around Alserkal Avenue in Al Quoz.

Downtown & Business Bay

ZAROOB LEBANESE $

Map p258 (☎04 327 6262; www.zaroob.com; ground fl, Jumeirah Tower Building, Sheikh Zayed Rd; dishes Dhs12-32; ⏲24hr; P; Ⓜ Emirates Towers, Financial Centre) With its live cooking stations, open kitchens, fruit-filled baskets, colourful lanterns and graffiti-covered steel shutters, Zaroob radiates the urban integrity of a Beirut street-food alley. Feast on such delicious no-fuss food as falafel (deep-fried chickpea balls), shawarma (spit-roasted meat in pita bread), flat or wrapped *manoushe* (Levant-style pizza) or *alayet* (tomato stew), all typical of the Levant. Nice terrace too.

★BAKER & SPICE INTERNATIONAL $$

Map p258 (☎04 425 2240; www.bakerandspiceme.com; Souk Al Bahar; mains Dhs80-150; ⏲8am-11pm; ; Ⓜ Burj Khalifa/Dubai Mall) A pioneer of the local-organic-fresh maxim in Dubai, this London import offers a seasonal bounty of dishes, prepared in-house and served amid charming, country-style decor and on a Dubai Fountain–facing terrace. The salad bar brims with inspired

DUBAI'S ICONIC BUILDINGS

Burj Khalifa (p81) The world's tallest building stacks up at a cloud-tickling 828m. For the design, American architectural firm Skidmore, Owings & Merrill LLP (SOM) found inspiration in the desert flower *Hymenocallis* or spider lily, whose patterning systems are embodied in Islamic architecture. The tower is designed as three petals arranged around a central core. As it rises from the flat base, the petals are set back in an upward-spiralling pattern.

Burj Al Arab (p97) The Burj was completed in 1999 and is set on an artificial island 300m from the shore. The 60-floor, sail-shaped structure is 321m high. A translucent fibreglass wall serves as a shield from the desert sun during the day and as a screen for an impressive light show each night. It remains *the* iconic symbol of Dubai.

Cayan Tower (p113) Stretching skyward for 307m, Cayan Tower isn't the tallest building in the Dubai Marina, but the 90 degree spiral over the course of its height does look pretty cool. The design is also functional, reducing wind forces and solar radiation on the building. It was designed by the same firm as the Burj Khalifa.

Dubai Creek Golf & Yacht Club (p61) When you cross the bridges over the Creek from Bur Dubai South, you'll notice the pointed white roof of the clubhouse set amid artificial, undulating hillocks. The idea behind this 1993 design was to incorporate a traditional element – the white sails of a dhow (wooden boat) – into the form and style of the building.

Dubai International Financial Centre (p83) Dubai's stock exchange and leading international financial institutions are housed in a complex of six buildings surrounding a central 80m-high triumphal arch called the Gate. Designed by the American firm Gensler Associates, it sits on an axis with the Jumeirah Emirates Towers and the World Trade Centre, effectively framing these two landmarks.

Dusit Thani Dubai (p186) (next to Interchange No 1) Sheikh Zayed Rd features many modern skyscrapers, but few are as eye-catching as this one. The 153m-high building has an inverted 'Y' shape – two pillars that join to form a tapering tower. It's meant to evoke the Thai joined-hands gesture of greeting, which is appropriate for this Thai hotel chain, but some think it looks more like a giant tuning fork.

Jumeirah Emirates Towers (p187) These twin triangular towers coated with silver aluminium panels and topped with needle-nose spires are among the most iconic buildings along Sheikh Zayed Rd. The taller of the two (355m) houses offices, while the other (305m) is an ultra-luxe business hotel. A three-storey shopping mall connects the two.

Jumeirah Beach Hotel (p189) This curvaceous S-shaped construction represents a wave, with the Gulf as its backdrop. The glimmering facades of the hotel and its close neighbour, the Burj Al Arab, are achieved by the use of reflective glass and aluminium. The two structures combined – a huge sail hovering over a breaking wave – symbolise Dubai's maritime heritage.

National Bank of Dubai (p54) This shimmering landmark was designed by Carlos Ott and completed in 1997, it combines simple shapes to represent a dhow with a billowing sail, while the real-life dhows plying the Creek are reflected in its gold-coated glass facade.

creations, the breakfasts are tops and the meat and fish dishes sustainably sourced.

LEILA LEBANESE **$$**

Map p258 (☎04 448 3384; http://leilarestaurant.ae; Sheikh Mohammed bin Rashid Blvd; mains Dhs23-68; ⏰9.30am-12.45am Mon-Sat, to 1.45am Sat & Sun; 📶; Ⓜ Burj Khalifa/Dubai Mall)

This Beirut import serves grannie-style rural Lebanese cafe cuisine adapted for the 21st century; light, healthy and fresh. The homey decor more than dabbles in the vintage department with its patterned wallpaper, crisp tablecloths and floral crockery. It's also a nice spot for breakfast and shisha.

EATALY ITALIAN **$$**

Map p258 (☎04 330 8899; www.eatalyarabia.com; lower ground fl, Dubai Mall; mains Dhs45-120; ⏰9am-11.30pm Sun-Wed, to 12.30am Thu-Sat; P 📶 👶; M Burj Khalifa/Dubai Mall) Italy's popular shop-cum-cafe has landed in Dubai Mall, bringing artisanal morsels from around the Boot to discerning palates. Stock up on pesto from Liguria, balsamico from Modena, olive oil from Sicily, and mozzarella and pasta made right in the store. Alternatively, stay and fill your stomach with pizza, panino or pasta freshly prepared at several food stations.

For kids it's fun to watch the action and perhaps finish up the meal with a trip to the Nutella bar.

THE LIGHTHOUSE MEDITERRANEAN **$$**

(☎04 422 6024; www.facebook.com/thelighthouseAE; Bldg 6, Dubai Design District; mains Dhs75-180; ⏰8am-11pm Sun-Wed, to midnight Thu & Fri, to 6pm Sat; 📶; M Burj Khalifa/Dubai Mall) The brainchild of Dubai-based chef Izu Ani, this cafe-shop hybrid is a beacon of good taste when it comes both to hand-selected designer gifts and to light meals mixing familiar and surprising ingredients. It's right in the hip Dubai Design District, served by free shuttle from Dubai Mall metro station.

THE DAILY BISTRO **$$**

Map p258 (☎04 561 9999; www.rovehotels.com/the-daily; Rove Downtown, 312 Happiness St; mains Dhs45-120, brunch Dhs99; ⏰6.30am-11.30pm; M Financial Centre, Burj Khalifa/Dubai Mall) Warehouse-style decor, floor-to-ceiling windows and an outdoor terrace – overlooking Burj Khalifa, no less – make an instant impression at this casual all-day spot. Add in warm service and easy-going food (shakshuka eggs, superfood salads, steak and chips) at very reasonable prices, and you know you're onto a winner. Wash it down with fresh juices, barista-made coffee and well-priced beer and wine.

NOODLE HOUSE ASIAN **$$**

Map p258 (☎04 319 8088; www.thenoodlehouse.com; ground fl, Boulevard Mall, Emirates Towers, Sheikh Zayed Rd; mains Dhs35-90; ⏰noon-midnight; P 📶; M Emirates Towers) This multibranch pan-Asian joint, where you order by ticking dishes on a tear-off menu pad, is a reliably good choice for a casual lunch or dinner. There's great variety – from roast duck to noodle soups and pad thai – and a spice-level indicator to please disparate tastes.

KARMA KAFÉ ASIAN **$$$**

Map p258 (☎04 423 0909; www.karma-kafe.com; Souk Al Bahar; mains Dhs60-200; ⏰3pm-2am Sun-Thu, noon-2am Fri & Sat; 📶; M Burj Khalifa/Dubai Mall) At this hip outpost a large Buddha guards the dining room dressed in sensuous burgundy with gold leaf accents. The menu hopscotches around Asia with classic and innovative sushi alongside such mains as tea-smoked salmon, Wagyu beef sliders from the robata grill, and black miso cod. The terrace has sublime Dubai Fountain views.

ASADO ARGENTINE **$$$**

Map p258 (☎04 428 7888; www.theaddress.com; ground fl, Palace Downtown, Mohammed bin Rashid Blvd; mains Dhs95-570; ⏰6.30-11.30pm; P 📶; M Burj Khalifa/Dubai Mall) Meat lovers will be in heaven at this rustic-elegant lair with stellar views of the Burj Khalifa from the terrace tables. Start with a selection of stuffed *empanadas* (bread pockets) before treating yourself to a juicy grilled Argentine steak or the signature baby goat, slowly tickled to succulent perfection on an outdoor charcoal grill. Reservations essential.

DINNER WITH A VIEW

The food may not be out of this world, but the views are certainly stellar from the world's highest restaurant, **At.mosphere** (Map p258; ☎04 888 3828; www.atmosphereburjkhalifa.com; 122nd fl, Burj Khalifa, Sheikh Mohammed bin Rashid Blvd; mains Dhs145-320; ⏰restaurant 12.30-3pm & 6.30-11pm, lounge noon-4.30pm & 6.30pm-2am; 📶; M Burj Khalifa/Dubai Mall). Book far ahead to enjoy the views and international fare with an emphasis on seafood.

The per-person minimum spend in the restaurant is Dhs500 at lunch and Dhs680 for dinner (Dhs880 for window table). If that's too dear, head one floor up to the lounge level where minimums are Dhs200 for breakfast, Dhs420 for afternoon tea and Dhs320 for dinner. No children under 10 are allowed. Dress nicely. The entrance is through the Armani Hotel.

WORTH A DETOUR

DUBAI AT THE RACES

Horses

Dubai racing's home is the spectacular **Meydan Racecourse** (04 327 0077, tickets 04 327 2110; www.dubairacingclub.com; Al Meydan Rd, Nad Al Sheba; premium seating Dhs50; races Nov-Mar; M Burj Khalifa/Dubai Mall) FREE, about 5km southeast of downtown Dubai. Spanning 1.5km, its grandstand is bigger than most airport terminals and lidded by a crescent-shaped solar-panelled roof. It can accommodate up to 60,000 spectators and integrates a five-star hotel, restaurants, an IMAX theatre and a museum.

Racing season starts in November but doesn't heat up until January, when the Dubai World Cup Carnival brings top horses and jockeys to Dubai. It culminates in late March with the elite Dubai World Cup, the world's richest horse race, with prize money of a dizzying US$10 million. Even if you don't like horse racing, attending a race presents great people-watching opportunities, because it attracts fans from a wide range of nationalities, ages and social backgrounds.

Meydan has a free-admission area where dress is casual. For the grandstand you'll need tickets and may want to dress up. Most races start at 7pm, but it's best to check the website for the exact schedule and tickets. There are also **stable tours** (04 381 3405; http://stabletours.meydan.ae; adult/child Dhs275/150; 7.30-11.30am Tue & Wed late Sep–mid-Apr) that let you meet the trainers and horses and get close-ups of the jockeys' dressing room and the parade ring.

To get here, take the 2nd interchange from Sheikh Zayed Rd, turn left onto Al Meydan Rd and follow the signs.

Camels

Camel racing is deeply rooted in the Emirati soul and attending a race is hugely popular with locals and visitors alike. The closest track to Dubai is **Al Marmoum** (04 832 6526; www.dcrc.ae; off Dubai–Al Ain Rd (Hwy E66); Nov-Apr), about 40km south en route to Al Ain. Races are usually held in the early morning on Fridays, but there is no fixed schedule. Check www.dubaicalendar.ae or ask at your hotel.

In April, the track hosts the hugely popular **Al Marmoum Heritage Festival** (http://almarmoomfestivals.ae; Apr) with numerous races featuring thousands of camels.

THIPTARA AT PALACE DOWNTOWN THAI $$$

Map p258 (04 428 7888; www.theaddress.com; Mohammed bin Rashid Blvd; mains Dhs120-290; 6-11.30pm; M Burj Khalifa/Dubai Mall) *Thiptara* means 'magic at the water' – very appropriate given its romantic setting in a lakeside pagoda with unimpeded views of the Dubai Fountain. The menu presents elegant interpretations of classic Thai dishes perked up by herbs grown by the chef himself. The green papaya salad, grilled black cod and green chicken curry are all solid menu picks.

Financial District

SUM OF US CAFE $$

Map p258 (056 445 7526; www.thesumofusdubai.com; ground fl, Burj Al Salam Bldg, 6th St; mains Dhs50-90; 8am-midnight; M World Trade Centre) This two-floor industrial-style and plant-filled cafe with outdoor seating roasts its own beans, bakes its own sourdough bread and serves food that is at once comforting and exciting. All-day breakfast choices include French toast with salted caramel sauce, while the cauliflower risotto makes for an interesting main dish.

★ZUMA JAPANESE $$$

Map p258 (04 425 5660; www.zumarestaurant.com; Bldg 06, Gate Village, Happiness St, DIFC; set lunches Dhs130, mains Dhs115-850; noon-3.30pm Sun-Thu, 12.30-4pm Fri, 12.30-4pm Sat & 7pm-midnight Sat-Wed, to 1am Thu & Fri; M Emirates Towers) Every dish speaks of refinement in this perennially popular bi-level restaurant that gives classic Japanese fare an up-to-the-minute workout. No matter if you go for the top-cut sushi morsels (the dynamite spider roll is a serious eye-catcher!), meat and seafood on the robata grill, or such signature dishes as miso-marinated black cod, you'll be keeping your taste buds happy.

Budget gourmets should go for the daily changing ebisu lunch menu (Dhs130). The lounge serves bites all day.

CARNIVAL BY TRESIND INDIAN $$$

Map p258 (04 421 8665; www.carnivalbytresind.com; podium level, Burj Daman Tower, DIFC; set menu lunch/brunch Dhs110/210; noon-3.30pm, 5pm-2am; ; Financial Centre) Fun is firmly on the agenda at this wildly popular restaurant, which offers a playful take on Indian molecular gastronomy. Behind the smoke and mirrors, you'll find some seriously scrumptious food, with many dishes created at your table and equally clever offerings for vegetarians. Prices are sensible for this part of town; the five-course set lunch is particularly good value.

AL NAFOORAH LEBANESE $$$

Map p258 (04 432 3232; www.jumeirah.com; lower fl, Boulevard, Jumeirah Emirates Towers, Sheikh Zayed Rd; mezze Dhs38-60, mains Dhs65-200; noon-3.30pm & 6-11.30pm; ; Emirates Towers) In this clubby, wood-panelled dining room the vast selection of delectable mezze is more impressive than the kebabs, but ultimately there are few false notes on the classic Lebanese menu. Even in summer you can sit on the terrace beneath an air-conditioned marquee.

HOI AN VIETNAMESE $$$

Map p258 (04 405 2703; www.shangri-la.com; 1st fl, Shangri-La Hotel, Sheikh Zayed Rd; mains Dhs120-185; 7pm-midnight daily, 12.30am-4pm Fri & Sat; ; Financial Centre) With an all-Vietnamese team in the kitchen, you can be sure the tastes are lusciously authentic at this upmarket restaurant. It's been around forever but continues to shine with flavour-intense dishes such as spicy seafood salad, lotus-leaf-wrapped sea bass and lemongrass-marinated duck.

Al Quoz

LIME TREE CAFE CAFE $

Map p260 (04 325 6325; www.thelimetreecafe.com; 4B St, Al Quoz; dishes Dhs24-40; 7.30am-6pm; ; Noor Bank) This comfy Euro-style cafe is an expat favourite for leisurely breakfasts, innovative sandwiches stuffed into their homemade Turkish pide and the irresistibly sinful cakes, most famously the double-layered carrot cake with cream-cheese frosting.

TOM & SERG INTERNATIONAL $$

Map p260 (056 474 6812; www.tomandserg.com; Al Joud Center, 15A St, Al Quoz 1; mains Dhs37-79; 8am-4pm Sun-Thu, to 6pm Fri & Sat; ; Noor Bank, FGB) This always-bustling warehouse-style cafe with concrete floors, exposed pipes and an open kitchen would fit right into Madrid or Melbourne, which is exactly where its proprietors hail from. The menu teems with global feel-good food like Moroccan chicken, eggs Benedict and a mean burger on a homemade bun. Great coffee too.

Close to the Alserkal Avenue gallery district.

DRINKING & NIGHTLIFE

Downtown has the hottest nightlife venues, with new ones coming online all the time. Shine your shoes, put on those vertiginous heels and bring the platinum credit card to get waved past the velvet rope.

Downtown & Business Bay

★WHITE DUBAI CLUB

(050 443 0933; www.whitedubai.com; Meydan Racecourse Grandstand Rooftop, Nad Al Sheba; 11pm-3am Tue, Thu-Sat) The Dubai spawn of the Beirut original did not need long to lure local socialites with high-energy rooftop parties under the stars. International spinmeisters shower party-goers with an eclectic sound soup, from house and electro to bump-and-grind hip-hop and R & B, all fuelled by dazzling projections and light shows.

It's the only Middle Eastern club on the Top 100 list of the British *DJ Mag*.

★BRIDGEWATER TAVERN SPORTS BAR

Map p258 (04 414 0000; www.jwmarriottmarquisdubailife.com/dining/bridgewatertavern; JW Marriott Marquis Hotel, Sheikh Zayed Rd;

4pm-2am; ; Business Bay) This happening joint has ushered the sports bar into a new era. Sure, there are the requisite big screens to catch the action, but it's packaged into an industrial-flavoured space with (mostly) rock on the turntables, shisha on the canalside terrace, and an elevated gastropub menu whose signature 'black' burger is so messy it comes with a bib!

BASE CLUB

(055 313 4999; www.basedubai.com; Dubai Design District; 10.30-3am Sep-May; Business Bay) This b-i-g next-gen nightclub holds forth under open skies in the Dubai Design District and can host up 5000 people for concerts and parties. Expect a top-notch sound system, a top line-up, pyrotechnics and shiny happy people.

TREEHOUSE BAR

Map p258 (04 438 3100; www.treehousedubai.com; Taj Dubai Hotel, Burk Khalifa Blvd; 6pm-1am Sat-Wed, to 2am Thu & Fri; Business Bay) At the top of the Taj, this luxe lair treats guests to unimpeded views of the Burj Khalifa, top-shelf drinks and an outdoor living room setting with potted plants, pillow-packed sofas, pink marble tables and even a candlelit mock fireplace. A chill spot for quiet conversation on weekdays, the action picks up with deep-house DJs on weekends.

MAJLIS CAFE

Map p258 (056 287 1522; ground fl, Gold Souk, Dubai Mall; 10am-midnight; ; Burj Khalifa/Dubai Mall) If you ever wanted to find out how to milk a camel (and who doesn't?), watch the video on the interactive iPad menu of this pretty cafe while sipping a camelccino (camel-milk cappuccino) or date-flavoured camel milk. Nibbles, desserts, chocolate and cheese, all made with camel milk, beckon as well.

CABANA BAR, LOUNGE

Map p258 (04 438 8888; www.theaddress.com; 3rd fl, Address Dubai Mall Hotel, Sheikh Mohammed bin Rashid Blvd; 8.30am-midnight; ; Burj Khalifa/Dubai Mall) A laid-back poolside vibe combines with urban sophistication and stellar views of the Burj Khalifa at this al fresco restaurant and terrace lounge. A DJ plays smooth tunes that don't hamper animated conversation. Cap off a Dubai Mall shopping spree at happy hour, which runs from 2pm to 8pm.

Financial District

★CIRQUE LE SOIR CLUB

Map p258 (050 995 5400; www.facebook.com/CirqueLeSoirDubai; Fairmont Hotel, Sheikh Zayed Rd; 10.30pm-3am Mon, Tue, Thu & Fri; World Trade Centre) Is it a nightclub, a circus or a cabaret? One of Dubai's hottest after-dark spots – and London spin-off – is actually a trifecta of all three, a madhouse where you can let your freak out among clowns, stilt-walkers, sword swallowers and Dubai party A-listers. Music-wise it's mostly EDM, but hip-hop Mondays actually draw some of the biggest crowds.

NIPPON BOTTLE COMPANY BAR

Map p258 (www.dusit.com/dusitthani/dubai; Dusit Thani Hotel, Sheikh Zayed Rd; 6pm-3am; Financial Centre) Finding this neon-lit Japanese bar, hidden speakeasy-style behind a bookcase off the lobby of the Dusit Thani Hotel, requires a clear head, which you may no longer have after sampling its potent cocktails and Japanese whiskies.

FIBBER MAGEE'S PUB

Map p258 (04 332 2400; www.fibbersdubai.com; Saeed Tower One, Sheikh Zayed Rd; 8am-2am; ; World Trade Centre) Been-around-forever Fibbers is an amiably scruffy morning to night pub with Guinness and Kilkenny on tap, all-day breakfasts plus a menu of international comfort food designed to keep brains in balance, and sports (rugby to horse racing) on the big screens. Traditional Irish music on Thursday nights puts a tear in many expat eyes.

CAVALLI CLUB CLUB

Map p258 (050 991 0400; http://dubai.cavalliclub.com; Fairmont Hotel, Sheikh Zayed Rd; 8.30pm-3am; ; World Trade Centre) Black limos jostle for position outside this over-the-top lair where you can sip Robert Cavalli vodka-based cocktails and dine on Italian fare served on Cavalli plates with Cavalli cutlery amid a virtual Aladdin's cave of black quartz and Swarovski crystals. Ladies, wear those vertiginous heels or risk feeling frumpy. Men, dress snappily or forget about it. The entrance is behind the hotel.

40 KONG BAR

Map p258 (04 355 8896; www.40kong.com; 40th fl, H Hotel, Sheikh Zayed Rd; 7pm-3am;

WORTH A DETOUR

IMG WORLDS OF ADVENTURE

Housed in an air-conditioned hangar the size of 28 football fields, **IMG Worlds of Adventure** (☎04 403 8888, 600 500 962; www.imgworlds.com; Sheikh Mohammed bin Zayed Rd (Hwy E311), City of Arabia; adult/child under 1.2m/child under 1.05m Dhs245/225/free; ⌚11am-10pm Sun-Wed, to 11pm Thu-Sat; P 👪) is the world's largest indoor theme park. The US$1 billion park is truly impressive, with more than 20 rides and attractions split across four themed zones – Marvel, Cartoon Network, Lost Valley Dinosaur Adventure and IMG Boulevard – and 28 dining outlets. Food is prepared on-site and the quality is surprisingly high, with a good range of healthy options.

Cartoon Network

Geared towards younger kids, it has child-friendly rides based around popular cartoon characters such as the Powerpuff Girls and the Amazing Ride of Gumball, as well as a Ben 10 5D cinema and LazyTown live show.

Marvel Zone

Thrill-seekers will find plenty to get hearts and adrenaline pumping. Thor Thunder Spin, a dizzying top-spin ride, will scare the bejeezus out of just about anyone. Thor is also part of the superhero battalion taking on the evil villain Ultra in the Avengers Battle of Ultron dark ride. Thumbs up also for Hulk Epsilon Base 3D that uses 360-degree projection screens and motion to take you through a fierce battle.

Lost Valley Dinosaur Adventure

Custom-developed for IMG, this imaginatively designed zone is inhabited by 69 state-of-the-art animatronic dinosaurs. If you run into one, ask nicely and it will gladly pose with you for your Instagram feed. A lot less friendly are its Jurassic buddies chasing after you on a jungle safari through the Forbidden Territory. For a truly white-knuckle experience, board the Velociraptor, a short but intense outdoor coaster that catapults you from zero to 100km/h in 2.5 seconds.

IMG Boulevard

The highlight here is the spine-chilling Haunted Hotel, a maze of rooms and corridors inhabited by living ghosts and ghouls. The minimum age is 15.

📶; Ⓜ World Trade Centre) Finance moguls and corporate execs mix it up at this intimate rooftop cocktail bar perched atop the 40th floor of the H Hotel with views of the World Trade Centre and Sheikh Zayed Rd. The twinkling lanterns and palm trees set romantic accents for post-work or post-shopping sundowners, paired with global bar bites.

☆ ENTERTAINMENT

★CINEMA AKIL CINEMA

Map p260 (www.cinemaakil.com; Alserkal Avenue, Al Quoz 1) Treating cineastes to smart indie flicks from around the world on a pop-up basis since 2014, this dynamic platform has now taken up permanent residence at the Alserkal Avenue. Screenings are often followed by Q&A sessions with directors.

LA PERLE BY DRAGONE PERFORMING ARTS

Map p258 (https://laperle.com; Al Habtorr City; tickets Dhs400-1600; 📶; Ⓜ Business Bay) A custom-designed theatre with a 270-degree angle makes for perfect sight lines even in the cheaper seats of this magical show centred on a aquatic stage where some 65 acrobats perform their stunning stunts. It is the brainchild of Franco Dragone, one of the original creators of Cirque du Soleil.

BLUE BAR LIVE MUSIC

Map p258 (☎04 310 8150; www.facebook.com/BlueBarNovotelWTC; Novotel World Trade Centre Dubai, Happiness St; ⌚noon-2am; 📶; Ⓜ World Trade Centre) Cool cats of all ages gather in this relaxed joint for some of the finest live jazz and blues in town, along with a full, reasonably priced bar line-up that includes signature cocktails named after jazz greats (try the Louis Armstrong–inspired Hello

Dolly). It's open daily with live concerts from 10pm Thursday to Saturday.

FRIDGE LIVE MUSIC

Map p260 (☎04 347 7793; www.thefridgedubai.com; Warehouse 5, Alserkal Avenue, Al Quoz 1; Ⓜ Noor Bank, FGB) Part of the Alserkal Avenue cultural campus, this talent-management agency runs a much beloved concert series (usually on Fridays) that shines the spotlight on local talent still operating below the radar. The line-up defines eclectic and may hopscotch from swing to opera, and jazz to pop, sometimes all in one night.

REEL CINEMAS CINEMA

Map p258 (☎04 449 1902; www.reelcinemas.ae; 2nd fl, Dubai Mall; 2D/3D films Dhs45/60, MX4D Dhs90, Platinum Movie Suite Dhs160; Ⓜ Burj Khalifa/Dubai Mall) Reel is one of the top flick-magnets in town screening mostly Hollywood blockbusters. It has 22 screens, including one featuring a state-of-the-art Dolby Atmos sound system, the over-18 Platinum Movie Suite with reclining leather chairs and table service, and an MX4D theatre whose seats have built-in motion effects.

THE JUNCTION THEATRE

Map p260 (☎04 338 8525; www.thejunctiondubai.com; Warehouse 72 , Alserkal Avenue, Al Quoz 1; Ⓜ Noor Bank, FGB) Since 2015, this pint-sized indie space has hosted some of Dubai's most exciting cultural programming, from plays to concerts, and comedy to dance, showcasing mostly local talent. Past productions have included George Orwell's *Nineteen Eighty-Four* and *Howzat,* the first play written in Dubai, which premiered here to much acclaim in 2016.

COURTYARD PLAYHOUSE THEATRE

Map p260 (☎050 986 1761; www.courtyardplayhouse.com; Courtyard Bldg, 4B St, Al Quoz 1; 👪; Ⓜ Noor Bank, FGB) This 70-seat community theatre (plus bean bags on busy nights) puts on a busy schedule of improv, stand-up comedy, kids theatre and live broadcasts from famous stages like the New York Met and London's National Theatre. It also offers acting, improv and comedy workshops geared towards the expat community.

SHOPPING

Dubai Mall's appeal is impossible to ignore, but there's also fabulous art in the Gate Village and on Alserkal Avenue, plus avant-garde fashions and furniture in the Dubai Design District.

KINOKUNIYA BOOKS

Map p258 (☎04 434 0111; www.kinokuniya.com/ae; 2nd fl, Dubai Mall; ⏲10am-midnight; 📶; Ⓜ Burj Khalifa/Dubai Mall) This massive shop is El Dorado for bookworms. Shelves are stocked with a mind-boggling half-a-million tomes plus 1000 or so magazines in English, Arabic, Japanese, French, German and Chinese.

★MIRZAM CHOCOLATE MAKERS CHOCOLATE

Map p260 (☎04 333 5888; www.mirzam.com; Warehouse 70, Alserkal Avenue, Al Quoz 1; ⏲10am-7pm Sat-Thu; 👪; Ⓜ FGB, Noor Bank)

DUBAI DESIGN DISTRICT

Creative folks have a new HQ in Dubai. The fresh-off-the-drawing board **Dubai Design District** (d3; ☎04 433 3000; www.dubaidesigndistrict.com; off Al Khail Rd, Business Bay; Ⓟ; Dubai Design District, Ⓜ Business Bay) has drawn both regional and international talent and brands, including hot shots like Adidas and Foster + Partners. Visitors can tap into this laboratory of tastemakers by checking out the edgy architecture and public art, browsing showrooms and pop-ups, eavesdropping on bearded hipsters in sleek cafes, checking out art exhibits in building lobbies, or attending a free screening, workshop or other cultural event. The website has a schedule.

D3 is part of the Dubai's ambitious plan to become a major player in the global design world. Indeed, what you see today is merely phase 1 of a three-phase project that should be finished by 2020. Phase 2 will add a vast 'Creative Community' section (to be designed by Norman Foster) with more galleries and art spaces aimed at nurturing local talent. The final phase will bring hotels, shops and an outdoor events space to a 1.8km-long section paralleling Dubai Creek.

SOUND TREATS AT DUBAI OPERA

Shaped like a traditional dhow – the sailing vessels that still ply the Gulf – **Dubai Opera** (Map p258; ☎04 440 8888; www.dubaiopera.com; Sheikh Mohammed Bin Rashid Blvd; Ⓜ Burj Khalifa/Dubai Mall) is the city's newest high-calibre performing-arts venue. Despite its name, it actually hosts a potpourri of shows, including musicals, ballet, comedy acts, rock bands and recitals. The 'bow' of the building contains a 2000-seat theatre and glass-fronted foyer overlooking Burj Lake.

There's a bar on the top floor. Ticket prices vary by show, and most start around the Dhs250 mark, with boxes entering the several thousands. But with excellent acoustics and unrestricted views from every maroon leather pew, there's no need to spend big money for good seats. No mandatory dress code, but you might want to dress nicely. Tickets are available online and at the box office.

The art of crafting fine chocolate is taken very seriously at this high-tech 'Willy Wonka' factory where all stages from roasting to handwrapping take place behind glass walls. Only single origin beans from such far-flung locales as Madagascar, Papua New Guinea, Vietnam, India and Indonesia are used. Sample the final product or sign up for a free tasting workshop, including one geared especially towards children.

RAW COFFEE COMPANY — COFFEE

(☎04 339 5474; www.rawcoffeecompany.com; Warehouse 10, cnr 7A & 4A Sts, Al Quoz 1; ⏲8am-5pm Sat-Thu, 9am-5pm Fri; 📶; Ⓜ Noor Bank) A keen coffee radar is required to track down this boutique roastery, down a hidden alley amid the dusty warehouses of Al Quoz. The building houses not only their roasting operation but also a cafe where local latterati gather for a chat and excellent organic and fair-trade bean-based drinks.

THE CARTEL — FASHION & ACCESSORIES

(☎04 243 2200; www.thecartel.me; Bldg 9, Dubai Design District; ⏲10am-8pm Sun-Thu, noon-8pm Sat; 📶; Ⓜ Business Bay) With chic new quarters in the edgy Dubai Design District, this concept boutique pushes the boundaries when it comes to fashion and accessories. Look for 'wearable art' by an international roster of over 60 avant-garde designers, including such local ones as Amber Feroz, Bint Thani and KBT Koncept.

CANDYLICIOUS — FOOD

Map p258 (☎04 330 8700; www.candylicious shop.com; ground fl, Dubai Mall; ⏲10am-midnight; 📶; Ⓜ Burj Khalifa/Dubai Mall) Stand under the lollipop tree, watch the candymakers at work or gorge yourself on gourmet popcorn at this colourful candy emporium stocked to the rafters with everything from jelly beans to halal sweets and gourmet chocolate. Sweet bliss. Just don't tell your dentist.

BALQEES HONEY — FOOD

Map p258 (☎04 441 6407; http://balqees.com; lower fl, Dubai Mall; ⏲10am-midnight; 📶; Ⓜ Burj Khalifa/Dubai Mall) Clued-in gourmets know that some of the world's best honey is Sidr, produced by nomadic beekepers in war-torn Yemen. At this little kiosk near the waterfall in Dubai Mall, you can stock up on this 'liquid gold' – and we mean this almost literally: their top product sells for more than Dhs600 per 290g glass (about 10oz).

FARMERS MARKET ON THE TERRACE — MARKET

Map p258 (☎04 427 9856; www.facebook.com/TheFarmersMarketOnTheTerrace; Bay Avenue Park, Burj Khalifa & Al A'amal Sts, Business Bay; ⏲8am-1pm Fri Nov-May; Ⓜ Business Bay) The carrots may have roots attached and dirt might stick to the fennel bulb, because both were still in the ground the previous day. Now they're vying for customers at this small farmers market, which brings organic, locally grown produce straight from grower to grazer.

SOUK AL BAHAR — MALL

Map p258 (www.soukalbahar.ae; Old Town Island; ⏲10am-10pm Sun-Thu, 2-10pm Fri; 📶; Ⓜ Burj Khalifa/Dubai Mall) Translated as 'market of the sailor', Souk Al Bahar is a small arabesque-style mall next to the Dubai Mall that sells mostly tourist-geared items. It's really more noteworthy for its enchanting design (arch-lined stone corridors, dim lighting) and Dubai Fountain–facing restaurants, some of which are licensed. Also handy: a branch of Spinneys supermarket in the basement.

GOLD & DIAMOND PARK JEWELLERY

Map p260 (☎04 362 7777; www.goldanddiamondpark.com; Sheikh Zayed Rd; ⏰10am-10pm Sat-Thu, 4-10pm Fri; Ⓜ FGB) An air-conditioned, less atmospheric alternative to the Deira Gold Souq, this buttoned-up business mall houses some 90 purveyors of bling. No bargaining here. If you can't find what you want, it's possible to commission a bespoke piece and have it ready in a couple of days. Refuel at the cafes ringing an outdoor courtyard.

NAYOMI CLOTHING

Map p258 (☎04 339 8820; www.nayomi.com; 1st fl, Dubai Mall; ⏰10am-10pm Sun-Wed, to midnight Thu-Sat; 📶; Ⓜ Burj Khalifa/Dubai Mall) One of Dubai's raciest stores stocks push-up bras, high-heeled feathery slippers, slinky night gowns, seductive beauty products (we like the 'Booty Parlor' line) and other nocturnal niceties from – surprise! – Saudi Arabia. In fact, Nayomi, which means 'soft' and 'delicate' in Arabic, is a major brand all over the Middle East, with 10 branches around Dubai alone.

SPORTS & ACTIVITIES

★PLATINUM HERITAGE TOURS TOURS

(☎04 388 4044; www.platinum-heritage.com; 3rd fl, Oasis Centre, Sheikh Zayed Rd, Al Quoz 1; ⏰office hours 8am-6pm; Ⓜ Noor Bank) This is a top purveyor of year-round culturally sensitive and eco-minded desert safaris (often aboard vintage Range Rovers!). A bestseller is the half-day Bedouin Culture Safari (Dhs495) that visits a nomadic Bedouin camp where you have a traditional breakfast with locals, get a falconry demonstration and meet salukis, Arabian hunting dogs (see p159 for more on salukis).

ARABIAN ADVENTURES TOURS

Map p258 (☎04 303 4888, 800 272 2426; www.arabian-adventures.com; Sheikh Zayed Rd, Emirates Holiday Bldg) Offers a wide range of tours, including sundowner tours, which include 4WD drives, barbecues and Arab-style entertainment. Also does day trips to the East Coast and into the Hajar mountains.

KNIGHT TOURS TOURS

(☎04 343 7725; www.knighttours.co.ae) Offers tours led by local guides/drivers who know the desert like the back of their hand. Activities include a day at the camel races, a camel caravan, Hatta mountain treks and a falcon show.

DUBAI ICE RINK ICE SKATING

Map p258 (☎04 437 1111; www.dubaiicerink.com; ground fl, Dubai Mall; per session incl skates Dhs60-100; ⏰10am-midnight; 👪; Ⓜ Burj Khalifa/Dubai Mall) This Olympic-size ice rink inside Dubai Mall is ringed with cafes and restaurants and can even be converted into a concert arena. Sign up for a private or group class if you're a little wobbly in the knees. There are DJ sessions for families in the afternoons as well as night-time disco sessions for shaking it up on the ice.

TALISE SPA SPA

Map p258 (☎04 319 8181; www.jumeirah.com; Jumeirah Emirates Towers, Sheikh Zayed Rd; ⏰9am-10pm; Ⓜ Emirates Towers) Finally, a spa squarely aimed at jet-lagged executives in bad need of revitalisation. There's the usual range of massages and spa treatments, plus a few esoteric ones. How about detoxifying with a Paprika Facial or turbo-recharging your body in a salty flotation pool? Botox without the needles? Margy's Collagen facial gets rid of those frown lines in no time (temporarily at least).

SPA AT PALACE DOWNTOWN SPA

Map p258 (☎04 428 7805; www.theaddress.com; Palace Downtown Dubai, Mohammed bin Rashid Blvd; ⏰9am-10pm; Ⓜ Burj Khalifa/Dubai Mall) Give in to your inner sloth in this intimate, sensuously lit spa where a signature treatment is the One Desert Journey (Dhs950), which involves a revitalising sand-and-salt scrub and a massage using an 'oussada' cushion filled with Moroccan mint. Once all that's done, you get to drift into semi-conscious bliss with a cup of tea in the relaxation room.

ARABIC LANGUAGE CENTRE LANGUAGE

Map p258 (☎04 331 5600; www.arabiclanguagecentre.com; 4th fl, Trade Centre Tower, Sheikh Zayed Rd; Ⓜ World Trade Centre) Runs various courses in Arabic from beginner to advanced levels.

Jumeirah

Neighbourhood Top Five

❶ **Madinat Jumeirah** (p98) Stepping into a modern Arabian souq with its sumptuous architecture, Venetian-style canals and Burj Al Arab backdrop.

❷ **Burj Al Arab** (p97) Sipping cocktails in this iconic landmark while enjoying the view and debating if the decor is kitsch or class.

❸ **Jumeirah Mosque** (p100) Learning about Islamic architecture and religion on a tour of this intricately detailed mosque.

❹ **Etihad Museum** (p99) Plugging into the making of the United Arab Emirates at this brand-new museum in a startlingly modern building next to the pavillion where the unification treaty was signed.

❺ **Kite Beach** (p100) Living the motto 'Life's a beach' along this glorious band of sand where an entire village of food trucks and cafes provides sustenance.

For more detail of this area see maps p254 and p256.

Lonely Planet's Top Tip

For the only chance of seeing the inside of a mosque as a non-Muslim in Dubai, show up for the low-cost tours of the Jumeirah Mosque, which are operated by the nonprofit Sheikh Mohammed Centre for Cultural Understanding (p68). Aside from admiring the grand architecture, you'll also get the opportunity to ask questions about the Islamic faith and Emirati culture.

Best Places to Eat

- Logma (p103)
- Pai Thai (p104)
- 3 Fils (p103)
- Ravi (p102)
- Al Fanar (p103)

For reviews, see p101.

Best Places to Drink

- Bahri Bar (p105)
- Grapeskin (p105)

For reviews, see p105.

Best Places to Shop

- BoxPark (p107)
- Mall of the Emirates (p107)
- City Walk (p107)
- Souk Madinat Jumeirah (p107)

For reviews, see p107.

Explore Jumeirah

Hemmed in by the turquoise waters of the Gulf, Jumeirah translates as 'the beautiful' and is practically synonymous with beaches, most famously Kite Beach. Its main drag is Jumeirah Rd, which runs straight as a ruler parallel to the Gulf from Jumeirah Mosque in the north to the Burj Al Arab. It's lined with boutiques, cafes and businesses catering mostly to a local clientele.

Although an older part of town, Jumeirah has of late been injected with pockets of urban cool by a number of new lifestyle malls along Al Wasl Rd (BoxPark, Galleria) while the City Walk development has created an entire new neighbourhood. Indie boutiques and the Italian-style Mercato Mall still make up the lure of Jumeirah Rd. The most interesting stretch begins just southwest of the Jumeirah Mosque, which is open to non-Muslims on guided tours.

The biggest change quite literally reshaping Jumeirah is the completion of the Dubai Canal, which now links Dubai Creek with the Gulf. New construction along both its banks and around its mouth will keep things dynamic for years to come.

As it stretches for many kilometres, Jumeirah has been officially subdivided into sections Jumeirah 1, 2 and 3 and Umm Suqeim 1, 2 and 3. For logistical reasons, we've also included the inland area around the Mall of the Emirates.

Local Life

- **City Walk** Join locals for coffee, a movie or a simple stroll around this new district with lots of cool street art.
- **BoxPark** No alcohol but lots of good vibes in the restaurants on this strip built from shipping containers.
- **Beaching** Head to Kite Beach to swim in the Gulf, get some exercise at the volleyball net, watch the kitesurfers and scarf a burger from the Salt food truck (p102).
- **Designer shopping** Check out what's humming on local and regional sewing machines on an indie boutique hop along Jumeirah Rd.

Getting There & Away

- **Metro** The closest stop to the Burj Al Arab and Madinat Jumeirah is Mall of the Emirates. For the Jumeirah Mosque, get off at World Trade Centre; for Kite Beach, get off at Noor Bank. You'll still need to catch a taxi to reach your final destination.
- **Bus** Bus 8 travels the entire length of Jumeirah Rd down to the Burj Al Arab. Other buses, including Nos 88 and C10, also travel along sections of the Jumeirah Rd.
- **Ferry** From the Dubai Canal Station, ferries travel thrice daily up the Dubai Canal, to Dubai Marina and to Bur Dubai.

IAN CUMMING / GETTY IMAGES ©

TOP SIGHT
BURJ AL ARAB

When Dubai's ruler Sheikh Mohammed commissioned the Burj Al Arab in the 1990s, his goal was to create an iconic symbol that would put the emirate on the map and make it recognisable all over the world. British architect Tom Wright looked to the sail of a classic regional cargo boat, called a dhow, for inspiration. The iconic design has a signature translucent fibreglass facade that serves as a shield from the desert sun during the day and as a screen for the impressive illumination at night. The 321m-high, 60 floor, Burj Al Arab opened in 1999 and was, at the time, the world's tallest hotel.

This iconic landmark sits on an artificial island off Jumeirah Rd and comes with its own helipad and a fleet of chauffeur-driven Rolls Royce limousines.

The Burj interior by British-Chinese designer Khuan Chew is every bit as over-the-top as the exterior is simple and elegant. The moment you step into the lofty lobby, a crescendo of gold-leaf, crystal chandeliers, hand-knotted carpets, water elements, pillars and other design elements put you into sensory overload. Some of the 24,000 sq metres of marble hail from the same quarry where Michelangelo got his material. The lobby atrium is tall enough to fit the Statue of Liberty within it.

The white metal crosspieces at the top of the Burj Al Arab form what is said to be the largest cross in the Middle East – but it's only visible from the sea. By the time this unexpected feature was discovered, it was too late to redesign the tower – the hotel had already put Dubai on the map and become the icon for the city. See the cross on a boat charter and decide for yourself. The scale is amazing.

If you're not staying in the hotel, you need a restaurant reservation to get past lobby security. Don't expect any bargains: there's a minimum Dhs350 spend for cocktails in the Skyview Bar (p106), while afternoon tea will set you back Dhs620. Check the website for details and to make a (compulsory) reservation.

DON'T MISS

- Afternoon tea at Skyview Bar
- Drinks at Gold on 27
- View of the building from Madinat Jumeirah or Sunset Beach

PRACTICALITIES

- Map p256, C1
- ☎04 301 7777
- www.burj-al-arab.com
- off Jumeirah Rd, Umm Suqeim 3
- Ⓜ Mall of the Emirates

S-F / SHUTTERSTOCK ©

TOP SIGHT

MADINAT JUMEIRAH

The architects of this luxurious resort village at the foot of the Burj Al Arab looked to Dubai's original creekside settlement in Bur Dubai for inspiration. Wind towers, abras, waterways and even a souq create modern Arabian flair in this complex that comprises three palatial hotels and dozens of private villas set in a richly landscaped garden.

Explore Madinat's 4km-long network of winding waterways on a leisurely 20-minute **cruise** (Map p256; Souk Madinat Jumeirah; adult/child Dhs85/50; ⏲10am-11pm Nov-Apr, 11am-11pm May-Oct) aboard a traditional-style abra (wooden boat) with cushioned benches. The desert seem far away as you glide past enchanting gardens of billowing bougainvillea, bushy banana trees and soaring palms, all set against the dramatic Burj Al Arab backdrop. Tours leave from the Souk Madinat waterfront (near the Left Bank bar). No reservations are necessary.

At the heart of the complex lies Souk Madinat Jumeirah (p107), a maze-like bazaar with around 75 shops lining wood-framed walkways. Although the ambience is too contrived to feel like an authentic Arabian market, the quality of some of the crafts, art and souvenirs is actually quite high. If you're in need of a bit of Western culture, see what's playing at the Madinat Theatre (p107). There are numerous cafes, bars and restaurants, the nicest of which overlook the waterways and the Burj Al Arab.

Friday brunch is a time-honoured tradition, especially among Western expats. The Madinat hotels Al Qasr (p189) and Mina A'Salam (p189) are famous for putting on some of the most most opulent spreads in town. Both dish up an unbelievable cornucopia of delectables – roast lamb, sushi, cooked-to-order seafood, foie gras, beautiful salads, mezze and all sorts of hot dishes, plus there are cheese and dessert rooms.

DON'T MISS

- Drinks or a meal with a view of the Burj Al Arab
- A spin around Souk Madinat Jumeirah
- An abra cruise along the resort's canal

PRACTICALITIES

- Map p256, B1
- ☎04 366 8888
- www.jumeirah.com
- King Salman Bin Abdul Aziz Al Saud St, Umm Suqeim 3
- Ⓜ Mall of the Emirates

SLAVA296 / SHUTTERSTOCK ©

TOP SIGHT
ETIHAD MUSEUM

Opened in January 2017, this striking modern museum engagingly chronicles the birth of the UAE in 1971, spurred by the discovery of oil in the 1950s and the withdrawal of the British in 1968. Documentary films, photographs, artefacts, timelines and interactive displays zero in on historic milestones in the years leading up to and immediately following this momentous occasion and pay homage to the country's seven founding fathers.

The museum building itself is an elegant design by the Canadian architectural firm Moriyama & Teshima. Its parabolic roof represents the sheet of paper upon which the declaration was written, while the seven golden columns in the entrance hall symbolise the pens with which it was signed. An expansive white travertine plaza link the building with the historic round Union House and the recreated guesthouse where the founding fathers stayed while the negotiations were under way. The original flagpole where the rulers gathered after the deal was done looms above a reflecting pool.

The generously proportioned below-ground galleries are accessed from the monumental entrance hall via a sweeping white marble staircase. On your right hangs a giant painting by Emirati artist Abdul Qader Al Rais that depicts the geography of the UAE. Just beyond are giant, eye-catching photographs of the rulers of the seven emirates that founded the nation, along with their family tree and personal effects such as Sheikh Zayed's cane and sunglasses and Sheikh Rashid's passport. Further on, you can catch 3D documentaries on the founding years, the original first page of the Constitution and a 'road to unification' digital timeline.

The name, by the way, has nothing to do with the airline: Etihad is simply the Arabic word for 'union'.

DON'T MISS

- Gallery of Rulers
- Tour of Union House
- Views of the building from the garden

PRACTICALITIES

- Map p254, H2
- ☎04 515 5771
- http://etihadmuseum.dubaiculture.ae
- Jumeirah St, Jumeirah 1
- adult/child Dhs25/10
- ⏲10am-8pm
- P
- M Al Jafiliya

SIGHTS

BURJ AL ARAB LANDMARK
See p97.

MADINAT JUMEIRAH AREA
See p98.

ETIHAD MUSEUM MUSEUM
See p99.

★JUMEIRAH MOSQUE MOSQUE
Map p254 (04 353 6666; www.cultures.ae; Jumeirah Rd; tours Dhs20; tours 10am Sat-Thu; P; M Emirates Towers, World Trade Centre) Snowy white and intricately detailed, Jumeirah is Dubai's most beautiful mosque and one of only a handful in the UAE that are open to non-Muslims – one-hour guided tours are operated by the Sheikh Mohammed Centre for Cultural Understanding (p220). Tours conclude with pastries and a discussion session during which you're free to ask any question about Islam and Emirati culture. There's no need to book. Modest dress is preferred, but traditional clothing can be borrowed for free.

2ND DECEMBER STREET STREET
Map p254 (btwn Jumeirah Rd & Satwa Roundabout; M Al Jafiliya) Quiet by day, 2nd December Street turns into one of Dubai's liveliest walking strips after dark with plenty of fine pickings for street food aficionados. Steer towards Al Mallah (p103) for shawarma, **Pars** (Map p252; 04 398 9222; 2nd December St, Satwa; mains Dhs45-120; 11am-midnight) for Iranian kebabs or just follow your instinct – or nose – to any of the little joints with blazing neon-signage lining the wide pavement. Also turn your head up to marvel at the house-sized murals created by artists in 2016 as part of the Dubai Street Museum (p102) project.

★DUBAI WALLS PUBLIC ART
Map p254 (City Walk; 24hr; M Burj Khalifa/Dubai Mall) FREE More than a dozen hot shots of the international street-art scene, including Aiko, Blek Le Rat, ROA and Nick Walker, have turned new urban-style quarter City Walk into an outdoor gallery. The project was sponsored by City Walk developer Meraas.

GREEN PLANET ZOO
Map p254 (www.thegreenplanetdubai.com; City Walk, Al Madina St; adult/child Dhs95/70; 10am-10pm Sat-Wed, 10am-midnight Thu & Fri; P; M Burj Khalifa/Dubai Mall) If you can build a ski slope in the desert, why not a rainforest too? Green Planet is an indoor tropical paradise intended to 'edutain' about biodiversity, nature and sustainability. More than 3000 animals and plants live beneath its green canopy, including birds, butterflies, frogs, spiders and snakes. The four-storey ecosystem is anchored by a giant fake tree covered in plants that will grow across it over time, making it look more like the real thing.

HUB ZERO AMUSEMENT PARK
Map p254 (800 637 227; www.hubzerodubai.com/en; City Walk, Jumeirah 1; master/hacker/child pass Dhs160/195/95; 2-10pm Sat-Wed, to midnight Thu & Fri; P; M Burj Khalifa/Dubai Mall) This high-tech indoor theme park is squarely aimed at serious gamers. Tickets buy access to 18 attractions, including a head-spinning VR experience, 3D dark rides, 4D cinema, race simulators, laser tag battles and a laser maze. The upper floor (free admission, pay as you go) has karaoke booths, pool tables and a 40-station area with the latest PC games. Nostalgic types can play retro games like Pac-Man and Space Invaders in the Time Warp Arcade.

★KITE BEACH BEACH
Map p256 (Sheikh Hamdan Beach; 2c St, off Jumeirah Rd, behind Saga World mall, Umm Suqeim 1; sunrise-sunset; M Noor Bank) FREE This long, pristine stretch of white sand, off Jumeirah Rd and next to a mosque, is superclean and has lots of activities, including kitesurfing, soap football, beach tennis, beach volleyball and kayaking. There are showers, wi-fi, toilets and changing facilities, plus lots of food trucks and cafes. Great views of the Burj Al Arab. It gets very busy on Friday and Saturday when a seaside market with crafts and gifts sets up.

SUNSET BEACH BEACH
Map p256 (Umm Suqeim Beach; Umm Suqeim 3; M FGB, Mall of the Emirates) FREE Just north of the Jumeirah Beach Hotel, Sunset is perfect for snapping that envy-inducing selfie with the Burj Al Arab as a backdrop. The wide, sandy strip has great infrastructure, including toilets, showers, changing cubicles and wi-fi via Smart Palms. There's also a short floodlit section for night-time swimming.

Sunset is also Dubai's last surfing beach, with small to medium waves that are perfect for beginners. It's backed by tranquil

DUBAI CANAL

Water was released into the Dubai Canal (also called Dubai Water Canal) on 1 November 2016, marking the culmination of an amazing feat of engineering that connects the mouth of Dubai Creek with the Gulf. The Creek's first 2.2km extension created the Business Bay district and was completed in 2007. In December 2013, construction kicked off on the last 3.2km segment that cuts from Business Bay below Sheikh Zayed Rd and through Safa Park before spilling into the sea at Jumeirah Beach.

While office and hotel high-rises are being built at a frantic pace in Business Bay (including the edgy **Dubai Design District**, p92), the waterfront on the final stretch will be lined with residences, boutique hotels, cafes, marinas and other public spaces. A promenade conducive to jogging and walking parallels both banks. A highlight is the illuminated and motion-operated **waterfall** (p83) that cascades down both sides of Sheikh Zayed Bridge from 7pm to 10pm, stopping only for passing vessels. The **Dubai Ferry** runs several times daily from Al Jaddaf Marine Station at the mouth of Dubai Creek to Jumeirah.

Umm Suqeim Park, which has lawns and a playground.

NIGHT BEACH BEACH

Map p256 (Umm Suqeim 1 Beach; sunset-midnight; MFGB) FREE Fancy a night-time swim with the twinkling Burj Al Arab as a backdrop? Since May 2017, you can now legally take a post-sunset dip along a 125m stretch of beach illuminated by 12m-high wind- and solar-powered floodlights ('Smart Power Poles') and staffed with lifeguards. Find it about 1km north of the iconic landmark.

LA MER BEACH

Map p254 (800 637 227; www.lamerdubai.ae; Jumeirah 1; 10am-midnight) FREE With shops, restaurants, a beachfront with hammocks and a huge playpark, La Mer is Dubai's newest beachfront destination. It's free to sunbathe or roam the complex. Kids will love the inflatable playground, and you're spoiled for choice when it comes to eating – try Motomatchi for Japanese desserts or go local at Treej Cafe.

NIKKI BEACH DUBAI BEACH

Map p254 (04 376 6162; www.nikkibeach.com/destinations/beach-clubs/dubai; Pearl Jumeirah Island; sunloungers with reservation weekdays/weekends Dhs150/300; 11am-9pm Sep-Jun; P; MAl Jafiliya) At this fashionable pleasure pit on the emerging Pearl Jumeirah residential peninsula, only the crisp all-white look is virginal. On weekends, the bronzed, beautiful and cashed-up descend on the Dubai branch of the famous Miami beach club to frolic in the vast pool, lounge on daybeds, load up on seafood and toast the sunset with bubbly. Weekdays are quieter.

MAJLIS GHORFAT UM AL SHEEF HISTORIC BUILDING

Map p254 (04 226 0286; near Al Mehemal & Al Bagaara Sts, Jumeirah 3; adult/child Dhs3/1; 7.30am-2.30pm Sun-Thu; MBusiness Bay, Noor Bank) This rare vestige of pre-oil times was built in 1955 as the summer retreat of Sheikh Rashid Bin Saeed Al Maktoum, the father of current ruler Sheikh Mohammed. The traditional two-storey gypsum-and-coral structure sports a palm-frond roof, a wind tower and window shutters carved from East African timber. The rug-lined *majlis* (reception room) itself is decorated with rifles, daggers, coffee pots, radios and clocks and offers a glimpse into royal leisure living. The palm garden features a traditional *falaj* irrigation system.

EATING

Jumeirah has some of the best eating in town, with a wonderful variety of restaurants from ethnic street bites on 2nd December St and urban bistros at BoxPark or City Walk to humble fish shacks on the waterfront and top-dirham dining shrines at the Burj Al Arab and Madinat Jumeirah.

THE ONE CAFE INTERNATIONAL $

Map p254 (600 541 007; www.theone.com; Jumeirah Rd, Jumeirah 1; mains Dhs39-55; 8am-8pm; ; MWorld Trade Centre) Deli dabblers will be in heaven at this stylish outpost upstairs at THE One home design store. All food is freshly prepared and calibrated to health- and waist-watchers without sacrificing a lick to the taste gods.

LOCAL KNOWLEDGE

URBAN ART ON 2ND DECEMBER ST

In 2016, 16 local and international street artists, including Hua Tunan, Ashwaq Abdulla and Inkman, mounted their cherry-pickers to turn the rather drab facades on 2nd December St into the glorious **Dubai Street Museum** (Map p254; 2nd December St, Satwa; 24hr; Al Jafiliya), with murals reflecting Dubai's Bedouin heritage. It marked phase one of a five-year government-funded project that will also add colour, beauty and urban pizzazz to other parts of the city.

Here are our top five murals:

Emirati children French artist Seth Globepainter created an endearing work depicting a pigtailed Emirati girl and boy in national dress standing on tiptoes while peering through a window. It's called 'Prohibited'.

Resting falcon Hua Tunan from China spray-painted this majestic sitting falcon (the UAE's national bird) in masterfully intricate detail.

Old man in boat Russian artist Julia Volchkova came up with this motif showing an elderly man in national dress rowing a wooden boat, possibly across Dubai Creek.

Founding fathers This work by Emirati woman artist Ashwaq Abdulla pays homage to Sheikh Zayed and Sheikh Rashid, two of the UAE's founding fathers.

Calligraphy quote Inkman from Tunis needed more than a week to beautify a ho-hum facade lot with this circular calligraphy quote from Sheikh Mohammed. It translates as: A positive spirit resides in our soul. It demands our attention and plays a strong role.

All-day breakfast, including delicious eggs benedict.

RAVI — PAKISTANI $

Map p254 (04 331 5353; Al Satwa Rd, Satwa; mains Dhs8-25; 5am-2.30am; ; World Trade Centre) Since 1978, everyone from cabbies to professional chefs has flocked to this Pakistani eatery, where you eat like a prince and pay like a pauper. Loosen your belt for heaped portions of grilled meats or succulent curries, including a few meatless option. Service is swift if perfunctory. Near the Satwa Roundabout. Cash only.

SALT — BURGERS $

Map p256 (www.find-salt.com; 2C St, Kite Beach, Umm Suqeim 1; sliders Dhs30-50; 11am-2am; ; Noor Bank) Salt started life as a roaming food truck serving delicious mini-burgers, before graduating to two silver Airstreams parked permanently at Kite Beach. Join the ever-present queue to place your order and then pull up some pallet furniture set right on the sand (or inside the air-conditioned glass cube, if the sun is starting to bite).

AL AMOOR EXPRESS — EGYPTIAN $

Map p256 (04 347 0787; Halim St, Al Barsha 1; mains Dhs10-56; 7.30am-2am; Mall of the Emirates) Vintage black-and-white photos of Egyptian actors keep an eye on diners here for their *koshari* fix (rice, macaroni and lentil 'porridge'), although it's more fun to order one of their famous cheese-, vegetable- or meat-stuffed *fiteer* pies and watch the baker sling and whirl the dough behind the counter.

MAJLIS CAFE — CAFE $

Map p254 (04 333 8183; Jumeirah Rd, Jumeirah 1; snacks under Dhs10, mains Dhs40; 8am-midnight Sat-Thu, noon-1am Fri; ; World Trade Centre) Secreted on the grounds of the fairytale Jumeirah Mosque (p100), this comfy-luxe lair lets you sink into white couches for a camelccino (cappuccino with camel milk) paired with Emirati sweets, ice cream or savoury finger food.

LIME TREE CAFE — CAFE $

Map p254 (04 325 6325; www.thelimetreecafe.com; Jumeirah Rd, Jumeirah 1; mains Dhs24-40; 7.30am-6pm; ; World Trade Centre) This comfy Euro-style cafe is an expat favourite famous for its luscious cakes (especially the carrot cake), tasty breakfasts, creative sandwiches (stuffed into their homemade Turkish pide), roast chicken and pastas. It's located next to Spinneys.

AL MALLAH — ARABIC $

Map p254 (04 398 4723; 2nd of December St, Satwa; sandwiches Dhs7-15; 6am-2.30am; Al Jafiliya) Locals praise the chicken shawarma and fresh juices at this been-here-forever traditional joint with shaded outdoor seating located on one of Dubai's most pleasant, liveliest and oldest walking streets.

KA'AK AL MANARA LEBANESE $

Map p254 (04 258 2003; www.facebook.com/kaakalmanara; 1st fl, Mercato Mall, Jumeirah Rd, Jumeirah 1; dishes Dhs18-32; 8.30am-midnight Sat-Wed, to 1am Thu & Fri; P; M Burj Khalifa/Dubai Mall) *Ka'ak* is flat sesame bread that's a street-food staple in Lebanon. This upbeat mall-based eatery serves them with various sweet and savoury fillings, sprinkled with *zaatar* or sumac, and toasted just right. Try the classic picon cheese spread or a fusion special like the chicken fajita *ka'ak*.

BOOKMUNCH CAFE CAFE $

Map p254 (04 388 4006; www.bookmunchcafe.com; Al Wasl Sq, Al Wasl Rd; mains Dhs38-68; 7.30am-10pm Sun-Wed, 8am-10.30pm Thu-Sat; M Business Bay) Literati young and old love this adorable bookstore-cafe combo geared towards families. It not only has a fabulous selection of children's books in several languages but also a progressive menu sure to please both tots and grown-ups. Menu stars include ginger-chilli-caramel shrimp, strawberry-kale salad and grandma's tarte tatin, and breakfast is all day.

OPERATION FALAFEL ARABIC $

Map p254 (04 343 9655; www.operationfalafel.com; Box Park, Al Wasl Rd, Jumeirah 2; falafel Dhs5-16, light dishes Dhs15-32; 8am-1.30am; 12, 15, 93, M Business Bay, Burj Khalifa/Dubai Mall) Despite the name, this hip home-grown chain doesn't stop at falafel, here served with a side of creamily nutty tahini or tucked into a pita or *saj* (flatbread) with hummus, pickles and mint leaves. Other respectable and delectable menu picks include shawarma, *fattoosh* salad and *zataar manakeesh* (Lebanese pizza).

There are six more branches around town, including The Beach at JBR and Downtown, both open 24 hours.

★LOGMA EMIRATI $$

Map p254 (800 56462; www.logma.ae; Box-Park, Al Wasl Rd, Jumeirah 1; mains Dhs60-70; 8am-1am; 12, 15, 93, M Business Bay) Meaning 'mouthful' in Arabic, this funky Emirati cafe is a great introduction to contemporary local cuisine. It's popular for breakfast dishes such as *baith tamat* (saffron-spiced scrambled eggs with tomato), wholesome salads (try the pomegranate mozzarella) and sandwiches made with khameer bread. Swap your usual latte for sweet *karak chai* (spicy tea) – a local obsession – or a date shake.

★3 FILS ASIAN $$

Map p254 (056 273 0030; http://3fils.com; Jumeirah Fishing Harbour, Al Urouba St, Jumeirah 1; sharing plates Dhs22-75; 1-11pm Mon-Wed, to midnight Thu-Sat; M Burj Khalifa/Dubai Mall) Singaporean chef Akmal Anuar turns out innovative yet unpretentious Asian-influenced small plates at this tiny, unlicensed spot – a perfect foil to Dubai's expensive, overblown eateries. There are around 25 seats inside and a pint-sized kitchen in the corner, but try to nab one of the outside tables overlooking the bobbing yachts in the marina. Be sure to book at weekends.

★BU QTAIR SEAFOOD $$

Map p256 (055 705 2130; off 2b St, Umm Suqeim Fishing Harbour, Umm Suqeim 1; meals Dhs40-125; noon-11.30pm; P; M Noor Bank, FGB) Always packed to the gills, this simple eatery is a Dubai institution famous for its dock-fresh fish and shrimp, marinated in a 'secret' masala curry sauce and fried to order. Belly up to the window, point to what you'd like and wait (about 30 minutes) for your order to be delivered to your table. Meals are priced by weight.

AL FANAR EMIRATI $$

Map p254 (04 344 2141; www.alfanarrestaurant.com; 1st fl, Town Center Mall, Jumeirah Rd, Jumeirah 1; mains Dhs42-68; noon-9.30pm Sun-Wed, to 10pm Thu, 9am-10pm Fri, to 9.30pm Sat; M Burj Khalifa/Dubai Mall) Al Fanar lays on the old-timey Emirati theme pretty thick with a Land Rover parked outside, a reed ceiling and waiters dressed in traditional garb. Give your taste buds a workout with such local classics such as *machboos* (casserole with rice), *saloona* (tomato-based stew) or *harees* (a porridge-like dish with meat).

PANTRY CAFE INTERNATIONAL $$

Map p254 (04 388 3868; www.pantrycafe.me; cnr Al Wasl Sq & Al Hadeeqa St, Jumeirah 2; mains Dhs50-140; 7.30am-10pm Sat-Wed, 8.30am-11pm Thu & Fri; M Business Bay) With its loft-like ceilings, concrete floors, red-brick walls and eco-aware attitude, the Pantry may scream 'Soho transplant' but is actually a laid-back lair serving the best of global comfort food (fish and chips, curry, risotto, pizza, burgers etc) plus eye-opening breakfasts. Also has a kids' menu.

COMPTOIR 102 HEALTH FOOD $$

Map p254 (☎04 385 4555; www.comptoir102.com; 102 Jumeirah Rd, Jumeirah 1; mains Dhs50-65, 3-course meal Dhs90; ⏰7.30am-9pm; 📶🖊; Ⓜ Emirates Towers) In a pretty cottage with a quiet patio out the back, this concept cafe comes attached to a concept boutique selling beautiful things for home and hearth. The daily changing menu rides the local-organic-seasonal wave and eschews gluten, sugar and dairy. There's also a big selection of vitamin-packed juices, smoothies and desserts. It's opposite Beach Centre mall.

SAMAD AL IRAQI IRAQI $$

Map p254 (☎04 342 7887; http://samadaliraqirestaurant.com; Jumeirah Rd, Beach Park Plaza, Jumeirah 2; mains Dhs50-95; ⏰9am-12.30am Sat-Thu, 1pm-1.30am Fri; Ⓜ Business Bay) This huge and fairly formal mall restaurant with decor inspired by ancient Iraq is locally adored for its excellent *masgouf* – wood-fired grilled fish, the national dish – but also serves Iraqi spins on traditional regional faves such as shawarma, biryani, kebab and grilled meats.

★PAI THAI THAI $$$

Map p256 (☎04 432 3232; www.jumeirah.com; Madinat Jumeirah, King Salman Bin Abdul Aziz Al Saud St, Umm Suqeim 3; mains Dhs55-175; ⏰12.30-2.15pm & 6-11.15pm; 📶; Ⓜ Mall of the Emirates) An abra ride, a canalside table and candlelight are the hallmarks of a romantic night out, and this enchanting spot sparks on all cylinders. If your date doesn't make you swoon, then such expertly seasoned Thai dishes as wok-fried seafood and steamed sea bass should still ensure an unforgettable evening. Early reservations advised.

★PIERCHIC SEAFOOD $$$

Map p256 (☎04 432 3232; www.jumeirah.com; Madinat Jumeirah, King Salman Bin Abdul Aziz Al Saud St, Umm Suqeim 3; mains Dhs125-450; ⏰12.30-3pm Sat-Thu & 6-11pm Sat-Wed, to 11.30 Thu & Fri; 📶; Ⓜ Mall of the Emirates) Looking for a place to drop an engagement ring into a glass of champagne? Make reservations (far in advance) at this impossibly romantic seafood house capping a historic wooden pier with front-row views of the Burj Al Arab and Madinat Jumeirah. The menu is a foodie's dream, with a plethora of beautifully prepared dishes.

LIMA DUBAI PERUVIAN $$$

Map p254 (☎056 500 4571; www.limadubai.com; City Walk, Jumeirah 1; mains Dhs90-200; ⏰noon-1am Sat-Tue, to 2am Wed-Fri; 📶; Ⓜ Burj Khalifa/Dubai Mall) Dubai is no stranger to the Peruvian food craze, but when Michelin-starred Virgilio Martinez opened his outpost, it marked another milestone. The food here is a triumph of creative spicing and boldly paired ingredients. In one signature dish, braised octopus cuddles up to green lentils, potato cream and kalamata olives. Pair with an impeccable pisco sour, and you've got a mighty fine dinner.

ZHENG HE'S CHINESE $$$

Map p256 (☎04 432 3232; www.jumeirah.com; Madinat Jumeirah, King Salman Bin Abdul Aziz Al Saud St, Umm Suqeim 3; mains Dhs110-390; ⏰noon-3pm & 6.30-11.30pm; 🅿📶🖊; Ⓜ Mall of the Emirates) Zheng He was an intrepid 15th-century Chinese seafarer and the food at his namesake restaurant at the Mina A'Salam is just as adventurous. The signature dish in the Sino-chic dining room is the roast duck carved tableside by a 'duck master'. Larger groups are tempted by lobster, turbot and denizens of the live fish tank. Large vegetarian and gluten-free selection to boot.

ROCKFISH SEAFOOD $$$

Map p256 (☎04 366 7640; www.jumeirah.com; Jumeirah Al Naseem, King Salman Bin Abdul Aziz Al Saud St, Umm Suqeim 3; mains Dhs65-175; ⏰8-11am, 12.30-3.30pm & 6.30-11.30pm; 🅿📶; 🚌81, Ⓜ Mall of the Emirates) With silver-and-white interiors and a sandy terrace with front-row views of Burj Al Arab, Rockfish serves up Mediterranean-style seafood in glam but unstuffy surroundings. The compact menu kicks off with *crudo* (raw seafood), moves on to salads and soups, and reaches a crescendo that is laced with Arabic influences.

NATHAN OUTLAW AT AL MAHARA SEAFOOD $$$

Map p256 (☎04 301 7600; http://almaharadubai.com; 1st fl, Burj Al Arab, Umm Suqeim 3; mains Dhs240-500, tasting menu Dhs950; ⏰12.30-3.30pm, 7-11.30pm; 🅿📶) A lift posing as a submarine drops you into a gold-leaf-clad tunnel spilling into one of Dubai's most extravagant restaurants. Tables orbit a circular floor-to-ceiling aquarium where clownfish flit and baby sharks dart as their turbot and monkfish cousins are being devoured. Only the finest seafood imported from the UK – and prepared with deft simplicity – makes it onto plates here.

LOCAL KNOWLEDGE

MOBILE KITCHEN FRENZY

Gourmet food trucks, the hipster export hit from the US, began rolling into Dubai in 2014 and quickly caused a minor food revolution. Now all sorts of contenders are popping up near sights, at festivals, on beaches, at markets and wherever else folk might be in need of quick sustenance.

The truck that launched it all was **Salt** (p102), a classic silver Airstream whose Wagyu burgers quickly garnered a cult following. Two Emirati women entrepreneurs came up with the concept and then relied on the power of social media to attract customers (dubbed 'Salters'). The truck is now a permanent fixture on Kite Beach, where it's been joined by a changing roster of other – still mobile – kitchens.

A corporate take on the street food truck craze is **Last Exit** (04 317 3999; www.lastexit.ae; Sheikh Zayed Rd (Hwy E11), near Interchange 11; mains Dhs10-50; 24hr; P), a series of themed food truck parks set up on the last exit of the highways leading out of Dubai. The original one is located on Hwy E11 (Sheikh Zayed Rd) en route to Abu Dhabi. With a kids' playground, prayer rooms and ATM machines as well as chains like Poco Loco and Baja Fresh in the mix, it's a far cry from the original improv concept. Here a few roaming faves still in keeping with the original concept:

Calle Tacos (www.calletacos.ae) This hard-to-miss tangerine-hued truck attracts loyal foodies inhaling such Mexican treats as nachos, burritos and, of course, tacos, served alongside 'secret' salsas created by the owners' families back in Mexico.

GObai (www.facebook.com/gobaifoodtruck) The name is a mash-up of Goa and Dubai and so is the menu, which lures munchers with fragrant curries to lamb burgers.

Casa Latina (www.facebook.com/pg/CasaLatinaFoodtruck) Caribbean and Latin American fare, including waist-expanding but oh-so-yum cheese sticks (*tequeños*).

The Shebi This silver Airstream peddles Indian-Lebanese fusion fare such as butter chicken shawarma, but is probably most famous for its pulled-beef burger topped with Sriracha mayo.

Vida Food Truck More Airstream action from this truck run by Downtown Dubai's Vida Hotel, which serves international comfort food such as mac and cheese or smoked brisket sandwiches.

DRINKING & NIGHTLIFE

Aside from the bars in and around Madinat Jumeirah and in a smattering of Western-style hotels, few places in Jumeirah serve alcohol, an exception being Nikki Beach Club (p101). Locals gravitate to the new urban walking areas like BoxPark and City Walk for coffee, shisha and mocktails.

BAHRI BAR — BAR

Map p256 (04 432 3232; www.jumeirah.com; Mina A'Salam, Madinat Jumeirah, King Salman Bin Abdul Aziz Al Saud St, Umm Suqeim 3; 4pm-2am Sat-Wed, to 3am Thu & Fri; ; M Mall of the Emirates) This chic bar drips with sultry Arabian decor and has a veranda laid with Persian rugs and comfy sofas perfect for taking in magical views. Daily drink deals and bands or DJs playing jazz and soul make the place a perennial fave among locals and visitors.

PROVOCATEUR — CLUB

Map p254 (04 343 8411, 055 211 8222; www.provocateurdubai.com; Four Seasons Resort, Jumeirah Rd, Jumeirah 1; 11pm-3am Wed-Fri & Sun; M Business Bay) At this ultra-posh party den, an eye-candy crowd lolls on curved floral banquettes beneath an LED ceiling pulsating to edgy EDM or old-school hip-hop and R & B. Think tough door, smart dress code, pricey drinks and top DJs.

GRAPESKIN — WINE BAR

Map p254 (04 403 3111; www.livelaville.com/dining/Grapeskin; La Ville Hotel & Suites, City Walk, Al Multaqa St, Jumeirah 1; 4pm-1am Sun-Wed, 3pm-1am Thu-Sat; ; M Burj Khalifa/Dubai Mall) At this stylish rustic wine bar imbued with a homey vibe you can match your wine to your mood. Most pours come from small vineyards and are served with fine cheeses, meats and platters. Chill to shisha on the terrace or join the post-work expat crowd for happy hour between 6pm and 8pm.

CALL TO PRAYER

If you're staying within earshot of a mosque, you might be woken around 4.30am by the inimitable wailing of the *azan* (the Muslim call to prayer) through speakers positioned on the minarets of nearby mosques. There's a haunting beauty to the sound, one that you'll only hear in Islamic countries.

Muslims pray five times a day: at dawn; when the sun is directly overhead; when the sun is in the position that creates shadows the same length as the object shadowed; at the beginning of sunset; and at twilight, when the last light of the sun disappears over the horizon. The exact times are printed in the daily newspapers and on websites. Once the call has been made, Muslims have half an hour to pray. An exception is made at dawn: after the call they have about 80 minutes in which to wake up, wash and pray before the sun has risen.

Muslims needn't be near a mosque to pray; they need only face Mecca. If devotees cannot get to a mosque, they'll stop wherever they are. If you see someone praying, be as unobtrusive as possible, and avoid walking in front of the person. All public buildings, including government departments, libraries, shopping centres and airports, have designated prayer rooms. In every hotel room arrows on the ceiling, desk or bedside table indicate the direction of Mecca. Better hotels provide prayer rugs, sometimes with a built-in compass.

SKYVIEW BAR — BAR

Map p256 (04 301 7600; www.burjalarab.com; Burj Al Arab; 1pm-2am Sat-Thu, from 7pm Fri) With minimum spends, and afternoon tea running at Dhs620 (Dhs720 for window seating), the tab at Burj Al Arab's Skyview Bar is as stratospheric as its lofty perch 200m above the sea. The minimum age is 21, booking ahead is essential and prepayment is required. As for the outlandish Liberace-meets–*Star Trek* interiors, all we can say is: 'Welcome to the Burj'.

The bar menu also includes such eccentric custom libations like 'Mrs Big' (with a nod to *Sex and the City*), which is delivered in a purple porcelain purse and served with three vials of 'nail polish' and a 'lipstick'.

FOLLY BY NICK & SCOTT — BAR

(04 430 8535; www.facebook.com/follydubai; Souk Madinat Jumeirah, King Salman Bin Abdul Aziz Al Saud St, Umm Suqeim 3; noon-2.30pm & 5-11pm Sun-Thu, noon-3.30pm & 5-11pm Fri & Sat; ; M Mall of the Emirates) This sprawling multistorey venue has a woodsy interior with an open kitchen, but it's really the three bars with killer views of the Burj Al Arab that steal the show. It's the latest venture by Nick Alvis and Scott Price, so expect quality nibbles (Dhs45 to Dhs110) to go with your cocktails, beer or biodynamic wines.

GOLD ON 27 — COCKTAIL BAR

Map p256 (04 301 7600; www.goldon27.com; Burj Al Arab, Umm Suqeim 3; 6pm-2am; ; M Mall of the Emirates) Signature cocktails at this bar on the 27th floor of the Burj Al Arab are crafted with local lore or landmarks in mind and often feature surprise ingredients – the whisky-based Light Sweet Crude contains a smidgen of foie gras and charcoal-infused truffle oil. A DJ helms the decks nightly from 8pm, but the action really only picks up around 10pm on Thursdays and Fridays. Prices are as sky-high as the location and reservations are essential. Book via the bar's app, and your reservation will be automatically activated at the hotel gates.

SHO CHO — BAR, CLUB

Map p254 (04 346 1111; www.sho-cho.com; Dubai Marine Beach Resort & Spa, Jumeirah Rd, Jumeirah 1; 7pm-3am Sun-Fri; ; M World Trade Centre, Emirates Towers) Although Sho Cho is primarily a Japanese restaurant, it's the heady lure of the cool Gulf breezes and potent cocktails on the terrace that continue to make this scene staple simply irresistible.

BRUNSWICK SPORTS CLUB — BAR

Map p256 (056 404 0685; http://brunswicksc.com; Level 2, Sheraton Hotel, Mall of the Emirates; noon-2am; M Mall of the Emirates) This hip bar has multiple screens to watch live sports, including Australian rules football and English Premier League, and industrial-style decor with exposed ducting, long wooden tables and some greenery for good measure. There's a great mix of international beers on tap, including lager, Guinness and German wheat beer, along with a dozen bottled varieties, and excellent Aussie pub grub.

ENTERTAINMENT

VOX MALL OF THE EMIRATES CINEMA

Map p256 (☎600 599 905; www.voxcinemas.com; 2nd fl, Mall of the Emirates, Sheikh Zayed Rd, Al Barsha 1; tickets Dhs35-160; ; Mall of the Emirates) This multiplex boasts 24 screens, including a 4D cinema with motion chairs, and wind, light and water effects; the region's first IMAX laser cinema; a colourful kids' cinema; and the superluxe Theatre by Rhodes where you can enjoy a meal conceived by Michelin-starred chef Gary Rhodes (Dhs295).

DUBAI COMMUNITY THEATRE & ARTS CENTRE THEATRE

Map p256 (DUCTAC; ☎04 341 4777; www.ductac.org; 2nd level, Mall of the Emirates, Sheikh Zayed Rd, Al Barsha; 9am-10pm Sat-Thu, 2-10pm Fri; Mall of the Emirates) This thriving cultural venue puts on all sorts of global diversions, from Shakespeare and classical concerts to Arabic folklore and art exhibits. Much support is given to Emirati talent, making this a good place to keep tabs on the local scene.

MADINAT THEATRE THEATRE

Map p256 (☎04 366 6546; www.madinattheatre.com; Souq Madinat Jumeirah, King Salman Bin Abdul Aziz Al Saud St, Umm Suqeim 3; Mall of the Emirates) The program at this handsome 442-seat theatre at Souk Madinat is largely calibrated to the cultural cravings of British expats. Expect plenty of crowd-pleasing entertainment ranging from popular West End imports to stand-up comedy, toe-tapping musicals, Russian ballet and kids' shows.

TURTLE WATCHING

The Jumeirah Al Naseem resort is the latest addition to Madinat Jumeirah and the home of the nonprofit **Dubai Turtle Rehabilitation Project** (www.jumeirah.com/turtles). It has nursed more than 560 injured or sick sea turtles back to health and released them into the Gulf. The turtles spend the last weeks before their release in the hotel's sea-fed lagoon. The enclosure is open to the public daily for free, and feedings take place at 11am on Wednesdays. Access is via the hotel. Keep an eye out for specimens of the endemic hawksbill turtle that limped onto the list of critically endangered species, with only 8000 nesting females known to exist worldwide.

SHOPPING

Jumeirah teems with indie boutiques along Jumeirah Rd and the new urban malls along Al Wasl Rd. Mercato Mall is noteworthy for its architecture, but for a better selection head to the Mall of the Emirates. Souk Madinat Jumeirah is pleasant but tourist-oriented.

SOUK MADINAT JUMEIRAH MALL

Map p256 (☎04 366 8888; www.jumeirah.com; King Salman Bin Abdul Aziz Al Saud St, Umm Suqeim 3; 10am-11pm; ; Mall of the Emirates) More tourist-geared boutique mall than traditional Arabian market, this handsomely designed souq is part of the Arab village-style Madinat Jumeirah resort and not a bad spot for picking up souvenirs. Options include camel toys at **Camel Company** (Map p256; ☎04 368 6048; www.camelcompany.ae; 10am-11pm), Bedouin daggers at **Lata's** (Map p256; ☎04 368 6216; 10am-11pm) and pashmina shawls at Jalabiyat Yasmine (p109). In some shops, bargaining is possible.

MALL OF THE EMIRATES MALL

Map p256 (☎04 409 9000; www.malloftheemirates.com; Sheikh Zayed Rd, Al Barsha; 10am-10pm Sun-Wed, to midnight Thu-Sat; ; Mall of the Emirates) Home to Ski Dubai (p109), a community theatre, a 24-screen multiplex cinema and – let's not forget – 630 shops, MoE is one of Dubai's most popular malls. With narrow walkways and no daylight, it can feel a tad claustrophobic at peak times (except in the striking Fashion Dome, lidded by a vaulted glass ceiling and home to luxury brands).

CITY WALK MALL

Map p254 (www.citywalk.ae; Al Safa Rd; 10am-10pm; ; Burj Khalifa/Dubai Mall) Dubai's newest pedestrianised shopping, dining and entertainment district boasts urban-style streets and a contemporary glass-roofed mall. Along with more than 60 shops, 30-odd cafes and restaurants, and a 10-screen cinema complex, there is a handful of family-friendly attractions, including the Green Planet (p100) biodome and Hub Zero (p100) gaming centre.

BOXPARK SHOPPING CENTRE

Map p254 (☎800 637 227; http://boxpark.ae; Al Wasl Rd; 10am-midnight or later; ; Business Bay) Inspired by the London original, this 1.3km-long outdoor lifestyle mall was built from upcycled shipping containers and has injected a welcome dose of urban cool into the Dubai shopping scene. The 220 units draw a hip crowd, including lots of locals, with quirky concept stores, eclectic dining, and entertainment options including a cinema with on-demand screenings.

URBANIST HOMEWARES

Map p254 (☎04 348 8002; www.facebook.com/Urbaniststore; BoxPark, Al Wasl Rd; ⏲10am-10pm Sun-Thu, to midnight Fri & Sat; Ⓜ Business Bay) The Syrian couple behind Urbanist dedicate the shop's shelf space to hand-curated items rooted in both tradition and modernity, and Western and Middle Eastern tastes. None of the pieces – from tiny gold earrings to tunics and fez-shaped stools – are run of the mill. It's all displayed in a vibrant space where industrial cool meets antique cabinets and mother-of-pearl mirrors.

TYPO STATIONERY

Map p254 (☎04 385 6631; http://typo.com; BoxPark, Al Wasl Rd; ⏲10am-10pm Sun-Thu, to midnight Thu & Fri; Ⓜ Business Bay) This is the kind of shop where 'notebooks' are still made from paper. Indeed, here they come in all shapes and sizes, from cutesy to corporate, along with lots of other fun but useful items like laptop bags, pencil cases and mobile phone covers.

GALLERIA MALL MALL

Map p254 (☎04 344 4434; www.galleria-mall.ae; Al Wasl Rd; ⏲10am-midnight; Ⓜ Burj Khalifa/Dubai Mall) The modern-Arabia design of this locally adored boutique mall is as much a draw as the shops, which include rare gems like the first UAE branch of Saudi homeware store Cities and hip local fashions by Zayan. Wrap up a visit with a healthy lunch at South African cafe Tashas or gooey cakes from Emirati-owned Home Bakery.

MERCATO SHOPPING MALL MALL

Map p254 (☎04 344 4161; www.mercatoshoppingmall.com; Jumeirah Rd, Jumeirah 1; ⏲10am-10pm; Ⓜ Financial Centre, Burj Khalifa/Dubai Mall) With 140 stores, Mercato may be small by Dubai standards, but it's distinguished by attractive architecture that looks like a fantasy blend of a classic train station and an Italian Renaissance town. Think vaulted glass roof, brick arches, a giant clock and a cafe-lined piazza. Retail-wise, you'll find upscale international brands and a Spinneys supermarket.

S*UCE FASHION & ACCESSORIES

Map p254 (☎04 344 7270; http://shopatsauce.com; ground fl, Village Mall, Jumeirah Rd; ⏲10am-10pm Sat-Thu, from 4pm Fri; Ⓜ Emirates Towers) Plain and simple they are not, the clothes and accessories at S*uce (pronounced 'sauce'), a pioneer in Dubai's growing lifestyle-fashion scene. Join fashionistas picking through regional and international designers and brands you probably won't find on your high street back home, including Alice McCall, Bleach and Fillyboo.

This is the original store. There are others in Dubai Mall, at The Beach at JBR and in the Galleria Mall.

HOUSE OF PROSE BOOKS

Map p254 (☎04 344 9021; www.houseofprose.com; Jumeirah Plaza, Jumeirah Rd, Jumeirah 1; ⏲10am-9pm Sat-Thu, 5-9pm Fri; Ⓜ Emirates Towers) At the original branch of this beloved local lit parlour, American bibliophile Mike McGinley has supplied readers with new and secondhand English-language books since 1993. After you're done, you can return your purchase for a 50% refund.

O CONCEPT FASHION & ACCESSORIES

Map p254 (☎04 345 5557; www.facebook.com/Oconceptstore; Al Hudheiba Rd, Jumeirah 1; ⏲10am-10pm; 📶; Ⓜ World Trade Centre) This Emirati-owned urban boutique-cum-cafe with shiny concrete floors and ducts wrapped in gold foil is a routine stop for fashionistas in search of up-to-the-second T-shirts, dresses, jeans and other casual-elegant fashions and accessories.

The cafe has delicious cappuccino and gluten-, sugar- and dairy-free desserts that actually taste good.

O' DE ROSE FASHION & ACCESSORIES

Map p256 (☎04 348 7990; www.o-derose.com; 999 Al Wasl Rd, Umm Suqeim 2; ⏲10am-8pm Sat-Thu; Ⓜ Noor Bank, FGB) Enjoy a sip of rose water upon entering this quirky concept boutique run by a trio of free-spirited cousins from Beirut. They share a passion for unusual things, as reflected in the store's line-up of ethnic-chic clothing, accessories, and art and home decor, most of it created by indie designers from around the region.

ZOO CONCEPT GIFTS & SOUVENIRS

Map p254 (☎04 349 5585; Shop M08-01 BoxPark, Al Wasl Rd, Jumeirah 2; ⏲10am-10pm Sun-Thu, to midnight Fri & Sat; 📶; 🚌12, 15, 93, Ⓜ Burj Khalifa/Dubai Mall) This concept store in trendy BoxPark stocks quirky gifts, gadgets, jewellery, clothes and accessories. Owner Hussein Abdul Rasheed curates an always-interesting mix of up-and-coming local labels like Hudoob (pop culture caps) and international brands such as Retrosuperfuture sunglasses, alongside panda-printed plates and knitted Coco Chanel dolls. There are also stores at Dubai Mall and Souk Al Bahar.

GARDEROBE VINTAGE

Map p256 (☎04 394 2753; www.garderobe.ae; Villa 596, Jumeirah Rd, Umm Suqeim 1; ⏱10am-8pm Sun-Thu; Ⓜ Noor Bank) Wallet-watching luxury lovers regularly pop by this stylish consignment boutique whose 'pre-loved' designer labels and accessories are in tip-top condition and often include gems by Chanel, Hermès, Alexander Wang and Gucci.

JALABIYAT YASMINE FASHION & ACCESSORIES

Map p256 (☎04 368 6115; www.jalabiatyasmine.com; Souk Madinat Jumeirah, King Salman Bin Abdul Aziz Al Saud St, Umm Suqeim 3; ⏱10am-11pm; Ⓜ Mall of the Emirates) This small boutique specialises in *jalabiyas* (traditional kaftans native to the Gulf) and other Arabic fashion, although most visitors will likely be drawn in by its huge selection of elegantly patterned shawls. The finest are handmade by weavers in Kashmir from genuine pashmina (cashmere) or shahtoosh (the down hair of a Tibetan antelope). Machine-made shawls start at Dhs150.

SPORTS & ACTIVITIES

WILD WADI WATERPARK WATER PARK

Map p256 (☎04 348 4444; www.wildwadi.com; Jumeirah Rd, Jumeirah 3; over/under 110cm tall Dhs310/260; ⏱10am-6pm Nov-Feb, to 7pm Mar-Oct; 👪; Ⓜ Mall of the Emirates) It's liquid thrills galore at Wild Wadi, where you can ride a water roller coaster (Master Blaster), plunge down a death-defying tandem slide (Jumeirah Sceirah) and get tossed around watery tornadoes (Tantrum Alley). Mellow types can chill on the lazy river while kids love romping around a vast water playground with smaller slides, water guns and a dumping bucket. Note that some rides have a 110cm minimum height requirement. One night a week the park is open only to women, girls, and boys under eight.

SPLASH 'N' PARTY WATER PARK

Map p256 (☎04 388 3008; www.splashnparty.ae; cnr 8A & 23A Sts, Umm Suqeim 1; day pass child & 1 adult weekday/weekend Dhs100/140, extra adult Dhs50 any day; ⏱9am-8pm Sun-Wed, to 9pm Thu-Sat; 👪; Ⓜ Noor Bank) This colourful park has plenty of splash pads, slides, water guns, tipping buckets and other water-based activities to keep tots entertained for hours. Parents can keep an eye on the action while chilling in the restaurant or at the juice bar. Popular for its themed birthday parties.

DESERT WINTER WONDERLAND

Picture this: it's 45°C outside, and you're wearing gloves and a hat and riding a chairlift through a faux alpine winter wonderland. Skiing in the desert? No problem. In Dubai, that is. **Ski Dubai** (Map p256; ☎toll free 800 386; www.theplaymania.com/skidubai; Mall of the Emirates, Sheikh Zayed Rd, Al Barsha; slope day pass adult/child Dhs310/285, snow park Dhs210; ⏱10am-11pm Sun-Wed, 10am-midnight Thu, 9am-midnight Fri, to 11pm Sat; 👪; Ⓜ Mall of the Emirates) has delighted everyone from slope-starved expats to curious tourists and snow virgins since opening in 2005 as the first indoor ski park in the Middle East.

Of course, Ski Dubai's 'mountain' is an ant hill when compared with the Alps, but it's challenging enough for beginners, fun for intermediate skiers and a novelty for more advanced skiers. Tackle five ski runs (the longest being 400m with a 60m drop) and a Freestyle Zone with jumps, rails and a 90m-long halfpipe, both accessed by chairlift. All equipment is provided, including socks and skis, although gloves and hats must be purchased in the integrated store unless you happen to have your own. Newbies can learn the basics in the ski school.

Snow bunnies of all ages can also have fun in the enchanting ice sculpture–dotted Snow Park. Race each other on parallel bobsled tracks, tumble downhill in a giant plastic snowball or soar above the slopes in a 150m-long zip line (for an extra fee). You'll also need to shell out a few extra dirham to meet the resident gentoo and king penguins that strut their stuff around the Snow Park several times daily.

For the best free views of Ski Dubai from the mall, head to the 1st-floor viewing gallery. There's also a full-on view of the slopes from the Après restaurant.

XDUBAI SKATEPARK SKATING

Map p256 (http://xdubai.com/skatepark; 2nd St, Kite Beach, Umm Suqeim 1; day pass Dhs35; ⏲10am-midnight, kids only 8-10am Fri & Sat; 👪; Ⓜ Noor Bank) Next to Kite Beach (p100), this good-sized canopy-covered skate park gets the adrenaline of youngsters flowing with two bowls (one 1.2m, the other 3.2m deep), rails, kickers, hubbas and various other street elements. It's suitable for beginners and advanced skaters. Helmets required for kids under 16.

MATTEL PLAY! TOWN PLAYGROUND

Map p254 (☎800 637 227; www.playtowndubai.com; City Walk; adult/child Dhs55/95; ⏲9am-6pm Sat-Wed, to 8pm Thu, 11am-8pm Fri; 👪; Ⓜ Burj Khalifa/Dubai Mall) In this adorable indoor playground, the milk-tooth brigade gets to build a house with Bob the Builder, put out fires with Fireman Sam, dance in front of a magic mirror with Angelina Ballerina and hang out with Barney and Thomas the Tank Engine. Parents, meanwhile, can nibble on a salad or lasagne at the cafe.

AL BOOM DIVING DIVING

Map p254 (☎04 342 2993; www.alboomdiving.com; Villa 254, cnr Al Wasl Rd & 33 St, Jumeirah 1; guided dives from Dhs250; ⏲10am-8pm Sun-Thu, to 6pm Fri & Sat; Ⓜ World Trade Centre) Al Boom is the largest dive centre in the UAE and offers the gamut of PADI certification courses as well as guided dives and night dives around the World islands off the coast of Dubai, shark dives at the Dubai Aquarium and reef dives off the East Coast and the Musandam Peninsula in Oman.

Their HQ is in Jumeirah, but they also operate dive centres at Le Royal Meridien Beach Resort & Spa, the One&Only Royal Mirage, the One&Only The Palm and the Dubai Aquarium.

SURF HOUSE DUBAI SURFING

Map p256 (☎04 321 1309, 050 504 3020; www.surfingdubai.com; Villa 110, 41A St, Sunset Beach; surfing/SUP lessons from Dhs150/200, rental per hr Dhs75; ⏲7am-7pm; Ⓜ FGB) 'Hang 10' central in Dubai is the Surf House, which not only stocks all the latest surf and stand-up paddleboards but also offers lessons in and equipment rental for both sports. With more than 3000 members, the venue doubles as a community hangout and includes a chill cafe, yoga studio and acoustic recording studio.

LOCAL KNOWLEDGE

YOGA ON THE BEACH

Downward dog and sun salutation with a view of the Burj Al Arab? Just sign up for the daily sunset yoga sessions (Dhs90) organised by the on-site **Talise Spa** (p110) and on Madinat Jumeirah's private beach. An even more spiritual journey awaits during Full Moon Yoga (Dhs99) – if you can get the timing right.

DUKITE KITESURFING

Map p256 (☎050 758 6992; www.dukite.com; Jumeirah Rd; Ⓜ Noor Bank) Respected outfits provides kitesurfing and stand-up paddleboarding (SUP) instruction and equipment rental. The shop is opposite Burger Fuel restaurant.

DUBAI KITESURFING SCHOOL KITESURFING

Map p256 (☎050 455 9098; www.dubaikiteschool.com; 2D St, Umm Suqeim 1; lessons private/group per hour Dhs300/250, full rental 1hr/day Dhs200/600; Ⓜ Noor Bank) Appropriately located on hip and action-oriented Kite Beach, this licensed and professionally run outfit offers kitesurfing lessons and also rents out the necessary gear to get you up and out on the water.

WONDER BUS TOURS BOATING

Map p254 (☎04 359 5656, 050 181 0553; http://wonderbusdubai.net; Mercato Mall, Jumeirah Rd, Jumeirah 1; adult/child 3-11yr Dhs170/120; Ⓜ BurJuman) These unusual sightseeing tours have you boarding the bright yellow amphibious Wonder Bus at the Mercato Mall, driving down to the Creek, plunging into the water, cruising past historic Bur Dubai and Deira and returning to the shopping mall, all within the space of an hour. Tours run several times daily.

TALISE SPA SPA

Map p256 (☎04 366 6818; www.jumeirah.com; Al Qasr Hotel, Madinat Jumeirah; ⏲9am-10pm; Ⓜ Mall of the Emirates) This world-class Arabian-themed spa has 26 gorgeous temple-like treatment suites and offers both classic and fanciful treatments as gold-clay body masks, sea-shell massages and holistic sensory stimulation sessions in an artist-designed 'AlphaSphere' pod. After your treatment, you're free to relax in the gender-separated sauna, steam room and pool.

Dubai Marina & Palm Jumeirah

Neighbourhood Top Five

❶ **The Walk at JBR** (p113) Strolling down this pleasant strip chock-a-block with family-oriented indie cafes, restaurants and shops, and combining this with a spin around The Beach, a chic new low-rise outdoor mall flanking a beautiful stretch of sandy beach.

❷ **Zero Gravity** (p119) Partying from day to night at this sizzling beach club.

❸ **101 Lounge & Bar** (p118) Catching the boat shuttle to the sleek lounge for bites and cocktails with a million-dollar view of the Dubai Marina skyline.

❹ **Asia Asia** (p115) Enjoying a canalside dinner or drink with gorgeous views of the glittering marina skyscrapers.

❺ **Dubai Marina Water Bus** (p121) Cruising around the marina by water bus, preferably at dusk or early evening.

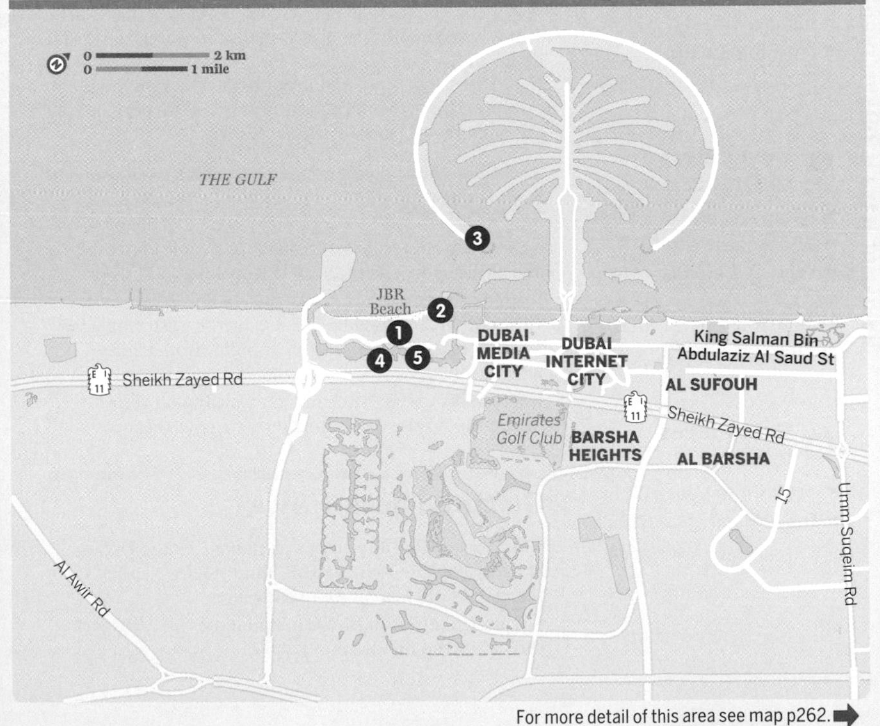

For more detail of this area see map p262.

Lonely Planet's Top Tip

A stroll along the Marina Walk is a lot of fun, but walking the entire undulating promenade would take the better part of the day. A great way to sample the ambience while saving your stamina and shoe leather is by hopping aboard the **Dubai Marina Water Bus** (p121). Part of Dubai's public transportation network (Nol cards are valid), it's like an inexpensive minicruise around this futuristic vertical neighbourhood and is best done at sunset or after dark.

Best Places to Eat

- Stay (p118)
- Tagine (p116)
- Rhodes W1 (p118)
- Fümé (p114)
- Toro Toro (p116)

For reviews, see p114.

Best Places to Drink

- Barasti (p119)
- Bliss Lounge (p120)
- Lock, Stock & Barrel (p119)
- Industrial Avenue (p120)

For reviews, see p119.

Best Places to Shop

- Ibn Battuta Mall (p123)
- Dubai Marina Mall (p123)

For reviews, see p123.

Explore Dubai Marina & Palm Jumeirah

Dubai Marina has become one of the most popular places to live in town, and its pedestrian-friendly areas also hold plenty of appeal for visitors. Carved from the desert, this is one of the world's largest artificial marinas, centred on a 3km-long canal flanked by a thicket of futuristic high-rises, including the twisting Cayan Tower. A stroll along the Marina Walk promenade is delightful, especially after dusk when you can gaze out at the glittering towers and bobbing yachts, stop by the dancing fountains and find your favourite dinner, drink or shisha spot.

Paralleling the beach are The Walk at JBR, a 1.7km-long strip of shops and family-oriented eateries, and The Beach at JBR, a chic open-air mall fronting a lovely sandy beach with great infrastructure. Just offshore is Bluewaters Islands, where the world's largest observation wheel, Ain Dubai, will soon start making its merry rounds. The Dubai Tram threads through much of the Marina.

Jutting into the Gulf is the Palm Jumeirah, an artificial island in the shape of a palm tree with a 2km-long trunk, 16-frond crown and 11km-long crescent-shaped breakwater. Built to increase Dubai's beachfront, it's home to luxury apartments, villas and hotels and punctuated by the garish but hugely popular Atlantis The Palm resort with its crowd-pleasing water park and aquarium.

Further south are the grounds of World Expo 2020, the emerging Al Maktoum International Airport and the theme parks of Dubai Parks & Resorts.

Local Life

- **Strolling** Evenings are perfect for people-watching and chilling on The Walk at JBR (p113) and Marina Walk.
- **Dinner with a view** Be dazzled by the glittering jewel box that is the Dubai Marina at night, from a lofty terrace table.
- **Beach it** Grab a towel and get working on your tan, then wrap up the day with a movie under the stars.

Getting There & Away

- **Metro** The Red Line stops at Damac for the Dubai Marina. For The Walk at JBR, the Jumeirah Lakes Towers station is a bit more convenient.
- **Tram** Dubai Tram links Dubai Media City, JBR and Dubai Marina on an 11km loop.

SIGHTS

AIN DUBAI FERRIS WHEEL

Map p262 (800 637 227; www.bluewatersdubai.ae; Bluewaters Island, Dubai Marina; M Jumeirah Lakes Towers, Jumeirah Beach Residence 2) After it opens (likely late 2018), Dubai will be able to lay claim to to yet another record: the world's tallest observation wheel. Ain Dubai will rise 210m on artificial Bluewaters Island off the coast of Jumeirah Beach Residence, making it 43m higher than current record-holder, the High Roller in Las Vegas. Up to 1400 passengers will get to enjoy 360-degree views of the Dubai skyline during the 48-minute rotation, seated in 48 enclosed cabins outfitted with stone floors and benches.

Some 9000 tonnes of German and Korean steel were used in construction of Ain Dubai, more than for the Eiffel Tower. It will be surrounded by the usual mix of shops, restaurants, hotels and residences.

THE BEACH AT JBR AREA

Map p262 (04 317 3999; www.thebeach.ae; Jumeirah Beach Residence, Dubai Marina; 10am-midnight Sun-Wed, to 1am Thu-Sat; P; M Jumeirah Lakes Towers, Damac, Jumeirah Beach Residence 1, Jumeirah Beach Residence 2) FREE Paralleling the beachfront for about 1km, The Beach is an open-plan cluster of low-lying, urban-style buildings wrapped around breezy plazas. Hugely popular with families on weekends, it mixes cafes and upmarket shops with a lively waterfront fun zone complete with a kiddie splash park, an outdoor gym, a crafts market and other diversions. A beach club rents out sunloungers, but you're free to spread your towel just about anywhere for free.

THE WALK AT JBR AREA

Map p262 (Jumeirah Beach Residence, Dubai Marina; M Jumeirah Lakes Towers, Damac, Jumeirah Beach Residence 1, Jumeirah Beach Residence 2) In a city of air-conditioned malls, this attractive outdoor shopping and dining promenade was an immediate hit when it opened in 2008. Join locals and expats in strolling the 1.7km stretch, watching the world on parade from a pavement cafe, browsing the fashionable boutiques or ogling the shiny Ferraris and other fancy cars cruising by on weekends.

JBR BEACH BEACH

Map p262 (Jumeirah Beach Residence, Dubai Marina; M Jumeirah Lakes Towers, Jumeirah Lakes Towers) FREE This clean, wonderful playground has plenty of facilities, including showers, toilets and changing rooms housed in distinctive panelled pods. Kids can keep cool in a splash zone, and there's even an outdoor gym for pumping, Since it's right next to The Beach at JBR (p113) and The Walk at JBR (p113), there's no shortage of food and drink outlets, although alcohol is only available in the hotels.

CAYAN TOWER ARCHITECTURE

Map p262 (Al Sharta St, Dubai Marina; M Damac, Marina Towers) It may not be the tallest residential tower in the Dubai Marina, but it's certainly a building with twist: a 90-degree spiral over the course of its height, to be precise. Aside from looking impressive, the design actually reduces wind forces on the building and reduces direct solar radiation.

PIER 7 NOTABLE BUILDING

Map p262 (04 436 1020; www.pier7.ae; Marina Walk, Dubai Marina; M Damac, Dubai Marina Mall) Linked to the Dubai Marina Mall via a glass-encased walkway, this circular tower gets its name from the seven restaurants – from Asian to French – on each of its floors. All but the lowest one have terrace tables for noshing with a view.

LOST CHAMBERS AQUARIUM AQUARIUM

Map p262 (04 426 1040; www.atlantisthepalm.com; Atlantis The Palm, Palm Jumeirah; adult/child 3-11yr Dhs100/70; 10am-10pm; P; Aquaventure) Rare albino alligators Ali and Blue are the latest stars in this fantastic labyrinth of underwater halls, enclosures and fish tanks that re-creates the legend of the lost city of Atlantis. Some 65,000 exotic marine creatures inhabit 21 aquariums, where rays flutter, jellyfish dance and giant groupers lurk. The centrepiece is the Ambassador Lagoon. For an extra fee, you can snorkel or dive with the fishes in this 11.5-million-litre tank.

Twice daily (at 10.30am and 3.30pm), scuba divers drop into the lagoon for an interactive **Aquatheatre** show and feeding session. Also available: behind-the-scenes tours with a stop at the fish hospital.

TOP SIGHT
AQUAVENTURE WATERPARK

Adrenaline rushes are guaranteed at this water park at Atlantis The Palm resort. A 1.6km-long 'river' with rapids, wave surges and waterfalls meanders through vast grounds that are anchored by two towers. A highlight is the ziggurat-shaped Tower of Neptune, with three slides, including the aptly named Leap of Faith, a near-vertical plunge into a shark-infested lagoon.

Thrill seekers will also want to steer towards the nearby Tower of Poseidon to be tossed and churned in the dark and twisty serpentines of the Aquaconda, the world's largest diameter raft slide. The same tower is also the launchpad for the gravity-defying Zoomerango slide that will catapult and plummet you relentlessly.

To keep an eye on the action, whoosh 20m above the park on the Atlantean Flyer zip-line (Dhs100). Although the park is clearly geared more towards teens and adults, those under 120cm tall will also find plenty of ways to keep cool. Aside from tamer rides and a wave pool, there's also an enormous playground where easy slides, water cannons and tipping buckets should generate plenty of squeals. Tickets also include same-day access to the sandy 700m-long Aquaventure beach.

DON'T MISS

- Leap of Faith
- Zoomerango
- Poseidon's Revenge
- Aquaconda

PRACTICALITIES

- Map p262, F1
- ☎04 426 1169
- www.atlantisthe palm.com
- Atlantis The Palm, Palm Jumeirah
- over/under 120cm tall Dhs260/215
- ⏲10am-sunset
- 🚌Aquaventure

EATING

Dubai Marina is dominated by sprawling beach resorts, each flaunting several top-end restaurants, bars and nightclubs. But you'll also find excellent eats away from the hotels, especially along the Marina Walk, The Walk at JBR and The Beach at JBR. Because of its compact nature, the area is conducive to hopping from one place to the next by foot.

Dubai Marina

BOUCHON BAKERY BAKERY $

Map p262 (☎04 419 0772; www.thebeach.ae; The Beach at JBR; pastries Dhs13-20, cakes Dhs20-24, mains Dhs50; ⏲8am-11pm Sun-Thu, to midnight Fri & Sat; 📶✍; Ⓜ Jumeirah Lakes Towers) This classy cafe – an outpost of celebrity chef Thomas Keller's popular US chain – serves fiendishly good pastries, cakes and macarons. Everything is baked fresh each morning in the glass-walled kitchen, with a well-priced selection of soups, salads and sandwiches and excellent coffee. Grab a table on the terrace or slide into a dark-leather booth indoors to escape the sun.

FÜMÉ INTERNATIONAL $$

Map p262 (☎04 421 5669; www.fume-eatery.com; level 1, Pier 7, Marina Walk, Dubai Marina; mains Dhs55-125; ⏲noon-2am Sat-Wed, 9am-2am Thu & Fri; 📶; Ⓜ Jumeirah Lakes Towers, 🚋Dubai Marina Mall) With its industrial-chic look, relaxed crew and global comfort food, Fümé brings more than a touch of urban cool to the Marina. The menu features plenty of creative dishes to keep foodies happy, including the bestseller: super-juicy beef chuck ribs smoked for six hours in a closed charcoal oven. No reservations.

It's next to Dubai Marina Mall.

MYTHOS KOUZINA & GRILL GREEK $$

Map p262 (☎04 399 8166; www.mythoskouzina.com; Level B1, Armada BlueBay Hotel, Cluster P, Jumeriah Lakes Towers; mains Dhs45-89; ⏲12:30-5pm & 7-11:30pm; Ⓜ Damac Properties) Kitted out like a traditional seaside taverna with whitewashed walls and rustic furniture, Mythos is a little slice of Santorini hidden away in the somewhat incongruous setting of JLT's Armada BlueBay Hotel. Order a selection of starters to share – the *keftedakia* (meatballs) are particularly good – then it's a toss-up between home-style favourites like moussaka and souvlaki and succulent grilled meat and seafood.

The area has become a hub for reasonably priced restaurants and bars in recent years, and Mythos is no exception. The small outdoor terrace lends itself to leisurely meals, although word is definitely out about this down-to-earth local, so it's best to book ahead.

ZAFRAN INDIAN **$$**

Map p262 (☎04 399 7357; ground fl, Dubai Marina Mall, Dubai Marina; mains Dhs32-130; ⊙noon-11pm Sat-Wed, to midnight Thu & Fri; P ; M Damac, Dubai Marina Mall) Devoid of mall-setting sterility, this contemporary Indian bistro packs a lot of sizzle into its kebabs, curries and biryanis, which are best enjoyed on the terrace. Menu stars include the butter chicken, chargrilled lamb kebabs and tandoori king prawns.

SUSHI ART JAPANESE **$$**

Map p262 (☎800 220, 04 448 9586; www.sushiart.ae; The Beach at JBR, Dubai Marina; nigiri per piece Dhs8-22, maki rolls Dhs17-49; ⊙11am-midnight; M Jumeirah Lakes Towers, Jumeirah Beach Residence 2) Sushi purist or not, you're sure to find your favourite among the huge, attractive selection of French-infused California-style bites at this minimalist cafe. A new collaboration with young Japanese chef Kei Kobayashi spices up the menu with such compositions as Gyu special roll starring teriyaki-laced seared beef and a pungent red-miso-cucumber salad.

MASSAAD BARBECUE LEBANESE **$$**

Map p262 (☎04 559 7895; www.massaadfarmtotable.com; ground fl, Amwaj block, The Walk at JBR, Dubai Marina; mains Dhs25-64; ⊙11am-1am; ; M Jumeirah Lakes Towers, Jumeirah Beach Residence 2) At this teensy country-style eatery most of the fresh ingredients – from lemons to chickens – are sourced from growers based in nearby Al Ain. Barbecued kebabs is the classic here, served either just with garnish or combined with fries, pickles and salad on a traditional wooden board called *tablieh*.

★**ASIA ASIA** FUSION **$$$**

Map p262 (☎04 276 5900; www.asia-asia.com; 6th fl, Pier 7, Dubai Marina; mains Dhs90-350; ⊙4pm-midnight or later; ; M Damac, Dubai Marina Mall) Prepare for a culinary journey along the Spice Road at this theatrically decorated restaurant entered via a candle-lit corridor that spills into an exotic booth-lined lounge with dangling birdcage lamps. Dim sum to tuna tataki and crispy duck – dishes here are alive with flavours from Asia and the Middle East. Bonus: the grand marina views from the terrace. Full bar.

THE CROFT BRITISH **$$$**

Map p262 (☎04 319 4794; www.thecroftdubai.com; 5th fl, Dubai Marriott Harbour Hotel & Suites, King Salman Bin Abdulaziz Al Saud St, Dubai Media City; mains Dhs90-165; ⊙5pm-1am Sun-Fri, 12:30-3.30pm Fri, 4pm-1am Sat; ; M Damac, Marina Towers) Chef Darren Velvick flies the flag for modern British cooking at this relaxed restaurant with an open kitchen and spacious terrace overlooking the lights of Dubai Marina. There's an emphasis on locally-grown and organic ingredients, along with craft beer, well-priced wine and a daily happy hour from 5pm to 8pm.

FISH BEACH TAVERNA SEAFOOD **$$$**

Map p262 (☎04 511 7139; www.fish-dubai.com; Le Meridien Mina Seyahi Beach Resort & Marina, King Salman Bin Abdul Aziz Al Saud St; mains Dhs110-160; ⊙noon-11pm Oct-Apr; M Nakheel, Mina Seyahi) With whitewashed walls, cobblestone paths and breezy blue and white decor, this charming beachfront restaurant conjures up thoughts of summer in the Greek Islands. The sharing-style menu is a pleasing mixture of Greek and Turkish dishes, along with fresh fish flown in three times a week from the Aegean Sea (which goes some way to explaining the hefty price tag).

MAYA MODERN MEXICAN KITCHEN MEXICAN **$$$**

Map p262 (☎04 316 5550; www.maya-dubai.com; Le Royal Meridien Beach Resort & Spa, Al Mamsha St, Dubai Marina; mains Dhs110-200, brunch without/with alcohol Dhs325/435; ⊙7pm-1am Mon-Sat; P ; M Damac, Jumeirah Beach Residence 1) Richard Sandoval, the man who introduced modern Mexican food to the US, is behind the menu at this casual-chic restaurant. Expect a piñata of flavours, from creamy guacamole (prepared tableside of course) to fish tacos with peanut sauce and chicken *mole poblano* to sizzling prawn fajitas. Tip: get there before sunset for top-shelf margaritas on the rooftop lounge. Great brunch too.

TAGINE MOROCCAN $$$

Map p262 (☎04 399 9999; http://royalmirage.oneandonlyresorts.com; The Palace, One&Only Royal Mirage, King Salman Bin Abdul Aziz Al Saud St, Dubai Media City; mains Dhs122-178; ⊙7pm-1am Tue-Sun; P ; M Dubai Internet City, Media City) Get cosy between lanterns, rugs and throw pillows at a low-slung table in the mood-lit dining room, then treat your taste buds while tapping your toes to the live Moroccan duo. Fez-capped waiters serve big platters of couscous and tagines with all the extras, including a vegetarian choice. The *mechoui* (cumin-laced roast lamb shoulder) is another fine menu pick.

EAUZONE ASIAN $$$

Map p262 (☎04 399 9999; http://royalmirage.oneandonlyresorts.com; Arabian Court, One&Only Royal Mirage, King Salman Bin Abdul Aziz Al Saud St, Dubai Media City; mains Dhs80-165; ⊙noon-3.30pm & 7-11.30pm; P ; M Nakheel, Palm Jumeirah) This jewel of a restaurant draws friends, romancing couples and fashionable families to a sublime seaside setting with shaded wooden decks and floating *majlis* (reception room) overlooking illuminated pools. Casual by day, it's hushed and intimate at night, perfect for concentrating on such pleasurable classics as lotus-wrapped sea bass or miso-glazed black cod.

TORO TORO LATIN AMERICAN $$$

Map p262 (☎04 317 6000; www.torotoro-dubai.com; Grosvenor House, Al Emreef St, Dubai Marina; small plates Dhs50-110, rodizio per person Dhs420; ⊙7pm-1am Sat-Wed, to 2am Thu & Fri; P ; M Damac, Jumeirah Beach Residence 1) The decor has as much pizzazz as the food at this pan-Latin outpost conceived by star chef Richard Sandoval. Feast on such small-plate top picks as lamb shank in adobo sauce, seafood ceviche or grilled octopus, or opt for the *rodizio* menu (a series of grilled meats carved at your table; four-person minimum). Huge selection of spirits and cocktails.

AL KHAIMA MIDDLE EASTERN $$$

Map p262 (☎04 317 6000; www.alkhaima-dubai.com; Le Royal Meridien Beach Resort & Spa, Al Mamsha St, Dubai Marina; mains Dhs125-295; ⊙6pm-1am Sat-Wed, to 2am Thu & Fri Sep-Jun; P ; M Damac) On balmy nights there are few places more tranquil than Al Khaima's linen-draped terrace tables. Classic mezze such as baba ghanoush (smoked eggplant dip), *kibbeh* (cracked wheat croquettes) and hummus are orchestrated into culinary symphonies and thus are the perfect overture for platters of kebabs prepared al fresco on a sizzling charcoal grill. Wind down the evening languidly puffing on a shisha.

BICE ITALIAN $$$

Map p262 (☎04 399 1111; Hilton Dubai Jumeirah, The Walk at JBR, Dubai Marina; pasta Dhs70-195, mains Dhs150-230; ⊙12.30-3.30pm & 7-11.30pm; P ; M Jumeirah Lakes Towers, Jumeirah Beach Residence 1, Jumeirah Beach Residence 2) Back in 1930s Milan, Beatrice 'Bice' Ruggeri first opened her *trattoria*, which evolved into the city's most fashionable by the 1970s. Today Dubai's BiCE carries on the tradition by adding creative touches to such classics as oven-baked sea bass and veal tenderloin with foie gras sauce. Nice touch: the olive-oil trolley.

INDEGO BY VINEET INDIAN $$$

Map p262 (☎04 317 6000; www.indegobyvineet.com; ground fl, Tower One, Grosvenor House, Al Emreef St, Dubai Marina; mains Dhs115-240, brunch with/without alcohol Dhs350/250; ⊙7pm-midnight; P ; M Damac, Jumeirah Beach Residence 1) India's first Michelin-starred chef, Vineet Bhatia, is the menu maven at this gorgeous, intimate dining room lorded over by big brass Natraj sculptures. Dishes straddle the line between tradition and innovation, usually with exciting results.

COUQLEY BISTRO $$$

Map p262 (☎04 514 9339; www.facebook.com/CouqleyUAE; Mövenpick Hotel, Cluster A, Jumeirah Lakes Towers; mains Dhs90-180; ⊙noon-2am; M Jumeirah Lakes) This friendly French bistro imported from Lebanon plays it safe with classic decor (vintage Parisian posters, red and green checked cushions) alongside a buzzy bar playing smooth jazz and indoor 'terrace' overflowing with faux vines. The menu is equally simple, with reasonably priced French comfort food, such as *magret de canard* (seared duck breast), duck confit, *moules frites* (mussels and fries) and foie gras.

EL CHIRINGUITO MEDITERRANEAN $$$

Map p262 (☎054 449 6464; www.elchiringuitoibiza.com/dubai; Rixos The Palm, East Crescent Rd, Palm Jumeirah; mains Dhs120-160, brunch with soft drinks/alcohol Dhs395/495; ⊙10am-midnight Tue-Sat, 10am-6pm Sun; P) Imported from Ibiza, this stylish beach club features a large open restaurant and

LET'S DO BRUNCH

Friday brunch is a major element of the Dubai social scene and just about every hotel-restaurant in town sets up an all-you-can-eat buffet with an option for unlimited wine or bubbly. Some indie eateries also do brunch but without alcohol. Here are our top indulgence picks in town. Bookings are essential.

The Motherlode

Expect to loosen your belt after enjoying the cornucopia of delectables at the Friday Brunch at **Al Qasr** (p189). Options include barbecued Wagyu burgers and global treats from Bangkok, Paris and Mexico. A live two-piece band provides entertainment. Brunch with soft drinks/alcohol costs Dhs495/595.

Spice Route Brunch

The food is as sumptuous as the decor at **Asia Asia** (p115) restaurant with terrace tables overlooking the Dubai Marina. Work your way from the raw bar to the sushi selection, then feast on crab cakes and shrimp tempura before hitting the slow roasted lamb or miso-marinated salmon. Held from 2pm to 5pm on Fridays, its prices range from Dhs295 with soft drinks to Dhs649 for champange.

Jazz Brunch

The cheap and cheerful brunch at **Jazz@PizzaExpress** (p123) has you filling up on Italian faves – antipasti, pasta, thin-crust pizza – ordered à la carte and brought to your table. Live jazz sets the mood. Brunch with/without alcohol costs Dhs199/129.

International Indulgence

Bubbalicious is the culinary bonanza orchestrated at the **Westin Dubai Mina Seyahi Beach Resort & Marina** (p192). It features everything from oysters to cheesecake, plus 10 live cooking stations and family-friendly entertainment such as acrobatic performances and a play area. Brunch with soft drinks/sparkling wine/champagne will set you back Dhs450/550/680.

Afternoon Revelry

The perfect brunch for sleepyheads, the Onshore Social at the **Zero Gravity** (p119) beach club doesn't kick into gear until the afternoon, taking revellers from day to night amid an avalanche of global faves, from dim sum to antipasti and lamb chops to decadent desserts. Stay on for sunset and night-time DJ beats. Brunch costs Dhs395, but if you want sparkling wine and pool and beach access, it's bumped up to Dhs666.

Fiesta Time

Brunch by the beach at Mas Mas Maya at **Maya Modern Mexican Kitchen** (p115). Fuel up on fajitas, fresh guacamole and tangy ceviche before capping your tummy with churros and ice cream. Includes pool and beach access to the Royal Meridien Beach Resort & Spa. Brunch is on from 12.30 to 4pm on Fridays and costs Dhs325 with soft drinks and Dhs475 with alcohol.

Carnivorous Delight

Fans of churrasco grills will be in heaven at the Hola Hola brunch at **Toro Toro** (p116), a sassy Latin American outpost at the Grosvenor House. Offering the regular menu's most popular dishes (including creamy guacamole and toothsome ceviche), this brunch is a great way to sample celebrity chef Richard Sandoval's culinary concoctions. Brunch with/without alcohol costs Dhs380/300.

central DJ booth, under a faux wisteria arch, leading down to a curvaceous pool and small beach. The menu hopscotches around the Med (salade niçoise, grilled fish, lobster rolls) with many plates suited for grazing and sharing.

BLUE ORANGE INTERNATIONAL **$$$**

Map p262 (☎04 511 7373; www.blueorangedubai.com; Westin Dubai Mina Seyahi Beach Resort & Marina, King Salman BinAbdul Aziz Al Saud St, Dubai Media City; mains Dhs60-180, Friday brunch with soft drinks/sparkling wine/champagne

Dhs450/550/680; ⌚12.30-3pm Sat-Thu, 6-10.30pm Sun-Wed, to 11pm Thu-Sat, brunch 1-4pm Fri; P 📶; M Nakheel) The Westin's all-day dining restaurant has a menu that aims at pleasing all, in an airy setting with citrus-coloured furniture on a white tiled floor and views over the pool. On Fridays, it hosts one of Dubai's most popular brunches, the Bubbalicious Brunch.

BARRACUDA SEAFOOD $$$

Map p262 (☎04 452 2278; www.facebook.com/barracudarestaurantuae; Silverene Tower, Marina Walk, Dubai Marina; mains Dhs50-215; ⌚noon-1am; 📶; M Jumeirah Lakes Tower, 🚊Dubai Marina Mall) Pick your '*poisson*' (mullet, sea bream, pomfret) from the ice display at this Egyptian seafood restaurant and have it prepared the way you like it. The classic style is oven-grilled with special spices, in a method called *singary* created by fishermen in Alexandria in the 1950s.

RHODES W1 BRITISH $$$

Map p262 (☎04 317 6000; www.rw1-dubai.com; Grosvenor House, Al Emreef St, Dubai Marina; mains Dhs140-280; ⌚7-11.30pm; P 📶; M Damac, 🚊Jumeirah Beach Residence 1) Michelin-decorated chef Gary Rhodes is famous for bringing British cuisine into the 21st century. At his plant-filled white-and-citrus-hued Dubai outpost, his dedication to spinning humble classics like butter-poached salmon and roast lamb into sophisticated, zeitgeist-capturing dishes shines brightly.

Palm Jumeirah

AL NAFOORAH LEBANESE $$

Map p262 (☎04 453 0444; www.jumeirah.com; ground fl, Jumeirah Zabeel Saray, West Crescent Rd, Palm Jumeirah; mezze Dhs40-55, mains Dhs65-215; ⌚2pm-midnight; P 📶) With its carved wooden archways, midnight-blue partitions and elegant tables, Al Nafoorah is no slouch in the looks department. The menu ticks all the Lebanese food boxes – hummus, grills, shawarma – all nicely executed and presented with panache. On balmy nights, the terrace tables with a view of Dubai skyline book up quickly.

★STAY FRENCH $$$

Map p262 (☎04 440 1030; http://thepalm.oneandonlyresorts.com; One&Only The Palm, West Crescent, Palm Jumeirah; mains Dhs190-290; ⌚7-11pm Tue-Sun; P 📶; M Nakheel, Dubai Internet City, 🚝Palm Atlantis) Three-Michelin-starred Yannick Alléno brings his culinary magic to Dubai in this subtly theatrical vaulted dining room accented with black crystal chandeliers. His creations seem deceptively simple (the beef tenderloin with fries and blackpepper sauce is a best-seller), letting the superb ingredients shine brightly. An unexpected stunner is the Pastry Library, an entire wall of sweet treats.

★101 LOUNGE & BAR MEDITERRANEAN $$$

Map p262 (☎04 440 1010; http://thepalm.oneandonlyresorts.com; One&Only The Palm, West Crescent, Palm Jumeirah; mains Dhs85-295, tapas Dhs35-80; ⌚11.30am-2am Mon-Sat; 📶; M Nakheel, Dubai Internet City, 🚝Atlantis Aquaventure) It may be hard to concentrate on the food at this marina-adjacent al fresco pavilion, with to-die-for views of the Dubai Marina skyline. Come for nibbles and cocktails in the bar or go for the full dinner experience (paella, grills, pastas). New: the ultraswish Champagne Bar. Ask about the free boat shuttle when making reservations.

LITTLE MISS INDIA INDIAN $$$

Map p262 (☎04 457 3457; www.fairmont.com/palm-dubai/dining/little-miss-india; Fairmont The Palm, Palm Jumeirah; mains Dhs60-185; ⌚6.30-11.30pm; 🖉) It's hard not to be impressed by the quirky decor in this Indian restaurant. The front of a colourfully painted truck dominates the exterior facade while the back serves as a lounge bar where cocktails with a creative Indian twist are offered up. The menu has plenty of veggie options and offers hearty, good-value Indian classics served by a very friendly staff.

DUBAI TRAM

The Dubai Tram (www.alsufouhtram.com) makes 11 stops in and around the Dubai Marina area, including near the Marina Mall, The Beach at JBR and The Walk at JBR. It also connects with the Damac and Jumeirah Lakes Towers metro stations and with the Palm Jumeirah Monorail at Palm Jumeirah station.

Trams run roughly every eight minutes from 6am to 1am Saturday to Thursday and from 9am to 1am on Friday. The entire loop takes 40 minutes. The fare depends on how many zones you travel through, starting with Dhs4 for one zone. Nol Cards must be used.

LIVING IT UP IN A BEACH CLUB

If you're not staying in a five-star resort, you can still get the full luxury beach 'day-cation' experience by snagging a day pass, as many hotels set aside a limited number for visitors. Reservations are required year-round. Generally speaking, your chances of getting one are much greater from Sunday to Wednesday than on the weekend (Thursday to Saturday). Rates often include a few dirham towards food and drinks. Butler service, cabanas, cold towels etc cost extra.

Club Mina (Map p262; ☎04 399 3333; www.clubminadubai.com; Le Meridien Mina Seyahi Beach Resort, King Salman Bin Abdul Aziz Al Saud St, Dubai Media City; day pass weekday/weekend adult Dhs225/350, child Dhs125/175; P 👪; M Nahkeel) Enjoy cocktails at the swim-up bar in one of the five pools beckoning in this family-friendly beach club jointly operated by the Westin and Le Meridien Mina Seyahi beach resorts. Little ones can frolic in two covered pools designed especially for them or let off steam in the kids' club. Active types can choose from the gamut of water sports options.

Zero Gravity (Map p262; ☎04 399 0009; www.0-gravity.ae; Al Seyahi St, Skydive Dubai Drop Zone, Dubai Marina; mains Dhs50-250; ⏱8am-2am; P 📶; M Damac) Keep an eye on the Dubai Marina skyline and the daredevils jumping out of planes at this sleek beach club-bar-restaurant next to Skydive Dubai, then cap a day of chilling and swimming in the sea and new infinity pool with a night of drinks, snacks and international DJs. Nice touch: the Friday-afternoon 'brunch'.

Fairmont Beach Club (Map p262; ☎04 457 3388; www.fairmont.com/palm-dubai; Fairmont The Palm, Palm Jumeirah; day pass weekday/weekend adult Dhs250/300, child Dhs150; ⏱6.30am-8pm; P 👪; M Nakheel) Both grown-ups and kids are well taken care of at this luxurious chill zone on the Palm Jumeirah trunk with 800m of beach and with grammable views back at the Dubai Marina skyline. Aside from several pools, tickets for Fairmont Falcon Juniors' Club comes with such activities as a splash park and a climbing wall, while older kids gravitate to the Xbox, Wii and PlayStation area.

DRINKING & NIGHTLIFE

This is a great area for going out at night, especially if you're in the mood for chilling by the beach, whether with cocktails or shisha. A number of beach clubs deliver day-to-night action, and there are even a couple of alternative dance venues.

★LOCK, STOCK & BARREL — BAR

Map p262 (☎04 514 9195; www.lsbdubai.com; 8th fl, Grand Millennium Hotel, Barsha Heights; ⏱4pm-3am Mon-Thu, from 1pm Fri, from 2pm Sat & Sun) Since opening in 2016, LSB has been racking up the accolades as living proof that there's room in bling-blinded Dubai for keeping-it-real party hangouts. Dressed in industrial chic, this two-level joint is the place for mingling with unpretentious folk over cocktails and craft beer, the occasional live band and fingerlickin' American soul food. Two-for-one happy hour daily from 4pm to 8pm.

★BARASTI — BAR

Map p262 (☎04 318 1313; www.barastibeach.com; King Salman Bin Abdul Aziz Al Saud St, Dubai Media City; ⏱11am-1.30am Sat-Wed, to 3am Thu & Fri; 📶; M Nakheel) FREE Since 1995, Barasti has grown from basic beach shack to top spot for lazy days in the sand and is often jam-packed with shiny happy party people knocking back the brewskis. There's soccer and rugby on the big screen, plus pool tables, water-sports rentals, a daily happy hour, occasional bands and drink specials on most weeknights.

SMOKY BEACH — CAFE

Map p262 (www.facebook.com/smokybeach; The Beach at JBR, Dubai Marina; shisha Dhs95; ⏱9am-5am; M Jumeirah Lakes Towers, 🚊 Jumeirah Beach Residence 2) Wriggle your toes in the sand while puffing on a shisha, nibbling on mezze or sipping an exotic mocktail in this chic and trendy spot. Prices are bit steep, but the location, friendly service and comfy white-wicker armchairs make it a worthwhile splurge.

INDUSTRIAL AVENUE CLUB

Map p262 (04 511 7139; www.industrialavenuedubai.com; Westin Dubai Mina Seyahi Beach Resort & Marina, King Salman bin Abdulaziz Al Saud St, Dubai Media City; 10pm-3am Thu & Fri) With its graffiti-slathered concrete walls, mismatched furniture and cool electronic tunes, this warehouse-style club tucked behind the China Grill bar channels Shoreditch and Berlin party grit reasonably well. Drinks prices are fair. Be warned: high heels don't do well on the uneven floor.

TAP HOUSE PUB

Map p262 (04 514 3778; www.thetaphouse.ae; Club Vista Mare, Palm Jumeirah; noon-1am Sun-Wed, to 2am Thu-Sat; ; Palm Jumeirah) This gastropub is as popular with the after-work crowd as it is with families on sunny Saturday afternoons. There's a dozen beers on tap, along with bottled European brews, tap-your-own 5-litre kegs and even beer-based cocktails (try the Leffe Fashioned – Jim Beam and bitters topped with Leffe Blonde). The breezy terrace boasts views of Burj Al Arab in the distance.

If you're taking the tram, it's a five-minute taxi ride from the tram stop to Club Vista Mare, a bustling boardwalk with seven licensed restaurants and bars. It's next to Tiara Residence.

LUCKY VOICE KARAOKE

Map p262 (800 58259; www.luckyvoice.ae; Grand Millennium Hotel, Barsha Heights; karaoke per hour Dhs50 for first 2 hrs, then Dhs30; 4pm-3am; ; Dubai Internet City) This UK import features private karaoke pods where groups of six to 25 people can belt out tunes from a huge playlist without (much) fear of embarrassment. Even if you're not into singing, come for ladies' nights, Friday brunch or on nights when the house band plays highly danceable funk, rock and soul classics.

The cost of the karaoke pod goes towards your food and drink tab.

STEREO ARCADE PUB

Map p262 (052-618 2424; www.stereoarcade.com; DoubleTree by Hilton, The Walk at JBR, Dubai Marina; pub & arcade 6pm-3am, club 10pm-3am Wed-Fri; ; Jumeirah Lakes Towers, Jumeirah Beach Residence 2) Part rock pub, part retro club, with an old-school arcade thrown in for good measure, this nightspot draws a fun, unpretentious crowd. The pub has live music six nights a week and the club blares out the best of the '80s, '90s and noughties, while the arcade has synth music and classic video games like Pac-Man and Street Fighter.

NOLA EATERY & SOCIAL HOUSE BAR

Map p262 (04 399 8155; www.nola-social.com; Level B1, Armada BlueBay Hotel, Cluster P, Jumeirah Lakes Towers; noon-3am; ; Damac Properties) With a huge marble-topped bar as its centrepiece and a daily happy hour (5pm to 8pm), the New Orleans–inspired Nola is popular with the after-work crowd. It's a good-looking spot in the bowels of the Armada BlueBay Hotel, with cosy vintage decor, teal booths, outdoor terrace and live jazz on Tuesday, Friday and Saturday nights.

Drinks are well-priced and the bartenders, decked out in old-school braces and bow-ties, add to the charm. If you're feeling peckish, there's decent Louisiana-style fare such as seafood jambalaya and Cajun grills.

TRIBECA BAR

Map p262 (050 345 6067; www.tribeca.ae; JA Ocean View Hotel, Al Mamsha St, Dubai Marina; 6pm-2am Sat-Mon, to 3am Wed, 5pm-3am Thu, 1pm-3am Fri; ; Jumeirah Lakes Towers, Jumeirah Lakes Towers) With metal-plated stools, palette tables and oversized art work in a warehouse-style setting, this place works hard to channel New York, but still manages to feel distinctly local. The healthy food menu pairs well with the expansive list of libations, including organic beer, wine and spirits. On Fridays, it hosts the Hiphop Karaoke party (www.facebook.com/hhkdxb).

REEM AL BAWADI SHISHA

Map p262 (04 452 2525; www.reemalbawadi.com; Marina Walk, Dubai Marina; shisha Dhs50; 9am-3am; Damac) This is the prettiest branch of a local minichain serving regional faves in a dimly lit, endearingly over-the-top *Arabian Nights* setting complete with costumed waiters. The spacious terrace is ideal for kicking back with a shisha while keeping tabs on the marina action. It's near Spinneys.

BLISS LOUNGE BAR

Map p262 (04 315 3886; www.blissloungedubai.com; Sheraton Jumeirah Beach Resort, Al Mamsha St/Te Walk at JBR, Dubai Marina; 12.30pm-2am; ; Jumeirah Lakes Towers) Sunset is the perfect time to stake out your turf at the circular bar or on a cushiony sofa in a tented 'pod' at this beachfront lounge with view of the Ain Dubai Ferris wheel. Kick back with a cold one or a shisha while nibbling on sushi and taking in some chill jazz or deep house courtesy of a resident DJ.

JETTY LOUNGE BAR

Map p262 (☎04 399 9999; www.royalmirage.oneandonlyresorts.com; One&Only Royal Mirage, The Palace, King Salman Bin Abdul Aziz Al Saud St, Dubai Media City; ⏲2pm-2am; 📶; Ⓜ Nakheel, 🚊Palm Jumeirah) From the moment you start following the meandering path through One&Only's luxuriant gardens, you'll sense that you're heading for a pretty special place. Classy without the pretence, Jetty Lounge is all about unwinding (preferably at sunset) on plush white sofas scattered right in the sand. There's a full bar menu and global snacks for nibbling.

SIDDHARTA LOUNGE BAR

Map p262 (☎04 317 6000; www.siddhartalounge.com; Tower 2, Grosvenor House, Al Emreef St, Al Saud St, Dubai Marina; ⏲12.30-3.30pm & 6.30-midnight Sat-Wed, 6pm-12.30am Thu & Fri; 📶; Ⓜ Damac) Part of Buddha Bar in the same hotel, Siddharta is an urban oasis and great spot to join Dubai's glam crowd in taking the party from daytime by the pool to basking in the glow of the Marina high-rises at night. Nice music, expertly mixed cocktails and swift service make up for the rather steep price tab.

BLUE MARLIN IBIZA UAE CLUB

(☎056 113 3400; www.bluemarlinibiza-uae.com; Golden Tulip Al Jazira Hotel, Ghantoot; ⏲1-11pm Fri; 📶) This Ibiza-style beachside 'meet' market is one of Dubai's top day-to-night dance clubs and worth the trek out of town on Fridays, especially when big-time DJs fuel the party. Expect lots of wrinkle-free, hormone-happy hotties showing off their tan.

CASA LATINA BAR

Map p262 (☎04 399 6699; www.facebook.com/pg/Casalatinaofficialpage; ground fl, Ibis Hotel Al Barsha, Sheikh Zayed Rd, Al Barsha 1; ⏲6pm-2am; 📶; Ⓜ Sharaf DG) With its alt-vibe, candlelit booths and inexpensive drinks, this Cuban-themed bar attracts a non-poser crowd that's more into the music than looking good. It also hosts two of the most happening monthly parties, the punk-indie-eclectic Bad House Party and the awesome Bassworx drum and bass session. Happy hour from 6pm to 8pm.

ATELIER M BAR

Map p262 (☎04 450 7766; www.atelierm.ae; 7th fl, Pier 7, Marina Walk, Dubai Marina; ⏲6pm-2am Sat-Mon & Wed, to 3am Tue, Thu & Fri; 📶; Ⓜ Damac, 🚊Dubai Marina Mall) Home-grown Atelier M delivers a double treat atop the circular Pier 7 building. The lift drops you at the restaurant, which serves respectable French-Asian fare, but for the party you need to

DUBAI MARINA CRUISING

Dubai Ferry Cruises (Map p262; ☎800 9090; www.rta.ae; Marina Walk, Dubai Marina; gold/silver ticket Dhs75/50; Ⓜ Damac) Dubai Ferry runs several mini-cruises from its landing docks near the Dubai Marina Mall. Aside from scheduled daily departures at 11am, 1pm and 6.30pm up the coast to Al Ghubaiba terminal on Dubai Creek, there's a 70-minute sightseeing trip to the Burj Al Arab at 3pm and sunset cruise to the Atlantis The Palm at 5pm.

Dubai Marina Water Bus (Map p262; www.rta.ae; Dubai Marina; tickets Dhs3-11, one-day pass Dhs25; ⏲10am-11pm Sat-Thu, noon-midnight Fri; Ⓜ Damac) For a scenic spin around the Dubai Marina, hop aboard the Water Bus, which shuttles between the Marina Walk, Marina Terrace, Marina Mall and Marina Promenade every 15 to 20 minutes. It's especially lovely at sunset or after dark, as boats float past the show-stopping parade of shimmering towers. Nol cards are valid.

Dhow Cruise (Map p262; ☎04 336 8407; www.tour-dubai.com; Tour Dubai, Marina Walk, below Al Gharbi St bridge, Dubai Marina; 1hr tour adult/child Dhs65/55, dinner cruises Dhs300/150; Ⓜ Jumeirah Lakes Towers, 🚊Dubai Marina Mall) Local company Tour Dubai runs guided one-hour boat tours with prerecorded English commentary aboard nostalgic dhows outfitted with colourful upholstered benches. There are eight tours daily between 10.30am and 5.30pm. In the evening, the dhows set sail for a two-hour dinner buffet with taped music. Alcohol is available.

head up to the rooftop lounge for killer views, the full spectrum of booze options and DJs keen on kicking up the energy.

PURE SKY LOUNGE BAR

Map p262 (☎04 399 1111; Hilton Dubai Jumeirah, The Walk at JBR, Dubai Marina; ⏰5pm-1am; 📶; Ⓜ Damac, 🚊 Jumeirah Beach Residence 1) When it comes to glorious views over The Beach at JBR and Palm Jumeirah, this chic indoor-outdoor lounge is in a lofty league on the 35th floor of the beachfront Hilton. White furniture accented with turquoise pillows channels a chill, maritime mood.

Try the signature Dubai Iced Tea and, if in a group, the Sharing Bomb Alaska, a devilish selection of eight desserts.

BUDDHA BAR BAR

Map p262 (☎04 317 6000; www.buddhabar-dubai.com; Grosvenor House, Al Emreef St, Dubai Marina; ⏰7pm-1.30am Sat-Wed, to 2.30am Thu & Fri; 📶; Ⓜ Damac, 🚊 Dubai Marina Mall) Dinner at perennially popular Buddha Bar always feels like a special occasion thanks to the theatrical design complete with a 7m-tall Buddha and the broad-spectrum Asian menu. But this is also a nightlife spot with an upstairs lounge, DJs three nights a week and superb handcrafted cocktails.

A good occasion to polish those shoes and get out the high heels.

ROOFTOP LOUNGE & TERRACE BAR

Map p262 (☎04 399 9999; http://royalmirage.oneandonlyresorts.com; Arabian Court, One&Only Royal Mirage, King Salman Bin Abdul Aziz Al Saud St, Dubai Media City; ⏰5pm-1am; 📶; Ⓜ Nakheel, 🚊 Palm Jumeirah) With its fabric-draped banquettes, Moroccan lanterns and oriental carpets, this lounge is one of Dubai's classiest sports bars. Catch live games in the circular bar, then report to the rooftop for chilling under the stars. There's also a good menu of mezze, in case you're feeling peckish.

OBSERVATORY BAR

Map p262 (☎04 319 4795; http://marriottharbourdubaidining.com; Dubai Marriott Harbour Hotel & Suites, King Salman Bin Abdul Aziz Al Saud St, Dubai Marina; ⏰noon-1am; 📶; Ⓜ Damac) Home of the guilt-free ladies' night where drinks have no more than 150 calories, the Observatory also scores with skyline lovers thanks to its eye-popping 360-degree views from the 52nd floor of the Marriott. Happy hour runs daily from 5pm to 10pm.

DEK ON 8 BAR

Map p262 (☎04 427 1000; www.mediaonehotel.com; Media One Hotel, Al Falak St, Dubai Media City; ⏰noon-midnight; 📶; Ⓜ Nakheel) Mingle with the after-work crowd beside the pool at this al fresco chill zone on the 8th floor of the Media One Hotel. Fashionable crowd, relaxed vibe, shisha and nice city views.

TAMANYA TERRACE BAR

Map p262 (☎04 366 9131; www.radissonblu.com/hotel-mediacitydubai; 8th fl, West Tower, Radisson Blu Hotel, Dubai Media City; ⏰5pm-2am Sun-Thu, 6pm-2am Fri & Sat; 📶; Ⓜ Nakheel) On the 8th floor of the Radisson, this is a fab spot for kicking off a long night of partying with sundowners against the backdrop of the forest of sparkling Marina skyscrapers. Mod furnishings, sassy lighting and international DJs fuel the ambience, especially during electro-heavy 'Night Vibes' on Fridays.

ARABIAN COURTYARD SHISHA

Map p262 (☎04 399 9999; http://royalmirage.oneandonlyresorts.com; One&Only Royal Mirage, Arabian Court, King Salman Bin Abdul Aziz Al Saud St, Dubai Media City; ⏰7pm-1am; 📶; Ⓜ Nakheel, 🚊 Palm Jumeirah) Reclining on beaded cushions and thick carpets and puffing on a shisha will make you feel as if you're in the *majlis* (reception room) of a local home, while mezze for nibbling and a live Arabic band complete the exotic experience. There's another shisha courtyard in the resort's Palace wing.

N'DULGE CLUB

Map p262 (☎04 426 0561; www.atlantisthepalm.com; Atlantis The Palm, Crescent Rd, Palm Jumeirah; ⏰9pm-3am Thu & Sat, 4pm-3am Fri; 🚝 Aquaventure) This massive club has something for everyone: a huge dance floor, a cabana-lined terrace for shisha and chilling, and a lounge for restoring energies with bar bites. It's popular with holiday-goers and with expats trying to stave off the post-Friday brunch stupor with hip-hop and R & B.

☆ ENTERTAINMENT

JAZZ@PIZZAEXPRESS LIVE MUSIC

Map p262 (☎04 441 6342; www.pizzaexpressuae.com; Cluster A, Jumeirah Lakes Towers; ⏰noon-1am Sat-Wed, to 3am Thu & Fri; 📶; Ⓜ Jumeirah Lakes Towers) It's really a pizza

WORTH A DETOUR

OUTLET SHOPPING

Everybody loves a bargain, but sometimes you just gotta drive a bit to get one. Dubai's two main outlet malls are worth the trip out into the desert.

Outlet Village (☎04 317 3999; www.theoutletvillage.ae; Jebel Ali Rd; ⏲10am-10pm Sun-Wed, to midnight Thu-Sat) Label lovers on a budget flock to this indoor outlet mall whose architecture was inspired by a Tuscan hillside village. Midrange to fancy brands from Banana Republic to Armani have shoppers reaching for their credit cards. It's about 30km south of the Dubai Marina, next to Dubai Parks and Resorts.

Dubai Outlet Mall (DOM; ☎04 423 4666; www.dubaioutletmall.com; Dubai–Al Ain Rd (Hwy E66); ⏲10am-10pm Sat-Wed, to midnight Thu & Fri) The first outlet mall in the Middle East is a bargain shopper's nirvana with 240 stores offering discounts ranging from 30% to 90%. Don't expect the latest season items (more like 'last' season) from such retailers as Diesel, Guess and Mango.

It's about 20km east of the Burj Khalifa. If you don't have your own transportation, ask at your hotel about the free shuttle provided by the mall.

joint tucked amid residential high-rises, but this pretence-free place gets hopping just about nightly with open-mic jam sessions, swing nights, acoustic songwriter nights and happening bands. It's next to Mövenpick Hotel.

MUSICHALL LIVE MUSIC

Map p262 (☎056 270 8670; www.jumeirah.com; ground fl, Jumeirah Zabeel Saray, West Crescent, Palm Jumeirah; mains Dhs170-290, minimum spend Dhs450; ⏲9pm-3am Thu & Fri; Aquaventure) It's not a theatre, not a club, not a bar and not a restaurant – the lavishly designed MusicHall is all those things. The concept hails from Beirut, where it's had audiences clapping since 2003 with an eclectic line-up of 10 live music acts – from Indian to country, and rock to Russian ballads. The food (fusion cuisine and international finger food) is an afterthought.

SHOPPING

Dubai Marina and Palm Jumeirah are not known as shopping havens, but there are a few malls as well as shops and boutiques along The Walk at JBR and The Beach at JBR to sate any browsing and spending urges.

IBN BATTUTA MALL MALL

Map p262 (☎04 390 9999; www.ibnbattutamall.com; Sheikh Zayed Rd, btwn Interchanges No 5 & No 6, Jebel Ali; ⏲10am-10pm Sun-Wed, to midnight Thu-Sat; ; MIbn Battuta) The shopping is good if nothing extraordinary, but it's the lavish and exotic design and architecture of this 400-shop mall that steal the show, which traces the way stations of 14th-century Arab explorer Ibn Battuta in six themed courts (China, Persia, Egypt, India, Tunisia, Andalusia). Anchor stores include Debenhams and Decathlon.

A new walkway links the mall to the metro station, and another extension under way at the time of writing will centre on a glass-covered courtyard and also add a new movie theatre and hotel.

GALLERY ONE ART

Map p262 (☎04 423 1987; www.g-1.com; The Walk at JBR, Dubai Marina; ⏲10am-10pm; MJumeirah Lakes Towers, Jumeirah Beach Residence 1) If you love art but can't afford an original, pick up a highly decorative print by well-known Middle Eastern artists without breaking the bank at this gallery shop. Some motifs are also available as greetings cards, posters, notebooks and calendars.

Other Dubai branches include those at Souq Madinat Jumeirah, Dubai Mall and Mercato Mall.

DUBAI MARINA MALL MALL

Map p262 (☎04 436 1020; www.dubaimarinamall.com; Dubai Marina Walk, Dubai Marina; ⏲10am-11pm Sat-Wed, to midnight Thu & Fri; ; MDamac) This mall has an attractive waterfront setting and a manageable 140 stores on four floors, so you won't get lost quite so readily as in its mega-size cousins. Its main architectural feature is the giant atrium where kids can trundle around in a toy train.

WORTH A DETOUR

DUBAI: THEME PARK CAPITAL

Not content with boasting the world's tallest building, an indoor ski slope and a palm-shaped island, Dubai is now also striving to become the theme park capital of the Middle East. In fact, an entire amusement park district, called Dubai Parks and Resorts (DPR), has sprung up in the southern suburb of Jebel Ali, about 30km southwest of Dubai Marina. The closest Metro station is UAE Exchange from where it's a 15-minute taxi ride to the park.

Motiongate (04 820 0000; www.motiongatedubai.com; adult/child Dhs330/280; 11am-8pm Sun-Wed, to 10pm Thu-Sat;) Whether you're seeking thrills or a family-friendly day out, this Hollywood-inspired theme park has something for everyone. The park is divided into four zones – DreamWorks, Lionsgate, Columbia Pictures and Smurfs Village – with 27 rides and attractions, including the world's first roller coaster inspired by *The Hunger Games*, river rapids, dark rides, 4D theatre rides, stage shows and kids' rides.

Bollywood Parks Dubai (04 820 0000; www.bollywoodparksdubai.com; adult/child Dhs285/245; noon-9pm Sat-Wed, to 10pm Thu & Fri;) Spread across five zones, Bollywood Parks celebrates Mumbai's legendary film industry. There's a handful of 3D and 4D rides based on blockbusters such as *Lagaan* and *Sholay*, along with a stunt show, interactive movie-maker experience and six restaurants. But it's really all about song and dance, with up to 30 live shows daily that are colourful, kitsch and utterly infectious.

Legoland Dubai (04 820 0000; www.legoland.com/dubai; adult/child Dhs295/250; 10am-6pm Sun-Thu, to 8pm Fri & Sat;) Designed for kids under 12, this colourful theme park has 40 rides and attractions across six themed areas. There's plenty to keep youngsters entertained including pedal cars and Duplo planes, while older kids will love the Dragon roller coaster and Power Tower 'free-fall' ride. Miniland is another highlight, with incredibly detailed miniature Lego versions of landmarks, such as the Burj Khalifa.

Legoland Water Park (04 820 0000; www.legoland.com; adult/child Dhs215/185; 10am-6pm;) This watery wonderland has more than 15 attractions, including the Joker Soaker playground with a 300-gallon bucket that dumps a downpour every few minutes. Along with tube rides and racing slides, there's a huge wave pool, lazy river with inflatable rafts and shaded Duplo area for toddlers. Facilities include a baby room with microwave, life jackets and tot-sized sunloungers.

GINGER & LACE FASHION & ACCESSORIES

Map p262 (04 368 5109; www.facebook.com/gingerandlace; Ibn Battuta Mall, Sheikh Zayed Rd, Jebel Ali; 10am-10pm Sun-Wed, to midnight Thu-Sat; MIbn Battuta) This indie shop in Ibn Battuta's India Court stocks an eclectic and rotating selection of colourful, whimsical fashion by high-spirited designers from around the globe. Much of the clothing is rather flashy, so dedicated wallflowers may want to look elsewhere.

SPORTS & ACTIVITIES

Hugging the Gulf, Dubai Marina and Palm Jumeirah are tailor-made for boating and water sports, but there are plenty of other popular outdoor diversions, including hitting the jogging trails, pumping iron by the beach, seaside yoga and parachuting out of an aeroplane. Out on Palm Jumeirah, a huge water park beckons.

AQUA FUN WATER PARK

Map p262 (http://aquafun.ae; Dhs120; 9am-6pm) Touted as the world's first inflatable water park, this small but challenging aqua park packs a punch. Don a lifejacket and get set to clamber, climb, slip and stumble over a network of floating obstacles. Popular with kids and adults alike, it's more challenging than it looks, and it's a great way to spend a few hours playing in the Gulf. Prepare to get wet.

SKYDIVE DUBAI SKYDIVING

Map p262 (04 377 8888; www.skydivedubai.ae; Al Seyahi St, Dubai Marina; tandem jump, video & photos Dhs2000; ⌚8am-4pm Mon-Sat; Ⓜ Damac) Daredevils can experience the rush of jumping out of a plane and seeing Palm Jumeirah and the Dubai skyline from the air by signing up for these tandem parachute flights. The minimum age is 18; weight and height restrictions apply as well.

For this ultimate thrill ride, you get to leap out of a turboprop at 4000m (harnessed to your instructor), scream your head off while free-falling for about one minute (an eternity!) until the parachute opens, and you glide gently back to earth in another five minutes. A third jumper immortalises your epic adventure on camera.

Opening hours vary seasonally, so check before you go.

SPLASH PAD WATER PARK

Map p262 (www.splashpaddubai.com; The Beach at JBR, Dubai Marina; per 1/24hr Dhs65/95; ⌚9am-8pm; 👪; Ⓜ Jumeirah Lakes Towers, 🚋 Jumeirah Beach Residence 2) Preschoolers can keep cool in the fountains, sprinklers, tipping buckets and other watery fun spots at this cheerfully coloured mini water park right next to the sand. The fenced-in area also includes a dry-play area with swings, see-saws and climbing frames.

EMIRATES GOLF CLUB GOLF

Map p262 (☎04 380 1234, 04 417 9800; www.dubaigolf.com; Interchange No 5, Sheikh Zayed Rd, Emirates Hills 2; Majlis/Faldo Sun-Thu Dhs995/595, Fri & Sat Dhs1200/695; Ⓜ Nakheel; 📶) This prestigious club has two courses: the flagship international championship Majlis course, which hosts the annual **Dubai Desert Classic** (☎04 383 3588; www.omegadubaidesertclassic.com; tickets Dhs75-175; ⌚Feb), and the Faldo course, which is the only floodlit 18-hole course in the country. Beginners can go wild on the par-three nine-hole course (peak/off-peak Dhs130/95).

Rates drop significantly from late May to mid-September.

YOGA BY THE SEA YOGA

Map p262 (☎800 637 227; www.thebeach.ae/whats-on/yoga-by-the-sea; South Lawn, The Beach at JBR, Dubai Marina; ⌚7-8am Mon, Wed, Fri & Sat Nov-Apr; Ⓜ Jumeirah Lakes Towers, 🚋 JBR Residence 2) FREE Novices and seasoned yogis alike flock to greet the day with sun salutations facing the serene waters of the Gulf. It's first-come, first-serve and hugely popular. Come at least half an hour early and bring your own mat and towel.

ONE&ONLY SPA SPA

Map p262 (☎04 315 2140; http://royalmirage.oneandonlyresorts.com; One&Only Royal Mirage, King Salman Bin Abdul Aziz Al Saud St, Dubai Media City; ⌚9.30am-9pm (women only until 1pm); Ⓜ Nakheel) Do you want to unwind, restore or elevate? These are the magic words at this exclusive spa with a dozen treatment rooms where massages, wraps, scrubs and facials are calibrated to achieve your chosen goal. Staff can help find the perfect massage or wrap for whatever ails you. A favourite is a session in the Oriental Hammam.

BEACH GYM GYM

Map p262 (☎04 323 2323; The Beach, Jumeirah Beach Residence, Dubai Marina; day pass Dhs60; ⌚6am-midnight Sun-Wed, to 11pm Thu-Sat; Ⓜ Jumeirah Lakes Towers, 🚋 Jumeirah Beach Residence 2) Work on your six pack and your tan at the same time at this outdoor gym right next to the waves, which has CrossFit equipment plus rope climbs, kettle bells, rowing machines and jumpboxes. It's busiest in the early morning and from late afternoon.

ATLANTIS ABRA RIDE BOATING

Map p262 (☎04 426 2000; www.atlantisthepalm.com; Atlantis The Palm, Palm Jumeirah; Dhs65; ⌚1-9pm; Ⓜ Palm Atlantis) If you want to see the humongous Atlantis complex from the water, sign up for this 20-minute ride in an electric abra that takes you from Nasimi beach to the end of the Aquaventure Waterpark. There's no need to book. Just show up.

PALM JUMEIRAH BOARDWALK WALKING

Map p262 (Palm Jumeirah; ⌚24hr) FREE This 11km paved promenade opened in November 2016 stretches across the entire Gulf-facing side of Palm Jumeirah's outer crescent and is popular for walks in the sea breeze. Food trucks provide refreshments, but for now there's little shade and cycling is – sadly – a no-no.

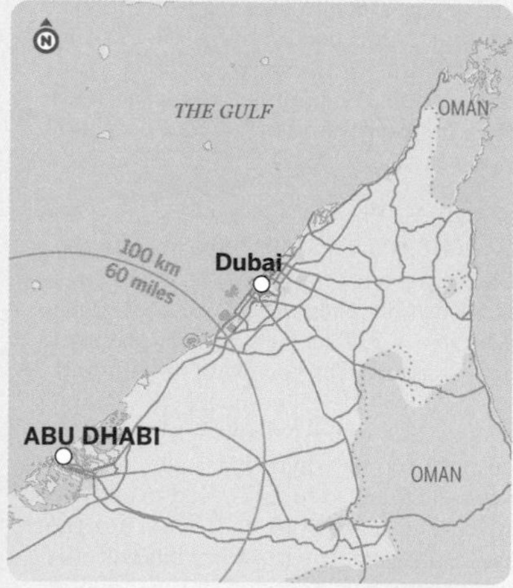

Abu Dhabi

TOP SIGHT

SHEIKH ZAYED GRAND MOSQUE

Rising majestically from beautifully manicured gardens and visible from each of the bridges joining Abu Dhabi Island to the mainland, the Sheikh Zayed Grand Mosque represents an impressive welcome to the city. Conceived by the first president of the United Arab Emirates, Sheikh Zayed, and marking his final resting place, the mosque accommodates 50,000 worshippers and is one of the few in the region open to non-Muslims.

Architecture

With more than 80 marble domes on a roofline held aloft by 1000 pillars and punctuated by four 107m-high minarets, Sheikh Zayed Grand Mosque is a masterpiece of modern Islamic architecture and design. More than 90,000 tonnes of pure white marble was used in its construction. Delicate floral designs inlaid with semi-precious stones, such as lapis lazuli, red agate, amethyst, abalone, jasper and mother-of-pearl, decorate a variety of marbles and contrast with the more traditional geometric ceramic details.

Interior

While it includes references to Mamluk, Ottoman and Fatimid styles, the overwhelming impression of the breathtaking interior is contemporary and innovative, with three steel, gold, brass and crystal chandeliers filling the main prayer hall with shafts of primary-coloured light. The chandeliers, the largest of which weighs approximately 11 tonnes, sparkle with Swarovski crystals and shine with 40kg of 24-karat galvanised gold.

Hand-Loomed Carpet

One of the prayer hall's most impressive features is the world's largest loomed carpet fashioned from Iranian cotton and New Zealand wool and flown in from Mashad, Iran, on two aeroplanes. The medallion design with elaborate arabesque motifs took 1200 craftspeople two years to complete, half of which was spent on hand-knotting the 5700 sq metres of woollen thread on a cotton base. That translates as 2.268 billion knots!

Mausoleum

Sheikh Zayed's mausoleum is on the approach to the mosque entrance, though only sitting presidents are allowed to enter. Prayers are continually recited by attendants here in one-hour shifts 24/7 (the cycles takes 1½ to two days to complete). While photographs of the mausoleum are not permitted, visitors are free to photograph all other parts of the mosque, but sensitivity should be shown towards those in prayer.

Visiting Etiquette

Visitors are welcome to enter the mosque except during prayer times. A worthwhile free 45-minute guided tour (in English and Arabic) helps explain some fundamentals of the Islamic religion while pointing out some of the stylistic highlights of the interior (otherwise comprehensive audio tours are available in 11 languages). Mosque etiquette requires all visitors to wear long, loose-fitting, ankle-length trousers or skirts, long sleeves and a headscarf for women. Those not dressed appropriately are asked to go into a changing room at security, where hooded abayas and kandouras can be borrowed for free.

DON'T MISS

- Hand-loomed carpet
- Swarovski chandeliers
- Inlaid floral designs decorating walls and pillars

PRACTICALITIES

- Map p151, B2
- ☎02 419 1919
- www.szgmc.ae
- off Sheikh Rashid Bin Saeed St
- admission free
- ⏲9am-10pm Sat-Thu, 4.30-10pm Fri, tours 10am, 11am, 2pm, 5pm & 7pm Sun-Thu, 5pm & 7pm Fri

Explore

The world's largest hand-loomed carpet, the fastest roller coaster, the highest high tea, the tower with the greatest lean, the largest cluster of cultural buildings of the 21st century – UAE capital Abu Dhabi isn't afraid to challenge world records. Welcome to an exciting city where nothing stands still... except perhaps the herons in its mangroves.

For those looking to engage with Gulf culture, Abu Dhabi offers opportunities to understand the UAE's history through museums, exhibitions, tours and food. But thankfully Emirati heritage isn't boxed and mothballed; it's also experienced through strolls around the dhow harbour, haggling in markets, absorbing the atmosphere at shisha cafes and strolling its lengthy and cinematic Corniche.

The Best...

➡ **Sights** Sheikh Zayed Grand Mosque (p127), Louvre Abu Dhabi (p156), Emirates Palace (p135), Abu Dhabi Heritage Village (p141), The Corniche (p129)

➡ **Places to Eat** Bait El Khetyar (p130), Zahrat Lebnan (p130), Zuma (p147), Butcher & Still (p147), Beach House (p158)

➡ **Activities** Kayaking through mangroves (p149), Ferrari World (p160), Yas Waterworld (p164), driving on the Yas Marina Circuit (p164)

Top Tips

➡ Abu Dhabi is fairly safe, and walkable day and night.

➡ Key areas are Breakwater, the Corniche and several blocks inland.

➡ Navigation is easy with a grid system, although road names are confusing.

➡ Big Bus Tour links main sights in suburbs and islands.

Getting There & Away

➡ **Air** Abu Dhabi International Airport (p216) is about 30km east of the city centre and served by more than 50 airlines flying to 85 cities.

➡ **Bus** The central bus terminal is about 4km south of the Corniche. RTA bus E100 leaves for Dubai's Al Ghubaiba bus station in Bur Dubai every 30 minutes from 4.30am to midnight (Dhs25, two hours).

➡ **Car** Abu Dhabi is 140km south of Dubai via Hwy E11.

➡ **Taxi** A taxi ride to Dubai or Al Ain costs around Dhs300 and can be booked in advance. Try **Abu Dhabi Taxi** (☎600 535 353; www.transad.ae).

Getting Around

➡ **Abu Dhabi City Bus** Operates on 14 routes around the clock. Useful routes: bus 5 links Marina Mall and Al Maryah Island via Al Zahiya; bus 54 links Al Zahiya and the Sheikh Zayed Grand Mosque. For trip planning, check http://dot.abudhabi.ae.

➡ **Yas Express** Free service links major attractions on Yas Island at least once hourly on three routes. See www.yasisland.ae for details.

➡ **Taxi** Cabs can be flagged down or ordered through the call centre (p128) (Dhs4 to Dhs5 fee). They are metered with a Dhs5 at flagfall (Dhs20 at the airport) plus Dhs1.82 per kilometre. There's a surcharge between 10pm and 6am and a Dhs12 minimum fare at times.

➡ **Water taxi** Traditional **water taxis** (Map p151; ☎050 133 2060; www.captaintonys.ae; ⏲4-10pm, 8pm-midnight during Ramadan), called abras, ply the waters of Khor Al Maqta, and also link to the Eastern Mangroves Hotel & Spa.

Need to Know

➡ **Area code** 02

➡ **Location** 140km southwest of Downtown Dubai.

➡ **Tourist Office** Abu Dhabi Tourism & Culture Authority (p227)

Al Markaziyah

Although Abu Dhabi teems with vibrant districts, if you had to put your finger on the one that represents its centre, then the area around the city's oldest building, Qasr Al Hosn, is surely it. At the beating heart of this central district is the World Trade Center, built on the site of the city's original souq. The district is busy day and night with city traders, office workers, shoppers and visitors.

SIGHTS

An effort by modern town planners to make the city green has resulted in numerous attractive parks and gardens, many of which are arranged along the inland side of the Corniche. A walk or cycle along the seaboard side of the Corniche is a good a way to view the main buildings of this district before plunging into the teeming city centre in and around Hamdan and Zayed the First Sts.

★QASR AL HOSN — FORT

Map p136 (White Fort; ☎02 697 6472; www.qasralhosn.ae; Sheikh Zayed the First St; ⌚9am-8pm) FREE Featured on the back of the Dhs1000 note, this iconic fort started life in 1760 as a watchtower that safeguarded a precious freshwater well. After an expansion, it became the ancestral home of the ruling Al Nahyan family in 1793 and remained a royal residence until 1966 (its historic watchtower is Abu Dhabi's oldest surviving structure). In a free, yearly-changing exhibit, photographs, archaeological finds, models and other objects chart the history of Abu Dhabi and its people.

KHALIFA MOSQUE — MOSQUE

Map p136 (Khalid Bin Al Walid St) In common with all mosques in the city, this beautiful mosque stands in nonalignment with the grid system, honouring the direction of Mecca instead. It is closed to non-Muslims.

★ABU DHABI CORNICHE — WATERFRONT

Map p136 The waterfront Corniche, with its white sandy beaches and generous promenade, stretches the entire length of the northwest shore of the city. Giving spectacular views of the iconic high-rise tower blocks assembled along the seafront, it also offers one of the city's main recreation opportunities with a dedicated walking and separate cycle path weaving in and out of the Corniche's landscaped gardens. Refreshments are available from the public beaches that punctuate the western section of the road.

CORNICHE BEACH — BEACH

Map p136 (www.bakeuae.com; Corniche Rd (West); adult/child Dhs10/5; ⌚8am-8pm) There are several gates to this spotlessly maintained, Blue-Flagged public beach. The turquoise sea, view of Lulu Island, palm trees and gardens make it an unexpected pleasure in the heart of a capital city. A lifeguard is on duty until sunset.

AL MARKAZIYAH GARDENS — PARK

Map p136 (Corniche Rd (West); ⌚24hr) Spread over three distinct areas, Al Nahyan Park, Family Park and Urban Park, Al Markaziyah Gardens forms a broad band of recreational lawns parallel to the Corniche. The facilities offer toddler and children play areas, fountains and shaded seating.

LAKE PARK & FORMAL PARK — PARK

Map p136 (Corniche Rd (East); ⌚24hr) FREE These two shady parks straddling 4th St and spreading along the Corniche provide a welcome respite to the intense traffic and crowds of downtown. The centrepiece of Lake Park is the 15m-high fountain; there is also a popular shisha cafe beside the lake. Formal Park has a maze, barbecue pits and an exercise track.

CAPITAL GARDENS — PARK

Map p136 (Muroor Rd, near Khalifa St; adult/child Dhs1/free; ⌚8am-10pm Sun-Wed, to 11pm Thu-Sat) This park in the heart of downtown offers two multipurpose playgrounds, a mini climbing wall and basketball and football areas; and there's an erupting fountain giving a bit of lively respite from the stifling heat of summer.

BURJ MOHAMMED BIN RASHID — NOTABLE BUILDING

Map p136 (Khalifa Bin Zayed the First St) This 92-floor, 382m giant among tower blocks forms part of the World Trade Center and is an important landmark in this mixed-use development marking the middle of downtown. Not only is this Abu Dhabi's tallest building (at least for now), but it may just be unique in having an indoor terraced garden on the 90th floor. The tower is the taller of two matching towers with distinctive sloping, elliptical roofs that look remarkable when lit at night.

ETISALAT HEAD OFFICE — NOTABLE BUILDING

Map p136 (www.etisalat.ae; cnr Sheikh Zayed the First & Sheikh Rashid Bin Saeed Al Maktoum Sts) This iconic 27-floor building, with a 'golf ball' as its crowning glory, makes an excellent landmark for navigating the city's grid system. Built in 2001, it houses the headquarters of the local telephone service provider.

Greater Abu Dhabi

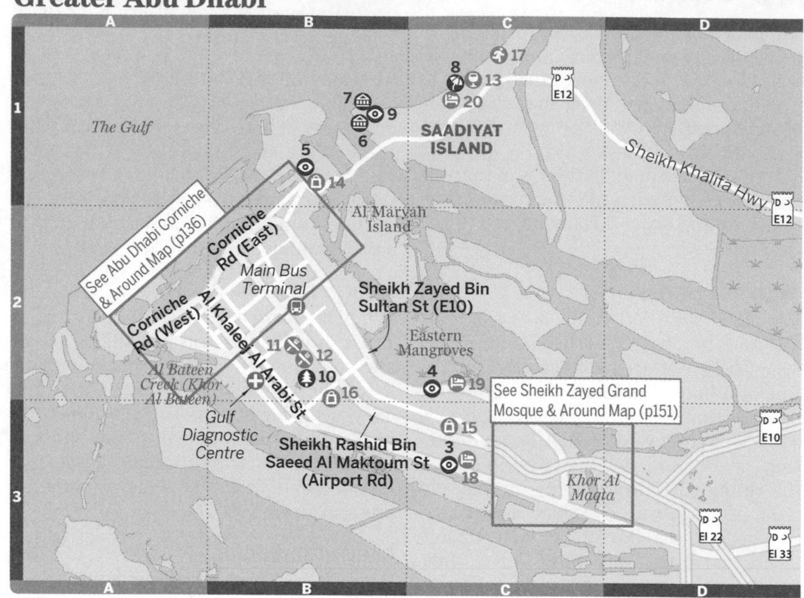

STREET SCULPTURES MONUMENT

Map p136 (2nd & Khalifa Sts) There was a time when no self-respecting Gulf city would be seen without a giant concrete coffee pot. Those days have gone, for better or for worse, but a little reminder of the pioneering days of oil riches and the city development they brought can be seen in the traffic island between the World Trade Center and Etisalat buildings.

EATING

Al Markaziyah is the quarter of cafes, coffee shops, curry houses, chop shops, kebab corners and shawarma stands. Strike out south of Zayed the First St and explore the teeming eateries north of Al Manhal district. The dozens of local, authentic options bear names like Syrian Palace, Lebanese Flower and Turkish Sheep. You can't go too wrong, but it's best to pick the busiest.

★BAIT EL KHETYAR JORDANIAN $

Map p136 (☎02 633 3200; Fatima Bint Mubarak St; shawarma Dhs6-35; ⏲8am-midnight Sun-Thu, 8am-noon & 1pm-midnight Fri) This can't-miss, mostly Jordanian hotspot makes Abu Dhabi's best shawarma, carved from two massive spits (one chicken, one beef) and served sandwiched, sliced or plated to legions of connoisseurs in simple yet stylish surrounds. Equally impressive is the house hummus (with chickpeas, tomatoes, onions and parsley) and *labneh* (yoghurt) with garlic. *Yalla!*

★ZAHRAT LEBNAN LEBANESE $

Map p136 (Lebanese Flower; ☎02 667 5924; near Zayed the First St, Al Manhal; mains Dhs22-55; ⏲7am-3am) Amid a cluster of Middle Eastern snack, grill and pastry outlets, a short walk from Al Husn Fort, the Lebanese Flower is a local legend, attracting a multinational clientele of city residents. The generous excellent-value plates of mezze include traditional favourites such as chicken livers, fried halloumi and tabbouleh. There's a pleasant family section upstairs.

CAFETERIA AL LIWAN SYRIAN $

Map p136 (☎02 622 1250; www.facebook.com/liwanabudhabi; Najda St; mains Dhs20-40; ⏲8.30am-11.30pm Sun-Thu, noon-1am Fri) This brilliant, cash-only budget eatery will exceed your expectations every chance it gets. It serves Damascene specialities (outstanding falafel, some of Abu Dhabi's best hummus, a beautiful beetroot *moutabel*) in a rustic but welcoming environment with graffitied walls, wood chairs and low-slung brass tables.

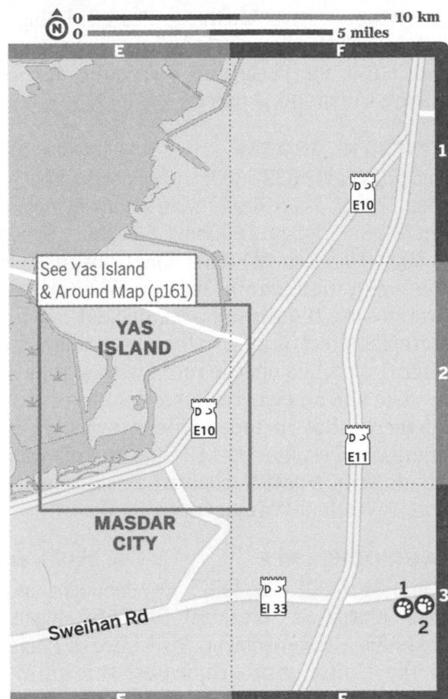

Greater Abu Dhabi

Sights

1	Abu Dhabi Falcon Hospital	F3
2	Arabian Saluki Centre	F3
3	Capital Gate	C3
4	Eastern Mangroves Promenade	C2
5	Fruit & Vegetable Market	B1
	Guggenheim Abu Dhabi	(see 7)
6	Louvre Abu Dhabi	B1
7	Manarat Al Saadiyat	B1
8	Saadiyat Public Beach	C1
9	UAE Pavilion	B1
10	Umm Al Emarat Park	B2

Eating

	18°	(see 3)
	Beach House	(see 20)
11	Café Arabia	B2
	Home Bakery	(see 12)
12	Salt	B2

Drinking & Nightlife

	Beach House Rooftop	(see 20)
13	Buddha-Bar Beach	C1
	De La Costa	(see 17)
	Relax@12	(see 18)

Shopping

14	Carpet Souq	B1
15	Paris Avenue	C3
16	Women's Handicraft Centre	B2

Sports & Activities

	Abu Dhabi Pearl Journey	(see 19)
	Anantara Spa	(see 19)
17	Saadiyat Beach Club	C1

Sleeping

18	Aloft Abu Dhabi	C3
19	Eastern Mangroves Hotel & Spa	C2
20	Park Hyatt Abu Dhabi Hotel & Villas	C1

ARABICA BOOZA ICE CREAM $

Map p136 (☎055 155 6295; ground fl, World Trade Center Mall; from Dhs15 for a small cup; ⊙10am-10pm) You might hear this small kiosk serving up *booza* (Syrian ice cream) before you see it. Staff wield a giant wooden pestle, rhythmically beating like a drum not only to attract attention but also to soften the ice cream. The original cream flavour is the hero, topped with pistachios as is traditional in Syria. Two or three other flavours, including chocolate, are also usually available.

TARBOUCHE AL BASHA LEBANESE $

Map p136 (☎02 628 2220; World Trade Center Souk; sandwiches Dhs24-30, mains Dhs14-110; ⊙8am-11.30pm) Smack in the middle of the World Trade Center Souk (p134) with pleasant food-court style seating, locally recommended Lebanese-leaning Tarbouche deals in an extensive list of kebabs (Iraqi, Turkish, Egyptian), good-value falafel and kebab sandwiches and an amazing thirst-quenching lemon and mint juice.

BUTT SWEETS SHOP BAKERY $

Map p136 (Hamdan St, next to Tawash Bldg; sweets from Dhs2; ⊙7am-10.30pm) Beloved for its name, this simple shop sells Pakistani sweets such as *jalebi* (deep-fried maida flour batter soaked in sugar syrup), *gulab jamun* (deep-fried curdled milk) and *rasgullah* (chhena and semolina dough cooked in light sugar syrup).

AL IBRAHIMI RESTAURANT INDIAN $

Map p136 (☎02 632 1100; www.ibrahimigroup.com; opposite Madinat Zayed Shopping & Gold Centre; biryanis Dhs16-24; ⊙noon-1am) This restaurant isn't going to win any prizes for decor, but it does muster up delicious authentic Indian, Pakistani, Iranian and Arabic dishes (particularly biryanis). There is an outside seating area where life chaotically passes by.

IDIOMS INTERNATIONAL **$**

Map p136 (☎02 681 0808; off Corniche Rd (West); mains Dhs35-65; ⏰9.30am-2am Sat-Wed, to 3am Thu & Fri; 📶) Despite being around for a few years, this hip eatery with its minimalist design is a breath of fresh shisha-flurried air. It does delicious soups, an international potpourri of main courses (fish and chips, lasagna, seafood pasta), creative mocktails and a long list of shisha flavours.

LEBANON MILL LEBANESE **$**

Map p136 (Lebanese Mill; ☎02 677 7714; 9th St; sandwiches Dhs5-15, mains Dhs18-37; ⏰noon-1am) The name on the door may not match that of the menu, but empty tables are as rare as hen's teeth in this simple but clean, family-friendly cafeteria that spoils palates with five types of shawarma, grilled kebabs and spit-roast chicken. Pair your meat with a plate of hummus, Arabic salad and a fruit juice, and you're in for one fine dining experience.

TAMBA INDIAN **$$**

Map p136 (☎02 672 8888; www.tambarestaurant.com; Level 6, The Hub, World Trade Center Mall; mains from Dhs42-232; ⏰noon-1am Sun-Thu, to 2am Fri & Sat; Ⓟ) Touted as traditional Indian food with a modern twist, Tamba's menu offers only the subtlest hint of what the surprise might be, and the sharing plate-style offering includes masala-rubbed Wagyu beef and smoked chicken with tomato gravy black pepper burrata. The location may seem uninspiring at first glance, but this rooftop gem is worth a visit.

BU! LATIN AMERICAN **$$**

Map p136 (☎02 666 8066; www.butrinity.com; 4th fl, The Hub, World Trade Center Mall; mains Dhs95-285; ⏰5pm-1am Sat-Wed, 5pm-3am Thu, 12.30-4.30pm & 5pm-1am Fri; 📶) Book ahead for a table at this stylish and trendy pan-Latin newcomer, an anchor of the newish dining and nightlife tower inside the World Trade Center Mall known as the Hub. It has excellent ceviche, fish and lobster tacos and other festive Latin staples (Brazilian fish stews, Peruvian fried rices, Argentine beef cuts); the salsa and merengue music ensure the mood is merry.

JONES THE GROCER INTERNATIONAL **$$**

Map p136 (☎02 639 5883; www.jonesthegrocer.com; 32nd St, Pearl Plaza Tower, ground fl; mains Dhs29-98; ⏰8am-11.30pm Sun-Thu, 9am-11.30pm Fri & Sat; 📶) This local outpost of the Australian chain has open kitchens overlooking the dining area decked out in stainless steel and earthy wood colours. There's a chilled cheese room with samples to taste and an eclectic homesickness cure-all menu that includes third-wave coffee, organic juices, lobster-tail mac and cheese, salads with *freekeh* (roasted green wheat) and Australian Wagyu rump steak.

LA BRIOCHE CAFÉ FRENCH **$$**

Map p136 (☎02 627 1932; www.labriocheuae.com; Khalifa St; breakfast Dhs23-52, mains Dhs19-85; ⏰6am-midnight; 📶) A slice of Paris in the United Arab Emirates, this mini-chain charmer is famous for its breakfasts but also makes healthy salads, bulging sandwiches and some of the best bread, croissants and pastries (baked fresh and local) in town. Service is swift and smiling, making this ideal for a takeaway to eat at Capital Gardens (p129), which are just 400m away.

★CHO GAO ASIAN **$$**

Map p136 (☎02 616 6149; www.facebook.com/chogaoasianexperience; Sheikh Hamdan Bin Mohammed St; mains Dhs46-138; ⏰noon-1am; 📶) This upbeat joint at the Crowne Plaza Abu Dhabi (p168) is a favourite as much for the tasty fare as for its ambience (all hardwoods and lemongrass, and a highly sociable vibe). The menu hopscotches from Japan to Singapore, China to Thailand and other Asian countries without missing a step. Whether it's curry, stir-fry or Peking duck, it all tastes fresh and flavourful.

KABABS & KURRIES INDIAN **$$**

Map p136 (☎02 628 2522; Khalifa bin Zayed the First St; mains Dhs25-72; ⏰noon-11pm; 📶) This appealing place on the ground floor of the Norman Foster–designed World Trade Center Souk serves up an extensive menu of tasty and refined Indian food inside and on the terrace.

SHAKESPEARE & CO INTERNATIONAL $$

Map p136 (☎02 639 9626; www.shakespeare-and-co.com; ground fl, Souq Central Market; breakfast Dhs58; ⏰7am-midnight; 📶) The decor in this chintzy, Edwardian-style diner may not give you much indication of the Gulf location, but its popularity with Arab diners certainly will. Renowned as a favourite breakfast venue, there's a full English (with turkey sausage and beef bacon) on offer, or Lebanese-style crepes.

MARAKESH MOROCCAN $$$

Map p136 (☎02 614 6000 ext 7334; www.cornichehotelabudhabi.com; Khalifa St, Corniche Hotel; 5-course menu Dhs220; ⏰7pm-3am; 📶) If the exotic Moroccan decor and the bona fide cuisine, including delicious tajines and couscous, aren't enough to bring you here, there's an excellent Moroccan band, belly dancer and singer. Evenings here are memorable and go late.

DRINKING & NIGHTLIFE

In Al Markaziyah, the drinking is either licensed and rooftop, or strictly nonalcoholic and ground floor. Either way, it's lively until the small hours.

RAW PLACE JUICE BAR

Map p136 (www.therawplace.com; World Trade Center Souk; juices Dhs15-48; ⏰7am-11pm Sun-Thu, 8am-11pm Fri) It's pricey, but this organic, cold-pressed juice chain churns out some seriously tasty bevvies fashioned from all manner of fresh fruits, vegetables and herbs (as well as cold-brew coffee, ginger shots and matcha). Once temperatures begin soaring, you won't care how much they cost.

LEVEL LOUNGE BAR

Map p136 (☎02 616 6101; www.crowneplaza.com; Sheikh Hamdan Bin Mohammed St; ⏰7pm-2am; 📶) This relaxing poolside rooftop lounge at the Crowne Plaza Abu Dhabi (p168) reopened after a full makeover in early 2018. New glass partitions and ceilings offer a piece of tower-top calm and cool even in the summer in the middle of the hectic city. It's a good local haunt for shisha and a chat with chill-out music.

COLOMBIANO COFFEE HOUSE COFFEE

Map p136 (☎02 633 7765; www.cchuae.com; Corniche Rd (West), Urban Park; coffee Dhs15-29; ⏰9am-2am; 📶) Sitting in the cafe part of this establishment, beside the pond in comfortable armchairs, is a pleasant and sociable experience, especially on warm nights before the full heat of summer.

CAFÉ LAYALI ZAMAN SHISHA

Map p136 (www.layalizaman.ae; Corniche Rd (West), Lake Park; shisha Dhs45-56; ⏰9am-2am Sun-Thu, 8am-noon & 2pm-2am Fri; 📶) This family-friendly shisha cafe serves a mix of continental, Lebanese and Italian fare, but it's really all about burning your eyes with local colour: the repetitive clank and table slaps of backgammon and playing cards echoes through a cloud of sweet shisha smoke that only thickens as the night wears on. It is ever-popular with locals, particularly later at night.

STRATOS LOUNGE

Map p136 (☎800 101 101; www.stratosabudhabi.com; 6th St, Le Royal Méridien Abu Dhabi; ⏰5pm-late Sun-Fri; 📶) This impressive revolving lounge gives a panoramic view of the city, although it can no longer command an uninterrupted vista. Has a good cocktail menu, ladies' night on Tuesdays (free prosecco), a popular Bollywood-themed evening on Thursdays and a sophisticated set up of plush high-back chairs.

SAX CLUB

Map p136 (☎02 674 2020; www.leroyalmeridienabudhabi.com; Khalifa Bin Zayed the First St; ⏰8pm-3.30am Mon-Fri; 📶) In the early evening, Sax lures chatty jet-setters huddled in intense tête-à-têtes and then cranks up the superb sound system to pack the dance floor with a glamtastic international crowd. Different promotions – Ladies' Night, Cabin Crew Night, Lebanese Weekend – keep things dynamic at this venue inside Le Royal Méridien Abu Dhabi.

TIARA RESTO CAFÉ SHISHA

Map p136 (Corniche Rd (West), Urban Park, Al Markaziyah Gardens; shisha Dhs50; ⏰10am-1am; 📶) This small cafe in Urban Park, just across from the Corniche, offers seating 'in the round' – or at least arranged in a crescent. An outside terrace looks on to the park's fountains – a decent spot for a late-night coffee and a chat with a friend in family-friendly company.

WORTH A DETOUR

A DAY IN THE DESERT

The great desert explorer, Wilfred Thesiger, claimed that no one could live like the Bedouin in the desert and remain unchanged. To get an inkling of what he meant, a day in the sand dunes, with their rhythm and their song (some whistle when it is windy), is a wonderful way to understand both Abu Dhabi's rich Bedouin heritage and also the city's remarkable growth against the physical odds.

Many tour companies offer exciting excursions into dunes and the oases of Abu Dhabi Emirate. They offer an opportunity to learn about Bedouin traditions, to ride a camel, and to appreciate the beauty of the desert and the surprisingly abundant life it harbours. Try to discourage companies from engaging in 'dune bashing': 4WD trips are a legitimate way of exploring the desert, but tearing up the dunes with speed as the only objective is not the healthiest engagement with this fragile environment. The following companies are recommended.

Emirates Tours & Safari (☎02 491 2929; www.eatours.ae; half-day desert safari adult/child Dhs290/200) Offers a half-day desert experience with barbecue.

Abu Dhabi Adventure Tours (☎055 484 2001; www.abudhabiadventure.com; evening desert safari per person Dhs250) If time allows, take its overnight tour to Liwa, home of the largest sand dune in the UAE.

Arabian Adventures (☎02 691 1711; www.arabian-adventures.com; per person from Dhs315) Sundowner tours leave late afternoon and return after dinner in the desert.

ENTERTAINMENT

CRISTAL LIVE MUSIC

Map p136 (www.cornichehotelabudhabi.com; Khalifa St, Corniche Hotel; ⏲5pm-2am; 📶) A resident pianist provides genteel entertainment in the dapper Cristal (from 9pm except Saturday). Dressed in polished oak and illuminated by candlelight and a fireplace, this is a haven of old-world charm in the heart of a frenetic city. Whisky and cigars are de rigueur for men, while the ladies sip French champagne.

SHOPPING

WORLD TRADE CENTER SOUK MALL

Map p136 (www.wtcad.ae; Khalifa Bin Zayed the First St; ⏲10am-10pm Sat-Wed, to 11pm Thu & Fri; 📶) Norman Foster's immensely pleasant reinterpretation of the traditional souq is a stylish composition of warm lattice woodwork, stained glass, walkways and balconies. On the site of the old central market, it connects with the modern World Trade Center Mall (p134) via a footbridge.

MADINAT ZAYED SHOPPING & GOLD CENTRE MARKET

Map p136 (www.madinatzayed-mall.com; 4th St; ⏲9am-10.30pm Sun-Thu, 4-10.30pm Fri) For first-time visitors to a gold souq, the window displays of bridal necklaces, earrings and belts, the trays of precious stones and the tiers of gold bangles are an attraction in their own right. For those familiar with dazzling arrays of jewellery, Madinat Zayed Shopping & Gold Centre offers another reason to visit – affordable pearls set in gold necklaces and rings.

WORLD TRADE CENTER MALL MALL

Map p136 (☎02 508 2400; www.wtcad.ae; Hamdan St; ⏲10am-10pm Sat-Wed, to 11pm Thu & Fri) Part of the World Trade Center, this pleasant shopping mall provides higher-end retail therapy to the complex's market counterpart. It includes a Holland & Barrett shop (for those looking for organic bits and bobs) and a new and popular upmarket dining and nightlife tower known as the Hub.

SPORTS & ACTIVITIES

CYACLE BIKESHARE BICYCLE HIRE

Map p136 (☎800 292 253; www.bikeshare.ae; Corniche Rd (East), Adia HQ; per 1/3 days Dhs15/40) One of handful of stations near the Corniche where you can hire a bike.

Breakwater & Around

The main attraction in this part of town is the Emirates Palace, one of the most opulent hotels in the Middle East. Lately it's been joined by other landmarks, including the clustered Etihad Towers and the lofty St Regis. Back down to earth, the landscaped Western Corniche is helping transform Abu Dhabi into an urban beach destination, while the Heritage Village is a reminder of the city's Bedouin roots.

SIGHTS

★EMIRATES PALACE NOTABLE BUILDING

Map p136 (☎02 690 9000; www.emiratespalace.com; Corniche Rd, West) FREE What the Burj Khalifa in Dubai is to the vertical, the Emirates Palace is to the horizontal, with audacious domed gatehouses and flying ramps to the foyer, 114 domes and a 1.3km private beach. Built for Dhs11 billion, this is the *big* hotel in the Gulf, with 1002 crystal chandeliers and 392 luxury rooms and suites. You don't have to check-in to check out the Emirates Palace, as it doubles as a cultural hub of the city.

UAE FLAGPOLE LANDMARK

Map p136 (Abu Dhabi Theater Rd) At 122m, this giant flagpole was the tallest free-standing flagpole in the world when it was constructed in 2001. It lost its title to the Raghadan Flagpole in Jordan in 2004 and is now a long way short of the world's tallest. That said, the Emirati flag makes a fine landmark and the small promenade beneath the pole offers one of the best photo opportunities in the city for an uninterrupted view of the skyline.

CORNICHE – AL KHALIDIYAH WATERFRONT

Map p136 (Corniche Rd (West); ⏲24hr) FREE When idling on a sunlounger, swimming in the sea or strolling under a canopy of trees, it's hard to believe that the Corniche was a dhow-loading bay for cargo and passengers until the 1970s. In 2004, land was reclaimed to form the 8km Corniche, and a decade later a major landscaping project transformed the seafront into a much-loved public amenity. The western end of the Corniche at Al Kahlidiyah offers the most facilities.

Parks, fountains, cycle tracks, walking paths and beaches snake along the waterside. Lots of benches, shady spots and exercise stations make this a popular destination for strollers and joggers, and there's a growing number of cafes.

SKY TOWER VIEWPOINT

Map p136 (☎02 681 9009; Marina Mall; ⏲9am-11pm) FREE You may pay a bit extra for a burger, sandwich or salad in the aerial Colombiano Coffee House at the top of this observation tower, but there's no charge for the panoramic view from 360-degree windows – unless you don't eat.

ZAYED CENTRE MUSEUM

Map p136 (☎02 665 9555; www.torath.ae; Bainunah St, Al Bateen; ⏲8am-2.15pm Sun-Thu) FREE This eclectic collection of artefacts and personal memorabilia documents the life of Sheikh Zayed, the founding father of the Emirates. The collection is housed in a rare assembly of old villas sporting traditional wind towers on the coast near the new Al Bateen developments. The small but fascinating museum, inside the Zayed Centre for Studies & Research complex, houses Zayed's favourite blue Mercedes and beat-up Land Rover, among other artefacts.

★ETIHAD ANTIQUES GALLERY GALLERY

Map p136 (☎02 667 1229; Villa 15, Al Huwelat St, Al Bateen; ⏲10am-1.30pm & 5-10.30pm Sun-Thu) FREE Collectors, art aficionados and antique-curious window shoppers converge on this fantastic space run by friendly German-Syrian Mohammed Khalil Ibrahim. An absolute showcase of Arabian and Middle Eastern art and antiques, you'll find 18th-century Orientalist paintings and Afghani brass-on-wood doors, 300-year-old bronze coffee pots and teapots, Ottoman and Persian swords dating back centuries – the list goes on and on.

ETIHAD MODERN ART GALLERY GALLERY

Map p136 (☎02 621 0145; www.etihadmodernart.com; Villa 15, Al Huwelat St, Al Bateen; ⏲10am-10pm Sun-Thu) FREE This hip modern art gallery showcases contemporary local and Arabian exhibitions and was the first privately funded gallery from the United Arab Emirates to host a large-scale

Abu Dhabi Corniche & Around

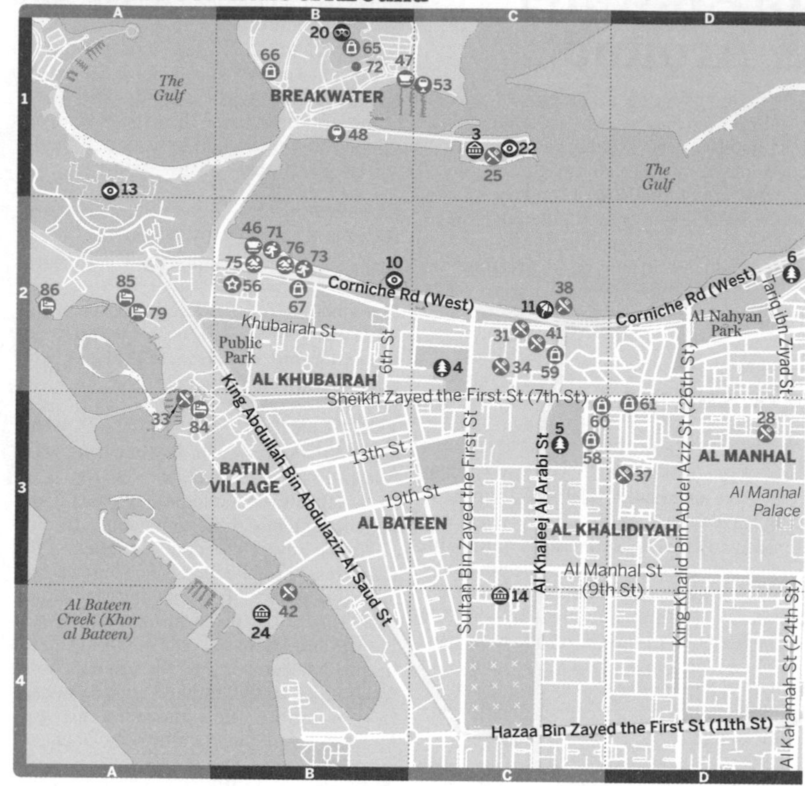

exhibition in Berlin. In addition to fine art, there's an excellent bohemian cafe, Art House Cafe (p141). Exhibitions change monthly except summer, when Art Souq showcases a wide variety of artists residing in the UAE.

AL KHALIDIYAH GARDEN — PARK

Map p136 (Sheikh Zayed the First (7th) St; ⏲8am-1am Mon-Sat, to midnight Sun) FREE With a few fruit-shaped climbing frames, this is a popular spot at weekends for local women and children (no boys over 10 years allowed).

AL KHALIDIYAH PUBLIC PARK — PARK

Map p136 (Khalidiyah Garden; btwn 16th & 30th (Al Khaleej Al Arabi) Sts; adult/child Dhs1/free; ⏲24hr) One of many popular, shady parks in Abu Dhabi, this park offers a respite from the heat of the Corniche in summer. There's a jogging track (20-minute circuit) and a variety of climbing frames and other attractions for youngsters.

EATING

When it comes to dining in and around Breakwater, the sky's the limit – literally, if you head for the Observation Deck at the Etihad Towers. That said, some of the best eating experiences are down to earth in the cheap-and-cheerful cafes dotted along the Corniche where there's a chance to join the city at rest.

SHISH SHAWERMA — ARABIC $

Map p136 (☎02 681 5733; www.shishshawerma.com; Corniche Rd (West), 2nd St; sandwiches Dhs10-25; ⏲10am-1am) On a bit of a backalley restaurant row behind Corniche Towers, this perennially popular and colourful fast-food shawarma joint gets the job done

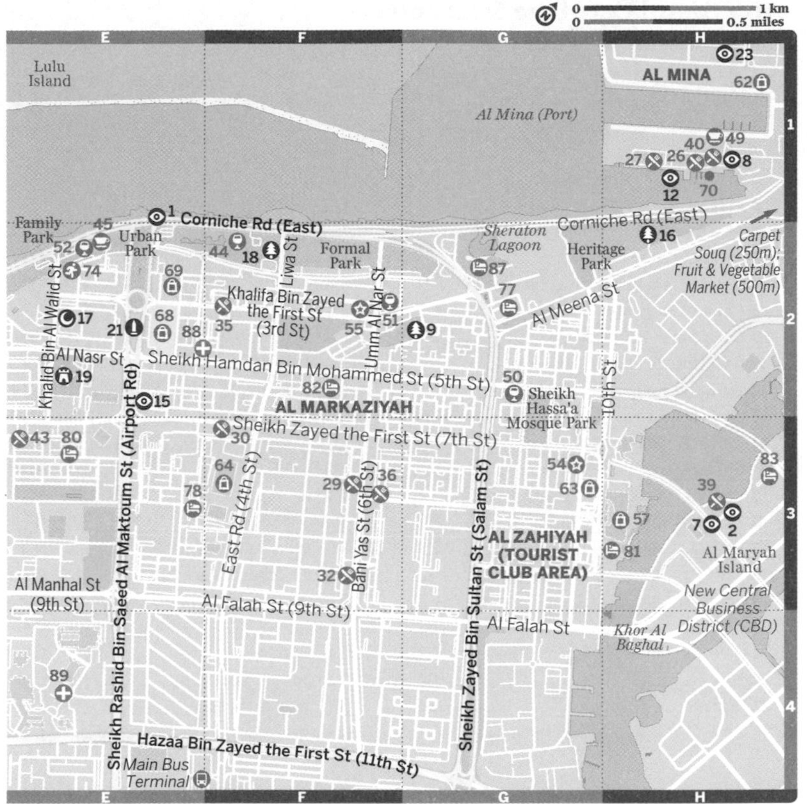

with succulent beef or chicken versions – spice 'em up with Mexican sauce and/or chilli paste – stuffed in fresh pita bread baked in a brick oven right at the counter.

AUTOMATIC RESTAURANT LEBANESE $

Map p136 (☎02 677 7445; 12th St, Al Khalidiya; mains Dhs8-60; ⏲10.30am-1am) No one has really got to the bottom of the name of this chain of popular restaurants selling the local equivalent of fast food. But the name matters not, as the food (dips, grills and rocket salads) is automatically trustworthy and delicious.

NOVA BEACH CAFÉ CAFE $

Map p136 (☎02 658 1870; www.facebook.com/novabeachcafe; Corniche Rd (West); mains Dhs28-75; ⏲9am-11pm) One of the few public places where you can have a coffee or meal overlooking the sea, this cafe has a devoted local following. If you're walking or cycling the Corniche, or looking for a bite between swims, this is a sociable venue where you can catch the sea breeze.

CAFÉ DU ROI FRENCH $

Map p136 (☎02 681 6151; www.cafeduroi.com; Corniche Rd (West); mains Dhs20-90; ⏲7am-midnight; 📶) With professional coffee and delicious pastries, croissants and sandwiches, plus several fluffy filled omelettes, this French-style cafe is the perfect spot for some leisurely lingering.

★LIVING ROOM CAFÉ CAFE $$

Map p136 (TLRC; ☎02 639 6654; www.thelivingroomcafeabudhabi.com; Khalifa Bin Shakhbout St (28th St), Khalidiya Village; mains Dhs20-85; ⏲7am-11pm Sun-Thu, 7.30am-11.30pm Fri & Sat; 📶👪) This award-winning, family-run venue began as a coffee-and-cake experience and has grown by word of mouth into a beloved restaurant. The emphasis

Abu Dhabi Corniche & Around

Sights

1 Abu Dhabi Corniche ... E1
2 Abu Dhabi Global Market Square ... H3
3 Abu Dhabi Heritage Village ... C1
4 Al Khalidiyah Garden ... C2
5 Al Khalidiyah Public Park ... C3
6 Al Markaziyah Gardens ... D2
7 Al Maryah Island Promenade ... H3
8 Al Mina Fish Market ... H1
Burj Mohammed Bin Rashid ... (see 68)
9 Capital Gardens ... G2
10 Corniche – Al Khalidiyah ... B2
11 Corniche Beach ... C2
12 Dhow Harbour ... H1
13 Emirates Palace ... A1
14 Etihad Antiques Gallery ... C4
Etihad Modern Art Gallery ... (see 14)
15 Etisalat Head Office ... E2
16 Heritage Park ... H2
17 Khalifa Mosque ... E2
18 Lake Park & Formal Park ... F2
19 Qasr Al Hosn ... E2
20 Sky Tower ... B1
21 Street Sculptures ... E2
22 UAE Flagpole ... C1
23 Warehouse 421 ... H1
24 Zayed Centre ... B4

Eating

Abu Dhabi Co-op Hypermarket ... (see 57)
25 Al Asala Heritage Restaurant ... C1
26 Al Dhafra Restaurant ... H1
Al Ibrahimi Restaurant ... (see 78)
27 Al Mina Modern Cuisine & Restaurant ... H1
Arabica Booza ... (see 68)
28 Automatic Restaurant ... D3
29 Bait El Khetyar ... F3
Biryani Pot ... (see 2)
Bu! ... (see 68)
Butcher & Still ... (see 83)
30 Butt Sweets Shop ... F3
31 Café Du Roi ... C2
32 Cafeteria Al Liwan ... F3
Cho Gao ... (see 82)
33 Cho Gao ... A3
Coya ... (see 83)
Crust ... (see 83)
Dai Pai Dong ... (see 2)
Finz ... (see 81)
Godiva Chocolate Café ... (see 2)
Idioms ... (see 41)
34 Jones the Grocer ... C2
Kababs & Kurries ... (see 69)
35 La Brioche Café ... F2
36 Lebanon Mill ... F3
Li Beirut ... (see 85)
37 Living Room Café ... D3
Marakesh ... (see 55)
Mezlai ... (see 13)
38 Nova Beach Café ... C2
39 Roberto's ... H3
40 Saudi Kitchen ... H1
Sayad ... (see 13)
Shakespeare & Co ... (see 69)
41 Shish Shawerma ... C2
Tamba ... (see 68)
Tarbouche Al Basha ... (see 69)
42 Tashas ... B4
Vasco's ... (see 75)
Virona ... (see 8)
43 Zahrat Lebnan ... E3
Zuma ... (see 2)

Drinking & Nightlife

Al Meylas ... (see 83)
Art House Cafe ... (see 14)
Belgian Beer Café ... (see 84)
Bentley Kitchen ... (see 2)
Butcher & Still ... (see 83)
44 Café Layali Zaman ... F2
45 Colombiano Coffee House ... E2
Eclipse Terrace Lounge ... (see 83)
46 Escape ... B2

is on family-friendly fare (there's a VIP children's menu and kids' corner), and the home-baked cakes, all-day breakfasts, toasted sandwiches and healthy salads will please those with a craving for something from mum's kitchen. It's inside Khalidiya Village.

CHO GAO ASIAN **$$**

Map p136 (02 666 6888; www.dining-intercontinental-ad.ae/restaurants/cho-gao; Marina Walk, Intercontinental Hotel, Al Khubeirah; mains Dhs52-148; noon-1am Sat-Wed, to 2am Fri & Sat; P) This outlet marks the second opening in the city of this much-loved restaurant, and this more desirable waterfront

47 Havana Café & Restaurant....................B1
Hemingway's....................(see 56)
48 Hookah Lounge....................B1
La Cava....................(see 2)
Le Café....................(see 13)
Level Lounge....................(see 82)
Maison Samira Maatouk....................(see 65)
49 Navona Restaurant & Coffeeshop....................H1
Observation Deck at 300....................(see 85)
50 Planet Café....................G2
Raw Place....................(see 69)
Ray's Bar....................(see 85)
51 Sax....................F2
Stratos....................(see 51)
52 Tiara Resto Café....................E2
53 Yacht Gourmet Restaurant....................C1

Entertainment
54 49er's The Gold Rush....................G3
55 Cristal....................F2
56 Jazz Bar & Dining....................B2
Novo Cinemas Abu Dhabi....................(see 57)
Vox Cinemas....................(see 65)

Shopping
57 Abu Dhabi Mall....................H3
58 Abu Dhabi Pottery Establishment....................C3
Avenue at Etihad Towers....................(see 85)
59 Centre of Original Iranian Carpets....................C2
60 Eclectic....................C3
61 Folklore Gallery....................D3
Galleria at Maryah Island....................(see 2)
Grand Stores....................(see 57)
62 Iranian Souq....................H1
Jashanmal....................(see 57)
63 Khalifa Centre....................G3
64 Madinat Zayed Shopping & Gold Centre....................F3
65 Marina Mall....................B1
66 Miraj Islamic Centre....................B1
67 Nation Galleria....................B2
Organic Foods & Café....................(see 67)
Wafi Gourmet....................(see 67)
68 World Trade Center Mall....................E2
69 World Trade Center Souk....................E2

Sports & Activities
70 Abu Dhabi Dhow Cruise....................H1
Beach Rotana Club....................(see 81)
71 Belevari Catamarans....................B2
72 Big Bus Abu Dhabi....................B1
73 Cyacle Bikeshare....................B2
74 Cyacle Bikeshare....................E2
Emirates Palace Spa....................(see 13)
75 Hiltonia Beach Club, Fitness & Spa....................B2
76 Nation Riviera Beach Club....................B2
Sense....................(see 2)

Sleeping
77 Al Diar Mina Hotel....................G2
78 Al Jazeera Royal Hotel....................E3
79 Bab Al Qasr....................A2
80 BackPacker Hostel Abu Dhabi....................E3
81 Beach Rotana Hotel....................H3
82 Crowne Plaza Abu Dhabi....................F2
Emirates Palace....................(see 13)
83 Four Seasons Abu Dhabi....................H3
84 InterContinental Abu Dhabi....................A3
85 Jumeirah at Etihad Towers....................A2
86 Khalidiya Palace Rayhaan by Rotana....................A2
87 Sheraton Abu Dhabi Hotel & Resort....................G2

Information
Abu Dhabi Tourism & Culture Authority....................(see 69)
88 Central Al Ahalia Pharmacy....................E2
Department of Culture and Tourism – Abu Dhabi....................(see 67)
89 Sheikh Khalifa Medical City....................E4

location makes Cho Gao Marina Walk the standout. Enviable marina views and a varied menu drawing on classic flavours from all over Asia with fresh and fragrant flavours mean this sociable and upbeat establishment remains a popular spot almost every night of the week.

TASHAS INTERNATIONAL **$$**

Map p136 (☎02 245 0890; www.tashascafe.com; Marsa, Al Bateen; mains Dhs56-190, tapas Dhs18-110; ⊙8am-11.30pm; 📶) This stylish South African transplant is one of the few places where Emiratis outnumber foreigners on any given night (no alcohol is served). Featuring both a chain-wide and Abu

Dhabi-specific menu, it's chock-full of creative and considerably yummy salads (the butternut is extraordinary), sandwiches, tapas, heartier mains and wonderful desserts (that hazelnut cheesecake!) served by a jovial, mostly African staff.

AL ASALA HERITAGE RESTAURANT EMIRATI $$

Map p136 (☎02 681 2188; www.alasalahrestaurants.com; mains Dhs28-65, buffet Dhs75; ⊙noon-midnight Sun-Thu, from 1pm Fri, buffet 1-5pm & 6.30-9pm Fri) Offering traditional *jasheed* (minced shark) and *harees* (meat and wheat 'porridge'), and *umm ali* (Arab bread pudding) in the Heritage Village, this restaurant, with its fine view of the Abu Dhabi skyline, caters mainly for tour groups sampling the buffet as part of their cultural tour. If unaccompanied by a tour guide, you'll be attentively looked after.

★LI BEIRUT LEBANESE $$$

Map p136 (☎02 811 5666; www.jumeirah.com; Corniche Rd (West), Jumeirah at Etihad Towers; set menu Dhs230-550, mains Dhs55-185; ⊙10am-3pm & 7pm-midnight Sep-May, dinner only Jul-Aug; 📶) One of the UAE's best Lebanese restaurants, Li Beirut will wow you with its fine dining take on Levantine deliciousness, which pairs cosily with several motherland wines – including the excellent Château Musar – and beers (Almaza, Beirut). From the scrumptious hot and cold mezze to memorable mains (*zaatar*-crusted rack of lamb, *freekeh* ragout-stuffed quail), a feast awaits. Book ahead.

★VASCO'S SEAFOOD $$$

Map p136 (☎02 692 4247; www.abudhabi.hilton.com; Corniche Rd (West); mains Dhs70-165; ⊙noon-3.30pm & 7-11pm Sun-Thu, from 10am Fri-Sat) With a patio overlooking the Gulf, hospitable staff and a delicious seafood-focused, fine-dining blend of regional and international cuisine, it's not surprising reservations are recommended. The Vasco twist to the menu is a good reminder of the early Portuguese influence in the region (Iberian-spice grouper, seafood cataplana); and the chilled lobster gazpacho is a revelation in this heat.

SAYAD SEAFOOD $$$

Map p136 (☎02 690 7999; www.emiratespalace.com; Emirates Palace, Ras Al Akhdar; mains Dhs110-495; ⊙6.30-11.30pm; 📶) Serving the city's finest seafood in a striking aquamarine setting (quite a contrast to the traditional marble and silk of the surrounding Emirates Palace), Sayad has earned a reputation as a top choice for a special occasion.

★MEZLAI EMIRATI $$$

Map p136 (☎02 690 7999; www.kempinski.com; Corniche Rd (West), Emirates Palace; mains Dhs70-330; ⊙1-10.30pm; 📶) Meaning 'old door lock', Mezlai, the UAE's first self-proclaimed Emirati restaurant, delivers a rare chance to enjoy local flavours in an upmarket and airy Bedouin-tent-inspired atmosphere. The Emirati food is prepared from organic and locally sourced ingredients. Favourites include lamb *medfoun* (shoulder of lamb, slow cooked in a banana leaf) and hamour or veal *machboos* (casserole) with spiced rice.

DRINKING & NIGHTLIFE

Drinking and nightlife in Abu Dhabi centres on coffee, a percolated smoke and lively conversation. Join the locals in their nightly pursuits in Breakwater's favourite shisha cafes, or for a more international experience, glam up for the many hotel bars and clubs that have a liquor licence and expect a minimum of 'smart casual' from their guests.

★OBSERVATION DECK AT 300 CAFE

Map p136 (☎02 811 5666; www.jumeirah.com; Corniche Rd (West), Jumeirah at Etihad Towers; entry Dhs85, high tea Dhs210, with champagne Dhs300; ⊙10am-7pm) This chic coffee shop on the 74th floor of Tower 2 of the iconic Jumeirah at Etihad Towers hotel serves the highest high tea in Abu Dhabi with a sublime panorama of city, sea and surrounds. The '300' refers to metres above ground. Admission includes Dhs50 towards food and drink.

★BELGIAN BEER CAFÉ BAR

Map p136 (☎02 666 6888; www.belgianbeercafe.com; Bainunah St, InterContinental Hotel; beers Dhs28-65; ⊙4pm-1am Sat-Tue, to 2am Wed; 📶) The Arabian peninsula is dire territory for hopheads, but the Belgian Beer Café, overlooking the marina at the InterContinental, boasts a satisfying suds selection,

TOP SIGHT
ABU DHABI HERITAGE VILLAGE

This reconstructed village gives an insight into the pre-oil era in the United Arab Emirates – a life that is in evidence in many parts of the Arabian Peninsula to this day. The walled complex includes all the main elements of traditional Gulf life: a fort to repel invaders from the sea, a souq to trade goats for dates with friendly neighbours and a mosque as a reminder of the central part that Islam plays in daily Arabic life.

Take a look at the *barasti* (palm-leaf) house, designed to catch the breeze through the palm frond uprights, an ox-drawn well without which settled life was impossible, and the ancient *falaj* (irrigation) system, which still waters the crops (note the stones for diverting the water) in the plantations of Al Ain and Liwa Oasis today.

Watch craftsmen at work at the tannery, pottery and glass-blowing workshop. Elsewhere, people hone the blades of *khanjars*, curved daggers that remain an important part of ceremonial costume across the region.

Finally pop into the museum with its traditional wind tower for cooling the interior. There are good displays of jewellery and paraphernalia of the pearl-diving industry, upon which Abu Dhabi was founded before pearls from Japan and the discovery of oil made pearling redundant.

Don't Miss

- Old Fort Museum
- Spice Shop
- Craftspeople demonstrations

Practicalities

- Map p136, C1
- www.torath.ae
- Abu Dhabi Theater Rd
- admission free
- 9am-4pm Sat-Thu, 3.30-9pm Fri

featuring five Belgian offers on draught and another 20 or so by the bottle.

RAY'S BAR BAR

Map p136 (02 811 5666; www.jumeirah.com; Corniche Rd (West), Jumeirah at Etihad Towers; cocktails Dhs40-80; 5pm-3am;) For a prime perspective on Abu Dhabi's audacious architectural vision, let the lift whisk you up to this 62nd-floor bar at Jumeirah at Etihad Towers (p169). If you arrive at sunset, you'll be dazzled by the light bouncing off these grand edifices. If the views and cocktails make you dizzy, the Asian tapas menu will restore balance to the brain.

HOOKAH LOUNGE SHISHA

Map p136 (02 666 1179; http://pentainvestment.net/project/hookah-lounge-abu-dhabi; Wavebreaker, opposite Marina Mall; 9am-1am Mon-Sat, to midnight Sun) Hookah Lounge sits right on the water's edge with spectacular views back across to the city. Shisha, unsurprisingly, is the main event here, though a menu of Lebanese snacks is available. You can also order from the menu of the neighbouring restaurant.

ART HOUSE CAFE CAFE

Map p136 (www.facebook.com/arthousecafead; Villa 15, Al Huwelat St, Al Bateen; mains Dhs20-55; 9am-11.30pm Sun-Thu, 10am-midnight Fri;) This arts and sustainability focused cafe inside Etihad Modern Art Gallery (p135) makes for an atmospheric pit stop while browsing art and antiques at Etihad Antiques Gallery (p135) next door. Coffee, wraps, salads and burgers make up the menu, but the coolest part is the tables and seats fashioned from recycled oil barrels and fuel canisters. It's a colourful, bohemian hangout.

ESCAPE CAFE

Map p136 (02 692 4344; www.abudhabi.hilton.com; Corniche Rd (West), Hiltonia Beach Club, Fitness & Spa; shisha Dhs70-80; 9am-1pm;) Hiltonia Beach Club's shisha cafe – open to the public – sits on prime beachside real estate with rather outstanding Abu Dhabi skyline views to accompany slightly pricier puffing (noon to midnight only), as well as light bites and heartier mains as the day wears on. DJs spin from 7pm to 11pm.

SHISHA CAFES

The scent of apple and vanilla commonly fills the midnight air, accompanied by the low rumbling and mumbled conversations of assembled puffers and gurglers, dragging on velvet hoses. This is not a psychedelic dream, it's a shisha cafe.

In Abu Dhabi, two sensations mark the hot and humid air of an Arabian evening: the wreaths of peach-scented smoke that spiral above the corner coffee houses and the low gurgle of water, like a grumbling camel, in the base of a water pipe. Shisha cafes are spread across the sea rim from the inland parks of the Corniche to the terraces of Breakwater and offer a wonderful, nonalcoholic opportunity to engage with local people.

The habit of shisha smoking, also known as hookah or hubble-bubble, originated hundreds of years ago in Persia and India.

Across the region, shisha cafes are often a male affair: men lounge in ubiquitous white plastic chairs, indolently watching football on the TV, and occasionally breaking off from sucking and puffing to pass a word of lazy complaint to their neighbour or hail the waiter for hot coals.

In Abu Dhabi, however, these cafes attract mixed company. Here, women in black *abayas* (full-length robes) with sparkling diamante cuffs drag demurely on velvet-clad mouthpieces, their smoking punctuating animated dialogue.

There is a popular misconception that because the smoke passes through water it is somehow filtered of toxins, but this is not the case. In fact, doctors argue that shisha is worse for your health than cigarettes, not least because a typical shisha session lasts for an hour and involves 200 puffs of nicotine, compared with only 20 for a regular cigarette.

If you're tempted to sniff out this redolent activity, here are our top five venues in the middle of the city.

Planet Café (p148)

Café Layali Zaman (p133)

Level Lounge (p133)

Yacht Gourmet Restaurant (below)

Havana Café & Restaurant (below)

MAISON SAMIRA MAATOUK COFFEE

Map p136 (www.maisonmaatouk.com; Marina Mall; coffee Dhs14-65; ⌚9am-10pm) Born in Lebanon in the '60s, Maison Samira Maatouk serves some of Abu Dhabi's finest coffee. Choose from an exquisite list of Turkish-style options (including the coveted Jamaican Blue Mountain), espresso or a high-dollar Arabic preparation (with saffron, cardamom and cloves, and served with dates; Dhs65). You can also customise your own coffee blend and pick up any of their signature roasts.

LE CAFÉ CAFE

Map p136 (☎02 690 7999; www.emiratespalace.com; Corniche Rd (West), Emirates Palace; high tea Dhs380-480; ⌚high tea 2-6pm; 📶) Try an Arabic twist on the classic English high tea with mezze, Arabic savoury pastries and baklava with a camelccino made with camel's milk (Dhs50) or a cappuccino sprinkled with 24-karat gold flakes (Dhs60). High tea of both classic and Arab variety is practically an institution at the Emirates Palace (p135), so book in advance.

YACHT GOURMET RESTAURANT SHISHA

Map p136 (☎02 222 2886; near Marina Mall, Marina Village; fresh fruit juice Dhs24, shisha Dhs32-45; ⌚24hr; 📶) Serving a variety of tasty fruit juices and basic Lebanese dishes, this is a very popular place for an evening of al fresco shisha in the mixed company of locals and a few foreigners in the know.

HAVANA CAFÉ & RESTAURANT CAFE

Map p136 (☎02 681 0044; Corniche Rd (West); shisha Dhs49-54; ⌚9am-2am Sun-Thu, to 3am Fri & Sat) With one of the very best views of night-time Abu Dhabi, the outside terrace at this highly popular shisha cafe is always teeming with appreciative puffers, smokers and gurglers. The service is attentive.

HEMINGWAY'S BAR

Map p136 (☎02 681 1900; www.abudhabi.hilton.com; Corniche Rd (West), Hilton Abu Dhabi; ⏰7pm-2am Sun-Wed, to 3am Thu & Fri; 📶) An international/Tex-Mex/Irish cantina popular with long-term expats, Hemingway's is the place to lounge in front of the big screen for beer, chips (albeit nacho chips) and football. There's a DJ spinning nightly from 7pm and happy hour from 4pm to 8pm Sunday to Wednesday and Friday.

SHOPPING

Breakwater and the western end of the Corniche run the gamut of enticing shopping opportunities, from the enormous Marina Mall to the craft-oriented boutiques of Al Khalidiyah.

★WAFI GOURMET FOOD

Map p136 (www.wafigourmet.com; Corniche Rd (West), Nation Galleria; ⏰9am-midnight Mon-Sat, from 8.30am Sun) Offering beautiful Medjool dates stuffed with pistachios, cashews, almonds or oranges; gorgeous marzipan, baklava and other Arabic sweets; take-home bottles of rose water; and a full-service deli, bakery and restaurant, Wafi Gourmet is one-stop shopping for foodies looking to take home the taste of Arabia.

MIRAJ ISLAMIC CENTRE ARTS & CRAFTS

Map p136 (☎050 250 3950; www.mirajabudhabi.com; Villa 14, Marina Office Park; ⏰9am-6pm) FREE Carpets, textiles, jewellery, sculpture, exquisite vases, marble inlay furniture and calligraphy are among the artworks from around the Islamic world displayed at this top-end gallery.

NATION GALLERIA MALL

Map p136 (☎02 681 8824; Corniche Rd (West), Nation Towers) This shopping experience is not just your average mall – it houses many unique stores, extravagant eateries and a huge Wafi Gourmet (p143), the celebrated Lebanese gourmet chain.

AVENUE AT ETIHAD TOWERS FASHION & ACCESSORIES

Map p136 (☎800 384 4238; www.avenueatetihadtowers.ae; Corniche Rd (West), Jumeirah at Etihad Towers; ⏰hours vary) Designer-led, luxury fashion items in an exclusive, opulent venue; this is boutique shopping at its finest.

CENTRE OF ORIGINAL IRANIAN CARPETS HOMEWARES

Map p136 (☎02 681 1156; www.coicco.com; Al Khaleej Al Arabi St; carpets from Dhs1200; ⏰9.30am-1.30pm & 5-9.30pm Sat-Thu, 5-9.30pm Fri) Spread over three floors, this carpet gallery has more than 4000 carpets to choose from, making it one of the largest collections of carpets in the Middle East. The shop's detailed website has a useful buyer's guide and glossary.

ORGANIC FOODS & CAFÉ MARKET

Map p136 (www.organicfoodsandcafe.com; Corniche Rd (West), Nations Towers; ⏰9am-11pm) 🍃 This organic store inside Nations Tower is Abu Dhabi's go-to for organic and natural food products and cosmetics.

ECLECTIC ANTIQUES

Map p136 (☎02 666 5158; www.facebook.com/eclectic.antiques.and.furniture; cnr Zayed the First & Sha'm Sts; ⏰10.30am-2pm & 5-9pm Sat-Wed, 11-7pm Thu) A delightful browsing experience with old furniture and textiles hobnobbing with new paintings, ceramics and sculpture by local Gulf artists. It's a royal pain to find, but it's on the mezzanine level (level 0 in the lift) of the Amanah Tower building.

ABU DHABI POTTERY ESTABLISHMENT CERAMICS

Map p136 (☎02 666 7079; www.abudhabipottery.com; 16th St; ⏰9am-1pm & 4.30-9pm Sat-Thu) A showcase for the collectable ceramics of Homa Vafaie-Farley, the venue also doubles as a pottery workshop with classes (from Dhs195) on offer.

FOLKLORE GALLERY ART

Map p136 (☎02 666 0361; www.folkloregallery.net; Zayed the First St; ⏰9am-1pm & 4-9pm Sat-Thu) Invest in a piece by up-and-coming local resident artists from a shop that started life mainly as a framing service in 1995.

MARINA MALL MALL

Map p136 (☎02 681 2310; www.marinamall.ae; ⏰10am-10pm Sat-Wed, to midnight Thu & Fri; 📶) Aside from more than 400 stores, this popular mall has plenty of entertainment options, including a multiplex cinema, a Bounce indoor free-jumping centre for kids, the Emirates Bowling Village and the Marina Eye Ferris wheel.

ENTERTAINMENT

JAZZ BAR & DINING LIVE MUSIC

Map p136 (02 681 1900; www.abudhabi.hilton.com; Corniche Rd (West), Hilton Abu Dhabi; mains Dhs105-155; 7pm-2am;) Cool cats flock to this sophisticated supper club at the Hilton Abu Dhabi that serves international cuisine in a modern art deco–inspired setting. But the venue is less about food and more about music – a four-piece jazz band plays from 9.30pm to an audience of sagely nodding aficionados. It's ladies' night Monday and Wednesday.

ABU DHABI CLASSICS CLASSICAL MUSIC

(800 555; www.abudhabiclassics.com; tickets Dhs80-350; Nov-May) This concert series brings top classical performances – including renowned international soloists and famous orchestras – to such venues as the Emirates Palace and Manarat Al Saadiyat in Abu Dhabi and the historic Al Jahili Fort in Al Ain.

VOX CINEMAS CINEMA

Map p136 (02 681 8464; www.uae.voxcinemas.com; Marina Mall; tickets Dhs35-150) Ultracomfortable cinema with Hollywood and Bollywood blockbusters in 2D, 3D and 4D. Tickets can be booked online.

SPORTS & ACTIVITIES

BIG BUS ABU DHABI BUS

Map p136 (02 449 0026; www.bigbustours.com; 24hr adult/child Dhs255/166, 48hr adult/child Dhs299/192; 9am-5pm) This hop-on, hop-off bus tour with recorded commentary is an easy way to get the lie of the land. The route passes all the major sights, including Sheikh Zayed Grand Mosque, the Corniche, the Heritage Village, Emirates Palace Hotel and Yas Island. Tickets include headphones and are sold online (at a discount) as well as at hotels and on the bus.

A separate shuttle, leaving every 90 minutes, covers Yas Island and Masdar City between 10am and 4pm daily. There is also a Friday-night bus (adult/child Dhs185/75) that leaves from the Marina Mall (at the Breakwater) at 7.15pm and takes two hours. You can board the bus at any stop, but the nominal starting point is the Marina Mall.

EMIRATES PALACE SPA SPA

Map p136 (02 690 7978; www.kempinski.com; Emirates Palace; 10am-11pm) For the ultimate indulgence, ask about the 5½-hour Day of Gold ritual. This includes a 24-karat-gold facial, an application of gold from head to toe and a massage using gold shea butter. If you don't come out feeling like Tutankhamun's mummy, it won't be for want of trying. Prices on request (sit down first).

NATION RIVIERA BEACH CLUB SWIMMING

Map p136 (02 694 4780; www.nationrivierabeachclub.com; Corniche Rd (West); day use per person/couple Sun-Thu Dhs160/265, Fri & Sat Dhs210/315; 6am-10pm) The plantation-style white pavilions and choice of subtropical planting make this upmarket club owned by St Regis Hotel instantly attractive. With steam room, sauna, Jacuzzi and a gym, there's plenty for those who just can't keep still. For those who can, the perfect beach, with its private, 200m unruffled shoreline, offers a peaceful view of Breakwater and beyond.

If you get hungry, popular Asian-fusion restaurant Asia de Cuba shares real estate here.

CYACLE BIKESHARE CYCLING

Map p136 (800 292 253; www.bikeshare.ae; in front of Nation Riviera Beach Club; per 1/3 days Dhs15/40; 24hr) One of some 50 bicycle ride-share stations in Abu Dhabi.

HILTONIA BEACH CLUB, FITNESS & SPA SWIMMING

Map p136 (02 692 4247; www.abudhabi.hilton.com; Corniche Rd (West); adult/child Fri & Sat Dhs125/50, Sun-Thu Dhs80/50; 8am-8pm) This recommended beach club occupies prime position at the western end of the Corniche. Set in beautifully landscaped gardens alongside a white-sand beach shaded by palm trees, the club offers three swimming pools, a gym and cafe. Punctuate a lazy day with a seafood salad and a glass of wine at the excellent restaurant, Vasco's (p140).

Admission, which is discounted after 3pm, includes towel, locker, shower facilities and access to the swimming pools.

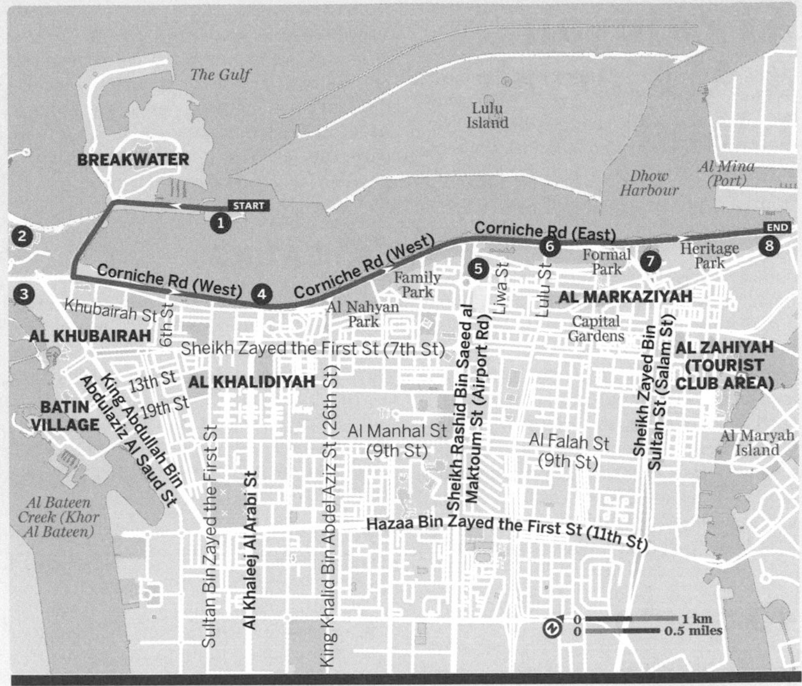

Neighbourhood Walk
A Stroll Downtown

START ABU DHABI FLAG
END HERITAGE PARK
LENGTH 10.5KM; FOUR HOURS

From the giant flag, the symbol of unity in this capital city, it's a brief walk to ❶ **Abu Dhabi Heritage Village** (p141). Here you can enjoy a glimpse of Emirati life before oil revenues transformed the country forever.

Follow the breakwater, which comes alive during the powerboat racing championships. Across the road, there's an oyster statue, a reminder of the city's former pearling industry. The view beyond is dominated by the ❷ **Emirates Palace** (p135) – hotel, spa, cultural centre and general city icon.

Joining the Corniche, you'll notice a billboard-sized poster of Sheikh Zayed, father of the nation. His 'benign dictatorship' brought development to Abu Dhabi and the country as a whole, as demonstrated by the architectural optimism of buildings such as ❸ **Etihad Towers**, clustered opposite.

Along the Corniche, you'll see similar expressions of confidence, such as Nation Towers, home to the St Regis. Beach clubs offer luxurious swimming, and the public ❹ **Corniche Beach** (p129) is Blue-Flagged for cleanliness. Take a break at the **Nova Beach Café** (p137) here.

Pause next at Rashid Bin Saeed Al Maktoum St. The inland procession of fine buildings includes the ❺ **Burj Mohammed Bin Rashid** (p129), the city's tallest tower, home to the World Trade Center, and the Etisalat building with its 'golf ball' crown.

Think you've been walking west to east? In fact the orientation is southwest to northeast, but this tends to be overlooked on maps. This stretch is beautifully landscaped and parallels attractive ❻ **Lake Park** (p129), connected by an underpass.

In a city where the shoreline has been dredged and reshaped, it's endearing to see that the *khor* (creek) beside the ❼ **Sheraton Hotel** (p168) has not been filled in. The Corniche passes over it, leaving this venerable hotel with its treasured beach.

Continue on to ❽ **Heritage Park** (p146) and a romantic view of the dhows floating two abreast in the harbour opposite.

Al Zahiyah & Al Maryah Island

Al Zahiyah, a district formerly known as 'Tourist Club Area' (and still referred to by many as such today), took on its previous name in the 1970s when the government built a beach (that no longer exists) to up the recreation ante for city residents. Today, one of the city's oldest neighbourhoods – now named 'colourful' in Arabic – remains a hubbub of trading and is chock-full of coffee shops, restaurants and hotels. Al Maryah Island, by contrast, is all shiny and new, with lofty skyscrapers and world-class facilities such as Cleveland Clinic Abu Dhabi. Take it all in along the scenic Al Maryah Island Promenade between CCAD, the Galleria Mall and the new Four Seasons Hotel.

SIGHTS

ABU DHABI GLOBAL MARKET SQUARE — NOTABLE BUILDING

Map p136 (Sowwah Sq; www.almaryahisland.ae; Al Falah St, Al Maryah Island) Home to more than 40 international companies, this cluster of glass-and-steel office monoliths on Al Maryah Island is the heart of Abu Dhabi's new financial centre. Also cradling the posh Galleria mall and a couple of five-star hotels, it sits just off the Al Zahiyah district and offers striking views of the city skyline from the waterfront promenade. Various other feats of engineering also vie for attention, including the Tetris-like Cleveland Clinic with its catwalk podium and distinctive diamond-glazing.

AL MARYAH ISLAND PROMENADE — WATERFRONT

Map p136 (24hr) FREE This 5.4km-long promenade bends gently round the western shore of the island and offers fantastic views of Abu Dhabi and the busy channel of water in between. Used as a venue for a lavish Christmas market and New Year's fireworks, and linking an assortment of cafes and bistros, the promenade is already a meeting place for Abu Dhabi's elite. Notable buildings include the upmarket Galleria mall and the Cleveland Clinic that almost manages to make healthcare look inviting.

HERITAGE PARK — PARK

Map p136 (24hr) This attractive family park straddles both sides of the far eastern end of the Corniche, with great views of the traditional dhow harbour across the water in Al Mina. With fountains and faux grottoes, barbecue facilities and play areas, it is a popular picnic site at weekends.

EATING

Restaurants representing just about every country involved in Abu Dhabi's modern development can be found in the malls and backstreets of Al Zahiyah, including British fish and chips, Baluchi mutton biryani, Indian vegetarian set lunches and Filipino chicken *adobo*. A government publication called *Where to Eat* lists all these restaurants by type.

ABU DHABI CO-OP HYPERMARKET — SUPERMARKET $

Map p136 (02 645 9777; www.abudhabicoop.com/english; 10th St, ground fl, Abu Dhabi Mall; 8am-midnight) Pick up barbecue supplies here and head to the Eastern Corniche or one of the city parks to cook them up.

DAI PAI DONG — CHINESE $$

Map p136 (02 813 5552; www.rosewoodhotels.com; Rosewood Hotel, Al Maryah Island; mains Dhs40-200, dim sum Dhs30-55; noon-3pm & 6-11pm Sun-Wed, to midnight Thu-Fri;) Amid dark, sexy interiors and an open kitchen, Dai Pai Dong's delicately flavoured, award-winning Chinese takes Hong Kong street eats to the next level. You'll find Asian foodies chasing Cantonese roasted duck, spicy braised chicken and wok-fried beef tenderloin with green tea and kumquat mojitos. Don't miss dim sum, either; or the wildly popular Saturday brunch (Dhs158 to Dhs258, noon to 4pm).

ROBERTO'S — ITALIAN $$

Map p136 (02 627 9009; www.robertos.ae/abudhabi; B3 Level, Rosewood Hotel, The Galleria Mall, Al Maryah Island; mains Dhs90-385; noon-3am) The pastas and risottos are already something of a legend around the capital, and even the most seemingly simple dishes are packed with rich and deep flavours. Roberto's Ravioli is our pick on the menu. The signature cocktails are worth staying for, best enjoyed on the outdoor terrace with waterside city views.

BIRYANI POT INDIAN $$

Map p136 (www.biryanipot.ae; Al Falah St, Galleria Mall, Al Maryah Island; mains Dhs24-66; ⏲10am-11pm Sat-Wed, to midnight Thu & Fri; 📶) Billed as gourmet Indian fast food, the 'pot' does indeed do yummy biryanis – including raved-about gluten-free organic versions with quinoa – alongside curries, tandoor grills and salads. The food-court setting isn't conducive to lingering unless you camp out on the terrace, which has water views.

GODIVA CHOCOLATE CAFÉ CAFE $$

Map p136 (☎02 667 0717; www.galleria.ae; Galleria at Maryah Island, Al Maryah Island; coffee Dhs25-45, sandwiches Dhs50-55; ⏲11am-10pm; 📶) What makes this indulgent cafe in the Galleria Mall an experience is the exceptional view of Abu Dhabi's Al Zahiyah district from the wall of windows in its mezzanine location. The beautiful cakes, pastries and chocolate-dipped strawberries are delights.

★BUTCHER & STILL STEAK $$$

Map p136 (☎02 333 2444; www.fourseasons.com/abudhabi/dining/restaurants/butcher_and_still; Four Seasons Abu Dhabi, Al Maryah Island; steak Dhs280-490; ⏲6pm-midnight; 📶) How good is this 1920s Chicago-inspired steakhouse at Four Seasons Abu Dhabi? We don't have enough space to tell you. American chef Marshall Roth sources his meat from the Temple Grandin–designed Creekstone Farms in Kansas (USA); when paired with his from-scratch béchamel-creamed spinach, you have a perfectly executed classic combination.

★ZUMA JAPANESE $$$

Map p136 (☎02 401 5900; www.zumarestaurant.com; Galleria at Maryah Island, Al Maryah Island; mains Dhs115-358; ⏲noon-3.30pm & 7pm-midnight Sun-Wed, to 1am Thu & Fri; 📶) The summit of Japanese cuisine in Abu Dhabi. Book ahead to enjoy the superb sushi and sashimi, the signature miso-marinated black cod or a hunk of meat cooked to perfection on the robata grill. Alcohol served (sake, finely curated cocktails and Hitachino, one of Japan's best craft beers). The beautiful bar, fashioned from striking Indonesian teak, is buzzy to boot.

A four-course business lunch, served Monday to Thursday, costs Dhs175.

CRUST INTERNATIONAL $$$

Map p136 (☎02 333 2222; www.fourseasons.com/abudhabi/dining/restaurants/crust; 1st fl, Four Seasons Abu Dhabi, Al Maryah Island; breakfast buffet Dhs140, Fri brunch buffet with soft drinks/house drinks/champagne Dhs275/385/545; ⏲6.30-11am daily, plus 12.30-4pm Fri) This breakfast spot for Four Seasons guests is also open to the public, though Crust really comes into its own for Friday brunch. A sumptuous international buffet includes freshly baked breads, decadent truffle mash, melt-in-your-mouth Wagyu bresaola, unbeatable crispy prawns and a seasonal rotation of desserts to die for. Clear your calendar – Friday brunch is a social, indulgent all-day experience.

FINZ SEAFOOD $$$

Map p136 (☎02 697 9011; www.rotana.com; 10th St, Beach Rotana Hotel; mains Dhs72-305; ⏲12.30pm-3.15am & 7-11pm; 📶) Amble down the jetty to this A-frame with terraces above the sea and enjoy some of the finest seafood in town. Whether chargrilled, steamed or baked, the results are invariably delicious in this recently made-over classic. Whole sea bass baked in salt for two remains a staple, but newer, surprisingly paired dishes (like scallops with short ribs) are worth considering.

COYA PERUVIAN $$$

Map p136 (☎02 306 7000; www.coyarestaurant.com/menu/abu-dhabi; Galleria, Four Seasons Abu Dhabi, Al Maryah Island; mains Dhs48-980; ⏲12.30-11pm, bar to 1.15am) Billed as modern Peruvian cuisine, the menu of sharing plates goes fusion, with inspiration from Latin America and the Far East. House specials include traditional ceviche and Peruvian sashimi, both achingly crisp and fresh. As vibrant as the food, the decor, along with impressive waterfront views, adds a heady but luxurious feel: an alluring concoction for a romantic night out.

DRINKING & NIGHTLIFE

Drinking and nightlife has a gritty edge to it in this part of town, with echoes of the city's expat, oil-pioneering past ingrained in the carpets of many a faded hotel. The new developments around Al Maryah Island have begun to change all that, however, attracting a new generation of city wheelers and dealers with cash to spend.

LA CAVA WINE BAR

Map p136 (☎02 813 5550; www.rosewoodhotels.com/en/abu-dhabi/dining/la-cava; Rosewood Hotel, Al Maryah Island; ⏲5pm-1am; 📶) Saunter down a dramatic candlelit staircase to this cellar-like hideaway in the Rosewood Hotel, probably Abu Dhabi's best destination for oenophiles in need. More than 1000 wine labels await, a handful of which are available by the glass (give Ixsir Altitudes Red from Lebanon a shot). Pair with the all-you-can-eat buffet of gourmet Spanish tapas, cheeses and desserts.

ECLIPSE TERRACE LOUNGE ROOFTOP BAR

Map p136 (☎02 333 2222; www.fourseasons.com/abudhabi/dining/lounges/eclipse_terrace_lounge; 3rd fl, pool level, Four Seasons Abu Dhabi, Al Maryah Island; ⏲11am-1am) Poolside Eclipse is a worthy spot to enjoy stunning views over the water and rooftops of the city. During the day it has a laid-back and relaxed vibe. The lounge comes alive for sundowners and then into the night with atmospheric chill-out tunes from the DJ as the understated but well-heeled, pre- and post-dinner crowd arrive.

BUTCHER & STILL COCKTAIL BAR

Map p136 (www.fourseasons.com/abudhabi/dining/restaurants/butcher_and_still; Four Seasons Hotel, Al Maryah Island; cocktails Dhs55-100; ⏲4pm-1am; 📶) A connoisseur's cocktail bar with a speakeasy vibe, Butcher & Still has a black marble bar, hardwood features and leather everywhere to pad the elbows. Smoked Manhattans and other creative Prohibition-era tipples, often made with house-mixed bitters, syrups and tinctures, dominate. Selected cocktails are shaken in an antique Tanqueray No 10 Imperial Shaker, one of only five in the world.

PLANET CAFÉ SHISHA

Map p136 (☎02 676 7962; Hamdan St; mains Dhs28-60, shisha Dhs35-60; ⏲7am-1am; 📶) A hugely popular, independent cafe that has nothing to write home about other than the sense of participating in a beloved local ritual. If you're keen on board games – or sinking into cosy orange couches – then you'll have to be quick off the mark to reserve one.

BENTLEY KITCHEN COCKTAIL BAR

Map p136 (☎02 626 2131; www.bentleybistro.com; Galleria at Maryah Island; mocktails/cocktails Dhs35/49; ⏲8am-2am; 📶) With a wicked assortment of carefully crafted mocktails and cocktails, this classy bar attracts a well-dressed clientele. Balance the drinks with upper-crust snacks, such as Wagyu flat-iron steak and hand-cut chips. The bistro offers a classic European menu (along with a new Greek side) with a suitably first-class view of Abu Dhabi's skyline.

AL MEYLAS LOUNGE

Map p136 (☎02 333 2222; www.fourseasons.com/abudhabi/dining/lounges/al_meylas; Four Seasons Abu Dhabi, Al Maryah Island; ⏲9am-1am) Located a step down from the long catwalk-style corridor, Al Meylas is the spot for a sophisticated afternoon tea with melt-in-your-mouth buttery scones and a glass of bubbles. Sit outside on the terrace in the cooler months to take in the sun-drenched city skyline – it becomes more spectacular as the sun goes down.

SHOPPING

With two of the city's main malls – and the massive Al Maryah Central Mall on its way – you're covered for fashion and interior design. Explore the area around Le Meridien. There's more on offer than marble aisles and shop windows – independent carpet, souvenir and craft shops here provide a refreshing break from the uniform mall experience.

GALLERIA AT MARYAH ISLAND MALL

Map p136 (☎02 616 6999; www.thegalleria.ae; Al Falah St, Al Maryah Island; ⏲10am-10pm Sat-Wed, to midnight Thu, noon-midnight Fri; 📶) This flashy contender in the business district on Al Maryah Island has dramatic looks (cathedral-high ceilings, sculptural roof) and a line-up of brands that should appeal to deep-pocketed couture lovers. Think Jimmy Choo, Prada and Dior. Nice touch: two food courts with terraces overlooking a pond.

ABU DHABI MALL MALL

Map p136 (☎02 645 4858; www.abudhabi-mall.com; 10th St; ⏲10am-10pm Sat-Wed, to 11pm Thu & Fri) This elegant mall has the expected 200 stores, cinemas and children's amusements, but it also has shops with a local twist. On level 3, buy sweets and nuts from Al Rifai (Dhs35 to Dhs185 per kilogram – try the biryani cashews), while on level 1 Bateel's dates (Dhs100 to Dhs136 per kilogram) make good gifts.

GRAND STORES DEPARTMENT STORE

Map p136 (www.grandstores.com; Abu Dhabi Mall; ⏲10am-10pm Sat-Wed, to 11pm Thu & Fri) To buy a gift for someone who has everything, you may like to hunt down silver- and gold-plated falcons, dhows or camels at this otherwise unremarkable speciality retailer.

JASHANMAL DEPARTMENT STORE

Map p136 (www.jashanmalgroup.com; Abu Dhabi Mall; ⏲10am-10pm Sat-Wed, to 11pm Thu & Fri) Set up by an Indian businessman in 1919 in Basra, Iraq, this wholesale and retail enterprise has become the Gulf's answer to Debenhams or Macy's.

KHALIFA CENTRE SOUVENIRS, HANDICRAFTS

Map p136 (10th St, Al Zahiyah; ⏲10am-1pm & 4-10pm Sat-Thu, 4-10pm Fri) For a wide range of souvenirs (shisha pipes, camel-bone boxes, stuffed leather camels, carpets and cushion covers), head to the Khalifa Centre, across the road from the Abu Dhabi Mall, where you'll find a dozen independent stores, mostly run by the expat Indian community, selling handicrafts and carpets.

ENTERTAINMENT

49ER'S THE GOLD RUSH LIVE MUSIC

Map p136 (☎02 645 8000; www.aldiarhotels.com; Al Diar Dana Hotel, cnr Zayed the First & Al Firdous Sts; ⏲noon-3am; 📶) This long-running nightclub has earned its spurs over the years, with its Wild West theme, Stetsons, bucking-bronco decorations, and built-in barbecue kitchen serving Texas-sized steaks and fries. There's a resident band and a DJ.

NOVO CINEMAS ABU DHABI CINEMA

Map p136 (☎02 645 8988; www.novocinemas.com; 10th St, 3rd fl, Abu Dhabi Mall; tickets Dhs35-55) This multiplex shows the latest Hollywood films, some in 3D.

WATER-BASED EXPLORATIONS

Noukhada Adventure Company (☎02 558 1889; http://noukhada.ae; kayaking tours adult/child from Dhs160/130; ⏲office 8.30am-5.30pm) Specialising in local exploration by paddle, this tour company runs popular kayaking trips through the local mangrove swamps. A 90-minute tour (Dhs160) is a great way to experience this unusual habitat. The two-hour ecotour (Dhs220) gives an even deeper understanding of this unique environment. There's even a monthly full-moon tour (adults only, Dhs200).

Abu Dhabi Pearl Journey (Map p130; ☎02 656 1000; www.adpearljourney.com; Sheikh Zayed Bin Sultan St; adult/child Dhs500/400; ⏲cruises 9am-8pm) Based at the marine promenade at **Eastern Mangroves Hotel & Spa** (p170), these walk-in tours ply the mangrove channels on a traditional dhow and leave hourly. Cruises include interactive presentations of Abu Dhabi's past as a pearling culture. They also demonstrate traditional seafaring songs and offer Arabic coffee and dates.

Captain Tony's (☎02 650 7175; http://captaintonys.ae; 90min sunset cruise adult/child Dhs250/150; ⏲4.30pm, times vary with season) Offering a wide range of cruises with an ecofriendly approach, this company runs a relaxing and popular sunset tour, ecotours to the mangroves, and a four-hour escape to a natural sandbar with sandwiches, umbrellas, deckchairs, buckets and spades. Stand-up paddleboarding and fishing is also on offer. Most departures are from Yas Marina.

Abu Dhabi Dhow Cruise (Map p136; ☎056 713 3703; www.abudhabidhowcruise.com; Dhow Harbour, Al Mina; dinner adult/child Dhs250/200, sunset adult/child Dhs65/45) This company offers lunch (1.30pm to 3pm), sunset (5.45pm to 6.45pm) and dinner cruises (8pm to 10pm). The food is simple fare but includes fresh fish. There is a minimum of 25 required for the lunch (other than Saturday) and sunset trips, which cruise along from the harbour. For an extra fee the company operates a pick-up service from major hotels.

SPORTS & ACTIVITIES

SENSE SPA

Map p136 (☎02 813 5537; www.rosewoodhotels.com; Rosewood Hotel; massages Dhs410-572, 30min milk bath Dhs202; ⏰10am-10pm) With nine treatment rooms, white leather lounges and traditional hammams, this is a temple of relaxation and therapy. It offers a masterclass in decadent design showcasing a marble soaking tub, bronze tiles, mist rooms, fibre-optic features and an infrared stone wall. Soak in a Cleopatra bath with goat's milk and the tub back home will never be the same again.

BEACH ROTANA CLUB SWIMMING

Map p136 (☎02 697 9302; www.rotana.com; 10th St, Beach Rotana Hotel & Towers; single/couple/child Fri & Sat Dhs220/320/95, Sun-Thu Dhs155/240/95; ⏰6am-11pm, pool 7am-10pm, beach 8am-sunset) With a small but pleasant beach, a grassy lawn, swimming pools and a wet bar/cafe, this club welcomes day visitors (though guests and members are prioritised if it gets crowded). There's an impressive view of the Al Maryah Island developments opposite.

Sheikh Zayed Grand Mosque & Around

In addition to the Sheikh Zayed Grand Mosque, there are sights scattered across the lower end of Abu Dhabi Island, but mostly they are not within walking distance. The Big Bus (p144) tour links the exhibition centre with the mosque and the Eastern Corniche but doesn't stray across to the mainland, so taxis or car hire may be the best way to visit this area.

SIGHTS

SHEIKH ZAYED GRAND MOSQUE MOSQUE

See p127.

MIRAJ – THE MUSEUM GALLERY

Map p151 (☎02 449 1041; www.mirajabudhabi.com; Sheikh Rashid Bin Saeed St; ⏰9.30am-6pm) FREE Showcasing beautiful objects from around the Islamic world (and India, Indonesia, Malaysia and beyond), including Persian carpets, calligraphy, ceramics and textiles, this private gallery-cum-museum is open for view, with most pieces also for sale. There's a lot to love throughout the labyrinthine galleries if you have the patience (and can tolerate the incessant lollygagging of the shop minders behind you – 'house rules').

SHEIKH ZAYED GRAND MOSQUE CENTRE LIBRARY LIBRARY

Map p151 (☎02 419 1919; www.szgmc.ae; off Sheikh Rashid Bin Saeed St; ⏰9am-6pm Sun-Thu) FREE Though it houses a few rare collections of Arabic calligraphy and copies of the Quran dating from the 16th century, this collection of manuscripts is intended primarily as a research centre, and there isn't much to see unless you are working on a thesis.

CAPITAL GATE LANDMARK

Map p130 (☎02 596 1234; www.capitalgate.ae; Al Khaleej Al Arabi St) Look out the window from many points in Abu Dhabi at night and you could be forgiven for thinking you've had one too many at the bar: reaching skyward in the city's southeast is this 35-floor, dramatically tilting skyscraper that holds the Guinness World Record as the world's most leaning tower (at 18 degrees westwards, it's over four times more wayward than the Leaning Tower of Pisa).

EASTERN MANGROVES PROMENADE WATERFRONT

Map p130 (New Corniche; Sheikh Zayed Bin Sultan St; E10) The seaward side of Sheikh Zayed Bin Sultan St has been developed into a promenade to rival Abu Dhabi's original downtown Corniche, with a series of landscaped gardens, parking bays, picnic areas and paths. Offering excellent views of Eastern Lagoon Mangrove National Park, this is a good place to watch birds or dangle a line in the water.

KHALIFA PARK PARK

Map p151 (www.adm.gov.ae; Al Salam St; adult/child Dhs1/free; ⏰3-10pm Sun-Thu, to 11pm Fri & Sat) This large and leafy park, not far from the Sheikh Zayed Grand Mosque (p127), has a number of attractions, including a football playing area, fountains, ponds and waterfalls, lots of shaded seating, a children's amusement park and a small train that trundles around the site.

Sheikh Zayed Grand Mosque & Around

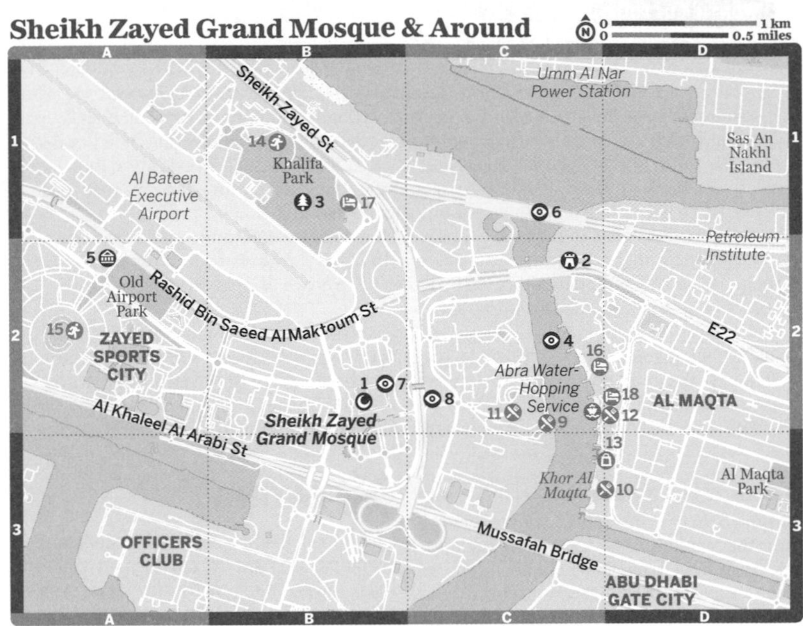

Sheikh Zayed Grand Mosque & Around

KHOR AL MAQTA WATERFRONT

Map p151 (Bain Al Jessrain) This historic waterway separates Abu Dhabi from the mainland, guarded by the now somewhat hidden Al Maqta Fort (p152) and a small watchtower, on a rocky promontory in the middle of the *khor* (creek). Luxury hotels and the charming Souk Qaryat Al Beri line the banks. Walking paths and abras (small traditional ferries) help visitors move between hotels and sights, while the snowy-white Sheikh Zayed Grand Mosque (p127) looms in the background.

WORTH A DETOUR

ABU DHABI FALCON HOSPITAL

Standing outside **Abu Dhabi Falcon Hospital** (Map p130; ☎02 575 5155; www.falconhospital.com; Sweihan Rd; 2hr tour adult/child Dhs170/60; ⊙tours 2pm Sat, 10am & 2pm Sun-Thu), watching anxious owners from across the region delivering their hooded 'patients' in person, you will quickly realise that this is a much-needed and much-loved facility. Falcons are an integral part of traditional Gulf culture and no expense is spared in restoring these magnificent birds to full health.

Tours include visits to the falcon museum, the examination room – including intimate glimpses into coping procedures – and the free-flight aviary. Tour reservations (bookable online) are mandatory. If you're willing to brave an arm, the well-behaved raptors will even perch for a photograph.

The hospital is about 6km southeast of Abu Dhabi airport. Coming from central Abu Dhabi, follow Airport Rd (E20) to Sweihan Rd in the direction of Falah City; about 3km past the junction with Hwy E11, turn right after the water tank (before exit 30A) and follow the signs to the hospital.

The hospital complex is also home to the **Arabian Saluki Centre** (p159).

SHEIKH ZAYED BRIDGE — BRIDGE

Map p151 Said to symbolise the flow of energy into the capital, this 842m-long modern bridge designed by Zaha Hadid is one of three gateways to Abu Dhabi. Its curvilinear form is reminiscent of sand dunes, and at night the lighting scheme gives a sense that the dunes are on the move.

AL MAQTA FORT & WATCHTOWER — FORT

Map p151 (Al Maqta Bridge; ⊙24hr; interior closed) FREE Despite being one of the oldest sights in Abu Dhabi, this 200-year-old guardian of the city was restored and then more or less abandoned after the visitors centre here closed (though word has it that a new, as-yet-undisclosed project is in the works). For now, although neglected, this old relic, with its companion watchtower on a rocky island in Khor Al Maqta (the so-called Abu Dhabi Grand Canal), is worth an up-close view – if you can find it!

★UMM AL EMARAT PARK — PARK

Map p130 (Mushrif Central Park; www.mushrifcentralpark.ae; 15th St; adult/child (under 3) Dhs5/free; ⊙8am-midnight) You almost walk away from this five-star urban park feeling like you've visited a museum. Manicured to perfection and full of design-forward and thoroughly interesting distractions, it more than justifies its admission fee. Highlights of the wonderful smoke-free space include a poignant memorial to the words of Sheikh Zayed; a sexy greenhouse with stupendous views; an animal barn with camels, goats, donkeys, llamas and the like; a botanical garden, and an outdoor performing-arts venue.

EATING

The hotels around Bain Al Jessrain offer a cornucopia of exotic cuisines in fine-dining venues, many with spectacular views of Sheikh Zayed Grand Mosque. Locally caught seafood and rich Middle Eastern flavours dominate menus. It's best to book for many of these restaurants, particularly during high seasons (around Western New Year and school holidays), Islamic Eid festivals and the Grand Prix weekend.

HOME BAKERY — CAFE $

Map p130 (www.homebakery.ae; Umm Al Emarat Park; mains Dhs30-55; ⊙8am-midnight; 📶) The United Arab Emirates is made up of a mere 10% Emiratis, and we'll be damned if you don't find nearly all of them at this trendy bakery inside the wonderful Umm Al Emarat Park (p152). The stylish haunt serves tea, coffee, juices, shakes and decadent cakes in addition to gourmet breakfasts and sandwiches.

SALT — FOOD TRUCK $

Map p130 (www.find-salt.com; Umm Al Emarat Park; burgers Dhs35-50; ⊙9am-2am) Born in Dubai at the hands of a female Emirati-Saudi partnership, the wildly friendly Salt food truck had people chasing it all over the United Arab Emirates before permanently landing a prime spot at Umm Al Emarat Park (p152; among other locations). The slick Airstream trailer does griddle-seared, grass-fed, hormone-free, halal, Wagyu-style beef miniburgers, along with fries, juices, ice cream and milkshakes.

★CAFÉ ARABIA MIDDLE EASTERN **$$**

Map p130 (☎02 643 9699; www.facebook.com/cafearabia; Villa No 224/1, 15th St, btwn Airport (2nd) Rd & Al Karamah (24th) St; mains Dhs32-55; ⏲8am-11pm Mon-Thu, 9am-11pm Fri-Sun; 📶) This homey cafe, housed in a three-floor villa, is run by a Lebanese arts enthusiast, Aida Mansour. Tasty pastries, fantastic breakfasts (shakshuka to die for) and Turkish coffee shine, but many come for the Arabian ambience, photographs, hanging lanterns, eclectic furniture and book-swap service. It's something of a community meeting place, and arts exhibitions and literary groups are hosted here.

USHNA INDIAN **$$**

Map p151 (☎02 558 1769; Souk Qaryat Al Beri, Bain Al Jessrain; mains Dhs55-230; ⏲12.30-11.30pm) 🍃 Romantic and elegant, this place hums with appreciation for the complex cuisine of India, brought to the United Arab Emirates by a large expat community. There are many curry houses across town, but this restaurant offers some of the most luscious variations, alongside beautiful views across the canal to the Grand Mosque, with a sustainable seafood commitment to boot.

MILAS EMIRATI **$$**

Map p151 (☎02 558 0425; www.milas.cc; Khor Al Maqta; mains Dhs30-95; ⏲9am-11.30pm; 📶) Dark wood, black glass and neon announce that this is an Emirati restaurant for the 21st century. Traditional dishes such as chicken *machboos* (casserole) and *deyay shiwa* (chicken marinated in saffron yoghurt) have been given a contemporary makeover. Thoughtful perks: wet handcloths, a complimentary *dangaw* (chickpea) appetiser and a post-meal perfume tray. It's on the 1st floor of Souk Qaryat Al Beri (p154).

★MIJANA LEBANESE **$$$**

Map p151 (☎02 818 8282; www.ritzcarlton.com; Khor Al Maqta; mains Dhs75-160; ⏲4pm-1am Tue-Sun) At the Ritz-Carlton, this swish venue offers contemporary Lebanese cuisine with interesting twists on favourite themes, such as beetroot *moutabel* (smoked aubergine dip), six varieties of hummus and *habra niyah* (raw mince lamb 'cooked' in fresh mint and garlic). Leave space for a shisha on the terrace with live Arabic music.

★BORD EAU FRENCH **$$$**

Map p151 (☎02 509 8511; www.shangri-la.com; Khor Al Maqta; mains Dhs105-265, 5-course blind tasting menu Dhs450, with wine Dhs750; ⏲6.30-11.30pm; 📶) Bord Eau at the Shangri-La Hotel is *le* restaurant for French fine dining in Abu Dhabi. The classic French fare (onion soup, foie gras, chateaubriand) is flawlessly executed with a modern twist and the flavours are calibrated to perfection. With simple elegance (including reproduction Degas ballerinas gracing the walls), the ambience matches the refined quality of the food.

18° MEDITERRANEAN **$$$**

Map p130 (☎02 596 1440; www.abudhabi.capitalgate.hyatt.com; Al Khaleej Al Arabi St, Hyatt Capital Gate, ADNEC; mains Dhs110-175; ⏲7-11.30pm, brunch noon-3pm Fri; 📶) Named after the degree of 'lean' in Abu Dhabi's famous Capital Gate (p150) skyscraper, and after the 18th floor on which it's situated, this Mediterranean-style restaurant

WAHAT AL KARAMA

The poignant **Wahat Al Karama** (Map p151; www.wahatalkarama.ae; 3rd St, Khor Al Maqta; ⏲9am-10pm, tours 11am & 5pm) FREE memorial, opposite the eastern side of the Grand Mosque, was inaugurated in 2016 in memory of Emiratis who have given their lives in service to the nation. Besides postcard-perfect views to the Grand Mosque, the main memorial features 31 massive aluminium-clad tablets in leaning stacks inscribed with poems and quotations from prominent UAE figureheads.

The Pavilion of Honour, an embedded polygon structure, is lined with a circular internal wall clad with more than 2800 aluminium plates inscribed with the names of the UAE's heroes. The Memorial Plaza is fashioned from Turkish travertine stone that forms a large circular pool of 15mm-deep water which reflects the Grand Mosque and memorial panels. Shuttle buses shuffle between the north car park of the Grand Mosque and Wahat Al Karama every 30 minutes between 10am and 6.30pm daily.

offers many Levantine favourites. Watch your dinner being cooked at the three interactive show kitchens or sit outside on the terrace and wonder how the food stays on the plate in this apparently leaning tower.

MARCO PIERRE WHITE STEAKHOUSE & GRILL STEAK $$$
Map p151 (02 654 3333; www.fairmont.com/abu-dhabi; Fairmont Bab Al Bhar; steaks Dhs175-545; 6pm-midnight;) Strictly carnivore in emphasis, this restaurant is the creation of British celebrity chef Marco Pierre White. A dramatic 'flame wall' gives the dining area a Dante-esque quality, but fortunately the culinary pyrotechnics produce heavenly results. The focus is squarely on quality cuts, prepared in both classic English style and innovative grilled variations.

BARFLY BY BUDDHA BAR ASIAN $$$
Map p151 (056 177 7557; http://barfly.ae; Venetian Village; mains Dhs75-280; 6pm-2am Sun-Wed, 6pm-3am Thu, 4pm-3am Fri, 4pm-1am Sat) In a beautiful waterfront setting, Barfly is a self-proclaimed supper club with a Far East–inspired menu, where dishes range from wok-seared sweet and sour prawns and Thai chilli chicken to international classics such as herb-crusted lamb chops and risotto. The sushi and sashimi really steal the show.

GIORNOTTE BREAKFAST $$$
Map p151 (02 818 8282; www.ritzcarlton.com; Ritz-Carlton Grand Canal; Fri brunch with/without drinks Dhs395/295; 1-4pm Fri) Live dance shows provide the entertainment for one of the city's best brunches. If that isn't entertainment enough, there are 27 live stations (chefs preparing food at counters in the restaurant), Wagyu beef carving, oyster-openings etc, not to mention trips to a dedicated dessert room.

SHO CHO JAPANESE $$$
Map p151 (02 558 1117; www.sho-cho.com; Souk Qaryat Al Beri, Bain Al Jessrain; mains Dhs61-148; noon-3am Sun-Thu;) A stylish Japanese restaurant with appropriate minimalist decor. Dishes are delicious, if a tad minimalist. Don't miss the seared sesame yellow-tail starter or the delicate and decorative maki sushi rolls. There's a DJ at weekends. Reservations are essential.

DRINKING & NIGHTLIFE

The numerous lounges and bars scattered around the hotels on the eastern side of Khor Al Maqta serve mocktails and cocktails. Most are within ambling distance of each other along the paths following the water's edge. Souk Qaryat Al Beri is at the heart of Bain Al Jessrain, offering coffee houses and cafes in a tasteful, modern rendition of an ancient souq.

★COOPER'S BAR
Map p151 (www.rotana.com; Park Rotana Abu Dhabi; pints Dhs24-42; noon-2.30am Sun-Wed, to 3.30am Fri & Sat;) A well-established bar, with an old-fashioned, wood-panelled, brass-trimmed ambience, this watering hole is renowned for its popular ladies' nights (Mondays to Fridays, though Tuesday is limited to teachers and cabin crew) with complimentary spirits.

RELAX@12 BAR
Map p130 (02 654 5183; Al Khaleej Al Arabi St, Aloft Hotel; cocktails Dhs48-60; 5pm-3am Wed-Fri, to 2am Sat-Tue) This stylish rooftop bar at the Aloft Abu Dhabi hotel (p169) indeed puts you in the mood for relaxing, with mellow sounds, comfy seating and an extensive drinks menu that won't eviscerate your wallet. Sushi as well as Chinese and Thai tapas-style dishes are available to help you stay stable, and there are different promotions almost every night.

SHOPPING

The streets of Al Maqta, inland from the Bain Al Jessrain tourist facilities, offer an insight into local life. Here *abaya* shops have the latest diamanté-encrusted fashions, colourful frock shops sell long dresses favoured by local women, tailors sell *kandoura* (long robes), and dozens of outlets have traditional perfumes and water pipes. For a more visitor-oriented shopping experience try Souk Qaryat Al Beri.

SOUK QARYAT AL BERI MARKET
Map p151 (02 558 1670; www.soukqaryatalberi.com; Khor Al Maqta; 10am-10pm Sun-Wed, 10am-11pm Thu, 3-11pm Fri) This 21st-century take on the classic souq gets a thumbs-up for its appealing Arabian architecture and waterfront location. The

WORTH A DETOUR

ABU DHABI'S CLEAN-TECH CITY

Near Abu Dhabi airport, **Masdar City** (Map p161; ☎800 627 327; www.masdar.ae; btwn Hwys E10 & E20; ⏲9am-5pm Sun-Thu) FREE is the world's first carbon-neutral, zero-waste city powered entirely by renewable energy. However, this is not your regular residential neighbourhood but rather a science community with a graduate-research university and companies focused on sustainability, clean tech and renewable energy. It's a great place to visit for the architecture and the sci-fi vibe.

Part of the fun is hopping on a pod-like driverless Personal Rapid Transit (PRT) vehicle at the car park for the short ride to the main campus (an expansion was under way at time of research to cover the whole campus). Pick up a map at the information desk upstairs from the PRT terminal (or download it from the website) for a self-guided tour. Several cafes and restaurants provide sustenance.

shops, which are popular with tourists and locals, stock many items with roots in Arabia, including oil-based perfumes, cookies made with camel's milk, chocolate-covered dates and handcrafted jewellery. Some small stalls sell souvenirs and craft items.

PARIS AVENUE FASHION & ACCESSORIES

Map p130 (☎02 653 4030; www.parisavenue.ae; Al Falahi Tower, Muroor; ⏲10am-8pm Sat-Thu) A favourite boutique that trends with the latest fashionable accessories from young graduate designers from Europe.

WOMEN'S HANDICRAFT CENTRE ARTS & CRAFTS

Map p130 (☎02 447 6645; Al Karamah (24th St); admission Dhs5; ⏲9am-3pm Sun-Thu) This government-run centre showcases textile weaving, embroidery, basket-making, silver-thread needlework and other time-honoured crafts traditional to the region. Shoes should be removed before entering the various workshops and permission sought for photographs. All items are for sale in the on-site shop. There is a henna bar for women; this temporary souvenir lasts about a week.

SPORTS & ACTIVITIES

ANANTARA SPA SPA

Map p130 (☎02 656 1146; www.abu-dhabi.anantara.com; Eastern Mangroves Hotel; 90min signature massage Dhs864; ⏲10am-11pm) With 15 treatment rooms and facilities for couples, the best part of this spa is the traditional Turkish hammam. A celebration of marble, mirrors and water features, the spa feels fit for royalty.

ZAYED SPORTS CITY BOWLING

Map p151 (☎02 403 4648; www.zsc.ae; Al Khaleej al Arabi St; per game from Dhs15; ⏲9am-1am) Housing the Khalifa International Bowling Centre, this huge complex has a somewhat-intimidating 40 lanes of play. Also on-site is an ice rink and professional tennis courts, venue of the Mubadala World Tennis Championship (p45), where you can play on the same court as your idol – though sadly not at the same time!

MURJAN SPLASH PARK WATER PARK

Map p151 (☎050 878 1009; www.murjansplashpark.weebly.com; Al Salam St, Khalifa Park; over/under 75cm Dhs45/free; ⏲noon-9pm) Offers a range of children's activities including water slides, water guns, 'lazy river ride' and trampolines. There's also a 'surf wrangler' for learning surfing with an instructor present.

Al Mina & Saadiyat Island

Saadiyat Island casts an interesting light on Abu Dhabi's cultural inheritance, past and present, and affords a glimpse of the city's future as artistic capital of the Gulf with the Abu Dhabi Louvre. The Al Mina port area is home to the old dhow harbour and interesting souqs, while Saadiyat Island's sandy beaches and protected coastal environment offer a world removed from urban life.

TOP SIGHT
LOUVRE ABU DHABI

Designed by Pritzker Prize–winning architect Jean Nouvel, the highly anticipated Louvre Abu Dhabi finally arrived in late 2017. The striking project features a contrasting medina-inspired sequence of white buildings flanking the centrepiece: an elaborate, 180m-wide filigree dome. The dome pays homage to desert-palm shading – its geometric openings represent interlaced palm leaves used in traditional roofing – and creates a cinematic 'rain of light' effect in the 23 galleries as the sun's rays pass throughout the day.

The galleries, which present a world-class collection of paintings, sculpture and objects from antiquity to the present, are laid out in 12 sequences highlighting universal themes and common influences, transcending geography, nationality and history. The 600 works have been selected from the Louvre's vast repositories (plus 300 on loan from other leading French museums). Highlights include a 3rd millennium BC standing Bactrian Princess, Osman Hamdi Bey's *A Young Emir Studying* (1878), a 1928 collage by Picasso titled *Portrait of a Lady* and Paul Gauguin's masterpiece *Children Wrestling*, among a wealth of French masterpieces.

Don't Miss

- The most ancient known photographic representation of a veiled woman
- A 3000-year-old Middle Eastern gold bracelet with a lion's head

Practicalities

- Map p130, B1
- http://louvreabudhabi.ae
- Cultural District, Saadiyat Island
- Dhs60

SIGHTS

In time, the main sights of Saadiyat Island will be clustered within walking distance of Manarat Al Saadiyat, a free-form cultural centre for the slowly evolving Abu Dhabi Cultural District. For now, this centre, the neighbouring UAE Pavilion and the new Abu Dhabi Louvre are the only cultural sights, but that will change with the eventual opening of the Guggenheim Abu Dhabi and the Zayed National Museum. Beaches and hotels are strung along the western shore beyond this area. The Yas Express links Saadiyat with Yas Island via the impressive Sheikh Khalifa Bin Zayed Hwy.

MANARAT AL SAADIYAT MUSEUM

Map p130 (☎02 657 5800; www.saadiyatculturaldistrict.ae; Cultural District, Saadiyat Island; ⏲9am-8pm) FREE Housed in a postmodern building with an eye-catching honeycomb mantle, Manarat Al Saadiyat ('place of enlightenment') houses four art- and culture-focused galleries. The temporary exhibitions often focus on future art and museum pieces due to be permanently stationed in upcoming headline-making museums such as the Guggenheim Abu Dhabi and the Sheikh Zayed Museum; as well as exhibiting the annual Emirati photography competition and the Abu Dhabi Art festival.

SAADIYAT PUBLIC BEACH BEACH

Map p130 (www.bakeuae.com; Saadiyat Island; adult/child Dhs25/15; ⏲8am-8pm) A boardwalk leads through a protected zone of coastal vegetation to this beautiful powdery white beach, home to nesting turtles, on the northwest coast of Saadiyat Island (near Park Hyatt Abu Dhabi). There's a lifeguard until sunset and a cafe, but no alcohol. Rent towels for Dhs10 and sunloungers for Dhs25.

UAE PAVILION NOTABLE BUILDING

Map p130 (☎02 406 1501; www.saadiyatculturaldistrict.ae; Cultural District, Saadiyat Island) FREE Shaped like two parallel sand dunes – smooth and curvaceous on the windward side, steep and rippled on the eroded side – this award-winning building by Sir Norman Foster and partners was designed for the 2010 Shanghai Expo. Now used as an exhibition space for touring cultural shows, this striking building is worth a visit. It comes into its own in November, when it hosts the Abu Dhabi contemporary art fair, along with Manarat Al Saadiyat (p156) next door.

GUGGENHEIM ABU DHABI MUSEUM

Map p130 (Saadiyat Island) Designed by award-winning architect Frank Gehry, the Guggenheim Abu Dhabi promises the same striking design that he's is famous for but with a nod to the traditional culture and design of the region. With 30,000 sq metres planned for exhibitions and galleries, the Guggenheim will be another jewel in Abu Dhabi's arts and culture crown. The opening date has been delayed since 2012, but curating the collection is already well underway with periodic pre-opening exhibitions at Manarat Al Saadiyat (p156).

AL MINA FISH MARKET MARKET

Map p136 (Dhow Harbour, Al Mina; ⏲7am-10pm) Never mind the prospect of lots of tasty seafood, this large fish market is a visual feast of colour, texture and design. Rhythmical arrangements of prawns, orange-spotted trevally, blue-shelled crabs, red snappers, pink Sultan Ibrahims and a host of unlikely edibles from the sea grace the ice bars here.

FRUIT & VEGETABLE MARKET MARKET

Map p130 (Al Mina; ⏲7am-midnight) This vast wholesale market, part of which is open-air, is the exchange point for melons from Jordan, potatoes from Turkey and onions from just about everywhere. A highlight is cruising along 'date alley', where shops sell around 45 varieties (from Dhs25 per kilogram). Giant *medjool* dates from Saudi Arabia cost Dhs70 to Dhs120 per kilogram, while medicinal *ajwa* dates fetch Dhs120 per kilogram. Try the plump, yellow *sucri* dates, which are prized for their sweetness.

WAREHOUSE 421 CULTURAL CENTRE

Map p136 (www.warehouse421.ae; Al Mina; ⏲10am-8pm Tue-Sun) FREE In a former port warehouse, this contemporary museum hosts exhibitions showcasing the UAE's art, culture, design and creativity scenes,along with workshops and film screenings in winter. It's a good bet for checking out the latest in cutting-edge Abu Dhabi art and culture. Look for the 18m-long cast-iron ship out the front.

DHOW HARBOUR HARBOUR

Map p136 (Al Mina) There's something fascinating about sitting by the harbourside watching the beautiful dhows (traditional wooden cargo boats) slip off to sea. At any time of day, there's work going on as fishers mend their nets, pile up lobster pots, hang out colourful sarongs to dry, unload fish and congregate for communal chats. As you survey the resting dhows strung together five abreast, you can almost forget Abu Dhabi's modern backdrop as its ancient past as a fishing village is revealed.

EATING

With limited residential areas on the island so far, eating is pretty much restricted to hotels and beach clubs. This is no hardship, however, as there are plenty of options to fit all budgets.

SAUDI KITCHEN MIDDLE EASTERN $

Map p136 (☎02 673 0673; Al Teelah St, Al Mina Port; mains Dhs30-70) This snug little den near the Mina Fish Market is decked out

LOCAL KNOWLEDGE

DIY FISH SUPPER

For a memorable lunch or supper for under Dhs50, buy your fish at the **Al Mina Fish Market** (p157) from the folk in blue (Dhs25 to Dhs35 per kilogram), and take it to the folk in red in the gutting and filleting station (Dhs2 per kilogram). Take the fillets next door (alongside the dry-fish section) and jostle with seafarers for your favourite spices. Then give your purchases to the cooks at one of the few restaurants, who will make it into a fire-hot Kerala fish curry or simply grill it rubbed in salt and lemon (Dhs15 per kilogram). Take the finished dish on to the dhow harbour outside and sit on a lobster pot to eat it! It doesn't get fresher than that.

WORTH A DETOUR

NURAI ISLAND

A 12-minute boat ride from Saadiyat Island, **Nurai Island** (☎02 506 6222; www.zayanuraiisland.com) is a piece of paradise that was awarded a 'Most Luxurious Project in the World' nod by *Newsweek* and is touted by the island's only tenant, the luxe **Zaya Nurai Island Resort** (1-/2-bedroom villas from Dhs4965/5700 incl unlimited boat transfers; @☎), as the Maldives of Arabia. It is indeed a postcard-perfect getaway, a lush, nearly 1-km-sq island with calm beaches, sun-toasted sands and top-end food and amenities.

Opened in 2015, this supremely idyllic getaway has 32 massive one- and two-bedroom villas that you'll need to be pried from at checkout. The modern villas, dressed in light and airy whites and pastels and best labelled as Scandinavia chic, feature private pools and poolside daybeds, deep soaking bathtubs and top-notch contemporary amenities, including a bike for each guest.

You can wheel around to five restaurants and bars (the Mexican-Lebanese executive chef is a true talent). There's a supreme spa with ocean-view treatment rooms; several beaches, including the rustic Smokin' Pineapple, which features overwater swings and hammocks, a bar and various water sports; and a trendy wine-stocked library. And the whole thing is mostly solar-powered to boot.

If you're not staying at the resort, you can enjoy a day here (10am to 11pm) for Dhs420.

with partitioned cushioned floor seating (no shoes please). It's the perfect place to try traditional, falling-off-the-bone lamb or chicken from the heart of the Peninsula such as *mandi* (slow-roasted for many hours and served with rice and chilli sauce) or *madfoon* (slow-roasted with nuts and raisins over rice).

AL MINA MODERN CUISINE & RESTAURANT SEAFOOD **$**

Map p136 (☎02 673 3390; Al Mina; mains Dhs45-65; ⊙noon-midnight) Most visitors steam on past this wonderful little restaurant in the hunt for its more famous neighbour, Al Dhafra Restaurant. That's a pity because the ambience here is every bit as authentic, with lots of old photographs on the wall, pet fish in the aquarium and the catch of the day delivered virtually from dhow to dinner plate.

VIRONA SEAFOOD **$**

Map p136 (Fish Market, Al Mina; set lunch Dhs7-13; ⊙11am-3pm) If you want a flavour of how seafood is enjoyed locally, nose round the back of the fish market, near the dry-fish section. This tiny Indian restaurant (name in Arabic only) serves as a canteen for harbour hands and traders, but they are accommodating to those looking to sample the delicious set platters of rice, fish, biryani, sambal and dal.

★BEACH HOUSE MEDITERRANEAN **$$**

Map p130 (☎02 407 1138; www.abudhabi.park.hyatt.com; Park Hyatt Abu Dhabi; mains Dhs115-205; ⊙12.30-11.30pm Sun-Thu, 9am-11pm Fri & Sat) Open for breakfast on weekends and lunch and dinner otherwise, this restaurant, with its emphasis on homey Mediterranean fare, has an enviable location amid the sand dunes on the Saadiyat Island coast. In the cooler months, go up to the Beach House Rooftop (p159) for arguably Abu Dhabi's best sunset views.

AL DHAFRA RESTAURANT MIDDLE EASTERN **$$**

Map p136 (☎02 673 2266; www.aldhafrauae.ae; Al Mina Port; buffet lunch/dinner from Dhs120/99, dinner cruise Dhs150; ⊙noon-5pm & 6.30-11.15pm; ☎) This aged, flamboyant gem, with its fading Arabian decor and hand-carved furniture, sports a sumptuous *majlis* (reception room) that has entertained princes and sheikhs over the decades. The lunch buffet offers one of the best opportunities in Abu Dhabi to sample local dishes, including *ouzi* (baked lamb) and *machboos* (chicken baked in rice).

It also runs a floating restaurant on board a traditional dhow (8.30pm to 10.30pm nightly) from Al Mina to the Breakwater and back. It's a fun setting for sampling Arabic dishes while sitting cross-legged on sedans and cushions and enjoying stunning views of Abu Dhabi's night-time skyline. It's near the fish market.

DRINKING & NIGHTLIFE

BEACH HOUSE ROOFTOP ROOFTOP BAR

Map p130 (☎02 407 1138; www.hyattrestaurants.com; ⏰5pm-1am Mon-Sun) Don't be deceived by the unassuming back staircase entrance. Climb to the top, and you'll be dazzled by incredible turquoise waters and panoramic ocean vistas. Atmospheric music at just the right volume and low, emotive lighting set the tone, though it's Mother Nature's stunning sunsets and gentle sound of waves lapping that really steal the show.

DE LA COSTA LOUNGE

Map p130 (☎02 656 3572; www.saadiyatbeachclub.ae; Saadiyat Beach Club; cocktails Dhs50-60; ⏰5pm-midnight Sat-Wed, to 2am Thu & Fri) With a beautiful vista, comfortable armchairs and sophisticated tipples, this is a delightful place to watch the sun go down across the water. Cooler months see DJs spinning on weekends.

BUDDHA-BAR BEACH LOUNGE

Map p130 (www.buddhabar.com; St Regis Saadiyat Island Resort, Saadiyat Island; Wi-Fi) The famous Asian-themed chillax lounge from Paris has brought its normally temporary beach-bar concept to Abu Dhabi – the first location to receive a permanent branch. This wildly popular spot has made a name for itself by setting its signature Asian-Mediterranean mix to a soundtrack of stirring lounge music with a Buddha statue or two for good measure.

NAVONA RESTAURANT & COFFEESHOP CAFE

Map p136 (Area 5, Dhow Harbour, Al Mina; coffee Dhs11-20, sandwiches Dhs18-45; ⏰9am-3am Sat-Thu, 11am-3am Fri) After a dusty morning slipping in and out of hot aisles of merchandise, haggling with stall-holders and photographing life along the harbour, you may fancy somewhere shady for a cold drink and a sandwich. Together with neighbouring Morka Restaurant, this unassuming cafe has indoor and outdoor seating and a chance to chat with expats from across the region.

SHOPPING

CARPET SOUQ MARKET

Map p130 (Al Mina; ⏰9am-11pm) Forget notions of bazaars selling fine Persian silk carpets – the carpet souq in Al Mina is far more authentic. This is where the average Gulf family buys a carpet for the *majlis* (reception room), a new portable prayer rug, a set of cushions or floor-level settees upholstered in traditional Bedouin geometric patterns of red, black and green.

LOCAL KNOWLEDGE

SALUKI – ARABIAN HUNTING DOGS

Prized for their hunting skills and speed over distance, salukis have for centuries been man's best friend to the Bedu, and after a visit to **Arabian Saluki Centre** (Map p130; ☎02 575 5330; www.arabiansaluki.ae; Abu Dhabi Falcon Hospital; ⏰9am-1pm Sun-Thu) FREE, it's easy to see why. Originating in China, the saluki is thought to be one of the first breeds of dog to be domesticated, and their speed, tolerance of high temperatures and intelligence made them the perfect companions for nomadic communities who used them to catch rabbits and other small game. While there's not much call for their skills in the desert these days, they remain a beloved part of the Arabian Peninsula heritage, with pure-bred, well-behaved dogs fetching thousands of dirhams. Many are bred to race and, according to the Guinness Book of Records, a saluki holds the record for four-legged speed at 68.8km/h, clocked in 1996. Their beauty is also prized and dogs are paraded before judges for their pride, stride and condition of coat.

The Arabian Saluki Centre is part of the **Abu Dhabi Falcon Hospital** (p152) and located about 6km southeast of Abu Dhabi airport.

IRANIAN SOUQ HOMEWARES

Map p136 (Al Mina; ⏰7am-midnight) If you've never been to a regional wholesale hardware market before, then this cramped collection of stalls huddled around the harbour edge is a fun destination. Giant aluminium cauldrons, floral melamine trays, Chinese plastic decorations, wickerware, Thermoses and copper coffee pots are just some of the assorted imports in this lively souq.

SPORTS & ACTIVITIES

SAADIYAT BEACH CLUB SPA

Map p130 (☎02 656 3500; www.saadiyatbeachclub.ae; Saadiyat Island; Sun-Thu day rate couple/adult/teen/child Dhs330/220/110/free, Fri-Sat Dhs720/420/210/free; ⏰beach 9am-sunset, other facilities to 8pm) This luxurious and exclusive beach club, spa and fitness centre is open to day visitors and offers a full spa experience, beautiful pools and an expanse of pristine beach. Protected hawksbill turtles nest along the coast and the occasional school of dolphins is spotted in the turquoise waters.

Yas Island & Around

Helping to define Abu Dhabi as a dynamic destination, Yas Island has blossomed into the activities hub of the capital. While the Grand Prix attracts a global audience in November, thrill-seekers visit year-round for Ferrari World's rides and simulations. As a rewarding contrast, a number of eco-friendly adventures are available in the mangrove stands dotting the edge of the beautiful Gulf.

SIGHTS

Yas Island has been developed entirely with the visitor in mind, so there's a wealth of information on what to see and do. The emphasis is less on sights than activities, and a half-day tour by bike, on the Big Bus or the free Yas Express is enough for a good flavour of the main points of interest if you haven't the time or inclination to get more involved.

★FERRARI WORLD ABU DHABI AMUSEMENT PARK

Map p161 (☎02 496 8000; www.ferrariworldabudhabi.com; Yas Leisure Dr; adult/child (under 1.3m) from Dhs295/230, with Yas Waterworld from Dhs315/250; ⏰11am-8pm) If you want bragging rights to having 'done' Formula Rossa, the world's fastest roller coaster, visit this indoor (perfect in summer) temple of torque and celebration of all things Ferrari in a spectacular building. Accelerating from 0km/h to 240km/h in 4.9 seconds, this is as close to an F1 experience as most of us are likely to get.

Other diversions includes the **Flying Aces** roller coaster, boasting the world's biggest loop and steepest/fastest incline cable lift; a **Ferrari Driving Experience** around the island with with a company-certified driver (from Dhs695 extra); and an imaginative 4D adventure. A fifth, fully-indoor roller coaster and a roof walk adventure were brewing at time of research. Between thrills, check out the car exhibitions or live shows.

WARNER BROS WORLD ABU DHABI AMUSEMENT PARK

Map p161 (www.wbworldabudhabi.com) Eyeing a July 2018 opening, the world's first Warner Bros–branded theme park should be a hit with kids and adults alike (DC Comics fans, we're talking to you). At least 29 immersive rides, entertaining shows and interactive attractions are confirmed, spread among six 'Lands': Warner Bros Plaza, Metropolis, Gotham City, Cartoon Junction, Bedrock and Dynamite Gulch – all indoors and air-conditioned.

YAS BEACH BEACH

Map p161 (☎056 242 0435; www.yasbeach.ae; adult/child weekday Dhs50/free, weekend Dhs100/free; ⏰10am-7pm) A surprisingly low-key corner of this high-tech island, Yas Beach is a lovely place to relax and enjoy the sea views, dabble in some water sports or generally chill with a cool beer. The kitchen rustles up grilled local fish and other tasty light bites. A DJ plays soothing sounds during Friday pool parties.

Day admission includes towel, sunbed, parasol and showers. Alcohol available.

Yas Island & Around

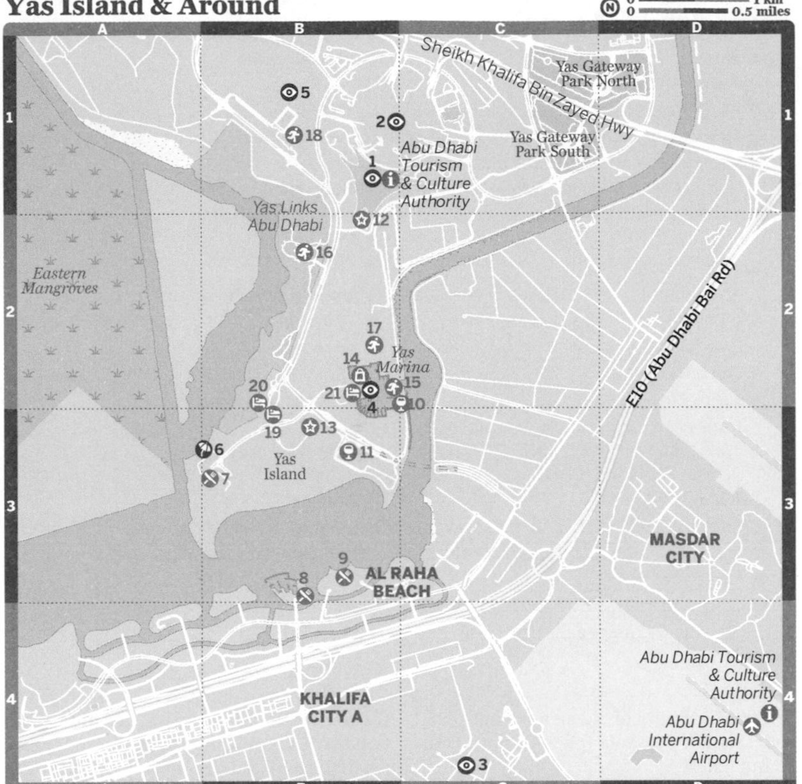

FUN WORKS AMUSEMENT PARK

Map p161 (☎02 565 1242; www.funworks.ae; Yas Mall, Yas Island West; ⏲10am-10pm Sat-Wed, to midnight Thu & Fri) With 6300 sq metres of bouncy buildings, rides, rooms to reconstruct, play stations and toys, this interactive play space targeted at fun learning is guaranteed to keep kids amused for hours.

MUSICAL FOUNTAINS FOUNTAIN

Map p161 (Yas Marina) FREE These fountains are fun for kids during the day and spectacular when set to music at night. Enjoy them on a promenade around the marina.

EATING

There are some truly memorable restaurants on Yas Island, serving the signature dishes of various famous international kitchens. Just as memorable for those with an interest in nature is a deli sandwich eaten in the company of herons and lurking dugongs on a sandspit out at sea.

TAWA BAKERY CAFE $

Map p161 (www.tawa.ae; Al Muneera Island Beach Plaza, Al Raha Beach; mains Dhs40-65; 📶) Strictly gluten-free, this trendy bakery on Al Muneer Beach does breakfast all day (French toast, eggs Benedict, huevos rancheros), a host of pizzas, sandwiches and pastas and some decadent desserts (banoffee pie, pistachio eclairs). It's a hip spot – exposed air ducts and bake pans as decor and all – and you even get a beach view.

C.DELI SANDWICHES $

Map p161 (www.rotana.com; Centro Yas Island; sandwiches Dhs32-42; ⏲24hr; 📶) If you don't fancy a full dinner at a restaurant but would still like something tasty, this tiny, all-day deli concept at the Rotana gives

Yas Island & Around

you the flexibility of a gourmet snack that you can take to your own favourite Yas Island haunt.

★NOLU'S CAFÉ CAFE $$

Map p161 (☎02 557 9500; www.nolusrestaurants.com; Al Raha Beach, Al Bandar; mains Dhs50-120; ⏲9am-11pm; 📶) With its starburst abstract panels, lime-green decor and a wholesome menu, this charmer feels more California than Abu Dhabi, but the secret recipes of the owner's Afghani mother add a delightfully regional spin. Try such little-known specialities as *aushak* (dumplings), *bolani* (stuffed flatbread) or killer saffron chicken, washed down with artisanal coffee, fresh juices or an activated charcoal matcha latte.

CAFE BATEEL MEDITERRANEAN $$

Map p161 (www.bateel.com; Pavilion Cascade Walk, Yas Mall; mains Dhs44-98; 📶) Hailing from Saudi Arabia and best known for its exquisite date speciality shops, the cafe arm of Bateel is worth seeking out. Its scrumptious, largely organic Mediterranean menu bridges Arabian peninsula pizzazz with an artisanal, farm-to-table twist from Umbria (Italy), served amid sophisticated and inviting olive interiors.

AQUARIUM SEAFOOD $$

Map p161 (☎02 565 0007; www.yasmarina.ae/aquarium; Yas Marina; mains Dhs65-165; ⏲noon-1am Sat-Wed, to 2am Thu-Fri; 📶) With extra-large aquariums gracing the interior of this casual-dining restaurant, there's no doubting its speciality. Tables on the terrace are coveted at night for views of the marina and the eccentric Yas Viceroy Abu Dhabi hotel. The Arabian-caught, Asian-prepared seafood includes myriad specials (all-you-can-eat paella, half-price lobster Mondays). Shisha available.

CIPRIANI ITALIAN $$$

Map p161 (☎02 657 5400; www.cipriani.com; Yas Marina; mains Dhs111-400; ⏲6pm-midnight) The cuisine at this renowned restaurant may be Italian (including a lot of signature dishes from world-famous Harry's Bar in Venice), but the view is distinctly Emirates. The terrace looks out over the grandstands of the Yas Marina Circuit (p164), designer yachts moored alongside, and the Yas Viceroy Abu Dhabi hotel (p170), with its mantle of amethyst and diamond lights.

Some Italians complain that, although high-quality, the food is presented at a trattoria rather than fine-dining level.

ROZANAH LEBANESE **$$$**

Map p161 (☎02 496 3411; www.rozanah.ae; Yas Marina; mezze Dhs22-50, mains Dhs54-95; ⏲7am-midnight Sun-Wed, to 1am Thu-Fri) This restaurant is in a perfect spot for watching the sunset, and its panoramic views are accompanied by delicious hot and cold mezze (eight types of hummus!) and a post-supper shisha. Movable walls and ceilings allow for al fresco dining in winter and air-con in summer.

DRINKING & NIGHTLIFE

Yas Island is a party place, lit up with lasers and innovative, ambient light shows, and with licensed bars offering themed nights in the hotels. If you like early nights, you have come to the wrong place!

★IRIS BAR

Map p161 (☎055 160 5636; www.irisabudhabi.com; Yas Marina; cocktails Dhs55-70; ⏲6pm-1am Mon-Tue & Sat, to 3.30am Wed-Sun; 📶) The wooden outdoor furniture gives a rustic angle to this trendy bar in the middle of a high-tech destination at the heart of Yas Island. A transplant from Beirut, its exquisite cocktails with proper ice shine – try the smoky negroni, featuring Campari, gin and vermouth infused for a week with orange, French thyme and sherry wood, respectively.

★MAD ON YAS ISLAND CLUB

Map p161 (☎055 834 6262; www.madonyasisland.com; Leisure Dr, near Yas Tunnel; ⏲11pm-3am Tue, Thu & Fri; 📶) The UAE's biggest nightclub packs a whole lotta wow into one large and luxurious room. The elongated hexagonal bar – a thing of beauty, especially when shades of violet and cerulean light beams cast their floating glow around the room – is flanked by two levels of table-service banquettes with an elevated DJ booth front and centre. See and be seen.

STARS 'N' BARS SPORTS BAR

Map p161 (www.facebook.com/starsnbarsabudhabi; Yas Marina; cocktails Dhs55-75; ⏲11.30am-2.30am Sun-Tue, to 3.30am Wed-Fri; 📶) Voted Abu Dhabi's best sports bar, this wildly popular and rowdy bar and grill is unapologetically American. With 24 taps, including craft selections from Brewdog, Anchor Steam and Brooklyn Brewery, it's certainly a beer destination, but it draws hordes for food, live music and shisha too. Throw in nearly 80 TVs and there's something – and something on – for everyone.

EMPIRE AT RUSH CLUB

Map p161 (☎050 501 5052; www.viceroyhotelsandresorts.com; Bridge Gallery, Yas Viceroy Abu Dhabi; ⏲11pm-3.30am Mon-Tue & Thu, from 10pm Fri; 📶) This stylish, rectangular den of decadence literally occupies a bridge directly over Yas Island's Formula One track. It's popular with a high-brow crowd flush with expats and Etihad cabin crews (they get a 50% drink discount). Ladies drink free on Monday nights, and if you dig Arabian beats, Tuesday is an East-meets-West free-for-all.

STILLS BAR & BRASSERIE BAR

Map p161 (☎02 656 3053; www.facebook.com/stillsbar; Yas Island Golf Plaza; ⏲3pm-2am Sun-Thu, from noon Fri & Sat; 📶) With live entertainment and the longest bar in Abu Dhabi, this is a happening spot for beer (17 taps), cocktails and a satisfying selection of upmarket pub grub, from burgers to fresh mussels. Based at the Crowne Plaza on Yas Island (p170).

☆ ENTERTAINMENT

VOX CINEMAS CINEMA

Map p161 (☎600 599 905; www.uae.voxcinemas.com; Level 1, Yas Mall, Yas Island West; tickets Dhs35-160; ⏲9am-midnight) If you like to smell the rubber on your car chase and feel the earth rumble as screaming tyres race across a 24.5m screen, then the 4D experience at Vox Cinema's 4DX Theatre won't disappoint. If you're a foodie who appreciates the finer things, a comfy seat at the luxurious Theatre by Rhodes nets you Michelin-starred cuisine too. Book online. There's also a private cinema for kids.

WORTH A DETOUR

CAMEL RACES IN AL WATHBA

Sporting colourful nosebags and matching blankets, camels are the stars of the show at the **Al Wathba Race Track** (☎02 885 8888; ⊙7.30am & 2.30pm Thu-Sat Oct-Apr), 45km southeast of Abu Dhabi. Races are great fun, even just to watch the enthusiasm of the owners who drive alongside the track cheering their beloved animals along. Arrive 30 minutes ahead of the starting block to absorb the prerace excitement.

DU FORUM CONCERT VENUE

Map p161 (☎02 509 8143; www.duforum.ae; Yas Leisure Dr) This striking indoor entertainment venue holds art exhibitions, concerts, comedy shows and sports events. Unlike the other Yas Island entertainment venue, Du Arena (p164), it is fully air-conditioned, allowing for big-ticket acts such as Tom Jones and events such as Oktoberfest to take place year-round.

DU ARENA CONCERT VENUE

Map p161 (☎02 509 8000; www.duforum.ae) This exceptional outdoor entertainment venue (formerly known as Yas Arena) regularly hosts big names of the regional and Western music world. With excellent acoustics and a unique cooling system, this venue has become one of the must-do stops on international tours. Tickets are available through UAE's Ticketmaster website (www.ticketmaster.ae).

SHOPPING

Mall shopping isn't the only buyer's experience worth having on the island – those in the know head for the seasonal local craft markets at the marina held on some Saturdays.

YAS MALL MALL

Map p161 (www.yasmall.ae; Yas West; ⊙10am-10pm Sat-Wed, to midnight Thu & Fri; 📶) Bright and spacious and with trees and a growing plant wall, Yas Mall is one of the newer additions to the Abu Dhabi megashopping scene. Look out for two 12m-high tree-themed sculptures by acclaimed South African artist Marco Cianfanelli, with leaves inspired by Arabic calligraphy. There's access to Ferrari World (p160), cinemas and a Carrefour hypermarket.

SATURDAY MARKET ARTS & CRAFTS

Map p161 (Yas Marina; ⊙1-6pm Sat) Tired of the impersonal mall experience? Then head for this open-air sporadically held market featuring crafts, printed cottons, watercolour paintings, novelty gifts and souvenirs from stalls arranged along the promenade.

SPORTS & ACTIVITIES

★YAS MARINA CIRCUIT ADVENTURE SPORTS

Map p161 (☎02 659 9800; www.yasmarinacircuit.ae; off Yas Leisure Dr; venue tours Dhs120, driving & passenger experiences Dhs440-4000; ⊙2hr tours 10am & 2pm Tue-Sat) Even if you're not in town in November for the Formula One Grand Prix, it's possible to experience the track year-round. Fancy yourself Lewis Hamilton as you drive the concourse at the wheel of – or as a passenger in – a Ferrari 458 GT (among several others) or go from 0km/h to 100km/h in two seconds in a dragster.

DRIVEYAS ADVENTURE SPORTS

Map p161 (☎02 659 9800; www.yasmarinacircuit.com; driver/passenger rides from Dhs1300/440; ⊙9am-11pm) Outside the racing calendar, DriveYas offers several opportunities on Tuesdays (winter only), Thursdays and Saturdays to experience the Yas Marina Circuit up close – so close, in fact, that there seems to be only a friction burn between you and the racetrack. Bookings should be be made a week in advance either online or by phone.

YAS WATERWORLD WATER PARK

Map p161 (☎02 414 2000; www.yaswaterworld.com; Yas Leisure Dr; adult/child from Dhs250/210, fast pass Dhs485/410; ⊙10am-6pm Nov-Mar, to 7pm Apr-May, Sep & Oct, to 8pm Jun-Aug) The UAE's most elaborate water park offers opportunities to get soaked on 45 rides, slides and other liquid attractions as you follow Emirati cartoon character Dana on her quest for a magical pearl. A wave pool, two lazy rivers and sunbeds offer relaxing alternatives to the rides if you're just looking to beat the Gulf heat.

STARTYAS/ TRAINYAS/GOYAS HEALTH & FITNESS

Map p161 (www.yasmarinacircuit.com; Yas Marina Circuit; ⌚6-10pm Tue, Wed & Sun) FREE Three days a week (Wednesdays is ladies only), Yas Marina Circuit opens its renowned Formula One track to all for free. Bring your running shoes, your bike, your tricycle – the 5.5km track is your oyster.

SEAWINGS SCENIC FLIGHTS

(☎04 807 0708; www.seawings.ae; scenic tour per person Dhs895) If you like to make a bit of a splash on entry, then consider arriving in Yas Island by seaplane. The scenic tour takes 25 minutes and takes off from the sea at either the Emirates Palace or Yas Marina. Flights can take up to nine passengers. Book online at least a few hours before you want to take off.

EYWOA WATER SPORTS

Map p161 (☎050 166 9396; www.eywoa.com; Yas Marina) Offering wakeboarding, wakesurfing, kitesurfing, stand-up paddleboarding, kayaking and towed inflatables, this company has its finger on the pulse of the latest ideas trending on H_2O.

YAS LINKS ABU DHABI GOLF

Map p161 (☎02 810 7710; www.yaslinks.com; visitor 18 holes Sun-Thu Dhs650, Fri & Sat Dhs950; ⌚practice facilities & clubhouse 6am-midnight) This beautiful 18-hole championship course, the first links course in the Middle East, was designed by Kyle Phillips and is partially set among mangroves.

SLEEPING

There are essentially two types of hotel in Abu Dhabi: the five-star luxury beach resort and the midrange city hotel. There is a growing trend for 'dry' hotels that do not serve alcohol, and these are generally good value too. Promotional discounts are on offer in beach resorts and city hotels throughout the year, especially during summer (April to September).

Al Markaziyah

BACKPACKER HOSTEL ABU DHABI HOSTEL $

Map p136 (☎050 490 4496; www.hostelinabudhabi.com; 6th St, Sector 14, Zone 2, Bldg 11, M fl, Unit M4; dm Dhs70; @📶) Dead simple and void of any and all personality, if BackPacker Hostel Abu Dhabi does one thing, it's dish out cheap sleeps. Four, six- and 10-bed segregated dorm rooms are offered. The common bathroom (we only saw one) isn't thrilling, but it's clean enough. If you're looking for a basic crashpad for a handful of dirhams, you've found it.

ROAD NAMES

Whether you're looking for Sheikh Zayed the First, 7th or Electra St will largely depend on what map you're using. The initiative to rename the city's roads (a term used interchangeably with 'streets') from the former numbering system has resulted in confusion, especially as some districts have been renamed too (including 'Tourist Club Area', now known Al Zahiyah).

Currently main roads are named after prominent Emirati figures while smaller roads reflect places. As former and current names are still common currency, here's a list of the main roads and their synonyms (without the suffix).

Sheikh Rashid Bin Saeed Al Maktoom 2nd, Airport

Sultan Bin Zayed the First 4th, East, Muroor, New Airport

Fatima Bint Mubarak St 6th, Umm Al Nar, Bani Yas, Baniyas

Sheikh Zayed Bin Sultan 8th, Al Salam, East Coast, Eastern Ring, New Corniche

Khalifa Bin Zayed the First 3rd, Khalifa, Sheikh Khalifa Bin Zayed, Al Istiqalal

Sheikh Hamdan Bin Mohammed 5th, Hamdan, Al Nasr, Al Khubairah

Sheikh Zayed the First 7th, Electra

Al Falah 9th, Old Passport Rd

1

ANGELO FERRARIS / SHUTTERSTOCK ©

2

4

BENNY MARTY / SHUTTERSTOCK ©

1. Abu Dhabi Heritage Village (p141)
Traditional, pre-oil era Gulf life is on display at this reconstructed village.

2. Corniche – Al Khalidiyah (p135)
The 8km Corniche was formed using reclaimed land, and the seafront is now a much-loved public amenity.

3. Sheikh Zayed Grand Mosque (p127)
One of only a few mosques in the region open to non-Muslims, the Sheikh Zayed Grand Mosque can accommodate 50,000 worshippers.

4. Louvre Abu Dhabi (p156)
The Louvre's galleries are home to a world-class collection of paintings, sculpture and objects from antiquity through to the present day.

3

CHRISTIAN HÄCKER / 500PX ©

AL JAZEERA ROYAL HOTEL HOTEL $

Map p136 (☎02 632 1100; www.aljaziraroyal.ae; opposite Madinat Zayed Shopping & Gold Centre; s/d from Dhs250/300;) With some of the cheapest rates in town, this friendly little 55-room hotel opposite the gold souq largely caters for Indian and Asian business clientele and has an excellent, low-key Indian-Arabic restaurant, Al Ibrahimi (p131), on-site. This is a good place to get a feel for local life, and appropriately it doesn't have a bar.

★**CROWNE PLAZA ABU DHABI** HOTEL $$

Map p136 (☎02 616 6166; www.crowneplaza.com; Sheikh Hamdan Bin Mohammed St; r from Dhs561; P@) This thoroughly amenable hotel, with its generous rooms – parquet flooring, marble bathrooms – and grand views of the city, knows exactly how to please its guests. The emphasis is on providing excellent service and a sociable experience, which is accomplished through its highly popular pan-Asian restaurant and lounge, Cho Gao (p132), popular Heroes pub and rooftop cocktail bar, Level Lounge (p133).

Al Mina & Saadiyat Island

★**PARK HYATT ABU DHABI HOTEL & VILLAS** RESORT $$$

Map p130 (☎02 407 1234; www.abudhabi.park.hyatt.com; Saadiyat Island; r from Dhs1575; P@) This beautiful low-rise luxury hotel offers a perfect retreat from the city. It encompasses a long stretch of white, sandy beach surrounded by a protected nature reserve. The infinity pool is flanked by open-air overwater cabanas that make you feel eye-to-eye with the ripples of the open Gulf. The 50-sq-metre standard rooms have daybed-strewn balconies, spacious bathtubs and twin sinks.

Al Zahiyah & Al Maryah Island

AL DIAR MINA HOTEL HOTEL $

Map p136 (☎02 678 1000; www.aldiarhotels.com; Al Meena St; r from Dhs350; @) This 90-room hotel caters for those on a budget, but that doesn't mean the facilities are scant. Rooms are perfectly decent, with double or twin beds, chilly air-con and well-worn hardwood furnishings and extra-large minibars (refrigerators, really). There are numerous bars on premises.

BEACH ROTANA HOTEL HOTEL $$

Map p136 (☎02 697 9000; www.rotana.com; 10th St; r from Dhs735; P@) Joined at the hip to Abu Dhabi Mall, this 565-room hotel is as much a favourite with leisure travellers as with conference-goers. Staff manage to keep several hundred guests happy when they have just spent a harrowing day with the credit card at the mall next door – and the snug beds are all too easy to sink into.

There's a Trader Vic's Polynesian-themed restaurant and German beer bar as well.

SHERATON ABU DHABI HOTEL & RESORT RESORT $$

Map p136 (☎02 677 3333; www.sheratonabudhabihotel.com; Corniche Rd (East); r from Dhs500; P@) A visitor could be forgiven for taking one look at the outside of this particularly rust-orange hotel and running off to the competition. That would be a pity, however, as this old warhorse is a city-centre icon in which you can unwind in the landscaped garden or dip a toe in the human-made private seawater lagoon.

Rooms are modern and feature roomy work stations, but the outdoor facilities are particularly noteworthy: a great pool and beach, several outdoor lounges and a cushioned amphitheatre that hosts nightly spinning DJs.

FOUR SEASONS ABU DHABI HOTEL $$$

Map p136 (☎02 333 2222; www.fourseasons.com/abudhabi; Al Maryah Island; r from Dhs995; P@) The Four Seasons' 2016 entry into the city's luxury-hotel landscape has milestone-level nods to local culture: the oblong baguettes layering its facade look like desert-evoking copper from a distance, but a closer look reveals rainbows of colourful hues summoning piles of souq fabric; a wavy articulated lobby wall light-shifts iridescently – a pearling industry nod; and the bound leather on its lobby cafe menus is the same as used in falcon caps.

Elsewhere the 200-room, art-inspired hotel (2000 pieces dot the property, 90% sourced locally) excels in every way: outstanding water and city views from nearly every vantage point; standard rooms curated to perfection with adjustable bedside tables, wonderful couches, veneer red-oak-accented furnishings and Peloponnese bathroom sponges; and knockout bar and dining options, including the wonderful Butcher & Still (p147), Washington, DC politico haunt **Cafe Milano** (☎02 333 2630; www.cafemilano.ae; mains Dhs85-265; ⊙noon-5.30pm Sun-Fri, 6-11.30pm Sat-Wed, to 12.30am Thu & Fri), a European-style cigar bar and Eclipse (p148), a poolside open-air club/lounge.

Breakwater

KHALIDIYA PALACE RAYHAAN BY ROTANA HOTEL $$
Map p136 (☎02 657 0000; www.rotana.com; Corniche Rd (West); r from Dhs650; P@🛜≋) Steeped in subtle Arabic character and harbouring a giant pool, landscaped gardens, facilities aimed at children and a relaxed atmosphere, this alcohol-free beachfront hotel has established a following among local families seeking a weekend getaway. There's an authentic Arabic restaurant, **Kamoon**, that's equally popular with locals. Ask for a Presidential Palace–facing room and prepare to be gobsmacked.

★EMIRATES PALACE HOTEL $$$
Map p136 (☎02 690 9000; www.emiratespalace.com; Corniche Rd (West); r from Dhs1900; P@🛜≋) While this remarkable Abu Dhabi landmark is a destination in its own right, offering excellent entertainment and restaurants, an overnight stay enhances what is already a class act. Features of the experience include 24-hour butler service, daily fresh flowers in the rooms, temperature-controlled swimming pools and resident-only beaches.

The concierge can book tickets, order a limousine and of course arrange helicopter transfers. A kids club helps entertain youngsters so ma and pa can spa in peace.

★INTERCONTINENTAL ABU DHABI HOTEL $$
Map p136 (☎02 666 6888; www.intercontinental.com/abudhabi; Bainunah St, Al Bateen; r from Dhs855; P@🛜≋) The InterContinental hotels in the Gulf region may not be the most 'des res' addresses in town, but they are invariably favourites with locals. The InterCon in Abu Dhabi is no exception, offering excellent service, large rooms, carefully targeted amenities (such as a private beach and marina) and the best fish restaurant and beer bar in town.

BAB AL QASR HOTEL $$$
Map p136 (☎02 205 3000; www.millenniumhotels.com; Corniche Rd (West); r from Dhs1095; P@🛜≋) With its five-floor-high minaret archway adorning its copper-toned facade, a lobby flanked with *mihrab*-style niches and marble inlay and hallway ceilings lined with Moroccan latticework, this 'Gate to the Palace', opened in 2016, is Abu Dhabi's luxury hotel most steeped in Arabian character. The 670 rooms are subtle, with rip-roaring views of both the Presidential and Emirati palaces.

JUMEIRAH AT ETIHAD TOWERS HOTEL $$$
Map p136 (☎02 811 5555; www.jumeirah.com; Corniche Rd (West); r from Dhs1150; P@🛜≋) This exceptional hotel, occupying one of a group of five landmark towers that rise from the end of the Corniche like polished organ pipes, lives up to the group's tagline – 'Stay different'. Aimed at top executives, international conference attendees and well-heeled visitors, the hotel has top-class restaurants – including Li Beirut (p140) – an observation deck, luxury spa, private beach and adjacent mall.

Sheikh Zayed Mosque & Around

★ALOFT ABU DHABI HOTEL $$
Map p130 (☎02 654 5000; www.aloftabudhabi.com; Al Khaleej Al Arabi St; d from Dhs615; P🛜≋) The loft-like rooms, landscaped pool and high-tech gadgetry in this hotel scream urban chic. Free wi-fi in all rooms, large TVs and iPod docking stations make this a convenient choice for getting some work done while attending a function at the adjoining ADNEC Exhibition Centre. The popular rooftop bar Relax@12 (p154) has killer views and cocktails.

PARK ROTANA ABU DHABI HOTEL $$
Map p151 (☎02 657 3333; www.rotana.com; Salam St, Khalifa Park; r from Dhs815; P@🛜≋) This fashionable business- and events-focused five-star hotel is conveniently located near the Grand Mosque and the exhibition centre, and features hallways and rooms flush with soothing abstract

WORTH A DETOUR

ARABIAN NIGHTS VILLAGE

The romantic **Arabian Nights Village** (☎02 676 9990; www.arabiannightsvillage.com; Arabian Nights Village Rd, Al Khatim Razeen; r Dhs1500;) is an oasis in the desert. Even though it loses some of its charm in high season when overnight tour groups dominate, it's so dreamy you might not care. The 38 boutique accommodations are divided between traditional Abu Dhabi–style houses, bamboo and palm-frond *barasti* dwellings and Bedouin tents. All are decked out in style, with minaret-style bathroom mirrors and luxe bedding.

The breakfast room is flush with Syrian and Turkish touches, there's an inviting pool and the whole dreamy place is surrounded by windswept desert. Prices include transfer in and out from Abu Dhabi – 124km to the northwest – breakfast and dinner, camel rides and sandboarding; ATV and dune bashing cost extra.

art. Built on the edge of Abu Dhabi's biggest park, a stroll before dinner is de rigueur.

TRADERS HOTEL, QARYAT AL BERI HOTEL **$$**

Map p151 (☎02 510 8888; www.shangri-la.com/traders; Khor Al Maqta; r from Dhs550;) With a pop-art vibe and bright colours in the lobby, this is a funky alternative to the standard marble and crystal of neighbouring hotels. After frolicking by the pool or on the beach, guests can retreat to rooms that are subdued but spacious.

★EASTERN MANGROVES HOTEL & SPA HOTEL **$$$**

Map p130 (☎02 656 1000; www.abu-dhabi.anantara.com; Sheikh Zayed Bin Sultan St; d from Dhs750;) Stepping into the lobby with its *mashrabiyya* (carved wood latticework) patterns and poolside oud player, it's clear that Arab hospitality is taken seriously at this luxe lair. Rooms overlook the eponymous mangroves (kayak tours available) and are soothingly furnished in matching nature tones. Work up an appetite in the infinity pool before grazing on international small plates in the rooftop Impressions restaurant-lounge.

FAIRMONT BAB AL BAHR HOTEL **$$$**

Map p151 (☎02 654 3000; www.fairmont.com/abu-dhabi; Khor Al Maqta; r from Dhs1185;) With stark glass facade and rectilinear night-lighting, this hotel resembles an office complex inside the vast, feng shui-ed atrium. The dramatic chandeliers and textured surfaces signal sophisticated accommodation. Rooms are richly dressed in wood and marble and have unparalleled views of Sheikh Zayed Grand Mosque (p127).

Yas Island

CENTRO YAS ISLAND HOTEL **$$**

Map p161 (☎02 656 4444; www.rotana.com; Golf Plaza; r from Dhs350;) A good-value option in the hotel cluster on Yas Island, this upbeat place with 359 compact rooms is a decent choice for the budget conscious and attracts a younger crowd. Rates include shuttle service to Yas Beach and access to the luxurious leisure facilities at the adjacent Yas Island Rotana.

CROWNE PLAZA ABU DHABI YAS ISLAND HOTEL **$$**

Map p161 (☎02 656 3000; www.ihg.com; r from Dhs570;) This friendly hotel with hospitable staff and comfortable rooms overlooks Yas Links (p165), the island golf course, and the Gulf beyond in a complex of hotels near Yas Marina Circuit (p164). Home to a popular nightspot, Stills (p163), and a Lebanese restaurant, **Barouk**, the hotel also hosts bike rental and bike-share – the perfect way of getting around the island attractions.

YAS VICEROY ABU DHABI HOTEL **$$$**

Map p161 (☎02 656 0000; www.viceroyhotelsandresorts.com; Yas Marina Circuit; r from Dhs1050;) This extravagantly shaped hotel sits in pole position on Yas Island, literally straddling the Yas Marina Circuit. The avant-garde, steel-and-glass structure with its corrugated mantel flung over the racetrack is dramatically studded with lights at night. The desert-rust interior is a haven of cool in the Gulf heat.

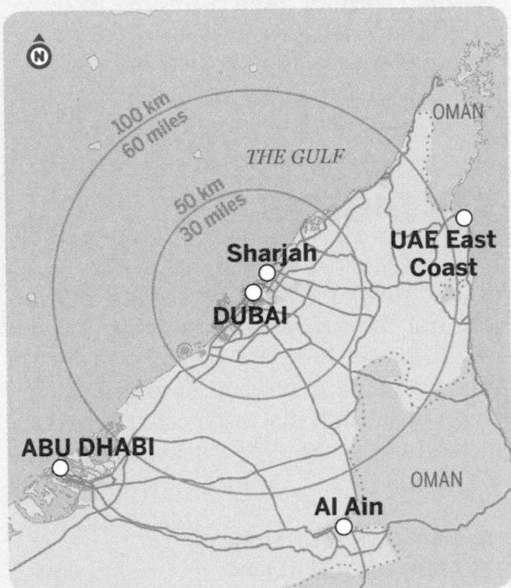

Day Trips from Dubai & Abu Dhabi

Sharjah p172

Dubai's northern neighbour is a cultured and heritage-oriented emirate that feels like a world apart, especially around the restored historic Heart of Sharjah and the nearby Arts Area.

Al Ain p175

The famous Al Ain oasis, with wonderful forts, museums, a model zoo and even ancient Bronze Age burial sites, offers a semi-rural retreat after the frantic pace of Dubai.

UAE East Coast p178

Sleepy fishing villages, rugged mountains, desert dunes, museums and the country's oldest mosque give the country's east coast serious nature getaway credentials.

Sharjah

Explore

Sharjah doesn't dazzle with glitz but with sensitivity towards its history and culture, which explains why Unesco declared it Cultural Capital of the Arab World in 1998, recognition reaffirmed in 2014, when it became Capital of Islamic Culture. Once you have penetrated the traffic-clogged outskirts of town, the historic old town is easy to navigate on foot. You'll need several hours to explore the heritage and arts areas, the souqs and excellent museums.

Aside from the main city of Sharjah, the enclaves of Dibba Al Hisn, Khor Fakkan and Kalba on the eastern coast also belong to the emirate.

One caveat: Sharjah takes its decency laws very seriously, so do dress modestly. That means no exposed knees, backs or bellies – and that goes for both men and women. It's also the only emirate that is 'dry' (ie no alcohol is available anywhere).

The Best...

- **Sight** Sharjah Museum of Islamic Civilization
- **Place to Eat** Sadaf (p174)
- **Place to Shop** Souq Al Arsah (p174)

Getting There & Away

- **Bus** Sharjah's main bus station **Al Jubail** (06 052 5252; Corniche St) is next to the fish and vegetable souq. It is served by bus E303 from Dubai's Union Square station in Deira every 15 minutes and by bus E306 from Al Ghubaiba station in Bur Dubai every 30 minutes (both Dhs, one hour). Buses to/from Abu Dhabi run every 30 minutes, take three hours and cost Dhs30.
- **Taxi** The main taxi stand in Sharjah is next to the bus station, but taxis can actually be flagged down anywhere in town. Trips to/from Dubai cost about Dhs50 plus a Dhs20 surcharge. Budget about Dhs350 to/from Abu Dhabi.

Need to Know

- **Area Code** 06
- **Location** 30km northeast of Downtown Dubai, 165km from Abu Dhabi.
- **Tourist Office Sharjah Commerce & Tourism Development Authority** (06 556 6777; www.sharjahmydestination.ae; Buheirah Corniche, 1st fl, Crescent Tower, Al Majaz; 7.30am-2.30pm Sun-Thu)

SIGHTS

Many of Sharjah's top sights are scattered around the partly walled-in **Heart of Sharjah** and the adjacent **Arts Area**, just off the Corniche. Both are part of a historical preservation and restoration project called Heart of Sharjah that is expected to be completed in 2025. See www.heartofsharjah.ae for details.

★SHARJAH MUSEUM OF ISLAMIC CIVILIZATION — MUSEUM

(06 565 5455; www.sharjahmuseums.ae; cnr Corniche & Arabian Gulf St; adult/child Dhs10/5; 8am-8pm Sat-Thu, 4-8pm Fri) Just about everything you always wanted to know about Islam is addressed in this well-curated museum in a stunningly converted souq right on the waterfront. The ground-floor galleries zero in on different aspects of the Islamic faith, including the ritual and importance of the hajj, and on Arab scientific accomplishments, especially in mathematics and astronomy. The upper floors navigate 1400 years of Islamic art and artefacts, including ceramics, woodwork, textiles and jewellery. Don't miss the zodiac mosaic below the central dome.

Audio guides are available for free in six languages.

★SHARJAH HERITAGE MUSEUM — MUSEUM

(06 568 0006; www.sharjahmuseums.ae; Heritage Area; adult/child Dhs10/free; 8am-8pm Sat-Thu, from 4pm Fri) This creatively curated museum goes a long way towards demystifying Emirati culture and traditions for visitors. Each of the five galleries examines different aspects of local life, from living in the desert, religious values, and birth and burial rituals to holiday celebrations, marriage and wedding ceremonies, and folk medicine. An abundance of quality original objects and excellent English panelling make a visit here a satisfying and educational experience.

CEREMONIAL DAGGERS: KHANJARS

The *khanjar* is a curved sheathed dagger that originated in Oman but is also worn by men in the UAE and other Gulf countries. Once used for personal protection and as a hunting tool, it is now a symbol of manhood and worn, attached to a belt, on ceremonial occasions. *Khanjars* were originally made from rhino horn, but today wood is most commonly used. Regular *khanjars* have two rings where the belt is attached and scabbards decorated with thin silver wire. The intricacy of the wire-thread pattern and its workmanship determine value. Sayidi *khanjars* have five rings and are often covered entirely in silver sheet, with little or no wire, and their quality is assessed by weight and craftsmanship. A *khanjar* ought to feel heavy when you pick it up. Don't believe anyone who tells you a specific *khanjar* is 'very old' – few will be more than 30 to 40 years old.

SHARJAH ART MUSEUM — MUSEUM

(☎06 568 8222; www.sharjahmuseums.ae; Arts Area; ⊙8am-8pm Sun-Thu, 4-8pm Fri) FREE The Arts Area is anchored by one of the region's largest and most dynamic art museums and the organiser of the Sharjah Biennial. Upstairs, a permanent exhibit presents a comprehensive survey of art created in the Arab world over the past 50 years. Other galleries house visiting exhibits of international calibre, and there's a nice cafe to boot.

BAIT AL NABOODAH — HISTORIC SITE

(☎06 568 1738; www.sharjahmuseums.ae; Heritage Area; ⊙closed for restoration) This 1845 house, a former pearl trader's home with a grand entranceway, elaborately carved decorations and an ample courtyard, is a fine example of early Emirati architecture and daily living. Though closed at the time of research, by the time you read this it may have reopened after extensive restoration.

AL QASBA — AREA

(☎06 556 0777; www.alqasba.ae; Al Qasba Canal) FREE This car-free canal-side development presents a family-friendly mix of cafes, carousels, boat rides, shops, a small musical fountain and a 60m-high Ferris wheel, the **Eye of the Emirates**. Come in the evening, but avoid Friday and Saturday nights if you don't like crowds. Art fans should check out the latest show at the **Maraya Art Centre**.

SHARJAH MARITIME MUSEUM — MUSEUM

(☎06 522 2002; www.sharjahmuseums.ae; Al Meena St; adult/child Dhs10/5, incl Sharjah Aquarium Dhs25/15; ⊙8am-8pm Sun-Thu, 4-8pm Fri) For a salty introduction to the UAE, visit this charming museum that displays enough traditional dhows, exhibits on pearling and fishing equipment to keep your imagination afloat for a half-hour or so.

SHARJAH AQUARIUM — AQUARIUM

(☎06 528 5288; www.sharjahmuseums.ae; Al Meena St; adult/child incl Sharjah Maritime Museum Dhs25/15; ⊙8am-8pm Mon-Thu & Sat, 4-10pm Fri) Enter an 'abandoned dhow' for close-ups of maritime creatures from the UAE's west and east coast without getting your feet wet. Moray eels lurk, blacktip reef sharks prowl, eagle rays flop and jellyfish dance around tanks that re-create Dibba Rock (when in season), mangroves, Shark Island's coral reefs and other local watery habitats. We like the touchscreens, but a few more labels wouldn't hurt.

SHARJAH DESERT PARK — ZOO

(☎06 531 1999; www.epaashj.ae; Hwy E88, Al Dhaid Rd; adult/child Dhs15/5; ⊙9am-6pm Sun-Mon & Wed-Thu, 2-5.30pm Fri) This desert park packs four venues into a 1-sq-km package, including a natural-history museum, a botanical museum and a children's farm where kids get to meet, pet and feed goats, camels and ducks, and ride ponies and camels.

The main attraction, though, is the **Arabia's Wildlife Centre**, a zoo showcasing the diversity of local critters. Vipers, flamingos, wildcats, mongooses, hyenas, wolves and the splendid Arabian leopard all make appearances.

Visitors get to observe most animals in air-conditioned comfort through glass panels (along with free-flying birds), making the centre a year-round destination. The park grounds also include a cafe and picnic facilities. It's on Al Dhaid Rd (Hwy E88), about 26km east of Sharjah.

THE ART OF HENNA

Henna body tattooing is a long-standing tradition dating back 6000 years, when women in central Turkey began painting their hands in homage to the Mother Goddess. The practice spread throughout the eastern Mediterranean, where the henna shrub grows wild. Today, Emirati women continue the tradition by decorating their hands, nails and feet for special events, particularly weddings. A few nights before the nuptials, brides-to-be are honoured with *layyat al-henna* (henna night). This is a women-only affair, part of a week of festivities leading up to the big day. The bride is scrubbed down, anointed head-to-toe with perfumes and oils, and shampooed with henna, jasmine or perfume. Her hands, wrists, ankles and feet are then tattooed with intricate floral designs, which typically last around six weeks. Lore has it that the duration of the tattoos is an indication to the mother-in-law of what kind of wife the bride will become. If she's a hard worker – and thus a more desirable daughter-in-law – the henna will penetrate deeper and remain longer.

EATING & DRINKING

KATIS RESTAURANT INDIAN **$**

(☎06 556 5650; Al Khan St, Al Khan; mains Dhs12-30; ⌚11.30am-3.30pm & 5.30pm-midnight) This tiny, seven-table, family-run joint with golden walls and dark wooden tables does well-executed home-cooked Indian fare, from butter chicken to prawn biryani plus beloved appetisers such as grilled tandoori momos (dumplings), chicken lollipops (drumsticks) and the wrap-like chicken kati roll. Chase them all with a fresh lime soda with mint. It's opposite Safeer Market.

SADAF IRANIAN **$$**

(☎06 569 3344; www.sadaffood.com; Al Mareija St; mains Dhs50-160; ⌚noon-midnight; 📶) The Sharjah branch of this popular minichain enjoys cult status among locals for its excellent, authentic Iranian cuisine. The spicy, moist kebabs are particularly good and the *zereshk polo meat* (rice with red barberries and chicken or meat) is another solid choice.

There are also plenty of other dining options on this street.

RATIOS COFFEE COFFEE

(http://ratios.coffee; Al Shanasiyah Souq, Heart of Sharjah; coffee Dhs14-25; ⌚8am-10pm; 📶) Caffeine nerds rejoice: this hipster Heart of Sharjah coffee house digs deep with single-origin beans sourced from El Salvador, Ethiopia and Indonesia, among others, and offers all the usual barista-focused preparations methods such as V60, Chemex, Aeropress and the like. In cooler months, there's a lovely back patio. In summer, go for the cold brew.

SHABABEEK LEBANESE **$$**

(☎06-554 0444; www.shababeek.ae; Block B, Qanat Al Qasba; mezze Dh18-26, mains Dh35-65; ⌚noon-11.30pm) With its deep-purple walls, black furniture and Arabic design flourishes, this chic and contemporary space is swish by Sharjah standards. Portions are not huge, but flavours are delicately paired and the creative selection goes way beyond the usual mezze and grills. Finish with the tangy rosewater sherbet.

SHOPPING

CENTRAL SOUQ MARKET

(Blue Souq; King Faisal Rd; ⌚9am-1pm & 4-11pm Sat-Thu, 4-11pm Fri) Near Al Ittihad Sq, the tile-embellished Central Souq occupies two long parallel buildings connected by indoor bridges. Shops on the ground floor hawk modern jewellery, watches and local and international clothing; upstairs is more regional flair, with rugs, pashminas and curios from the Arab world. Visit in the evening, when the place fills with locals.

SOUQ AL ARSAH MARKET

(Courtyard Souq; www.heartofsharjah.ae/souq-al-arsah.html; Heritage Area; ⌚9am-9pm Sat-Thu, 4-9pm Fri) One of the oldest souqs in the UAE (about 50 years), this once crawled with traders from Persia and India and local Bedouin stocking up on supplies, their camels fastened to posts outside. Despite a facelift it's still atmospheric, though vendors now vie for tourist dirham with pashminas, *dhallahs* (coffee pots), herbs and spices, old *khanjars* (daggers) and traditional jewellery in air-conditioned comfort.

Al Ain

Explore

About two hours east of Abu Dhabi, Al Ain is fed by natural springs and set among oases and plantations, garnering it the nickname 'Garden City'. The birthplace of the United Arab Emirates' founding father Sheikh Zayed was once a vital stop on the caravan route between Oman and the Gulf. Visitors flock to its forts, museums, zoo and smattering of Unesco World Heritage sites. Unlike Abu Dhabi, Dubai and Sharjah, Al Ain lacks ultramodern skyscrapers and as a result feels more culturally authentic. The fact that it's home to the UAE's highest proportion of Emirati nationals (clocking in at a whopping 30%) also helps. A highlight is the drive up the mountain road snaking to the top of Jebel Hafeet, treating you to sweeping views of the arid splendour that is the Empty Quarter along the way.

The Best...

➡ **Sights** Al Ain Zoo (p176)

➡ **Place to Eat** Tanjore (p176)

➡ **Place to Drink** Rooftop (p177)

Getting There & Away

➡ **Bus** Al Ain's new central bus station is near Al Ain Oasis opposite the fish market. Express bus X90 shuttles back and forth to Abu Dhabi every 45 minutes (Dhs25, 1½ hours). Al Gazal runs minibuses between Al Ain and Dubai's Al Ghubaiba bus station in Bur Dubai hourly (Dhs20).

➡ **Taxi** Budget about Dhs270 for the trip to/from Dubai and Dhs300 to/from Abu Dhabi. The main taxi stand is next to the bus station. Shared taxis leave across the street from the bus station and are considerably cheaper (Dhs35 to Dubai or Sharjah; Dhs30 to Abu Dhabi).

Need to Know

➡ **Area Code** 03

➡ **Location** 150km southeast of Downtown Dubai and 170km east of Abu Dhabi.

➡ **Tourist Office Information Centre** (☎03 711 8311; www.visitabudhabi.ae; Al Jahili Fort; ⏰9am-5pm Sat-Thu, 3-5pm Fri)

SIGHTS

Al Ain is quite tough to navigate because of its many roundabouts. Brown signs directing visitors to the major tourist attractions are helpful, but a few more wouldn't hurt. Be on the lookout for His Highness Sheikh Khalifa Bin Zayed Al Nahyan Masjid – this impressive new mosque, one of the UAE's largest, will hold some 20,000 worshippers when it is completed by 2018.

AL AIN PALACE MUSEUM MUSEUM

(☎03 751 7755; Al Ain St; ⏰8.30am-7.30pm Tue-Thu, Sat & Sun, from 3pm Fri) FREE This nicely restored, rambling palace was Sheikh Zayed's residence from 1937 to 1966. The simple yet elegant cinnamon-coloured compound is divided into private, guest and official quarters by courtyards and landscaped with cacti, magnolia trees and palms. You can step inside the *majlis* (reception room) where Zayed received visitors, roam around the huge kitchen, see the canopied matrimonial bed and snap a photo of the Land Rover he used to visit the desert Bedouin.

AL JAHILI FORT HISTORIC SITE

(Mohammed Bin Khalifa St; ⏰9am-5pm Tue-Thu & Sun, 3-5pm Fri) FREE Surrounded by a lush park, this fairy-tale fort was constructed in the 1890s as the summer residence of Sheikh Zayed I (1836–1909) and expanded by the British in the 1950s. The original parts are the square fort in the far-left corner of the courtyard and the wedding-cake-tiered tower opposite. It won the prestigious Terra Award for the best Earthen Architecture in the world in 2016.

Today the compound houses a tourist centre with temporary exhibitions (Zayed I, UAE Armed Forces etc) and a superb exhibit of photographs taken by British explorer Sir Wilfred Thesiger during his multiple crossings of the Empty Desert in the 1940s.

AL AIN NATIONAL MUSEUM MUSEUM

(☎03 764 1595; Zayed Bin Sultan St; adult/child Dhs3/1; ⏰8.30am-7.30pm Tue-Thu, Sat & Sun, from 3pm Fri) This charmingly old-fashioned museum is perfect for getting up to speed on the ancient past of the Al Ain region. Highlights of the archaeological section include weapons, jewellery, pottery and coins excavated from 4000-year-old tombs at nearby Al Hili and Umm Al Nar. The ethnography galleries zero in on various aspects of the daily life of the Bedouin and settled people, including education, marriage and farming.

There is beautiful silver jewellery, traditional costumes and a harrowing display of simple circumcision instruments with lots of sharp points and hooks – ouch!

AL AIN OASIS OASIS

(☎03 712 8429; ⏰8am-5pm) **FREE** Eight gates lead into the great date plantations of this famous oasis – the UAE's first curated Unesco World Heritage site – with some 150,000 trees of around 100 varieties. Simply wander around this tranquil, jungly maze, away from the hubbub of the city, and keep an eye out for the 3000-year-old *falaj* natural irrigation system lacing the grounds. It's easy to get lost – if you do, ask a security guard for a lift on a buggy (offer a tip).

There's a small cafe and a winter-only gift shop and horse and pony rides. The oasis is off Zayed bin Sultan St.

HILI ARCHAEOLOGICAL PARK ARCHAEOLOGICAL SITE

(Mohammed Bin Khalifa St, Hili; ⏰4-11pm) **FREE** Honoured as a Unesco World Heritage Site in 2011, these remarkable vestiges of a settlement and tombs dating back some 5000 years to the Umm Al Nar period open up a window on early life in the region. On the edge of town, they've been integrated into a peaceful park. A highlight is the Great Hili Tomb, whose two entrances are decorated with carvings of humans and antelopes.

The park is about 12km north of Al Ain's centre.

EATING & DRINKING

★TANJORE INDIAN $$

(☎03 704 6000; Al Salam St, Danat Al Ain Resort; mains Dhs32-90; ⏰12.30-3pm & 7-11pm Tue-Sun; 📶) Al Ain's best Indian restaurant, Tanjore at the **Danat Al Ain Resort** (http://alain.danathotels.com; r from Dhs400; P📶🏊) will have your taste buds doing cartwheels. Fuelled by an arsenal of aromas, the chicken tikka masala (or biryani), the fiery chicken Chettinad and the lobster masala are among the dishes rivalling any curry in India. Kudos for the attentive service, understated folkloric decor and up-and-coming Sula Indian wines.

AL FANAR EMIRATI $$

(☎03 766 5200; www.alfanarrestaurant.com; Souq Al Zafarana; mains Dhs49-79; ⏰9am-10pm Sat-Wed, 9am-midnight Thu, 9am-noon & 1-11pm

TOP SIGHT
AL AIN ZOO

Al Ain's remarkable zoo is the region's largest and most acclaimed; its spacious enclosures, inhabited by indigenous and exotic species, are impressively authentic. Observe grazing Arabian oryx, big-horned Barbary sheep, rhinos, hippos, tigers, lions and more. Some were born at the zoo, which has a well-respected conservation and breeding program. Highlights include giraffe feedings, a fascinating walk-through lemur experience and the world's largest human-made safari, a 217-hectare landscape housing more than 250 African and Arabian animals.

Other additions include the Sheikh Zayed Desert Learning Centre, which is a sustainably built multimedia exhibition housing five interactive galleries: Sheikh Zayed Tribute Hall, Abu Dhabi's Desert over Time, Abu Dhabi's Living World, People of the Desert and Looking to the Future. There's also a variety of cafes and restaurants and a Children Discovery Garden, among others, with renovations/expansion ongoing at time of writing.

Don't Miss

- Giraffe feedings
- Walk-through lemur experience
- Safari tour

Practicalities

- ☎03 799 2000
- www.alainzoo.ae
- off Zayed Al Awwal & Nahyan Al Awwal Sts
- adult/child from Dhs50/20
- ⏰9am-8pm, longer in winter

CAMEL MARKET

It's dusty, noisy, pungent and chaotic, but never mind: Al Ain's famous **camel market** (Zayed Bin Sultan St; ⏲7am-sunset) FREE is a wonderful immersion in traditional Arabic culture. All sorts of camels are holed up in pens, from wobbly legged babies that might grow up to be racers to imposing studs kept for breeding. The intense haggling is fun to watch. Trading takes place in the morning, but it's usually possible to see the corralled animals all day long.

Some traders may offer to give you a tour (for money), but you're free to walk around on your own. Taking photographs will also elicit requests for payment. Haggling should bring the often exorbitant asking price down to Dhs10 or Dhs20. Women should dress conservatively.

The market is about 8km south of central Al Ain, behind Bawadi Mall and part of the Al Ain Central Market, which also trades in goats and other animals.

Fri;) Part of a mini UAE chain, this is a good place to start if you're looking to dig into Emirati cuisine. Locals go for dishes such as *robyan* biryani (shrimp with rice, onions and coriander), *samek mashwi* sea bream (grilled spiced whole fish), *jasheed* (minced baby shark with onions and spices) and various lamb-shank biryanis.

MAKANI CAFE LEBANESE **$$**

(03 768 6666; Khata Al Shikle St, Hilton Al Ain; mains Dhs15-165; ⏲6pm-2am) Meaning 'my place' in Arabic, this Hilton Abu Dhabi outpost has a delightful atmosphere, with plenty of palms and comfortable rattan-style furniture. The fare – from falafel and lamb-kofta sandwiches to the mixed seafood grill – is simple but satisfying. Live Arabic music creates a fitting accompaniment, as do shisha and a Lebanese wine or two.

SHAHRYAR IRANIAN **$$**

(03 737 0077; Othman Bin Affan St; mains Dhs34-98; ⏲noon-midnight) On the 1st floor of Al Ain Mall, this simple, spotless eatery serves reliable Iranian staples, including kebabs, rice dishes and a tasty salad combo with tabbouleh, hummus and *fattoush* (with strips of bread). Leave room for the *faloodeh* dessert (a Persian spin on ice cream).

ROOFTOP BAR

(03 713 8888; www.therooftopalain.com; Aloft Hotel, Hazza Bin Zayed Stadium Development; cocktails Dhs40-45; ⏲6pm-2am;) Al Ain's latest hotspot, the Rooftop sits – you guessed it! – on top of the hip new Aloft hotel and backs right up against the Hazza Bin Zayed Stadium. It's an atmospheric open-air pool party, with the blue-lit waters lighting the whole place up like a disco lounge after sundown.

Call ahead to book a poolside cabana or grab a cocktail and ogle the desert views, which stretch all the way to Jebel Hafeet.

TRADER VIC'S BAR

(03 754 5111; Zayed Bin Sultan St, Al Ain Rotana Hotel; cocktails Dhs28-48; ⏲12.30-3.30pm & 7.30pm-1am) Sip exotic rum concoctions while taking in the trippy tiki decor and enjoying a wide choice of tasty bar snacks at this happening spot at the **Al Ain Rotana Hotel** (www.rotana.com/alainrotana; d from Dhs800; P). Still hungry? Consider booking a table for dinner, when a live Cuban band will get your toes tapping between courses (music starts 9pm Monday to Saturday).

SPORTS & ACTIVITIES

WADI ADVENTURE WATER PARK

(03 781 8422; www.wadiadventure.ae; Jebel Al Hafeet St; adult/child Dhs50/25, attractions Dhs25-150; ⏲11am-8pm Sun-Thu, 10am-8pm Fri & Sat) Unleash your inner daredevil at this water park, which features the region's first human-made white-water rafting facility. It also offers a variety of water sports, including surfing, kayaking and swimming. Admission buys access to pools, restaurants and a low-ropes course only.

Reserve ahead if you want to brave white water aboard a raft (Dhs100 per 1½ hours), ride the 200m-long zip line (Dhs50 per hour) or ride the giant swing with its stomach-turning 14m drop (Dhs25).

WORTH A DETOUR

JEBEL HAFEET

This jagged 1240m-high limestone mountain rears out of the plain south of Al Ain. Its arid crags are home to red foxes, feral cats and the rock hyrax, which resembles a large rabbit but is, improbably, related to the elephant; and 5000-year-old single-chamber domed tombs that are part of Al Ain's Unesco World Heritage sites. A 12km-long paved road – completely lit after dark – corkscrews to the Mercure Grand Jebel Hafeet and a couple of coffee houses at the summit.

There are several pullouts to admire the views along the way. The virulently green slopes at the bottom of the mountain are fed by natural hot springs emanating from the mountainside. A small resort with a lake and giant fountain has grown up around the springs, with segregated bathing, camping and picnicking opportunities. The Qemat Jebel Hafeet Restaurant & Cafeteria offers a good perch alongside the wadi with its shaded terrace and tasty snacks.

The top of Jebel Hafeet is about 30km from central Al Ain, including the 12km stretch of mountain road. From the town centre, head west on Khalifa bin Zayed St towards the airport, then follow the brown signs.

UAE East Coast

Explore

Time seems to move much more slowly on the UAE's eastern coast, whose beaches are a popular getaway for nationals and expats keen to escape the daily razzmatazz. Although there are a few five-star resorts, the vibe is decidedly old school and low key. International tourism has suffered, as visitors prefer the glitzy resorts of Dubai or the new properties of up-and-coming neighbouring emirate of Ras Al Khaimah.

Facing the Indian Ocean (more specifically, the Gulf of Oman), the east coast belongs almost entirely to the emirate of Fujairah, interrupted only by the three small Sharjah enclaves of Dibba Al Hisn, Khor Fakkan and Kalba. While the businesslike capital, Fujairah, has a couple of heritage sites, tourism is concentrated further north, especially around Al Aqah, where the rugged Hajar Mountains dip down to long, sandy beaches with excellent swimming, snorkelling and diving.

The Best...

- **Sight** Al Badiyah Mosque
- **Place to Eat** Al Meshwar
- **Place to Stay** Le Méridien Al Aqah Beach Resort

Getting There & Away

- **Bus** E700 buses link Fujairah City and Deira's Union Bus Station in Dubai roughly hourly (Dhs25, two hours). Return buses and shared taxis leave when full from the bus stop just just east of Choithrams Supermarket on Sheikh Hamad Bin Abdullah Rd (Dhs30, 1¼ hour). There's no direct route from Abu Dhabi.
- **Taxi** A taxi from Dubai will cost about Dhs250. A taxi from Fujairah City to Al Aqah beach costs around Dhs80.

Need to Know

- **Area Code** 09
- **Location** 120km east of Downtown Dubai, 270km northeast of Abu Dhabi.
- **Tourist Office Fujairah Tourism & Antiquities** (09 223 1554; www.fujairahtourism.ae; Fujairah World, near Fujairah Museum; 7.30am-2.30pm Sat-Wed)

SIGHTS

AL BADIYAH MOSQUE MOSQUE

(Dibba Rd, Hwy E99; 9am-5pm) FREE Badiyah (also spelt Bidyah and Bidiya), 8km north of Khor Fakkan, is famous for its tiny 1446 mosque. The modest stone and mud structure, adorned with four pointed domes and resting on a single internal pillar, is considered the oldest mosque in the UAE.

Non-Muslims are free to take a peek but must be modestly dressed and take off their shoes; women must also cover their hair. Free *abayas* (full-length robes for women) may be borrowed from the attendant.

The prayer hall has a lovely contemplative feel, enlivened by a red carpet with white dots and leather-bound books stacked into wall niches. The mosque is built into a low hillside along the coastal road just north of Badiyah village and guarded by two ruined watchtowers. It's well worth walking up here for sweeping views of the Hajar Mountains and the Gulf.

CORNICHE BEACH

Khor Fakkan is home to a busy container port. Still, the town is not without its charms, especially along the corniche, which extends for several kilometres and is flanked by palm trees, gardens, kiosks and a playground, making it popular with families for picnics and waterfront strolls.

WADI WURAYAH NATIONAL PARK

Tucked into the Hajar Mountains between Dibba, Khor Fakkan and Masafi, Wadi Wurayah (Wurayah Canyon) is a true natural treasure that was designated the UAE's first Mountain Protected Area by the World Wildlife Fund (WWF) in 2009.

EATING

AL MESHWAR LEBANESE **$$**

(☎09 222 1113; Hamad bin Abdullah Rd; mezze Dhs15-35, mains Dhs37-170; ⏲9am-1am) With its Fred Flintstone exterior, this perennially popular local restaurant is easily spotted. It's just as well, for the Lebanese fare is finger-licking good, from the tangy hummus and copious other mezze (go for the outstanding mixed platter for Dhs65) to grilled meats and fluffy *sambousek* (meat pies). Shisha lounge downstairs; family dining upstairs.

IRANI PARS RESTAURANT IRANIAN **$$**

(☎09 238 7787; Corniche Roundabout; mains Dhs20-75; ⏲9.30am-12.30am) Locals give this simple restaurant the thumbs up for its generous portions of grills served with fluffy rice. Try the classic stews such as the herb-based *ghormeh sabzi.*

SPORTS & ACTIVITIES

AL BOOM DIVING DIVING

(☎09 204 4925; www.alboomdiving.com; Le Méridien Al Aqah Beach Resort; dives from Dhs400, 3pm snorkel trip Dhs150; ⏲8am-6pm) Al Boom is an excellent diving operation with several dive sites covering most of the UAE plus a once-monthly Musandam dhow trip.

ABSOLUTE ADVENTURE OUTDOORS

(☎04 392 6463; www.adventure.ae; Karsha; day trips from Dhs350; ⏲Oct-Apr) Located near the Golden Tulip Hotel in Oman, this well-named outfit organises a wide range of activities, including kayaking tours, trekking, mountain biking and camping in the Hajar Mountains.

All bookings must go through their head office in Dubai well in advance due to border-crossing formalities.

AL MARSA DIVING

(☎02 683 6550; www.almarsamusandam.com; dives from Dhs400, sunset cruise Dhs150; ⏲8am-1pm & 3-6pm) Based in Oman (with their main UAE office in Sharjah), this reliable local diving operator offers a wide range of courses, including scuba diving, advanced courses, rescue and dive-master courses. Also offers dhow trips, including a sunset cruise. Border-crossing bureaucracy must be handled in advance.

SLEEPING

LE MÉRIDIEN AL AQAH BEACH RESORT RESORT **$$$**

(☎09 244 9000; www.lemeridien-alaqah.com; Dibba Rd, Hwy E99; d from Dhs1200; P📶🏊) With a beautiful location embracing a private beach and standard yet spacious 48-sq-metre rooms, this resort is practically a destination in its own right. Spend days diving, waterskiing, playing volleyball or simply lazing on the sand or by one of the UAE's largest pools and then pick your favourite from among the five on-site restaurants at dinnertime.

A massive kids' play area means the adults can catch a break as well.

Sleeping

Butler service, Rolls Royce limousines, champagne baths – your imagination is the only limit when it comes to luxe lodging in Dubai. Yet the tiny turbo emirate offers the entire gamut of places to unpack your suitcase, including boutique hotels, heritage B&Bs, quality midrange hotels and, of course, just about every international hospitality brand under the sun.

Accommodation Options

Dubai has more than 100,000 beds, a number that's still growing in the run-up to World Expo 2020. With so much competition, standards are generally high, and even most budget hotels deliver decent-sized rooms with at least a modicum of style, a private bathroom, cable TV and wi-fi.

Midrange hotels often have superb facilities, including a pool, multiple restaurants, a gym, satellite TV and a bar. Top-end hotels boast the full spectrum of international-standard amenities, plus perhaps a scenic location, great views and ritzy designer decor. Budget hotels cluster in Deira; most are fine for a one- or two-night stay, although the cheapest may also be places where sex workers conduct their business.

Beach resorts come with private beaches, fancy spas and an entire village worth of restaurants and bars. City hotels, especially in the Financial District, tend to flaunt corporate flair, with design and amenities to match.

Free wi-fi is commonplace, with only a few hotels charging as much Dhs100 per day for access. Some hotels still restrict free access to the public areas.

Most hotels have at least one snack bar or restaurant, although only the international four- and five-star properties serve alcohol.

By law, unmarried men and women are not permitted to share a room, but in reality most international hotels turn a blind eye. Having two different last names is no tip-off, as most married Arab women keep their name.

Hotel Apartments

Although designed for long-term stays, hotel apartments are a great way for wallet-watching travellers to economise in comfort. Available in various configurations from studios to two-bedroom apartments, they come with cooking facilities and room cleaning. Facilities such a gym or pool are fairly standard, but on-site restaurants or bars are not. There are two main clusters of hotel apartments: in the Mankhool area in Bur Dubai behind the BurJuman mall and in Al Barsha just south of the Mall of the Emirates.

Boutique & Heritage Hotels

In a city where a 'bigger is better' mentality rules, boutique hotels have been slow to catch on, but there is a growing number of charismatic heritage hotels. Located in Bur Dubai and Deira, they're essentially B&Bs set up in historic courtyard buildings and offering ample authenticity and sense of place. Travellers in need of buckets of privacy, high comfort levels or the latest tech amenities, however, may not feel as comfortable here.

Room Rates

Room rates fluctuate enormously, spiking during festivals, holidays and big events and dropping in the summer months.

The best beds often sell out fast, so make reservations as early as possible if you've got your eye on a particular place. You can book most properties online with a best-price guarantee.

Lonely Planet's Top Choices

One&Only The Palm (p191) Sumptuous resort with Moorish-style design accents and lavish Arabian-style.

Rove Downtown (p186) Budget-friendly urban base with Burj Khalifa views.

Palace Downtown (p187) Romantic inner-city pad with easy access to top shopping and dreamy views of Burj Khalifa.

Al Qasr Hotel (p189) Posh player with A-lister clientele, 2km of private beach and canalside dining.

XVA Hotel (p185) Connect to the magic of a bygone era in this art-filled heritage den.

Best By Budget

$

Rove City Centre (p183) Hip yet down-to-earth with amenities more typical of posher players.

Ibis Mall of the Emirates (p188) Predictably basic but comfortable and in a primo location.

Premier Inn Dubai International Airport (p183) Easy in, easy out at this airport-adjacent budget designer hotel.

$$

Centro Barsha (p188) An excellent value-for-money pick beloved by urban adventurers.

Beach Hotel Apartment (p188) Rare bargain with a killer location and easy access to tanning and shopping.

Pearl Marina Hotel Apartments (p190) All the charms of Dubai Marina at your feet without having to rob a bank.

Media One Hotel (p190) High-octane hotspot with mod design, party pedigree and unpretentious attitude.

$$$

Grosvenor House (p192) Art deco–inspired hotel draws local trend-chasers to its hip bars and restaurants.

Park Hyatt Dubai (p184) Class act surrounded by lush landscaping with superb facilities and golf course access.

Mina A'Salam (p189) A warm beachfront port of call for blue-sky holiday cravers.

Raffles Dubai (p186) Slick, chic decor with water features and top-rated Japanese rooftop restaurant and lounge.

Best Beach Hotels

Jumeirah Beach Hotel (p189) Excellent choice for families and active types with kids' club and free access to Wild Wadi Waterpark.

Al Qasr Hotel (p189) Pure luxury with Arabian flair, a giant swimming pool, mile-long beach and top-notch spa.

One&Only Royal Mirage (p191) Refined and grown-up resort with lush gardens fronting a splendid beach.

Le Meridien Mina Seyahi Beach Resort & Marina (p190) Oldie but goodie with breezy rooms and a white-sand beach and popular beach bar.

Best City Escapes

Desert Palm Resort & Hotel (p191) Easy retreat from the urban hubbub makes for a perfect desert staycation.

One&Only The Palm (p191) Cocoon of quiet sophistication with kiss-worthy skyline views.

Al Maha Desert Resort (p191) Five-star Bedouin hideaway with sensuous spa.

Jumeirah Zabeel Saray (p192) Feel like royalty at this palace-style retreat.

NEED TO KNOW

For accommodation in Abu Dhabi, see p165.

Price Ranges

The following price ranges refer to a double room with a private bathroom in high season (November to March). Unless otherwise stated, breakfast is included in the price. Rates do not include municipal tax (10%), service charge (10%) and the tourism tax (Dhs7 to Dhs20 per day).

$	under Dhs500
$$	Dhs500–1000
$$$	over Dhs1000

Check-in & Check-out

Flights arrive in Dubai at all hours, so be sure to confirm your check-in time with the hotel before arrival. The earliest check-in is generally at 2pm, although if the room is ready, early access is usually no problem. Checkout is 11am or noon, though some hotels will give you an extra hour or two for free if you check with reception.

Useful Websites

- **Lonely Planet** (www.lonelyplanet.com/united-arab-emirates/dubai/hotels) Recommendations and bookings.
- **Visit Dubai** (www.visitdubai.com) The official tourist authority site also has accommodation booking function.
- **Dnata** (www.dnatatravel.com) Major travel agency for the Middle Eastern market, based in Dubai.

Where to Stay

NEIGHBOURHOOD	FOR	AGAINST
Bur Dubai	Value-priced hotel apartments cluster behind BurJuman Mall, international budget and midrange chains hug the main streets, and heritage boutique hotels are near the Creek.	Can be soulless away from Meena Bazaar (the souq area), lacking the atmosphere of Deira and the glitz of modern Dubai.
Deira	Atmospheric area near the Creek and souqs. The nicest places overlook the Creek; those closer to the airport often have excellent rates. Easy Dubai Metro access.	Noisy and chaotic. Budget choices can be brothels. Heavy traffic and nightmare parking during busy times of the day.
Downtown Dubai & Business Bay	In the midst of major sightseeing and shopping magnets, superb luxury hotels, excellent restaurants and trendy nightlife.	Horrendous rush-hour traffic; some distance from the sea. Expensive.
Dubai Marina & Palm Jumeirah	Super-ritzy beach hotels around the Marina and on the Palm; midrange places in Dubai Media City and Dubai Internet City. Terrific views, nightlife and food scene.	Cookie-cutter international chains can seem anonymous and don't provide a sense of place. Resorts on Palm Jumeirah are a long way from anywhere. Paucity of budget options.
Jumeirah	Good for beachfront hotels and Burj Al Arab views. Hotel apartments cluster next to Mall of the Emirates.	Many hotels are a taxi ride from the nearest metro station. Shortage of budget options on the beach.

Deira

Deira is close to the airport and therefore popular with visitors on stopovers. There are plenty of older, smaller, budget places in and around the souqs, although some can be quite – how shall we say? – shady. Nicer properties can be found along the Creek as far south as Dubai Festival City.

★ROVE CITY CENTRE HOTEL $
Map p246 (04 561 9100; www.rovehotels.com; 19B & 24B Sts; r Dhs410; P; M Deira City Centre) This fast-growing budget chain offers superb value for money with a killer Old Dubai location close to the souqs, Dubai Creek, great ethnic eats, public transport and the airport. Families will appreciate the adjoining rooms, the outdoor pool, free board games and 24-hour laundry. Crisp, contemporary rooms are good-sized, with floor-to-ceiling windows.

AHMEDIA HERITAGE GUEST HOUSE B&B $
Map p244 (04 225 0085; www.ahmediaguesthouse.com; Al Ras Rd; r from Dhs350; ; M Al Ras) Rooms outfitted with Persian carpets on white-tiled floors, rich drapes and cosy beds (some of them four-poster) make you feel like you've dropped into a fairy tale. This charmer sits in the heart of historic Deira, close to the Spice and Gold Souqs.

PREMIER INN DUBAI INTERNATIONAL AIRPORT HOTEL $
(04 885 0999; https://global.premierinn.com; 52nd St, opposite Terminal 3; r from Dhs485; P@; M Airport Terminal 3) If your plane lands late or leaves early, the Dubai airport outpost of this UK-based budget chain is a convenient place to check in. It delivers modern if pocket-sized digs, appealingly accented with the company's trademark purple. Plane-spotters can indulge their obsession while floating in the rooftop pool. Free airport shuttles run every 30 minutes.

MARCO POLO HOTEL HOTEL $
Map p244 (04 272 0000; www.marcopolohotel.net; Al Muteena St; r from Dhs310; P; M Union, Baniyas Square) Behind the shiny dark-glass facade awaits an updated city hotel close to the airport and thus handy on stopovers. The carpeted rooms won't win style awards but are comfortable and big enough for short stays. Great eats are just steps away, and if you don't feel like leaving, you've got numerous feed-and-drink spots right in the lobby.

CORAL DUBAI DEIRA HOTEL HOTEL $
Map p244 (04 224 8587; www.hmhhotelgroup.com; Al Muraqqabat Rd; d from Dhs450; P@; M Al Rigga) In a handy location near some of Deira's best budget eats, the good-value Coral hides considerable comforts behind its business demeanour. The tone is set with the free welcome juice and continues all the way up to the good-sized rooftop pool. Handy assets include free parking and wi-fi, but rooms could use touching up. No alcohol.

LANDMARK HOTEL BANIYAS HOTEL $
Map p244 (04 228 6666; www.landmarkhotels.net/baniyas; Baniyas Sq at 14th Rd; d from Dhs260; @; M Baniyas Square) Just off Baniyas Sq, this is one of the better hotels in a hyper-busy business district near the Gold Souq. Rooms have laminate flooring, warm colours and enough space to feel comfortable, if not to do cartwheels. Instead, get the heart pumping in the well-equipped rooftop gym sitting next to a small pool with an atmospheric panorama of Deira.

RODA AL BUSTAN HOTEL $
Map p246 (04 282 0000; www.rotana.com; Casablanca St, Garhoud; r from Dhs425; P@; M Airport Terminal 1, GGICO) Everything works like a well-oiled machine at this business hotel handily situated about 1.4km from the airport. Rooms are classically elegant, and there are several restaurants on-site and more within walking distance. If you're here on a layover, the good-sized pool, tennis courts and gym might come in handy for counteracting stiff joints.

DUBAI YOUTH HOSTEL HOSTEL $
(04 298 8151; www.uaeyha.com; 39 Al Nahda Rd, Al Qusais; dm/s/d HI members Dhs110/200/260, nonmembers Dhs120/230/270; P@; M Stadium) Dubai's only Hostelling International–affiliated hostel is just north of the airport, far from most Dubai attractions but only 300m from a metro station and a mall. The range of facilities (pool, tennis court, coffee shop and laundry) is

impressive. Private rooms in the newer wing (Hostel A) come with TV, fridge and bathroom.

Amenities in the four-bed dorms in the older wings (Hostels B and C) are minimal. It's located between Lulu Hypermarket and Al Bustan Mall. No smoking, alcohol or visitors allowed. Check-in is from 2pm to 4am.

RADISSON BLU HOTEL HOTEL **$$**

Map p244 (☎04 222 7171; www.radissonblu.com; Baniyas Rd; r from Dhs800; P@🛜🏊; MUnion, Baniyas Square) This Creek-side stalwart was Dubai's first five-star hotel when it opened in 1975 and still fits as comfortably as your favourite jeans. All 276 rooms feature balconies. It was undergoing a makeover during our last visit, but will retain its range of excellent restaurants.

SHERATON DUBAI CREEK HOTEL & TOWERS HOTEL **$$**

Map p244 (☎04 228 1111; www.sheratondubaicreek.com; Baniyas Rd; r from Dhs680; P@🛜🏊; MUnion) Make sure you score a Creek-facing room for maximum enjoyment of the sparkling views through floor-to-ceiling windows. The angularity of the oversized rooms is softened by arabesque swirls in the carpet and mirrored doors on the wardrobes. Of the on-site restaurants, Ashiana (p58), which serves updated Indian fare, is the best.

HILTON DUBAI CREEK HOTEL **$$**

Map p244 (☎04 227 1111; www.hilton.com; Baniyas Rd, Al Rigga; r from Dhs680; P@🛜🏊; MAl Rigga) In a building designed by Bastille Opera architect Carlos Ott, this glass-and-chrome hotel offers a smart alternative to the usual white-marble opulence so common in Dubai. After a day of turf-pounding you can retreat to rooms with leather-padded headboards, grey-granite baths, fabulous beds and Creek views. Rates include a shuttle to the beachfront sister property Hilton Dubai Jumeirah.

RIVIERA HOTEL HOTEL **$$**

Map p244 (☎04 222 2131; www.rivierahotel-dubai.com; Baniyas Rd; d from Dhs650; @🛜; MBaniyas Square) Though updated, this old-timey hotel can't quite compete in the amenity department. However, it gets bonus points for its Creek location, proximity to the Deira souqs and ample breakfast buffet. Rooms feature carpets, patterned wallpaper and bold colour accents and overlook either the Creek or the souqs. No alcohol.

★PARK HYATT DUBAI RESORT **$$$**

Map p246 (☎04 602 1234; https://dubai.park.hyatt.com; Dubai Creek Club St, Dubai Creek Golf & Yacht Club; d from Dhs1100; P@🛜🏊; MDeira City Centre) The mile-long driveway through a lush date-palm grove is the first hint that the Park Hyatt is no ordinary hotel – an impression quickly confirmed the moment you step into the domed and pillared lobby. Tiptoeing between hip and haute, it has oversized pastel rooms with subtle arabesque flourishes and balconies for counting the dhows plying the Creek. Close to the airport.

The spa and restaurants are all top notch and the golf-course setting further lends an air of exclusivity.

Bur Dubai

One of the cheapest areas to stay in Dubai, Bur Dubai counts heritage B&Bs, the city's oldest hotel, modern budget and midrange chains and plenty of hotel apartments in the Mankhool area, near the BurJuman mall, among its lodging options.

ORIENT GUEST HOUSE HERITAGE HOTEL **$**

Map p248 (☎04 351 9111; www.orientguesthouse.com; Al Fahidi Historical District, Al Fahidi St; r from Dhs444; 🛜; MAl Fahidi) This romantic B&B in a former private home beautifully captures the feeling of old Dubai. The 11 smallish rooms are entered via heavy wooden doors and surround a central courtyard that doubles as a cafe and breakfast spot. Furnishings exude traditional Arabic flair and feature richly carved wooden armoires, four-poster beds with frilly drapes and tiled floors. It's off Al Fahidi St.

BARJEEL HERITAGE GUEST HOUSE GUESTHOUSE **$**

Map p248 (☎04 354 4424; www.barjeelguesthouse.com; Shindagha Waterfront; r from Dhs400; 🛜; MAl Ghubaiba) Right on the historic Shindagha waterfront, where Dubai's royal family used to live, this charismatic retreat lets you connect with Dubai's past in a beautifully restored *barjeel* (wind-tower) building. In typical local style, rooms wrap around a quiet courtyard and feature romantic four-poster beds; suites have a *majlis*-style sitting area. Rates include English or Arabic breakfast.

GOLDEN SANDS HOTEL APARTMENTS APARTMENT $

Map p248 (04 355 5553; www.goldensandsdubai.com; Al Mankhool Rd; studio apt from Dhs300; @; BurJuman) This Dubai hotel apartment pioneer has 750 studios and one- or two- bedroom serviced apartments with kitchenettes and balconies spread over a dozen boxy midrises behind the BurJuman mall. All have ample space, but some units could use sprucing up, especially the bathrooms. It's in a residential area with lots of other hotel apartments around.

FOUR POINTS BY SHERATON BUR DUBAI HOTEL $

Map p248 (04 397 7444; www.fourpointsburdubai.com; Khalid bin al Waleed Rd, Mankhool; r from Dhs370; P@; Al Fahidi) A long stone's throw from a metro station, this Four Points has carpeted rooms decked out in soothing yellows and anchored by supremely comfortable beds with marshmallow-soft feather pillows. You'll find an adequate gym, a small pool, a hot tub and a stellar Indian restaurant, Antique Bazaar (p72).

MAJESTIC HOTEL TOWER HOTEL $

Map p248 (04 359 8888; www.dubaimajestic.com; Al Mankhool Rd; r from Dhs430; P@; Al Fahidi) Despite its ho-hum location on a busy street, this hotel scores highly for comfort, design and a 'with it' vibe thanks to a happening Greek restaurant and the best live-music club in town. All rooms come with plush beds and heavy drapes in neutral colours; the 'classic' ones are tiny, so book 'deluxe' if you need more elbow room.

SAVOY CENTRAL HOTEL APARTMENTS APARTMENT $

Map p248 (04 393 8000; www.savoydubai.com/savoy-central; Al Rolla Rd, Meena Bazaar; r from Dhs340; P@; Al Ghubaiba, Al Fahidi) These roomy studios with kitchenettes and big purple sofa beds put you within steps of fabulous budget eats, the Bur Dubai souqs and major historic sights, including the Dubai Museum. The rooftop pool is perfect for splashing under the stars. Free wi-fi in the lobby and pool only.

RAINBOW HOTEL HOTEL $

Map p248 (04 357 2172; www.rainbowhoteldubai.com; Khalid bin al Waleed Rd; r from Dhs250; P; Al Fahidi) With their white-tiled floors and heavy curtains, the Rainbow's 40 rooms exude a retro charm that complements the spirit of the hotel's historic-centre location, steps from the souqs, the Dubai Museum, the Creek and lots of fabulous hole-in-wall expat eateries. Despite its small size, the property brims with facilities, including a small rooftop pool, sauna and gym.

XVA HOTEL HERITAGE HOTEL $$

Map p248 (04 353 5383; www.xvahotel.com; s/d from Dhs360/675; ; Al Fahidi) This charmer occupies a century-old wind-tower house smack dab in the Al Fahidi Historic District (p67), off Al Fahidi St. Its 13 compact rooms sport whitewashed walls decorated with art that picks up on local themes like the Henna Room or the Dishdash Room. Most open onto a courtyard (making them rather dark) with a cafe where breakfast is served.

ARABIAN COURTYARD HOTEL & SPA HOTEL $$

Map p248 (04 351 9111; www.arabiancourtyard.com; Al Fahidi St; r from Dhs550; P@; Al Fahidi, Al Ghubaiba) Opposite the Dubai Museum, this hotel is an excellent hub for city explorers. The Arabian theme extends from the turbaned lobby staff to the design flourishes in the decent-sized rooms, some of which catch glimpses of the Creek across the souq. Facilities include a pub, a much-lauded Indian restaurant, a swimming pool, a spa and a gym. One child under 11 stays free.

MÖVENPICK HOTEL & APARTMENTS BUR DUBAI HOTEL $$

Map p252 (04 336 6000; www.movenpick.com; 19th & 12A Sts, Oud Metha; r from Dhs650; P@; Oud Metha, Dubai Healthcare City) A lobby decorated in shades of charcoal and cream leads to a sweeping *Gone with the Wind* staircase and from there to 255 good-sized and well-lit rooms dressed in sumptuous chocolate, cherry and vanilla. There's half a dozen restaurants, including the excellent Chutneys (p72) for Indian fare.

It's opposite the American Hospital, close to the airport; plane spotters especially will love the rooftop pool.

★RAFFLES DUBAI HOTEL $$$

Map p252 (☎04 324 8888; www.raffles.com/dubai; Sheikh Rashid Rd, Wafi City, Oud Metha; r from Dhs1110; P@; MDubai Healthcare City) Built in the shape of a pyramid, Raffles is a stylish hotspot with magnificent oversized rooms (with balconies) blending Asian and Middle Eastern design accents, and bathrooms dressed in natural Egyptian stone, boasting whirlpool tubs and walk-in showers. Zeitgeist-capturing in-room touches include lighting controlled from a bedside console, iPod docking stations and free superfast wi-fi.

FOUR POINTS BY SHERATON DOWNTOWN DUBAI HOTEL $$$

Map p248 (☎04 354 3333; www.fourpointsdowntowndubai.com; 4C St, off Al Mankhool Rd; r from Dhs1300; P@; MAl Karama, Al Fahidi) An excellent value-for-money pick, this outpost has rooms spacious enough for a small family beyond its chrome-and-marble lobby. The location is a bit nondescript, but extras such as comfy mattresses, big flat-screen TVs, and a rooftop gym and pool compensate.

Downtown Dubai

Staying in Downtown Dubai puts you smack dab in the city's vortex of vibrancy. Aside from the big international chains, you'll also find a few home-grown players imbued with a local sense of place. With few exceptions, you'll need to shell out top dirham.

★ROVE DOWNTOWN HOTEL $

Map p258 (☎04 561 9999; www.rovehotels.com/hotel/rove-downtown; 312 Happiness St; r Dhs470; P; MFinancial Centre, Burj Khalifa/Dubai Mall) Tailor-made for wallet-watching globetrotters, Rove is a hip launch pad with sassy, contemporary decor and such millennial must-haves as a an outdoor pool for chilling, a 24-hour gym, a industrial-styled cafe plus a hangover-friendly 2pm checkout. Pay a little extra for rooms with Burj Khalifa views.

All rooms have a single sofa bed suitable for children and many rooms are interconnected. Children under six eat free at the restaurant's weekend brunch buffet (adult/child over 6 years Dhs99/49).

IBIS WORLD TRADE CENTRE HOTEL $

Map p258 (☎04 332 4444; www.accorhotels.com; Sheikh Zayed Rd, Financial District; r from Dhs430; P@; MWorld Trade Centre) Of the several Dubai branches of this good-value chain, this one behind the World Trade Centre is the most central. After the airy feel and modern design in the public areas, the ship's-cabin-sized rooms are a bit of a let-down, but it's hard to find a hotel that's cleaner or more comfortable at this price.

JW MARRIOTT MARQUIS HOTEL DUBAI HOTEL $$

Map p258 (☎04 414 0000; www.marriott.com; Happiness St, Business Bay; r from Dhs820; P@; MBusiness Bay) Standing 355m tall, the mammoth Marriott is the world's tallest hotel with 1600 rooms split across two jagged towers inspired by the trunk of a date palm. Cathedral-like loftiness also dominates much of the public areas, while rooms have floor-to-ceiling windows to better appreciate the stunning views.

DUSIT THANI DUBAI HOTEL $$

Map p258 (☎04 343 3333; www.dusit.com; 133 Sheikh Zayed Rd; r from Dhs870; P@; MFinancial Centre) Shaped like an upside-down tuning fork, one of Dubai's most architecturally dramatic towers hides traditional Thai decor behind its futuristic facade. Although it's geared towards the business brigade, urban nomads will also appreciate the lovely interplay of warm woods, earthy tones and rich fabrics in the oversized rooms and the stellar views from the rooftop pool.

CARLTON DOWNTOWN HOTEL $$

Map p258 (☎04 506 9999; www.carltondowntown.com; Sheikh Zayed Rd, DIFC; r from Dhs700; P@; MFinancial Centre) Close to DIFC and the Dubai Metro, this hotel tower is a value-priced crash pad for urban explorers with several restaurants and bars, Dubai's highest open-air rooftop pool with killer views, a spa and a well-equipped gym. Rooms are good-sized and modern, and even the smallest have a desk and a sofa for lounging.

JUMEIRAH EMIRATES TOWERS HOTEL $$

Map p258 (☎04 330 0000; www.jumeirah.com; Sheikh Zayed Rd, Financial District; d from Dhs750; P@; MEmirates Towers) An eye-catching steel-and-glass high-rise harbours one of the top-ranked business hotels in the

Middle East. Glide up in the panoramic lift to sumptuous, high-tech rooms with power views, a black-and-grey aesthetic and a sleek, exec-oriented layout. Women might prefer the Chopard ladies' floor, where pink replaces grey and in-bath fridges let you chill your caviar face cream.

Rates include shuttle and admission to Jumeirah's private beach and Wild Wadi Waterpark (p109).

SHANGRI-LA HOTEL **$$**

Map p258 (☎04 343 8888; www.shangri-la.com/dubai; Sheikh Zayed Rd, Financial District; r from Dhs900; P@🛜≋; MFinancial Centre) Shangri-La is the mythical paradise first described in James Hilton's 1933 novel *Lost Horizon*. In Dubai, it's a business hotel imbued with an understated sexy vibe. Rooms are a winner in the looks department, with their sycamore furniture, soft leather headboards, local art work and deep soaking tubs.

FAIRMONT DUBAI HOTEL **$$**

Map p258 (☎04 332 5555; www.fairmont.com/dubai; Sheikh Zayed Rd, Financial District; r from Dhs850; P@🛜≋; MWorld Trade Centre) This city slicker wows, especially at night when its four-poster towers are dipped in coloured lights. With a direct link to the Financial Centre, it courts high-powered execs and even has rooms with an extra-large desk to help you ink that deal. Wi-fi is charged at Dhs100 per day.

The two rooftop pools are lovely indulgence zones while Cirque Le Soir (p90) and Cavalli Club (p90) are two of the hottest night clubs in town.

NOVOTEL WORLD TRADE CENTRE HOTEL **$$**

Map p258 (☎04 332 0000; www.novotel.com; Happiness St; r from Dhs880; P@🛜≋; MWorld Trade Centre) The functional but comfortable Novotel adjoins the convention centre and has generic if well-thought-out rooms with a sofa that pulls out in case you've got the kids tagging along. The rectangular swimming pool is sufficient for laps, and there's a decently equipped gym. The Blue Bar (p91) is a top spot for live jazz.

★PALACE DOWNTOWN HOTEL **$$$**

Map p258 (☎04 428 7888; www.theaddress.com; Sheikh Mohammed Bin Rashid Blvd, Old Town Island; d from Dhs2100; P@🛜≋; MBurj Khalifa/Dubai Mall) City explorers with a romantic streak will be utterly enchanted by this low-lying, luxe lakefront contender with its winning alchemy of old-world class and Arabic aesthetics. Rooms are chic and understated, styled in easy-on-the-eye natural tones, and boast balconies overlooking Dubai Fountain. With the Burj Khalifa and Dubai Mall steps away, it's also a perfect launch pad for shopaholics.

VIDA DOWNTOWN DUBAI BOUTIQUE HOTEL **$$$**

Map p258 (☎04 428 6888; www.vida-hotels.com; Sheikh Mohammed Bin Rashid Blvd; r from Dhs1300; P@🛜≋; MBurj Khalifa/Dubai Mall) This crash pad for next-gen creatives and entrepreneurs has upbeat public areas with cool lamps and other urban accents that smoothly segue to white, bright rooms and huge open bathrooms with both a tub and walk-in shower. All electronics are controlled by the TV, there's a 24hr gym to combat fat and fatigue, and a daybed-lined pool for chilling.

MANZIL DOWNTOWN HOTEL **$$$**

Map p258 (☎04 428 5888; www.vida-hotels.com/en/manzil; Sheikh Mohammed Bin Rashid Blvd; r from Dhs1300; P@🛜≋; MBurj Khalifa/Dubai Mall) Arabesque meets mid-century modern at this lifestyle hotel that draws global hipsters with high-tech touches, design cachet and thoughtful services. Rooms marry crisp white minimalism with Middle Eastern lamps and design touches, as well as bathrooms with giant rain showers and free-standing tubs. If you're jetting in on a late flight, the 24-hour gym might help you loosen up.

ADDRESS DUBAI MALL HOTEL **$$$**

Map p258 (☎04 438 8888; www.theaddress.com; Sheikh Mohammed Bin Rashid Blvd; r from Dhs1500; P@🛜≋; MBurj Khalifa/Dubai Mall) A mod interpretation of Arabic design traditions, this fashionable hotel is directly connected to the Dubai Mall. Lug your bags back to spacious rooms where sensuous materials – leather, wood and velvet – provide a soothing antidote to shopping exhaustion. Besides ultracomfy beds and a balcony, you'll find the gamut of lifestyle essentials, including iPod docking stations and Nespresso machines.

The gym and business lounge are both open around the clock. For guests with children, room rates include a two-hour stay in the on-site **QIX kids' club**.

Jumeirah

Luxury lovers should steer towards the Burj Al Arab or the hotels at Madinat Jumeirah. The cluster of midrange hotels and hotel-apartments next to the Mall of Emirates offer great value for money.

CENTRO BARSHA HOTEL $

Map p256 (04 704 0000; www.rotana.com/centrobarsha; Rd 329, Al Barsha 1; d from Dhs450; P ; M Sharaf DG) About 500m from the Mall of the Emirates, this is the Rotana brand's entry into the budget design-hotel category. Rooms are compact but stylish and outfitted with all the key lifestyle and tech touches, including satellite TV and IP phones. Kick back in the comfy cocktail bar, the 24-hour gym or by the pleasant rooftop pool.

IBIS MALL OF THE EMIRATES HOTEL $

Map p256 (04 382 3000; www.ibis.com; 2A St, Al Barsha 1; r from Dhs320; P @ ; M Mall of the Emirates) Classic Ibis: a good deal with low-frill but sparkling-clean rooms. If you'd rather drop your cash in the adjacent mall than loll by the pool or nosh on pillow treats, this is not a bad place to hang your hat. Just remember that you can't hang much more than that in the shoebox-sized rooms. On-site bar.

HOLIDAY INN EXPRESS HOTEL $

Map p254 (04 407 1777; www.ihg.com; Jumeirah Rd, near 2nd December Rd; r from Dhs340; P ; M Al Jafiliya) It's a Holiday Inn Express, so you know you're not getting the Ritz. Still, the overall look at this well-run property is clean and contemporary, starting in the Bauhaus-meets-Arabia lobby and transitioning nicely to snug rooms with a fridge and floor-to-ceiling windows overlooking the port and Pearl Jumeirah construction. No pool but free shuttle to the beach.

LA VILLA NAJD HOTEL APARTMENTS APARTMENT $

Map p256 (04 361 9007; www.lavillahospitality.com/Najd; btwn 6A & 15 Sts, Al Barsha 1; apt from Dhs285; P @ ; M Mall of the Emirates) One of the older among the hotel apartments near the Mall of the Emirates, Najd has 64 tiled-floor apartments that make maximum use of space, packing a living room, bedroom, kitchen, full bathroom and guest bathroom into a relatively compact frame. Ask for a unit overlooking Ski Dubai (p109). Basic gym, nice rooftop pool.

LA VILLE HOTEL & SUITES BOUTIQUE HOTEL $$

Map p254 (04 403 3111; www.livelaville.com; Al Multaqa St, City Walk; r from Dhs960; P ; M Burj Khalifa/Dubai Mall) This chic boutique contender fits well with the urban lifestyle concept of City Walk but has the distinction of actually serving alcohol in its food outlets that include the rooftop lounge Look Up and the rustic-elegant Grapeskin bar (p105) next to the leafy courtyard. The 88 rooms have an uncluttered feel, a vanilla-chocolate colour scheme and panoramic windows. It's part of Marriott's Autograph Collection.

DUBAI MARINE BEACH RESORT & SPA RESORT $$

Map p254 (04 346 1111; www.dxbmarine.com; Jumeirah Rd, Jumeirah 1; r from Dhs500; P @ ; M World Trade Centre) You'll sleep well at this oldie-but-goodie beachside resort with villas set among pools and tropical gardens. The beach is rather small, but there's a water-sports centre and an entire village worth of restaurants, bars and nightclubs for grown-ups, including **Boudoir** (Map p254; 04 345 5995; www.clubboudoirdubai.com; 10pm-3am) and Sho Cho (p106). Rooms are rather small but immaculately kept; get one with a balcony.

DONATELLO HOTEL HOTEL $$

Map p256 (04 340 9040; www.donatello-hoteldubai.com; cnr 19th & 21st Sts, Al Barsha; apt from Dhs450; P ; M Sharaf DG) About 500m from the Mall of the Emirates, this modern hotel is a great base for power shoppers. Stow away your loot in stylish, carpeted rooms with classic reddish-brown furniture, patterned wallpaper and a small sitting area. Reflect upon the day's adventures during a massage in the spa or while splashing around the rooftop pool.

BEACH HOTEL APARTMENT APARTMENT $$

Map p254 (04 345 2444; www.beachhotelapartment.ae; Al Hudhaiba Rd, Jumeirah 1; apt from Dhs600; P ; M World Trade Centre) Terrific service-minded staff, a sunny rooftop pool and a good location give this place a considerable edge. You'll be steps from the beach, Jumeirah Mosque and trendy cafes and boutiques, as well as a Spinneys supermarket in case you want to make use of your kitchen. The cheaper rooms face the atrium.

AL KHOORY EXECUTIVE HOTEL HOTEL $$

Map p254 (☎04 354 6555; www.corp-executive-al-khoory-hotel.dubaihoteluae.com; cnr Al Wasl & Al Hudhaiba Rds, Jumeirah 1; r from Dhs450; P @ 🛜; M World Trade Centre) Although the lobby exudes buttoned-up business flair, this mid-size hotel actually has plenty in store for leisure travellers, including a superb location a mere 10-minute walk from the beach, Jumeirah Mosque and shopping on Jumeirah Rd. Other assets include a better-than-average gym. Standard rooms are smallish but comfy.

CHELSEA PLAZA HOTEL HOTEL $$

Map p254 (☎04 398 2222; www.chelseagroupdubai.com/chelseaplaza; Satwa Roundabout, Satwa; r from Dhs540; P @ 🛜 ≋; M Al Jafiliya, World Trade Centre) In the heart of polyethnic Satwa, the Chelsea has traditionally furnished rooms with patterned carpets, shiny-dark furniture and floor-to-ceiling windows. Bathrooms come with both tubs and big showers. Catch up on games over a pint at the dimly lit sports bar or keep fit on the health club's circuit-training machines or via some laps in the decent-sized pool.

★**AL QASR HOTEL** HOTEL $$$

Map p256 (☎04 366 8888; www.jumeirah.com; Madinat Jumeirah, King Salman Bin Abdul Aziz Al Saud St, Umm Suqeim 3; r from Dhs1300; P @ 🛜 ≋; M Mall of the Emirates) If cookie-cutter hotels don't cut it, try this polished pad styled after an Arabian summer palace. Details are extraordinary, from the lobby's Austrian-crystal chandeliers to mirror-polished inlaid-marble floors. Rooms sport arabesque flourishes, rich colours and cushy furnishings, while balconies overlook the waterways of Madinat Jumeirah. Top marks for the 2km-long private beach and one of the biggest pools in town.

Children can make new friends in Sindbad's Kids Club or whoosh down the slides at Wild Wadi Waterpark (p109); the admission is included in room rates.

MINA A'SALAM HOTEL RESORT $$$

Map p256 (☎04 366 8888; www.jumeirah.com; Madinat Jumeirah, King Salman Bin Abdul Aziz Al Saud St, Umm Suqeim 3; r from Dhs1000; P @ 🛜 ≋; M Mall of the Emirates) The striking lobby is an overture to the full symphony of relaxed luxury awaiting in huge, amenity-laden rooms with arabesque design flourishes and a balcony overlooking Madinat Jumeirah. Guests also have free access to the adjacent sister property Al Qasr (p189), including the pools, the 2km-long private beach and the kids club, as well as to Wild Wadi Waterpark (p109).

JUMEIRAH BEACH HOTEL RESORT $$$

Map p256 (☎04 348 0000; www.jumeirah.com; Jumeirah Rd, Umm Suqeim 3; r from Dhs1500; P @ 🛜 ≋; M Mall of the Emirates) Shaped like a giant wave, this family-oriented resort on a 1km-long private beach is tailor-made for active types, with four pools, plenty of water sports, an entire fitness building and tennis courts. Little ones can romp around Sinbad's Kids Club or keep cool at the adjoining Wild Wadi Waterpark (p109) which has free admission for hotel guests. Sea-facing rooms look out over the Burj Al Arab.

KEMPINSKI HOTEL MALL OF THE EMIRATES HOTEL $$$

Map p256 (☎04 341 0000; www.kempinski.com/en/dubai/mall-of-the-emirates; Sheikh Zayed Rd, Mall of the Emirates, Al Barsha 1; r from Dhs1250; P @ 🛜 ≋; M Mall of the Emirates) Linked to the Mall of the Emirates, the Kempinski exudes modern European sophistication and is a perfect launch pad for a shopping immersion. The monumental marble lobby contrasts with the warmly furnished rooms, which come with iPads, Nespresso machines and other zeitgeist-compatible features. Higher categories have marble bathrooms with enormous tubs and walk-in rain showers.

A big hit, especially with Arabian guests, are the alpine-style 'Aspen Chalet' apartments overlooking Ski Dubai (p109).

BURJ AL ARAB HOTEL $$$

Map p256 (☎04 301 7777; www.burj-al-arab.com; Jumeirah Rd, Umm Suqeim 3; ste from Dhs6200; P @ 🛜 ≋; M Mall of the Emirates) This sail-shaped landmark regularly hosts pop stars, royalty, billionaires and the merely moneyed. The lobby with its eye-catching waterfall and opulent decor is the overture to the 202 richly decorated suites. The recently completed North Deck added two huge pools and 400 sunloungers.

Suites are bi-level, and even the smallest measure 170 sq metres and come with a personal butler. The decor is l-u-s-h, with moiré silk walls, mirrored ceilings over the beds, curlicue high-backed velvet chairs and inlaid bathroom tiles displaying scenes of Venice. And all that gold? Yes, it's the real 24-karat thing.

Dubai Marina & Palm Jumeirah

Dubai Marina and Palm Jumeirah teem with five-star properties catering to the leisure brigade. Inland, along Sheikh Zayed Rd, and in Barsha Heights and Dubai Internet City, you'll also find midrange local properties and international chains.

GRAND MIDWEST TOWER HOTEL **$**

Map p262 (04 436 2000; www.grandmidwest.com; Sheikh Zayed Rd, Dubai Internet City; r from Dhs260; P @ ; M Dubai Internet City) Despite the corporate feeling, this tower is a top-value pick thanks to fall-over-backwards friendly staff and generously sized studios and apartments. All are sheathed in warm hues and outfitted with stylish kitchens, ultra-comfy beds, fast wi-fi, and balconies. It's next to a metro station and there's a distant view of the Burj Al Arab from the pool deck.

MARINA DREAM HOSTEL HOSTEL **$**

Map p262 (9th fl, Dream Tower 1, Al Marsa St, Dubai Marina; dm from Dhs95; P ; M Jumeirah Lakes Towers) Not your classic hostel, this place in a Marina high-rise consists of dorms in apartments, with men and women on different floors. It's a hop, skip and jump from a metro station and a short walk from the beach. Rates include a cooked breakfast, wi-fi, linen, towels and access to a swimming pool and gym. Book via www.hostelworld.com or www.hostels.com. It's above a 24/7 grocery store.

LE MERIDIEN MINA SEYAHI BEACH RESORT & MARINA RESORT **$$**

Map p262 (04 399 3333; www.lemeridien-minaseyahi.com; King Salman Bin Abdul Aziz Al Saud St, Dubai Media City; r from Dhs800; P @ ; M Nakheel, Mina Seyahi) This beachfront hotel is a sentimental favourite and nirvana for active types with water sports, tennis courts and an enormous state-of-the-art gym. The giant free-form pool is as lovely as the meandering palm-tree-lined gardens and calm beach, while rooms are dressed in cool white and have floor-to-ceiling windows with sea views.

It's home of Barasti (p119), a hugely popular beach bar. A kids' club lets grown-ups relax while their offspring make new friends in a safe environment.

RIXOS PREMIUM DUBAI HOTEL **$$**

Map p262 (04 520 0000; http://premiumdubai.rixos.com; The Walk, Jumeirah Beach Residence; r from Dhs750; P @ ; M Damac Properties, Jumeirah Beach Residence 1) Set bang on the beach, this super-stylish hotel has rooms decorated in gold and silver tones with pops of colour and floor-to-ceiling windows (book a room on the south side for views of the Ain Dubai observation wheel). There's a buzzy vibe, with a beach club, a glam nightclub and the sprawling Lock, Stock & Barrel pub.

MEDIA ONE HOTEL HOTEL **$$**

Map p262 (04 427 1000; www.mediaonehotel.com; Al Falak St, Dubai Media City; r from Dhs500; P @ ; M Nakheel, Marina Tower) Match your mood to the room: Hip, Cool, Calm or Chill-Out. This lifestyle hotel loads up on all the zeitgeist essentials global nomads crave, like IP phones, iPod docking stations and smart TVs. The pool area is a lovely chill area that also draws locals with ladies' nights, shisha and other events. It's behind the American University.

PEARL MARINA HOTEL APARTMENTS APARTMENT **$$**

Map p262 (04 447 1717; www.pearlmarinahotel.com; Al Marsa St, Marina Waterfront, Dubai Marina; apt from Dhs600; P ; M Jumeirah Lakes Towers) Tucked into the far end of the Dubai Marina, the Pearl may not be as flashy as its high-rise neighbours, but who cares? The price tag is only a fraction of that of the big names, giving you more dirham to spend on fun, food and fashion. The fabulous beach and The Walk at JBR are only steps away.

GLORIA HOTEL HOTEL **$$**

Map p262 (04 399 6666; www.gloria-hotels.com; Sheikh Zayed Rd, Dubai Internet City; ste/apt from Dhs600/700; P @ ; M Dubai Internet City) Next to a metro station, the popular Gloria actually flaunts numerous assets that'll make you want to stay put, including a top-notch gym, a 25m rooftop pool and a surprisingly good buffet restaurant. There are more than 1000 suites and apartments with kitchen with varying decor depending on whether you go for a Californian, Classic, Modern or Mediterranean design theme. No alcohol.

DESERT DREAMS

Just a short drive from the traffic jams, construction sites and megamalls are three stellar desert resorts. If you crave a little peace and quiet, these resorts will let you experience a calmer, less-hurried side of Dubai.

Al Maha Desert Resort & Spa (☎04 832 9900; www.al-maha.com; Dubai Desert Conservation Reserve, Dubai–Al Ain Rd (Hwy E66); full board from Dhs4100; P @ ᯤ ≋) It may only be 65km southeast of Dubai (on the Dubai to Al Ain Rd), but Al Maha feels like an entirely different universe. Gone are the skyscrapers, traffic and go-go attitude. At this remote desert eco-resort it's all about getting back to some elemental discoveries about yourself and where you fit into nature's grand design.

Part of the Dubai Desert Conservation Reserve (DDCR), Al Maha is one of the most exclusive hotels in the UAE and named for the endangered Arabian oryx, which is bred as part of the DDCR's conservation program. The resort's 42 luxurious suites are all stand-alone, canvas-roofed bungalows with handmade furniture and private plunge pools. Each one has its own patio with stunning vistas of the beautiful desert landscape and peach-coloured dunes, punctuated by mountains and grazing white oryx and gazelles.

Rates include two daily activities, such as a desert-wildlife drive, an archery session or a camel trek. Private vehicles, visitors and children under 10 are not allowed.

Bab Al Shams Desert Resort & Spa (☎04 809 6498; www.meydanhotels.com/babalshams; Al Qudra Rd; r from Dhs1250; P @ ᯤ ≋) Resembling a fort and blending into the desertscape, Bab Al Shams is a tonic for escapists seeking to indulge their *Arabian Nights* fantasies. Its labyrinthine layout reflects both Arabic and Moorish influences; the 115 rooms are gorgeous, spacious and evocatively earthy, with pillars, lanterns, paintings of desert landscapes and prettily patterned Bedouin-style pillows.

While this is the perfect place to curl up with a book or meditate in the dunes, those who enjoy a more active holiday will also find plenty to do. A wonderful infinity pool beckons, as do the luscious Satori Spa and eight restaurants. Children between five and 12 years old can make new friends in Aladdin's Kids Club. Off-site activities pay homage to Emirati heritage with desert tours, falconry, archery, and horse and camel rides. Bab Al Shams is about 45 minutes south of Dubai off Hwy E611, near Endurance Village.

Desert Palm Resort & Hotel (☎04 323 8888; Al Awir Rd; r from Dhs1700, villa from Dhs4500; P ᯤ ≋) Feel the stress nibbling at your psyche evaporate the moment you step inside this luxe boutique retreat, just a short drive outside Dubai and set on a private polo estate. You can opt for either a 'palm room' with floor-to-ceiling windows overlooking the polo field or go for total privacy in one of the villas with a private pool.

Either way, you'll feel quite blissed out amid copper-toned decor, fancy linens and vast green landscapes. There's also an infinity pool, an on-site spa and a gourmet deli for picking up tasty treats to enjoy on the terrace or as a desert picnic.

ONE&ONLY THE PALM BOUTIQUE HOTEL **$$$**

Map p262 (☎04 444 1180; www.thepalm.oneandonlyresorts.com; West Crescent, Palm Jumeirah; r from Dhs3400; P ᯤ ≋; M Nakheel) The stunning Dubai skyline looms across the Gulf, yet this romantic and megaposh gem offers a complete retreat from the city. Exuding the feel of an exclusive private estate, it has rambling gardens, several pools and Moorish-influenced suites daubed with teal and purple colour accents and outfitted with all requisite 21st-century tech touches. Privacy is key throughout.

The mainland is at least a 30-minute drive away, but there's a free boat shuttle to the sister property One&Only Royal Mirage (p191).

ONE&ONLY ROYAL MIRAGE RESORT **$$$**

Map p262 (☎04 399 9999; www.royalmirage.oneandonlyresorts.com; King Salman Bin Abdul Aziz Al Saud St, Dubai Media City; r from Dhs1950; P @ ᯤ ≋; M Nakheel, 🚊 Media City) Not the newest resort but still a class act all around, the Royal Mirage consists of the Moorish-style Palace, the romantic Arabian Court and the ultra-discreet Residence & Spa hideaway. All are cocooned by richly landscaped gardens and flanked by a 1km-long sandy beach. Opulently furnished rooms with patios face the sea and are sheathed in soothing natural shades.

A boat shuttle departs hourly to the even-more-luxe sister hotel One&Only The Palm (p191) on Palm Jumeirah.

LE ROYAL MERIDIEN BEACH RESORT & SPA RESORT **$$$**

Map p262 (☎04 399 5333; www.leroyalmeridien-dubai.com; Al Mamsha St, Dubai Marina; r from Dhs1200; P@🛜🏊; MDamac, 🚊Jumeirah Beach Residence 1) An older but well-kept 500-room resort flanks a gorgeous beach and counts extensive gardens, three pools, a Roman-themed spa and an excellent kids' club among its assets. Although all rooms have Gulf-facing balconies, the traditional decor in many of them hasn't aged well, so be sure to get a recently spiffed-up one where dark woods meet tranquil pastels.

GROSVENOR HOUSE HOTEL **$$$**

Map p262 (☎04 399 8888; www.grosvenorhouse-dubai.com; Al Emreef St, Dubai Marina; r from Dhs1100; P@🛜🏊; MDamac) Twin-towered Grosvenor House was the first hotel to open among the jumble of the Marina's sky-punching towers. The public areas are sleek, grown-up and angular in a vague art deco aesthetic, but rooms feel warm and homey with their cream and brown hues brightened by red accents. The range of quality bars and restaurants is extraordinary.

Grosvenor guests also get full access to the pool and beach of the nearby sister hotel, Le Royal Meridien (p192).

JUMEIRAH ZABEEL SARAY HOTEL **$$$**

Map p262 (☎04 453 0000; www.jumeirah.com; West Crescent Rd, Palm Jumeirah; r from Dhs1200; P@🛜🏊) With its domed ceiling, golden pillars and jewel-like lamps, Zabeel Saray's lobby is as lavish and majestic as an Ottoman palace. The rich decor transfers in subtler ways to the rooms, where everything is calibrated to take the edge off travel. Distinctive asset: the 59m-long infinity pool. Little ones love hanging out at Sinbad's Kids Club.

The spa is one of the finest relaxation stations in town and comes complete with a Turkish hammam and a salt-water lap pool. A great selection of restaurants makes for contented tummies. The only downside is the remote location: the nearest metro station is about a 20-minute taxi ride away.

WESTIN DUBAI MINA SEYAHI BEACH RESORT & MARINA RESORT **$$$**

Map p262 (☎04 399 4141; www.westinminaseyahi.com; King Salman Bin Abdul Aziz Al Saud St, Dubai Media City; r from Dhs1050; P@🛜🏊; MNakheel, 🚊Mina Seyahi) A top choice for water sports enthusiasts, this sophisticated beach resort feels like a cross between an Arabian summer palace and an Italian palazzo. With classic furniture and vanilla and cocoa hues, the oversized rooms look sharp yet homey. The five pools include a 150m-long lagoon-like winding pool for lazing (the others are for kiddies and for swimming laps).

The hotel shares facilities, including a water sports centre, with the neighbouring Le Meridien Mina Seyahi.

ADDRESS DUBAI MARINA HOTEL **$$$**

Map p262 (☎04 436 7777; www.theaddress.com/en/hotels/the-address-dubai-marina; Dubai Marina Mall, Dubai Marina; r from Dhs1600; P@🛜🏊; MDamac, 🚊Dubai Marina Mall) This place has the sophistication of a city hotel, but its location on the Marina Walk with direct access to the Marina Mall also pulls in a solid crowd of leisure lovers. You'll sleep well in modern rooms dressed in homey natural tones and equipped with the gamut of mod cons.

The huge infinity pool on the 4th floor has head-spinning views of the boats and twinkling high-rises.

RITZ-CARLTON DUBAI HOTEL **$$$**

Map p262 (☎04 399 4000; www.ritzcarlton.com/dubai; The Walk at JBR, Dubai Marina; r from Dhs1200; P@🛜🏊; MDamac, 🚊Jumeirah Beach Residence 1) When this timelessly elegant Mediterranean villa-style resort first opened in 1998, Dubai Marina was still the middle of nowhere. Now it's dwarfed by high-rises, but the mature gardens and tall palms create a visual berm. Rooms and suites are carpeted, dressed in pastel shades and accented with Arabic design features. All have a terrace or patio.

Understand Dubai & Abu Dhabi

Dubai & Abu Dhabi Today

Dubai and Abu Dhabi are at an exciting juncture. Behind them lie the bad old days of regional unrest, global recession and economic vulnerability. Ahead lies the prospect of enhanced stability, stronger regional ties and closer integration with the international community. With prestigious cultural and infrastructure projects under way, this is an excellent time to visit this city that's at the heart of Arabia while being a world away from neighbouring troubles.

Best on Film

Mission: Impossible – Ghost Protocol (2011) Tom Cruise scales the Burj Khalifa in this 'Mission' thriller.

Star Trek – Beyond (2016) Dubai stands in as the city of the future encountered by the Star Trek cew on their explorations of deep space.

Syriana (2005) Dubai stands in for Iran in this political thriller that earned George Clooney his first Oscar as Best Supporting Actor.

Naqaab (2007) Bollywood suspense thriller largely shot in and around Jumeirah Beach.

Wall Street: Money Never Sleeps (2010) The sequel to the 1987 Michael Douglas classic *Wall Street* was partly filmed in Dubai.

Best in Print

Arabian Sands (Wilfred Thesiger; 1959) Timeless account of British explorer's desert crossings of the 1940s.

Dubai: The Story of the World's Fastest City (Jim Krane; 2009) Review of Dubai's rags-to-riches story.

Dubai: Gilded Cage (Syed Ali; 2010) Scholarly and critical examination of Dubai's rapid transformation.

From Rags to Riches: A Story of Abu Dhabi (Mohammed Al-Fahim; 2011) A memoir of the city written by an Emirati.

Arts & Culture

It's easy to think of a country that makes headlines with robocops, flying cars and palm-shaped islands as a cultural wasteland. But Dubai and Abu Dhabi are both making concerted efforts at sharpening their creative profiles. The recent openings of the Dubai Opera and the Louvre Abu Dhabi are only the most visible stepping stones. Meanwhile, the Dubai Design District is quickly becoming a regional laboratory for the world's finest creative tinkerers, while Art Dubai and Abu Dhabi Art have catapulted from a little-noticed art fairs to global events in less than a decade. In Dubai, the local arts community now has a key nexus on Alserkal Avenue, an urban campus of upcycled warehouses that's home to contemporary galleries championing local and regional artists.

Dubai as Early Adopter

Already famous for having the most luxurious stable of police cars, Dubai is now positioning itself as a testing ground for futuristic modes of transport. The police fleet itself has been augmented by an autonomous robot police car that will act as a mobile surveillance unit. Self-driving smart vehicles are expected to account for 25% of all traffic by 2030. The emirate is also experimenting with multicopters and drones to provide a flying taxi service and is reportedly exploring the possibility of building the world's first Hyperloop, a vacuum-sealed pod transportation system that would cut the trip from Dubai to Abu Dhabi to 12 minutes. Whether any of it will ever get off the ground, so to speak, remains to be seen of course, but in a city unafraid of testing the boundaries of innovation, it just might.

Gearing up for World Expo 2020

When Dubai won the right to hold the first World Expo in the Middle East in 2020, the announcement was celebrated with massive fireworks at the Burj Khalifa. It was a major triumph for the tiny emirate driven by humongous vision and ambition. Preparations to welcome the world between 20 October 2020 and 10 April 2021 are in full swing on the 4.38-sq-km site in a newly planned district called South Dubai, halfway to Abu Dhabi. The fair's guiding principle 'Connecting Minds, Creating the Future' is as high-minded as it is urgent: the need for collaboration across cultures, countries and religions to come up with sustainable solutions for the world's biggest problems.

Political Role

Overall, Dubai and the UAE have benefited from being a stable political force in a region beset by war and violence. The country's military is, however, involved in a number of regional conflicts, including the international fight against Al Qaeda and Isis, as well as the Saudi-led operation against Shiite Houthi rebels in Yemen. The death of 45 UAE troops by a rebel-fired missile strike in 2015 marked the highest number of combat casualties suffered since the country's founding in 1971 and even spurred the creation of a new national holiday – Martyr's Day (30 November). In 2017 the UAE, along with Bahrain and Egypt, joined Saudi Arabia in cutting diplomatic ties with Qatar, closing off air, land and sea borders and suspending flights by government-owned airlines Emirates and Etihad. The stalemate remains unresolved at the time of writing.

Pursuit of Happiness

When Ohood Bin Khalfan Roumi became the UAE's first ever Minister of Happiness in 2016, her appointment elicited more than a few chuckles. But Roumi knows that her role is no laughing matter. And so does Dubai ruler (and UAE vice president and prime minister) Sheikh Mohammed Bin Rashid Al Maktoum, who thought of the post. The latest United Nations World Happiness Report ranked the UAE 21 out of 150 countries – the highest for an Arab nation but apparently not good enough. In keeping with the emirate's superlative-striving nature, Sheikh Mohammed wants to make Dubai the happiest place on earth (watch out Disneyland!) and has founded the Smart Dubai campaign to come up with ways to improve people's lives. One of the most visible initiatives it has rolled out so far involves the Happiness Meters at airports, museums, malls, beaches and other public places. It allows people to click on emojis (smiling, unhappy, indifferent) to register their level of contentment with the experience.

if UAE were 100 people

9 would be Emirati
17 would be other Arabs and Iranians
3 would be Western European
71 would be South Asian

belief systems

(% of population)

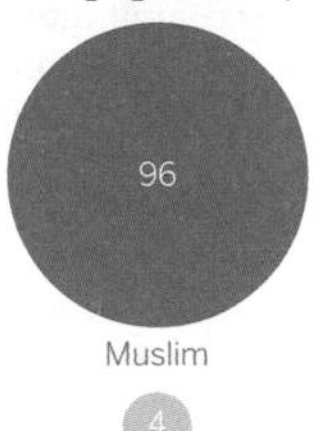

population per sq km

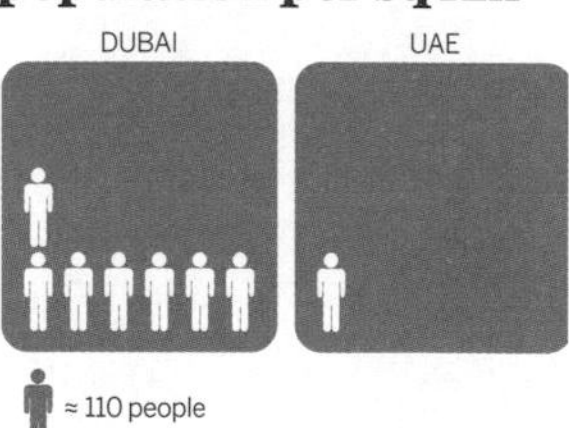

History

Travel along the main arteries of Dubai and Abu Dhabi, and it's hard to picture these cities before their modern incarnations. The term 'rags to riches' is used widely to describe their rapid development, but there's very little evidence now of the pre-oil days except in pockets of largely reconstructed heritage sites. History here has not been laid down in buildings and monuments but in customs and manners – these take longer to fathom, perhaps, but their foundations run just as deep.

Trade Roots

Spearheads and other archaeological evidence suggest that human settlement in the region began early, with *Homo sapiens* arriving in the region by around 100,000 BC, attracted by the savannah-like grasslands that dominated much of the Arabian Peninsula. These hunter-gatherer groups burned fires and reared livestock, forming the first organised communities in the region.

Inevitably, when organised communities innovate to survive they produce items desirable to other communities: in other words, they trade. As early as 6000 BC loose groups of Stone Age and Bronze Age individuals set up intricate trade routes between Arabia, Mesopotamia and the Indus Valley. They traded largely in copper mined in Magan (the ancient name of Oman) and exchanged goods with the Dilmun Empire (centred on modern-day Bahrain). It's easy to simplify the lives of the ancients, but the early seafaring traders of the Gulf were no barbarians: they spent their mineral wealth on fine glass, ate too many dates and suffered bad teeth. They took the time to thread beads, enjoyed complex legends, and expressed their interest in life through their administrations of death.

All trace of the great Magan civilisation ceased after the 2nd millennium BC, with some historians speculating that the desertification of the area hastened its demise. But the die was cast: this was to be a land of trading routes, where frankincense from the south, transported by camel caravan across the great deserts of the interior, was swapped for spices and textiles from India, silk and porcelain from China, and

TIMELINE

3000 BC

Dilmun, the first great civilisation in the Arabian Peninsula, is founded off the coast of Bahrain. It extends across today's UAE to the hills of Oman and facilitates regional trading.

AD 570

Prophet Mohammed is born in the same year that the Ma'rib dam in Yemen burst its banks. These twin events lead to the great Arab diaspora.

700–850

The Umayyads introduce Arabic and Islam to the Gulf region. Mecca and Medina lose their earlier political importance but grow as the spiritual homes of Islam.

bitumen from the Dead Sea. Visit any souq in Dubai or Abu Dhabi today and the pots and pans, electronic gadgetry, gold necklaces, plastic buckets and inlaid boxes, none of which are produced locally, are evidence of how trade continues to run through the blood of the region.

Foreign Influence

Given that today one out of every four people in the world is Muslim, there can be no greater moment of historical importance on the Arabian Peninsula than the birth of the Prophet Mohammed in the year AD 570. And if you are in any doubt as to the lasting legacy of the religion he founded, just listen to call to prayer reverberating through Dubai and Abu Dhabi five times a day. Mammon may have a foothold in today's malls, but a deep respect for Islam is at the heart of daily life, as evidenced by the innumerable mosques built in the last decade and, more to the point, the number of people frequenting them.

In historical terms, the arrival of Islam in the Gulf was significant for two reasons. Its ports helped facilitate the outward flow of Islam, transporting Prophet Mohammed's teachings across the waters of the Arabian Sea by dhow, uniting people in worship of the 'one true god' and the condemnation of idols. Equally, the same ports welcomed an inward flow of pilgrims in search of spiritual renewal during the annual hajj to Mecca and Medina. The ebb and flow of pilgrims brought a different kind of exchange, a cultural interaction with a succession of powerful dynasties such as the Umayyads and the Abbasids from the north. Their influence helped define the early nature of Gulf settlements and encouraged trade to flourish.

Given the lively trade of the region, it's not surprising that the Peninsula attracted the attention of European powers too. In 1498 a great Omani seafarer, Ahmed bin Majid, unwittingly helped a Portuguese explorer, Vasco da Gama, to navigate the Strait of Hormuz. The Portuguese took advantage of this knowledge by annexing Yemen's Socotra Island, occupying Oman and colonising Bahrain. Travel along the Gulf today and Portuguese forts appear with regularity: cut inland and there's no trace of them. The Portuguese were only interested in protecting their trade routes and made no impact on the interior of Peninsula countries at all. When they were eventually ousted by the mid-17th century, they left not much more than a legacy of military architecture and the Maria Theresa dollar – an important local currency.

The Portuguese were followed in the 17th and 18th centuries by the French and the Dutch, who understood the strategic significance of the Gulf coast in terms of protecting their own trade routes to the east. Other powerful entities, such as the Wahhabi tribes (of what is

Historical Reads

From Trucial States to United Arab Emirates by Frauke Heard-Bey

The Arabs by Peter Mansfield

Arabian Sands by Wilfred Thesiger

Pearl diving sounds romantic, but it was an industry founded on suffering. A diver's life was one of hardship and the rewards no match for the dangers involved. Most divers were East African slaves, and profits went into the pockets of the boat owner.

850–1300

Arabia's old trade routes collapse and the Peninsula declines in wealth and importance. Under the control of Tartar moguls, Persian and Ottoman Turks, petty sheikhdoms bicker over limited resources.

1580

Gasparo Balbi, a Venetian jeweller, investigates the region's potential for pearling and visits a town in the Gulf called 'Dibei'. Pearling eventually becomes the region's economic mainstay.

1793

The Bani Yas, the main power among the Gulf's Bedouin tribes and the ancestors of today's Emirati ruling families, move their capital to Abu Dhabi.

1805–92

The British engage in a number of skirmishes along the 'Pirate Coast' of Abu Dhabi and Dubai. The local sheikhdoms capitulate to become British protectorates called the 'Trucial States'.

now Saudi Arabia), the Ottoman Empire and the Persians were also attracted by the Gulf's strategic importance. But it was the British who most successfully staked a claim in the region's future.

The Trucial Coast

There were around 350 shops in Deira by 1908 and another 50 in Bur Dubai, where the Indian community was concentrated. To this day, the Bur Dubai Souq shows a strong Indian influence, and Bur Dubai is home to the only Hindu temple in the city.

On the one hand, the various treaties and 'exclusive agreements' that Britain signed with the emirs of the Arab Peninsula kept the French at bay and thereby safeguarded British trading routes with India. On the other hand, the British helped maintain the claims to sovereignty of the emerging Gulf emirates against Turkish and Persian interests, and from the ambitions of the eventual founder of Saudi Arabia, Ibn Saud. In exchange for British protection, the local sheikhs relinquished all jurisdiction over their foreign affairs. As a result of these treaties, or truces, Europeans called the area 'the Trucial Coast', a name the territory retained until the 1971 federation that created the United Arab Emirates (UAE).

So what had become of these two Gulf cities during these international machinations? Fresh water was discovered in Abu Dhabi Island in 1793, encouraging the powerful Al Nahyan family out of the desert oasis of Liwa to the coast. Until then, the ruling Al Nahyan tribe, part of the Bani Yas tribal confederation, had lived a Bedouin lifestyle, looking after camels and goats, tending small plantations in the oasis and generally living a frugal life in a desert environment. The story goes that, during their nomadic peregrinations, they were led by a gazelle to Abu Dhabi ('father of the gazelle', in Arabic), an island blessed with fresh water. This made life by the coast sustainable and the family put down roots by the coast, building the foundations of what was destined to become today's city.

Dubai, meanwhile, was little more than a small fishing and pearling hamlet, perched on a disputed border between two local powers – the seafaring Qawassim of present-day Ras Al Khaimah and Sharjah, to the north, and the Bani Yas tribal confederation to the south. In 1833, under the leadership of Maktoum bin Butti (r 1833–52), a tribe from Abu Dhabi overthrew the Creekside village of Dubai, thereby establishing the Al Maktoum dynasty, which still rules the emirate of Dubai today. For Maktoum bin Butti, good relations with the British authorities in the Gulf were essential to safeguard his small sheikhdom against attack from the larger and more powerful surrounding sheikhdoms. In 1841 the Bur Dubai settlement was expanded to Deira on the northern side of the Creek, although throughout the 19th century it largely remained a tiny enclave of fishermen, pearl divers, Bedouins, and Indian and Persian merchants. Interestingly, the Indians and Persians (now Iranians)

1833

Some 800 members of the Al Maktoum family arrive in Bur Dubai and establish power under Maktoum bin Butti. When smallpox breaks out in 1841, many people move across the Creek to Deira.

1930

The pearling industry collapses on the heels of the Great Depression of 1929–34 and the introduction of Japanese cultured pearls.

1951

The British establish the Trucial States Council, which brings together the leaders of the sheikhdoms that will later form the UAE.

1960

The first commercial oil field is discovered at Babi in Abu Dhabi. Six years later, oil is discovered in Dubai, spurring a period of rapid economic growth for both emirates.

PASSING THE TORCH

Overseeing Dubai's transformation into a 21st-century metropolis is the third son of the dynasty, Sheikh Mohammed bin Rashid al Maktoum, who was the face of modern Dubai even before he succeeded his older brother as ruler in 2006. Having ruled Dubai as a de facto leader since the mid-1990s, Sheikh Mohammed has brought consistency and continuity to Dubai in a period of tremendous social, cultural and economic change. In February 2008, he named the third of his children, his son Hamdan bin Mohammed al Maktoum, also known as 'Fazza', as crown prince. As his likely successor, Sheikh Hamdan has increasingly taken on leadership roles in various fields and initiatives. Handsome, athletic and outgoing, Fazza has a huge presence on social media with more than three million followers on Instagram alone.

In Abu Dhabi, Sheikh Khalifa bin Zayed al Nahyan, a highly regarded philanthropist, was elected to the role of UAE president when his father died in 2004. He has spent more than a decade continuing the great man's work, quietly transforming the city into an international metropolis and the assured capital of the UAE.

are still largely the custodians of the area, providing the Creek with much of its modern character.

Throughout the 19th century, both towns developed significantly, largely thanks to the income from the pearl industry. Sheikh Zayed bin Mohammed (Zayed the Great) helped Abu Dhabi become the most significant of the Gulf emirates, assisted in this regard by his relationship with the British. But Dubai was soon to catch up under the visionary ruler, Sheikh Maktoum bin Hasher al Maktoum (r 1894–1906). It was he who gave foreign traders tax-exempt status, leading to the establishment of Dubai as a duty-free port, a move that catapulted the emirate ahead of its rivals. Disillusioned traders from Persia crossed the Strait of Hormuz to take advantage of tax-free trade, becoming permanent residents in the area known as the Bastakia Quarter.

Sheikh Rashid, the driving force behind Dubai's phenomenal growth and 'father of (modern) Dubai', died in 1990 after a long illness and was succeeded as emir by his son, Sheikh Maktoum bin Rashid al Maktoum. Maktoum had already been regent for his sick father for several years and continued Dubai's expansion.

From Protectorate to Federation

By the beginning of the 20th century both Dubai and Abu Dhabi were well established, with populations approaching 10,000. Both towns were hit hard by the collapse of the pearling trade, the mainstay of the Gulf economy for decades. The trade had fallen victim to the Japanese discovery in 1930 of a method of artificial pearl cultivation as well as to the Great Depression of 1929–34.

Dubai's Sheikh Saeed al Maktoum (r 1912–58) realised that alternative sources of revenue were necessary, so while Abu Dhabi threw in its lot with the exploration for oil, Dubai began embracing the concept of

1968

The British announce their intention to withdraw from the Trucial States by 1971, leaving local leaders to discuss the shape of a future nation.

1971

After negotiating a federation with neighbouring emirates, Sheikh Zayed (ruler of Abu Dhabi) becomes the founding president of a united UAE. Sheikh Rashid (ruler of Dubai) advances to prime minister.

1990

Upon the death of Sheikh Rashid his son, Sheikh Maktoum, takes over as Dubai's ruler. His brother, incumbent ruler Sheikh Mohammed, succeeds the flamboyant sheikh in 2006.

2004

Sheikh Zayed dies. The father of the nation is deeply mourned across the UAE and succeeded by his son, Sheikh Khalifa bin Zayed Al Nahyan.

re-export. This involved the importing of goods (particularly gold) that entered and exited Dubai legally but were sold on to other ports abroad tax-free – a dubious practice akin to smuggling according to some, but highly lucrative for Dubai.

Visitors to Dubai will no doubt notice enormous posters of a smiling Arab. This is Sheikh Zayed bin Sultan al Nahyan, the first president of the UAE. Revered by his people, and often called 'father' by Emiratis, his compassion, modesty and wisdom commanded huge respect across the Middle East.

The wealth generated from trade in yellow gold in Dubai was quickly trumped by the riches earned from black gold in Abu Dhabi. The first commercial oil field was discovered at Babi in Abu Dhabi in 1960, and six years later Dubai struck it lucky too. The discovery of oil greatly accelerated the modernisation of the region and was a major factor in the formation of the UAE. In 1951 the Trucial States Council was founded, for the first time bringing together the rulers of the sheikhdoms of what would eventually become a federation.

When Britain announced its departure from the region in 1968, the ruler of Abu Dhabi, Sheikh Zayed bin Sultan al Nahyan, took the lead in forming alliances among the seven emirates that made up the Trucial States as well as Bahrain and Qatar. The latter two went on to their own independence, but on 2 December 1971 the United Arab Emirates was created. It consisted of the emirates of Dubai, Abu Dhabi, Ajman, Fujairah, Sharjah and Umm Al Quwain; Ras Al Khaimah joined in 1972. Impressively, given the volatility in the region, the UAE remains to this day the only federation of Arab states in the Middle East.

Establishing a Stable State

Oil-rich Abu Dhabi, the largest of the emirates, and Dubai carried the most weight in the new federation, but each emir remained largely autonomous. Sheikh Zayed became the supreme ruler (president) of the UAE, and Sheikh Rashid of Dubai assumed the role of vice president.

The fledgling nation had its share of teething problems, with border disputes between the emirates continuing throughout the 1970s and '80s, together with negotiations about the levels of influence and independence enjoyed by each emirate. The relationship between the two leading emirates has not been without its troubles either. Achieving an equitable balance of power, as well as refining a unified vision for the country, was much debated until 1979 when Sheikh Zayed and Sheikh Rashid finally compromised to reach an agreement.

The result was a much stronger federation in which Dubai remained a bastion of free trade while Abu Dhabi imposed a tighter federal structure on the other emirates. Zayed remained as president, while Rashid agreed to also take on the title of prime minister as a symbol of his commitment to the federation.

2008

The world financial crisis severely affects Dubai's economy. Abu Dhabi lends a helping hand in a gesture that demonstrates the bond between the two emirates.

2010

The Burj Khalifa opens. At 828m it's the world's tallest building with 163 floors and the highest outdoor observation deck in the world.

2013

Dubai wins the right to hold the Expo 2020 world fair under the theme 'Connecting Minds, Creating the Future'.

2017

The highly anticipated Louvre Abu Dhabi opens in a spectacular building by Jean Nouvel.

Politics & Economy

The United Arab Emirates (UAE) is a federation of seven autonomous states – Dubai, Abu Dhabi, Sharjah, Ras Al Khaimah, Fujairah, Umm Al Quwain and Ajman – each governed by hereditary absolute monarch called a sheikh. Among the emirates, Dubai has the highest profile abroad, but Abu Dhabi is the indisputable capital, with the greatest wealth and the largest territory. A certain tribal rivalry between them has helped spur the union on.

Federal Politics

Despite Dubai becoming so strong over the last few years, it has had to fight to preserve as much of its independence as possible and to minimise the power of the country's federal institutions.

Politically, the relative interests of the seven emirates are fairly clear. Oil-rich Abu Dhabi is the largest and wealthiest emirate and has the biggest population. As such it is the naturally dominant member of the federation. Dubai is the second-largest emirate by population, with both an interest in upholding its free-trade policies and a pronounced independent streak. The relationship between the two emirates was redefined during the financial turmoil of 2008–09 when the capital came to Dubai's rescue on several occasions. The other emirates are dependent on subsidies from Abu Dhabi, though the extent of this dependence varies widely.

The Decision-Makers

The seven rulers of the UAE form the Supreme Council, the highest body in the land. The council ratifies federal laws and sets general policy. New laws can be passed with the consent of five of the seven rulers. The Supreme Council also elects one of the emirs to a five-year term as the country's president. After the death in late 2004 of Sheikh Zayed, the founder and first president of the country, power passed peacefully to his son, Sheikh Khalifa bin Zayed al Nahyan.

The president of the UAE is traditionally drawn from the Al Nahyan tribe, the ruling family of Abu Dhabi, while the prime minister is of the Al Maktoum ruling family, from Dubai.

There is also a Council of Ministers, or cabinet, headed by the prime minister (the ruler of Dubai) who appoints ministers from across the emirates. The more populous and wealthier emirates such as Abu Dhabi and Dubai have greater representation.

The cabinet and Supreme Council are advised, but can't be overruled, by a parliamentary body called the Federal National Council (FNC). It has 40 members, apportioned among the seven emirates. Since 2006, half of the members are elected, while the other 20 are directly appointed by the ruler of each emirate. The FNC debates proposed legislation and the federal budget. During the most recent elections in 2015, voter turnout came to 35%, marking an improvement over the 26% that went to the polls in 2011. The number of people eligible to vote rose steadily from a mere 7000 in the 2006 election to 135,308 in 2011 and 224,279 in 2015. The ultimate goal is universal suffrage. Of the nine female FNC members, only one was elected, the other eight were appointed.

Benign Autocracy

During the 2011 uprisings across the region, there was much talk about democracy but not much appetite to see it implemented. It may go against the grain of Western assumptions, but democracy is not as universally desired in the region as the media would have us believe. Perceived as promoting the interests of the individual over those of the community, democracy is considered by many in this part of the world to run contrary to tribal traditions, where respect for elders is paramount. In common with other parts of the Middle East, the people of the UAE tend to favour strong, centralised government under an autocratic leader – what has been dubbed 'benign dictatorship'. Of course, benign dictatorship is only as good as the person in charge, and Dubai has been lucky in this respect, enjoying a half century of visionary and dynamic leadership.

Dubai's tourism, some suggest, was built on a clever exploitation of the stop-over market, on the back of an excellent airline. Offering passengers a chance to break their journey and enjoy some tax-free shopping, Dubai has now become a destination in its own right.

When Sheikh Mohammed bin Rashid al Maktoum of Dubai was named one of the world's 100 most influential people by *Time* magazine in 2008, it came as no surprise. Having spent several years as a de facto ruler while he was crown prince, Sheikh Mohammed was the obvious candidate for the top job when his brother, Sheikh Maktoum, died in early 2006. Although he is surrounded by some of the greatest minds in the Gulf, as well as political and economic experts imported from all over the world, there's no uncertainty about where executive power lies. 'Sheikh Mo', as he is affectionately called, has a flair for generating publicity for the city and was deeply involved in the planning and construction of landmark projects such as the Burj Al Arab, Palm Jumeirah and Burj Khalifa. He is also the architect of Vision 2020, a road map created in 2013 to double the number of visitors to the emirates to 20 million per year by 2020, as well as being the driving force behind Dubai's bid to host World Expo 2020.

Visitors from Western countries may feel uncomfortable with the large-scale portraits of rulers in hotel lobbies and on billboards around town. Yet these are not simply the propaganda tools of an autocratic regime; many people in Dubai revere their rulers. Few world leaders are able to drive themselves around town, as Sheikh Mohammed does, without a bodyguard and without any fear of being attacked. Although dissenting voices aren't tolerated and the local media is uncritical, most people admire the emirs for creating a haven of peace and prosperity in a troubled part of the world.

A Diversified Economy

The UAE has the world's sixth-largest oil reserves and the fifth-largest natural gas reserves, although these are unevenly distributed between the emirates. While 95% of the country's oil fields lie beneath the sands of the emirate of Abu Dhabi, Dubai has had to make do with a mere five patches in the Gulf. It is thought that at current levels of extraction, reserves will last for another 93 years but, as the dramatic drop in oil prices since 2015 has shown, the country cannot afford to be complacent about its continuing wealth.

In common with Gulf neighbours, therefore, the UAE is looking at alternative sources of energy and ways of diversifying the economy. Dubai's strategy for diversification has shown particular foresight, largely thanks to the vision and ambition of Sheikh Mohammed bin Rashid al Maktoum. Dubai's reserves of oil and gas were never that large, but the resources were used wisely to finance a modern and efficient infrastructure for trade, manufacturing and tourism. Today, revenues for oil and gas account for less than 2% of Dubai's GDP.

ABU DHABI'S BLACK GOLD

You only have to sniff the air during the F1 race weekend at Yas Marina Circuit to recognise that Abu Dhabi is a capital city that celebrates its fuel.

Abu Dhabi's Oil Wealth

The oil reserves of the UAE are estimated to be 98 billion barrels, 92 billion of which belong to Abu Dhabi. Within the space of 50 years, oil has transformed the capital from a fishing village into, according to the Sovereign Wealth Fund, the richest city in the world. With US$773 billion in cash in the bank and over US$10 trillion invested, it's little wonder that this wealthy emirate is able to splash the cash.

Oil's Origins

So where does all the oil come from? Extensive flooding millions of years ago led to the remains of marine life being deposited in layers of sediment across Arabia's land mass. When dead organic matter is trapped under the land's surface with a lack of oxygen to prevent it from decaying to water and carbon dioxide, the raw material of hydrocarbons is produced – this is the origin of oil and gas.

The conversion from dead organic matter to a hydrocarbon is subject to many particular conditions including depth and temperature. Arabia's geology is uniquely supportive of these conditions, and 'nodding donkeys' (drilling apparatus, capable of boring holes up to 5km deep) can be seen throughout the interior. In Abu Dhabi's dhow harbour, you can sometimes spot offshore platforms, used for tapping into hidden seams of 'reservoir rock', being towed in for maintenance.

How Long Will it Last?

The media across the region agonise over reserves reaching their peak and whether modern technologies such as fracking will reduce the dependency on Arab oil. Given that the economies of the Gulf rely to a lesser or greater extent on oil and gas – just look at the hit the UAE took when the 2010 oil glut saw oil prices fall from US$125 per barrel to a mere US$30 in 2016 – this is one issue that can't be left to *insha'allah* (God's will). As such, Abu Dhabi and its neighbours are busy diversifying their economies and actively exploring alternative technologies (most notably in pioneering Masdar City) to ensure they exchange today's black gold for tomorrow's sound future.

Economic Challenges

Until September 2008 it looked as though Dubai had the Midas touch. But then the global financial crisis struck and the emirate's economy collapsed like a proverbial house of cards. After real estate prices plummeted by as much as 50%, the emirate was unable to meet its debt commitments. However, markets stabilised quickly after the Abu Dhabi government rode to the rescue with a US$10 billion loan. As a symbol of gratitude, in January 2010 Sheikh Mohammed renamed Burj Dubai, the world's tallest building, 'Burj Khalifa', in honour of the UAE president and ruler of Abu Dhabi, Sheikh Khalifa bin Zayed al Nahyan.

Dubai climbed quickly out of recession, proving its perennial critics wrong. By 2014 its GDP was growing at a robust 4.3% per annum. Its numerous free-trade zones played a significant factor in the rebound. Companies based in these zones are lured by the promise of full foreign ownership, full repatriation of capital and profits, no corporate tax for 15 years, no currency restrictions and no personal income tax. One of the largest free-trade zones is Jebel Ali in southern Dubai, which is home to 5500 companies from 120 countries.

Dubai did feel the impact of the significant drop in oil prices from 2015, but also has economic building blocks that are not dependent on the vagaries of the oil market. Starting in 2018, the introduction of a 5%

Dubai's current ruler, Sheikh Mohammed bin Rashid Al Maktoum ('Sheikh Mo'), is a keen fan of falconry and equestrianism and runs the Godolphin Stables; he is estimated to be worth US$4 billion.

CENSORSHIP

While the UAE constitution allows for freedom of speech, in practice the government uses its powers to limit this right. According to the independent watchdog organisation Freedom House, the UAE government may censor both domestic and foreign publications before distribution and prohibit criticism of the government, UAE rulers and ruling families, and friendly foreign governments. Access to websites considered indecent, such as those featuring pornography, online dating or LGBT content, is also blocked, as is any domain associated with Israel. In consequence, local journalists working in Dubai are used to practising self-censorship.

Free voice calls made via WhatsApp, Skype and other VoIPs are usually blocked since they are not recognised 'licensed providers'. There have been periods in the past when the ban was periodically lifted, however. Some users employ a virtual private network (VPN) to access VoIP voice mail. Text messaging via these apps usually works.

value-added tax will further add to the revenue stream. So far, Dubai has mostly managed to control its debt load and to play the long game, with the many World Expo 2020 projects going full steam ahead.

Once a Trader, Always a Trader

Throughout history, trade has been a fundamental part of Dubai's economy. The emirate imports an enormous amount of goods, primarily minerals and chemicals, base metals (including gold), vehicles and machinery, electronics, textiles and foodstuffs. The main importers into Dubai are the US, China, Japan, the UK, South Korea and India.

Exports are mainly oil, natural gas, dates, dried fish, cement and electric cables. Top export destinations are the other Gulf States, Iran, India, Japan, Taiwan, Pakistan and the US.

Dubai's re-export trade (where items such as white goods come into Dubai from manufacturers and are then sent onwards) makes up about 80% of the UAE's total re-export business. Dubai's re-exports go mainly to Iran, India, Saudi Arabia, Kuwait, China and Afghanistan.

Economics on the Web

www.ameinfo.com

www.uaeinteract.com

www.emirateseconomist.blogspot.com

World's Largest Airport

Dubai never shies away from superlatives, which is why it should be no surprise that it is building the world's biggest airport. Upon final completion (estimated to be 2027), Al Maktoum International Airport in Jebel Ali will boost the emirate's annual passenger potential to an estimated 160 million by 2035, and be capable of handling more than 12 million tonnes of cargo annually. It is costing around US$34 billion to build and will eventually be 10 times the size of Dubai International Airport and Dubai Cargo Village combined.

Identity & Culture

A criticism levelled at Dubai and Abu Dhabi is that they are so lacking in national identity 'you could be anywhere'. This must be said by those who've never visited, or by those who mistakenly think high-rise sophistication is the sole preserve of Western cultures. Arrive at the airports with their bold design, extravagant spaces and grand public art; their welcoming, polite immigration officers; their prayer rooms, perfumes, nuts and dates, and frankly 'you couldn't be anywhere else'!

Bedouin Heritage

Emiratis celebrate their cultural identity through falconry, animal husbandry, horse- and camel-racing and escapes to the desert. The Bedouin bond with animals may be an obvious indication of a link with the past, but there are more subtle ways in which this heritage is kept alive. Go to a conference, and you are likely to be offered coffee and dates, or at the very least offered the welcome that is implicit in those traditional symbols of 'bread and salt'. Visit a neighbour, and they will see you to the lift well in a gesture of safe passage.

Sensing that shedding the visible symbols of their old way of life gave the wrong message about their emirate, the government of Dubai has since worked hard to reinstate them. Forts have been renovated, old buildings preserved, heritage villages and cultural centres promoted, and songs and dances reinstated during national day events. Even though the application to have the historic sections along Dubai Creek in Bur Dubai and Deira declared a Unesco World Heritage Site has been rejected twice, it has only spurred the government to try harder. In fact,

TODAY'S MODERN BEDOUIN

There are few Bedouin in the United Arab Emirates who live up to their name as true desert 'nomads' these days, but there are still communities who live a semi-traditional life on the fringes of the Empty Quarter. Their survival skills in a harsh terrain and their ability to adapt to changing circumstances are part of their enduring success. Most of today's Bedouin have modernised their existence with 4WD trucks (it's not unusual to find the camel travelling by truck), fodder from town and purified water from bowsers. All these features have limited the need to keep moving. Some have mobile phones and satellite TV and most listen to the radio. Many no longer move at all.

Old Habits Die Hard

Despite changes to their living experience, Bedouin remain the proud people of the desert and many of their customs and values, dating from the earliest days of Islam, remain unchanged. They rear livestock and trade with fellow tribespeople. Some live in goat-hair tents with the women's harem curtained off. The men's section serves as the public part of the house where guests are shown hospitality, an enduring feature of the Bedouin tradition. It's here that all the news and gossip – a crucial part of successful survival in a hostile environment – is passed along the grapevine.

the entire Shindagha Historic District and heritage buildings in Deira are closed for a major revamp and upgrade to showcase the emirate's past in more modern, accessible and meaningful ways.

These are not just gestures to attract and entertain tourists: they fulfil a role in educating young Emiratis about the value of their culture and heritage. After all, in the words of Sheikh Zayed, the father of the nation, 'He who does not know his past cannot make the best of his present and future for it is from the past that we learn'.

Islamic Values

A Life Informed by Religion

Islam is not just the official religion in the UAE: it is the cultural lifeblood. Religion is more than something performed on a Friday and put aside during the week: it is part of everyday life. It guides the choices an individual makes and frames the general context in which family life, work, leisure, care of the elderly and responsibility towards others take place. As such, Islam has played a socially cohesive role in the rapidly evolving UAE, providing support where old structures (both physical and social) have been dismantled to make way for a new urban experience.

For the visitor, understanding this link between religion and daily life can help make better sense of often misunderstood practices. Take dress, for example. Islam prescribes modest dress in public places for both men and women. The origin of the custom of covering the body is unclear – it certainly pre-dates Islam and to a large degree is an excellent way to deal with the ravaging tropical sun. Similarly, Muslims are forbidden to consume anything containing pork or alcohol. These strictures traditionally made good sense in a region where tapeworm was a common problem with pork meat and where the effects of alcohol are exaggerated by the extreme climate.

Presenting the public face of their families remains the traditional prerogative of men. The home is set up with this in mind with a *majlis* (reception room), used by men to entertain guests. The fact that the genders continue to be segregated should not be misconstrued as subjugation of one gender by another.

Practical Faith

You don't have to be in Dubai long to notice the presence of the 'third party' of Islam in all human interaction. Every official occasion begins with a reading from the Holy Quran. A task at work begins with an entreaty for God's help. The words *al-hamdu lillah* ('thanks be to God') frequently lace sentences in which good things are related. Equally the words *insha'allah* (God willing) mark all sentences that anticipate the future. These expressions are not merely linguistic decoration; they evidence a deep connection between society and faith.

Social Interaction

Respect for Elders

Emiratis value the advice of their elders. Traditional tribal leaders, or sheikhs, continue to play an important social function in terms of providing for the less well off, settling local disputes and giving patronage where required. The term *wasta*, translated loosely as 'influence', is frequently bandied about. *Wasta* is generally bestowed by sheikhs on family or tribal members and differs little from the preferential treatment that exists in many Western societies, except that it is more overt and considered more acceptable. Seeking favours from the well-connected has helped consolidate the power of key families, not least the Maktoums, the ruling dynasty of Dubai.

THE FIVE PILLARS OF ISLAM

The general tenets of a Muslim's faith are expressed in the five pillars of Islam.

Shahadah The profession of faith: 'There is no god but God, and Muhammad is the messenger of God.'

Salat Muslims are required to pray five times every day: at dawn (*fajr*), noon (*dhuhr*), mid-afternoon (*asr*), sunset (*maghrib*) and twilight (*isha*). During these prayers a Muslim must perform a series of prostrations while facing Mecca. Praying is preceded by ritual ablutions.

Zakat Muslims must give a portion of their income to help the poor. This is considered an individual duty in Dubai, as opposed to a state-collected income tax redistributed through mosques or religious charities favoured in some communities.

Sawm It was during the month of Ramadan in AD 610 that Muhammad received his first revelation. Muslims mark this event by fasting from sunrise until sunset throughout Ramadan. During the fast a Muslim may not take anything into his or her body. Food, drink, smoking and sex are forbidden.

Hajj All able Muslims are required to make the pilgrimage to Mecca at least once, if possible during a specific few days in the first and second weeks of the Muslim month of Dhul Hijja, although visiting Mecca and performing the prescribed rituals at any other time of the year is also considered spiritually desirable.

Marriage

A Muslim man is permitted by Islam to have up to four wives (but a woman may have only one husband). As with many practices within Islam, this one originally came about due to practical considerations: the ability of a man to take more than one wife enabled men to marry women who had been widowed (and thus left without a provider) due to war, illness or natural disaster. Most Emiratis have only one wife, however, not least because Islam dictates that each spouse must be loved and treated equally. Besides, housing and child-rearing are expensive – perhaps that's one of the reasons why the average number of children in a modern Emirati family has declined from five to two.

Urban life puts a particular strain on city marriages, with the high divorce rate revealing a fault line between traditional and modern values. Growing infidelity between partners, unrealistic expectations about living the urban dream, the difficulties of cross-cultural unions and long commutes are some of the many reasons cited for marriage break-ups.

Emirati women in the UAE pilot fighter jet planes, work as police officers, undertake research, serve as ambassadors, run corporations and participate in Antarctic exploration. Seven of 29 members of the UAE cabinet are women.

Role of Women

Modern life has provided new opportunities for women beyond care of the family, largely thanks to the equitable nature of education in the UAE. More women than men graduate from the region's universities, and many go on to work in a variety of roles, including as doctors, engineers, government ministers, innovators and corporate executives. Several initiatives have further elevated women's participation in the nation's development. In 2012 the UAE cabinet made it compulsory for corporations and government entities to appoint women to their boards of directors. The region's first military college for women opened in 2014. Nearly one quarter of cabinet posts are currently filled by women and in 2016, the Federal National Council became the region's first to be led by a woman.

Despite such advances, women still have to contend with social and legal constraints, a situation the Gender Balance Council, founded by Sheikh Mohammed in 2015, is tasked with remedying. It strives to bring the UAE into the world's top 25 countries on the UN's gender equality index by 2021 (it currently ranks 46 out of 159 countries).

The Workplace

Most Emiratis work in the public sector, as the short hours, good pay, benefits and early pensions make for an attractive lifestyle. The UAE government is actively pursuing a policy of 'Emiratisation', however, which involves encouraging Emiratis to work as entrepreneurs and employees in the private sector.

Until more locals take up the baton of small and medium enterprise, it will be hard for the government to decrease the dependency on an imported labour force, but equally it is hard for this to happen while Emiratis are employed only in a token capacity in the private sector. At some point, a leap in the dark will be inevitable to allow for local people to assume the roles for which they are being trained.

Multicultural Population

You can't talk about the identity of the Emirates without factoring in the multinational composition of the population. Across the UAE expats comprise around 80% of the population. In Dubai, therefore, the visitor experience is largely defined by interaction with the myriad nationalities that have been attracted to the Gulf in search of a better (or at least more lucrative) life.

Different nationalities have tended to dominate specific sectors of the workforce: people from the Philippines are employed in health care, construction workers are predominantly from Pakistan, financial advisers are from India, while Western countries have traditionally supplied technical know-how. Discussion prevails as to who benefits most from the contract between employer and employee, with serious concerns about the welfare particularly of construction and domestic workers. Some steps have been taken to right the wrongs of those in low-paid work, but it's fair to say that conditions for many remain far from ideal.

On the positive side, the international composition of the resident population has resulted in a vibrant multiculturalism. This is expressed in different religious festivals (including Diwali and Christmas), and gives the opportunity to experience the food and customs of each community in restaurants and shops. A visit here is likely to involve memorable conversations that allow the visitor to travel the world in an afternoon.

Environment

It may seem odd to discuss the environment when talking about a major metropolis, but peer out from the observation decks of Burj Khalifa in Dubai and the hinterland immediately makes an impression. The cities are discrete specks in a desert that nips at the heels of civilisation, mocking human attempts to tame it. Exploring the desert is therefore more than just a fun day out – it provides defining context.

The Land

Geologists speak of the Peninsula in terms of two distinct regions: the Arabian shield and the Arabian shelf. The shield, which consists of volcanic sedimentary rock, makes up the western third of today's Arabian Peninsula. The shelf is made up of the lower-lying areas that slope away from the shield, from central Arabia to the waters of the Gulf. Dubai and Abu Dhabi sit on the very edge of this Arabian shelf.

Geologists believe that the Peninsula originally formed part of the larger land mass of Africa. A split in this continent created both Africa's Great Rift Valley and the Red Sea. As Arabia slipped away from Africa, the Peninsula began to 'tilt', with the western side rising and the eastern edge dropping, a process that led to the formation of the Gulf.

There are no permanent rivers in the United Arab Emirates (UAE), but natural springs create oases in the desert. Al Ain (about 150km south of Dubai) and Liwa (340km southwest) grew up around date plantations. Shading citrus trees and grain crops, the plantations are watered via elaborate irrigation networks (*falaj*). A working *falaj* at Majlis Ghorfat Um Al Sheef (p101) in Jumeirah demonstrates how these channels work for the benefit of the whole community.

Ecosystems

Desert

The harsh lands of Arabia have for centuries attracted travellers from the Western world, curious to see the great sea of sand known as the 'Empty Quarter' or 'Rub al Khali'. Straddling the UAE, Saudi Arabia, Oman and Yemen, the dunes form a magnificent landscape that changes in colour and texture as the sun and wind project their own dramas on the ridges of sand.

A portion of the Empty Quarter, including one of the highest dunes in the northern sands, lies within the territory of Abu Dhabi, and a sealed road winding from the oasis towns of Liwa to the fringe of the sands makes this environment easily accessible by car from Dubai and Abu Dhabi. For those able to spare the time to camp in this terrain, there is the chance to see some of the desert's shy residents. The dunes are home to various reptiles, including vipers, monitor lizards (up to 1m long) and spiny-tailed agamas.

At dawn, the tracks of hares, hedgehogs and foxes illustrate that many species of mammals have adapted to this unforgiving environment. Many have large ears, giving a broad surface area from which

Although second-largest of the seven emirates, Dubai is quite small in comparison, extending over only 4114 sq km. Compare that to Abu Dhabi, which is at 67,340 sq km the largest emirate in the UAE, occupying more than 80% of the country's total area.

to release heat, and tufts of hair on paws that enable walking on the blistering sands.

To this day, people come to the desert expecting 'sand, sand, sand, still sand, and only sand and sand again'. The Victorian traveller who wrote those words (Kinglake) curiously had only passed through gravel plains at that point, but so strong is the connection between the words 'desert' and 'sand', he felt obliged to comment on what he thought he should see rather than on what was there. For anyone who looks beyond roadside plantings, it will become quickly apparent that the term 'desert' encompasses far more than simply sand. In fact, most of the UAE is comprised of flat gravel plains, punctuated with thorny, flat-topped acacia trees and herbal plants, interrupted by notorious salt flats, known as *sabkha*.

Seas

The Gulf has a character all its own, thanks to its largely landlocked location. Flat, calm, and so smooth that at times it looks solid like a piece of shiny coal, it tends to be shallow for up to a kilometre from the shore. With lagoons and creeks edged with valuable mangroves, this is an important habitat for waders and gulls. It is also conducive to human development: much of the rim of the Gulf, particularly surrounding Dubai and Abu Dhabi, has been paved over or reclaimed for land use.

Sabkha is a salt-crusted quagmire of water-saturated land. It looks hard and even polished to the eye, but attempt to ride a camel across it or drive a vehicle on it and the surface quickly disintegrates.

While dredging for this purpose (some 33 million cu metres of seabed was distributed for the World project alone) has had a detrimental effect on marine life, and particularly on fragile coral reefs, the waters off Dubai and Abu Dhabi still teem with around 300 different species of fish. Kingfish, hammour, tuna, sardines and sharks are regulars of the fish market, but thankfully turtles are no longer hunted for food. Endangered green and hawksbill turtles used to nest in some numbers on Dubai's beaches and their tracks can still be seen on the protected beaches of Saadiyat Island in Abu Dhabi. The Dubai Turtle Rehabilitation Project (www.dubaiturtles.com), based at Jumeirah Al Naseem in Madinat Jumeirah, is actively engaged in protecting the species and in nursing sick and injured specimens back to independent life in the Gulf.

City Parks

Perhaps few would consider a city park as part of the natural environment, and in the Gulf states it could be argued there is nothing natural about these landscaped areas. Indeed, most of the planting is imported from neighbouring subtropical countries, and each specimen is individually irrigated with piped water.

Despite their artificiality, however, the many city parks dotted around Dubai and Abu Dhabi have proved havens for insects and birds. Although surrounded by high-rises and roaring highways, Dubai's Ras Al Khor Wildlife Sanctuary continues to be the home of a flamboyance

DUBAI DESERT CONSERVATION RESERVE

The 225-sq-km **Dubai Desert Conservation Reserve** (www.ddcr.org) accounts for 5% of the emirate's total land. The reserve was established in 1999 and has been involved in projects to reintroduce mountain gazelles, sand gazelles and Arabian oryx. It's possible to stay inside the reserve at **Al Maha Desert Resort & Spa** (p191), designed as a model for superluxury ecotourism.

The reserve is divided into four zones, the third of which is only open to resort guests and the fourth to a small number of desert tour operators, including **Arabian Adventures** (p94), offering a less costly admission than overnighting at the resort.

DESERT YES, DESERTED NO

Visiting any wilderness area comes with responsibility and no more so than in a desert, where the slightest interference with the environment can wreak havoc with fragile ecosystems. The rocky plains of the interior may seem like an expanse of nothing, but that is not the case. Red markers along a road, improbable as they may seem on a cloudless summer day, indicate the height of water possible during a flash flood. A month or so later, a flush of tapering grasses marks the spot, a temporary home to wasp oil beetles, elevated stalkers and myriad other life forms.

Car tracks scar a rock desert forever, crushing plants and insects not immediately apparent from the driver's seat. Rubbish doesn't biodegrade as it would in a tropical or temperate climate. The flower unwittingly picked in its moment of glory may miss its first and only opportunity for propagation in seven years of drought.

With a bit of common sense, however, and taking care to stick to existing tracks, it's possible to enjoy the desert without damaging the unseen communities it harbours. It also pays to turn off the engine and just sit. At dusk, dramas unfold: a fennec fox chases a hedgehog, a feral dog trots out of the wadi without seeing the snake slithering in the other direction, tightly closed leaves relax in the brief respite of evening and a dung beetle rolls its reward homewards.

of pink flamingoes and a major stopover on the migration path between Europe, Asia and Africa. More than 320 migratory species pass through in spring and autumn, or spend the winter here. Species native to Arabia include the crab-plover, the Socotra cormorant, the black-crowned finch lark and the purple sunbird – the last of which is a common resident in any park where aloe is grown.

Environmental Issues

Protected Areas

The idea of setting aside areas for wildlife runs contrary to the nature of traditional life on the Peninsula, which was, and to some extent still is, all about maintaining a balance with nature, rather than walling it off. The Bedouin flew their hunting falcons only between certain times of the year and moved their camels on to allow pasture to regrow. Fishermen selected only what they wanted from a seasonal catch and threw the rest back. Farmers let lands lie fallow so as not to exhaust the soil.

Modern practices including sport hunting, trawler fishing and the use of pesticides in modern farming have had such an impact on the environment over the past 50 years, however, that all governments in the Gulf region have recognised the need to protect the fragile ecosystems of their countries. This has resulted in the creation of protected areas (10% of regional land mass), but, with tourism on the increase, there is a strong incentive to do more.

Among its Peninsula neighbours, the UAE leads the way with 5% of the Emirate of Dubai established as a protected area. In addition, the Dubai Desert Conservation Reserve has helped reintroduce the Arabian oryx, hunted almost to extinction in the last century.

Botanical Reads

Handbook of Arabian Medicinal Plants by S A Ghazanfar

Vegetation of the Arabian Peninsula by S A Ghazanfar & M Fisher (eds)

Reducing the Global Footprint

Dubai loves being Number One, but being slapped with the distinction of having the world's largest ecological footprint was not a record it craved, which is why now one of its government's many ambitions is to become the world's most sustainable city by 2050. Whether it will get there remains to be seen, but a number of initiatives indicate that it's certainly on the right track.

MANGROVES

The Eastern Mangroves off the northeast coast of Abu Dhabi is the largest mangrove forest in the UAE, but Dubai also has an important area of this unique habitat with the Ras Al Khor Wildlife Sanctuary. Some key facts:

What are mangroves? A mangrove is a type of subtropical, low-growing tree with high salt toleration that lives with roots immersed in the high tide.

Are all mangroves the same? No, there are 110 species. The grey mangrove is the most common in Abu Dhabi and Dubai.

Why are they protected? This fragile ecosystem is a haven for wildlife and helpfully protective of shorelines commonly eroded by tides.

What lives in these forests? Mangroves provide a safe breeding ground for shrimps, turtles and some fish species, and habitats for migrating birds.

Any other uses? Historically, they provided a rich source of fuel and building material. The hard wood is resistant to rot and termites – ideal for building boats and houses.

Are they endangered? Yes, but thanks to local conservation efforts and deliberate replanting schemes the mangroves have grown in size over recent years.

The launch of the emission-free Dubai Metro in 2010 was just the beginning. Meanwhile, on the outskirts of the city, a new community called Sustainable City (www.thesustainablecity.ae) has sprung up that recycles its own water and waste and generates a surplus of energy. Deep in the desert, the Dubai government is building the world's largest (what else?) solar energy park by 2030. Its first solar plant opened in March 2017 and supplies electricity for about 50,000 homes. And many more schemes are in the works that Dubai hopes to showcase at its World Expo in 2020 where, not coincidentally, sustainability is a major theme.

Meanwhile, Masdar City (p155), Abu Dhabi's flagship environmental project, is a progressive testing ground for sustainable urban living solutions and aims to become the world's first carbon-neutral, zero-waste community powered entirely by renewable energy. And some 175km southwest of the UAE capital, in the deep desert, Shams 1 ('Sun' 1) is a huge 100 megawatt concentrated solar power plant that generates enough energy for 20,000 households as a step towards Abu Dhabi's goal of creating 7% of its power via renewable energy by 2020.

Visitors can play their part in water conservation by taking simple measures, such as having quick showers rather than bathing; cutting down on laundry of towels and bed linen; using the half-flush button, where possible, on toilets; and turning the tap off when brushing teeth.

Water

With palm-lined avenues, luscious lawns, parks and flowerbeds, it may be difficult to remember that Dubai is built in one of the most arid deserts on earth. The city receives no more than one or two days of rain per year and the ground water is highly saline – almost eight times as saline, in fact, as sea water. Virtually all (98%) of the city's drinking water is supplied, therefore, from desalination.

You'd think that the lack of natural reserves would have led to low water usage but, at 550L per day, the UAE has one of the highest per-capita rates of water consumption in the world. Recognising the challenges involved in indulging the city's seemingly endless thirst for water, the UAE government launches periodic awareness campaigns to encourage citizens to consume less, but the answer may lie with further technology.

When it rained in Dubai and Abu Dhabi for five days straight in February 2017, it wasn't the result of a natural process but of cloud seeding. Indeed, the country has dabbled in cloud seeding since the late 1990s but didn't get serious until launching the UAE Research Program for Rain Enhancement Science in 2015. It awards research grants to scientists all over the world to study how to, essentially, make rain.

The Arts

Rightly or wrongly, nations tend to be judged less by their contribution to their own artistic milieu than by their participation in contemporary dialogues that are largely Western in origin. The cities of the Gulf clearly feel this pressure to engage in the globalisation of the arts, as the openings of the Louvre Abu Dhabi and the Dubai Opera demonstrate. Go looking only for contemporary exhibitions, however, and you'll run the risk of missing the art that means the most to the locals.

Function & Form

If you chose one feature that distinguishes art in the Arab world from that of the Western tradition, it would have to be the close integration of function with form. In other words, most Arab art has evolved with a purpose. That purpose could be as practical as embellishing the prow of a boat with a cowrie shell to ward off 'evil eye' or as nebulous as creating intricate and beautiful patterns to suggest the presence of God and invite spiritual contemplation. Purpose is an element that threads through all Gulf art, craft, music, architecture and poetry.

Craft Heritage

Crafts have traditionally been a notable art form in the Gulf, thanks in part to the influence of Bedouin heritage. The nomadic pre-oil lifestyle of a section of the population dictated a life refined of excess baggage, and so creativity found its most obvious expression in poetry, song, storytelling and portable, practical craft.

In crafts such as jewellery, silver-smithing, weaving, embroidery and basket-making, function and form combine in artefacts that document a way of life. Take jewellery, for example – the heavy silver so distinctively worn by Bedouin women was designed not just as a personal adornment but as a form of portable wealth. Silver amulets contained rolled pieces of parchment or paper bearing protective inscriptions from the Quran to guarantee the safety of the wearer. These were considered useful against the perils of the 'evil eye' – the envy or malice of others.

At the end of the life of a piece of jewellery the silver was traditionally melted down and traded in as an ultimate gesture of practicality. In the same vein it is a sad fact about practical craft that once the need for it has passed, there is little incentive to maintain the skills. Why bother with clay ewers when everyone drinks water from plastic bottles? Aware of this fact, local craft associations have sprung up in the hope of keeping local crafts alive.

Ayyalah is a typical Bedouin dance. Performed to a simple drumbeat, men link arms, wave camel sticks or swords, sway back and forth and sing of the virtues of bravery in battle.

Competing Internationally

It's easy to criticise the Emirates for buying into the international arts scene when they invest little in encouraging contemporary arts at home, but they are hardly to blame. There isn't a city to be taken seriously

THE ORAL TRADITION

If you want to discover what gets the locals clapping, what makes them sway to the beat during national days and holidays, and what makes them fall utterly silent after talking all the way through a formal address by a visiting dignitary, it's not classical music or Western visual arts. It's Arabic poetry. If you get the chance to attend a recitation when visiting Dubai or Abu Dhabi, it shouldn't be missed.

Traditionally dominating Middle Eastern literature, all the best-known figures of classical regional literature are poets, including Omar Khayyam and Abu Nuwas. Poets were regarded as possessing knowledge forbidden to ordinary people and served the purpose of bridging the human and spirit worlds. To this day, even the the TV-watching young are captivated by a skilfully intoned piece of verse.

Poetry is part and parcel of the great oral tradition of storytelling that informs the literature of all Peninsula countries, the roots of which lie with the Bedu. Stories told by nomadic elders served not just as after-dinner entertainment, but also as a way of binding generations together in a collective oral history. As such, storytelling disseminated the principles of Islam and of tribal and national identity.

around the globe that doesn't have an opera house or a pavilion at the Venice Biennale, regardless of whether these pieces of imported Western culture are relevant. When the opera house first opened in neighbouring Muscat, a third of the audience left after the interval unaware that the performance continued, underwhelmed by musicians they couldn't see (in the orchestra pit) and mildly offended by the unrobing of the soprano in a brothel scene – a topic so *haram* (forbidden) locally as to be verging on the subversive.

This example serves to show that there is an almost unbridgeable gap between function and form in contemporary arts in the region. This leads one to surmise that the world-class exhibitions and performances on offer are largely there to impress visitors and to prove to cynics abroad that there is a cultural depth to these cities that can only be measured in Western terms.

For the cultural elites of Dubai and Abu Dhabi, these are therefore happy days. The openings of the Louvre Abu Dhabi and the Dubai Opera have added more than a world-class high-brow touch. The annual Art Dubai and Abu Dhabi Art festivals attract some of the most celebrated international galleries, artists and dealers. Regional art is also getting the spotlight in the galleries of Alserkal Avenue and the Gate Village in Dubai and at the Etihad Modern Art Gallery in Abu Dhabi.

For all the criticism, this investment in global arts is to be welcomed as with it comes a greater integration between East and West, and an opportunity to showcase more traditional local art forms to an international audience. This in turn helps preserve the traditions that matter most to local people.

Top Art Galleries & Exhibition Spaces

Louvre Abu Dhabi (p156)i

Third Line (p84)

Gallery Isabelle van den Eynde (p85)

Carbon 12 (p85)

Etihad Modern Art Gallery (p135)

Survival Guide

Transport

ARRIVING IN DUBAI & ABU DHABI

Most visitors arrive by air, with flights coming in from many major international cities. The approximate duration time from London is seven hours, from Sydney it's 14 hours, from New York 12 hours and from Ottawa 14 hours. Dubai serves as a popular stopover hub between Europe and Asia.

There is road access from Oman via Al Ain, about 150km southeast of Dubai. You will be required to show your passport and visitor visa (if applicable). Check with the UAE consulate or at www.dubai.ae for the latest information. The UAE also shares a border with Saudi Arabia at Sita/Ghuwaifat, but only GCC (Gulf Cooperation Council) citizens are permitted to cross here.

Flights, cars and tours can be booked online at lonelyplanet.com/bookings.

Air

Dubai International Airport

In Deira, near the border with the emirate of Sharjah, **Dubai International Airport** (DXB; Map p216; ☎04 224 5555; www.dubaiairports.ae) is the busiest airport in the world, handling some 84 million travellers. It has three terminals:

Terminal 1 Main terminal used for major international airlines.

Terminal 2 For small airlines and charters mainly en route to Iran, Eastern Africa and some Eastern European countries.

Terminal 3 Used exclusively by Emirates Airlines.

TAXI

Taxis wait outside each arrivals terminal 24/7. A surcharge of Dhs25 applies to rides originating at the airport, plus Dhs1.96 per kilometre. Expect to pay about Dhs50 to Deira, Dhs60 to Bur Dubai, Dhs70 to Downtown Dubai, Dhs110 to Madinat Jumeirah and Dhs130 to Dubai Marina.

DUBAI METRO

The Red Line stops at terminals 1 and 3 and is the most efficient way to get across town by public transport. Trains run roughly between 5.30am and midnight (until 1am on Thursdays and Fridays). On Fridays, train service starts at 10am. Up to two pieces of luggage are permitted. A Nol card must be purchased at the station.

BUS

The bus is only really useful at night when metro service stops. The handiest route is bus C1, which runs 24 hours to Deira, Bur Dubai and Satwa from terminals 1 and 3. Buy a Nol card in the arrivals terminal. For route planning, see www.wojhati.rta.ae.

Al Maktoum International Airport

Dubai's second airport, **Al Maktoum** (DWC; ☎04 224 5555; www.dubaiairports.ae; off Sheikh Mohammed Bin Rashid Al Maktoum Rd (E611); 📶; Ⓜ UAE Exchange) is a work in progress in the southern part of the emirate near Jebel Ali. The fiscal downturn of 2008–10 significantly delayed construction and pushed the completion date to 2027. For now, it's mostly used by cargo planes and receives only a smattering of commercial flights.

BUS & METRO

Bus F55 links the airport with the Ibn Battuta metro station hourly. It's served by the Red Line, which goes all the way to Dubai International Airport. At night, bus F55A goes from the airport to Satwa bus station.

TAXI

Taxis wait outside the passenger terminal. Expect a fare of Dhs70 for Dubai Marina, Dhs110 for Downtown Dubai and Dhs120 for Bur Dubai.

Abu Dhabi International Airport

About 30km east of the city centre **Abu Dhabi International Airport** (Map p161; ☎02 505 5555; www.abudhabiairport.ae) is served by more than 50 airlines flying to 85 cities. It has three terminals, including Etihad's exclusive base, Terminal 3. A vast expansion, the Midfield Terminal, is expected to open in 2019. Free wi-fi throughout.

BUS

Air-conditioned bus A1 picks up from outside the arrivals area of all terminals every 40 minutes around the clock (one hour, Dhs4) and travels via the central bus station all the way into town as far as Al Zahiyah. Etihad passengers can use free shuttle buses to and from Dubai and Al Ain (show your boarding pass).

TAXI

Taxis cost Dhs75 to Dhs85 for the half-hour trip to the city centre, including flagfall of Dhs25.

GETTING AROUND DUBAI

For details on getting around Abu Dhabi, see p128.

Bicycle

German company **Nextbike** (Byky; ☎04 238 4344; www.nextbike.net; 1/2/5/24hr Dhs20/25/40/80; ⏰24hr) has teamed up with local provider Byky (www.bykystations.com or www.nextbike.net/en) to provide a bike-sharing service in the Dubai Marina, Downtown Dubai and on Palm Jumeirah. First register online and then when you're ready to rent a bike, call the hotline and type in the bike's ID number to obtain the code needed to open the combination lock. Bikes must be returned to another station. Prices are staggered, with one hour costing Dhs20 and 24 hours Dhs80. The website has full details.

Boat

Abra

Abras are motorised traditional wooden boats linking Bur Dubai and Deira across the Creek on two routes:

Route 1 Bur Dubai Abra Station (Map p248; www.rta.ae) to **Deira Old Souk Abra Station** (Map p244); operates daily between 6am and midnight; rides take five minutes.

Route 2 Dubai Old Souk Abra Station (Map p248; www.rta.ae) to **Al Sabkha Abra Station** (Map p244; Baniyas Rd); operates around the clock; rides take about seven minutes.

Abras leave when full (around 20 passengers), which rarely takes more than a few minutes. The fare is Dhs1, and you pay the driver en route. Chartering your own abra costs Dhs120 per hour.

Air-conditioned abras also link **Al Jaddaf Marine Station** (Ⓜ Creek) with the **Dubai Festival City Abra Station** every 10 to 20 minutes from 7am to midnight. The fare is Dhs2 and rides take about six minutes.

In addition, pricey, tourist-geared sightseeing abras offer short rides around Burj Lake, Madinat Jumeirah and the Atlantis The Palm.

Dubai Ferry

The Dubai Ferry operates on two interlinking routes and provides a fun way for visitors to see the city from the water.

Dubai Marina to Al Ghubaiba (Bur Dubai) Route These 90-minute mini-cruises depart at 11am, 1pm and 6.30pm from the **Dubai Marina Ferry Station** (Map p262) and the **Al Ghubaiba Ferry Station** (Map p248; ☎800 9090; www.rta.ae; Shindagha Waterfront). The route passes by Madinat Jumeirah, the Burj Al Arab and Port Rashid. Other options from either station include an afternoon-tea trip at 3pm and a sunset cruise at 5pm. The fare for any of these trips is Dhs50 (children Dhs25).

Dubai Canal Route Links Al Jaddaf Marine Station with Dubai Canal station at 10am, noon and 5.30pm and at noon, 2pm and 7.30pm in the other direction. Stops include Dubai Design District, Al Wajeha, Marasi and **Sheikh Zayed Rd** (Map p258). Fares depend on number of stations travelled; the entire one-way route is Dhs50.

Both routes connect at the Dubai Canal station. The fare from here to either Al Ghubaiba or Dubai Marina is Dhs25. Fares and schedules change frequently; check www.dubai-ferry.com for the latest information.

Dubai Water Bus

Air-conditioned water buses link four stops around the Dubai Marina every 15 to 20 minutes from 10am to 11pm Saturday to Thursday and from noon to midnight on Friday. Fares range from Dhs3 to Dhs5 per stop or Dhs25 for a day pass. Nol Cards are valid.

TRAVELLING BETWEEN DUBAI & ABU DHABI

Dubai's Roads & Transport Authority (www.rta.ae) operates air-conditioned (often overcrowded) buses to other emirates between 6am and 11pm. Bus E100 to Abu Dhabi leaves from **Al Ghubaiba** (Map p248; Al Ghubaiba Rd; Ⓜ Al Ghubaiba) bus station in Bur Dubai every 20 minutes. The journey takes two hours and costs Dhs25. Buses arrive at Abu Dhabi's **central bus terminal** (Map p130; www.dot.abudhabi.ae; Rashid Bin Saeed Al Maktoum St), which is about 4km south of the Corniche. Maps, timetables and a journey planner are available at www.dubai-buses.com.

Bus

The RTA operates local buses on more than 120 routes primarily serving the needs of low-income commuters. Buses are clean, comfortable, air-conditioned and cheap, but they're slow. The first few rows of seats are generally reserved for women and children. Fares range from Dhs3 to Dhs8.50 and Nol Cards must be used.

For information, check http://dubai-buses.com; for trip planning, go to www.wojhati.rta.ae.

Car & Motorcycle

Driving in Dubai itself is not for nervous nellies given that local behind-the-wheel styles are rather quixotic and negotiating seven- or eight-lane highways can be quite scary at first. Distances can be deceiving. Heavy traffic, detours and eternal red lights can quickly turn that 5km trip into an hour's journey.

However, well-maintained multilane highways, plentiful petrol stations and cheap petrol make car rental a worthwhile option for day trips from Dubai.

For navigating, Google Maps works reasonably well. A local alternative is the RTA Smart Drive app, downloadable free from Google Play and Apple app store.

There are seven automated toll gates (Salik; www.salik.gov.ae/en), each costing Dhs4, set up along Dubai's highways, including two along Sheikh Zayed Rd: Al Barsha near the Mall of the Emirates and Al Safa near Burj Khalifa. All rental cars are equipped with sensors that record each time you pass a toll point. The cost is added to your final bill.

Hire

There are scores of car-rental agencies in Dubai, from major global companies to no-name local businesses. The former may charge more but give peace of mind with full insurance and 24/7 roadside assistance. You'll find the gamut at the airport and throughout the city. Most major hotels have desks in the lobby.

To hire a car, you must be over the age of 21 (25 for some fancier models) and have a valid driving licence and credit card. Depending on your country of origin, you may also need to produce an international driving licence. Some companies require that the national licence has been held for at least one year.

Daily rates start at about Dhs200 for a small manual car, including comprehensive insurance and unlimited mileage. Expect surcharges for airport rentals, additional drivers, one-way hire and drivers under 25 years of age. Most companies have child safety seats for a fee, but these must be reserved. It's usually more economical to prebook your car from home with an online car rental brokers such as Auto Europe (www.autoeurope.com) or Holiday Autos (www.holidayautos.com).

Insurance

You will be offered a choice of insurance plans. Opt for the most comprehensive type, as minor prangs are common here. Make sure you have the car rental company's number for roadside assistance.

Parking

Standard parking zones are indicated by two-tone curb markings (black and turquoise).

Dubai's parking system is divided into zones.

Zone A Roadside parking in commercial areas, Dhs4 per hour, enforced 8am and 10pm.

Zone B Car parks in commercial zones, Dhs3/8/20 per hour/3 hours/24 hours, enforced 8am to 10pm.

Zone C Roadside parking in non-commercial zones, Dhs2/8 per hour/3 hours, enforced 8am to 10pm.

Zone D Car parks in non-commercial zones, Dhs2/8/10 per hour/3 hours/24 hours, enforced 8am to 10pm.

Tickets are purchased from an orange machine and displayed on your dashboard. They take coins, prepaid cards sold at supermarkets in denominations of Dhs30 or Dhs100 and the Nol Card (prepaid public transport pass; see www.nol.ae).

The fine for not buying a ticket is Dhs150; for overstaying it's Dhs100.

Road Rules

- Driving is on the right.
- The speed limit is 40km/h to 60km/h on city streets, 70km/h to 90km/h on major city roads and 100km/h to 120km/h on dual-lane highways.
- Seatbelts are compulsory, and it is illegal to use a handheld mobile phone while driving.
- There's a zero-tolerance

DON'T DRINK & DRIVE!

Drinking and driving is never a good idea, but in the UAE you'd be outright crazy to do so. Let's make it absolutely clear: if you've had as much as one sip, you've had too much. The UAE has a zero-tolerance policy on drink-driving (ie the blood alcohol limit is 0%), and if your vehicle is stopped and you're found to have been driving under the influence of alcohol (or a narcotic substance), you'll be facing a stiff fine (minimum Dhs20,000), jail time and deportation.

policy on drinking and driving (0% is the blood alcohol limit).

- Never make an offensive hand gesture to another driver; it could end in deportation or a prison sentence.
- Tailgating, although common, is illegal and can result in a fine.
- Don't cross yellow lines.
- If you're involved in a traffic accident, it's a case of being guilty until proven innocent, which means you may be held by the police until an investigation determines whose fault the accident was.

Rush Hour

Traffic congestion in Dubai can be a nightmare at peak hours, ie between 7am and 9am, 1pm and 2pm and most of the evening from 5pm onwards. Roads are also clogged on Friday afternoon, especially around shopping malls, beaches and family attractions.

TICKETS & PASSES

The RTA network is divided into seven zones, with fares depending on the number of zones traversed. Travel requires the purchase of a Nol ticket or card (*nol* is Arabic for 'fare') at ticket stations or from vending machines before boarding. Cards must be tapped onto the card reader upon entering and exiting at which point the correct fare will be deducted. Two types of tickets are relevant to visitors:

Nol Red Ticket (Dhs2, plus credit for at least one trip) Must be pre-loaded with the correct fare each time you travel; can be recharged up to 10 times; may only be on a single mode of transport at a time. Fares: Dhs4 for one zone, Dhs6 for two zones, Dhs8.50 for three or more zones, Dhs20 for the day pass.

Nol Silver Card (Dhs25, including Dhs19 credit) With pre-loaded credit, this works on the pay-as you-go principle with fares deducted. Get this card if you're going to make more than 10 trips. Fares are Dhs3 for one zone, Dhs5 for two zones and Dhs7.50 for three or more zones.

For full details, see www.nol.ae.

Metro

Dubai's metro (www.dubaimetro.eu) opened in 2010 and has proved a popular service.

Red Line Runs for 52.1km from near Dubai International Airport to Jebel Ali past Dubai Marina, mostly paralleling Sheikh Zayed Rd.

Green Line Runs for 22.5km, linking the Dubai Airport Free Zone with Dubai Healthcare City.

Intersection of Red & Green Lines At Union and Khalid Bin Al Waleed (next to BurJuman shopping mall) stations.

Onward Journey At each station, cabs and feeder buses stand by to take you to your final destination.

Frequency Red Line trains run roughly every 10 minutes from 5am to to midnight Saturday to Wednesday, to 1am Thursday, and from 10am to 1am on Fridays. Green Line trains start slightly later at 5.30am from Saturday to Thursday.

Cars Each train consists of four standard cars and one car that's divided into a women-only section and a 'Gold Class' section where a double fare buys carpets and leather seats. Women may of course travel in any of the other cars as well.

Tickets Nol (fare) cards can be purchased at the station and must be swiped before exit.

Fares These vary from Dhs2 for stops within a single zone to Dhs6.50 for stops within five zones.

Routes All metro stations stock leaflets, in English, clearly mapping the zones.

Penalties If you exit a station with insufficient credit, you will have to pay the equivalent of a day pass (Dhs14). Inspectors regularly check cards have been swiped and will issue an on-the-spot Dhs200 fine for ticket evasion.

Monorail

The elevated, driverless Palm Jumeirah Monorail (www.palm-monorail.com) connects the Palm Jumeirah with Dubai Marina. There are three stations: Palm Gateway near the bottom of the 'trunk', Al Ittihad Park near the Galleria Mall and Atlantis Aquaventure at the Atlantis hotel. The 5.45km trip takes about 12 minutes and costs Dhs20 (Dhs30 return trip); cash only. Trains run every 15 minutes from 9am to 10pm. The monorail links to the Dubai Tram at Palm Gateway.

Taxi

Dubai is a taxi-centric city, and you're likely to find yourself in need of a cab at some point. Government-licensed vehicles are cream-coloured and operated by **Dubai Taxi Corporation** (☎04 208 0808; www.dubaitaxi.ae). They are metered, air-conditioned, relatively inexpensive and the fastest and most comfortable way to get around, except during rush-hour traffic. Taxis can be hailed in the street, picked up at taxi ranks or booked by phone. You'll also see private taxis with different-coloured roofs (eg Arabia Taxi has a green roof). These are licensed and fine to use.

Dubai's public transport authority RTA has introduced a free Smart Taxi App from which you can book the nearest taxi based on your location. It's available on Google Play and Apple App Store.

Fares

➡ Flagfall for street taxis is Dhs8 between 6am and 10pm and Dhs9 between 10pm and 6am.
➡ The starting fare for prebooked taxis is Dhs8, which increases to Dhs12 during peak times: 7am to 10am and 4pm to 10pm Saturday to Wednesday and 4pm to midnight Thursdays and Fridays.
➡ The per km fare is Dhs1.82.
➡ The minimum fare per ride is Dhs12.
➡ Trips originating at the airports have a flagfall of Dhs25 and a per kilometre charge of Dhs1.96.
➡ Salik toll of Dhs4 per gate is automatically added to the fare.
➡ Tip about Dhs5 or Dhs10 or round the fare up to the nearest note. Carry small bills because drivers may not be able to make change otherwise.
➡ Drivers accept credit cards.

Reaching Your Destination

Most taxi drivers are expats from South Asia but speak at least some English. However, destinations are generally not given via a street address but by mentioning the nearest landmark (eg a hotel, mall, roundabout or major building). If you're going to a private residence, phone your host and ask them to give the driver directions.

Drivers new to the streets of Dubai may have trouble finding their way around. If they don't use a navigational system, Google Maps, RTA Smart Drive or some other web-based mapping app, use the one on your mobile to help them find your destination (which you've downloaded first, of course, to avoid roaming fees).

Women & Taxis

It's generally fine for women to ride alone in a taxi, even at night, although you should not sit in the front as this might be misunderstood. Although drivers rarely get touchy or physically aggressive, some may try to hit on you, especially if you're young, attractive and/or not conservatively dressed. Use common sense and your experience to deal with the situation. If you prefer, book a pink-roofed cab with a woman driver – a so-called **Ladies Taxi** (☎04 208 0808).

Uber & Careem

As in other metropolises, taxis are facing stiff competition from mobile ride-hailing apps such as Uber (www.uber.com) and Dubai-based Careem (www.careem.com), founded here in 2012 and now operating throughout the Middle East. Cost-wise, there's very little difference, but Uber and Careem tend to have much nicer cars that often come with free water, phone chargers and more clued-in drivers.

Tram

The Dubai Tram (www.alsufouhtram.com) makes 11 stops in and around the Dubai Marina area, including near the Marina Mall, The Beach at JBR and The Walk at JBR. It also connects with the Damac and Jumeirah Lakes Towers metro stations and with the Palm Jumeirah Monorail at Palm Jumeirah station.

Trams run roughly every eight minutes from 6am to 1am Saturday to Thursday and from 9am to 1am on Friday. The entire loop takes 40 minutes. The fare depends on how many zones you travel through, starting with Dhs4 for one zone. Nol Cards must be used.

Walking

Negotiating Dubai by foot, even combined with public transport, is highly challenging because of the lack of pavements, traffic lights and pedestrian crossings. Not to mention summer heat! It is not unheard of here to be forced to take a taxi, merely to reach the other side of the road.

Tours

If you're a Dubai first-timer, letting someone else show you around is a fun and efficient way to get your bearings, see the key sights quickly and obtain a general understanding of the city. Dubai offers a growing number of guided explorations to match all sorts of interests.

If you just want to get a quick introduction to the city, take the hop-on hop-off tour offered by **Big Bus Dubai** (☎04 340 7709; www.bigbustours.com; 24hr ticket adult/child US$69/41, 48hr US$73/47, one week US$83/54). For a rather unusual sightseeing tour, sign up with **Wonder Bus Tours** (p110) for a combined land-water exploration. Those seeking more substance should check out the cultural tours offered by the non-profit **Sheikh Mohammed Centre for Cultural Understanding** (p68), including a visit to Jumeirah Mosque. Hardcore foodies should sign on with Arva Arved's **Frying Pan Adventures** (p71) for a mouth-watering immersion in Dubai street food culture. To see Dubai from the water, consider a dinner cruise with **Al Mansour Dhow** (p58) or **Bateaux Dubai** (Map p244; ☎04 814 5553; www.bateauxdubai.com) or simply board the public **Dubai Ferry** (p121) for trips down the Dubai Canal or along the coastline from Bur Dubai to Dubai Marina.

Directory A–Z

PRACTICALITIES

Currency

UAE dirham (Dhs) is divided into 100 fils. Notes come in denominations of five, 10, 20, 50, 100, 200, 500 and 1000. There are Dhs1, 50 fils, 25 fils, 10 fils and 5 fils coins.

Newspapers & Magazines

Newspapers Four English-language dailies are published in the UAE: *The National*, *Gulf News*, *Khaleej Times* and *Gulf Today*.

Business *Emirates Business 24/7* (www.emirates247.com) is a government-owned publication covering business news.

Entertainment The weekly *Time Out Dubai* (www.timeoutdubai.com) and *Time Out Abu Dhabi* (www.timeoutabudhabi.com) as well as the monthly *What's On Dubai* (www.whatson.ae) are the main listings and lifestyle magazines.

Lifestyle *Friday* (http://fridaymagazine.ae) is a free weekly supplement to *Gulf News*.

Tap Water

Tap water is safe to drink in Dubai and Abu Dhabi.

Many people prefer the taste of bottled water, which is cheap and available everywhere, but it's good to be mindful of plastic use. Organisations like Goumbook (www.goumbook.com) have started initiatives trying to reduce reliance on plastic in the region.

Accessible Travel

In recent years, the government has launched several initiatives to make Dubai more accessibility friendly, most notably the Dubai Disability Strategy 2020. Most buildings are wheelchair-accessible, but drop-down curbs are still rare, and practically non-existent in Bur Dubai and Deira.

International airports Both are equipped with low check-in counters, luggage trolleys, automatic doors, lifts and quick check-in. Dubai International has a special check-in gate for travellers with special needs and a meet-and-assist service.

Public transport A limited supply of 'special needs taxis' – vans with wheelchair lifts – are available from **Dubai Taxi** (☎04 208 0808; www.dubaitaxi.ae), but they must be ordered several hours in advance. Some local buses and all water taxis are wheelchair-accessible. Dubai's metro has lifts and grooved guidance paths in stations and wheelchair spaces in each train compartment. Most parking areas contain spaces for drivers with disabilities.

Accommodation International chains and all top-end hotels have rooms with extra-wide doors and adapted bathrooms. Even budget hotels have lifts.

Sights & attractions Shopping malls are accessible, as are most bars and restaurants. Some beaches, including Kite Beach and Sunset Beach, have boardwalks leading through the sand to the waterfront. In Abu Dhabi, the big sights, such as Sheikh Zayed Grand Mosque, the Emirates Palace, Yas Island and Masdar City, all have facilities for those in wheelchairs.

Customs Regulations

The following is a quick rundown on what you may and may not bring into Dubai or

Abu Dhabi. For the full story, see www.dubaicustoms.gov.ae.

Anyone aged over 18 years is allowed to bring in the following duty-free:

➡ 400 cigarettes plus 50 cigars plus 500g of loose tobacco.

➡ 4L of alcohol or two cartons (24 cans) of beer (non-Muslims).

➡ Gifts not exceeding Dhs3000 in value.

You are *not* allowed to bring in:

➡ Alcohol if you cross into the UAE by land.

➡ Narcotics of any kind.

➡ Electronic cigarettes.

➡ Materials (ie books) that insult Islam.

➡ Firearms, pornography or Israeli products.

You must declare to Customs:

➡ Cash (or equivalent) more than Dhs100,000.

➡ Gifts with a value of more than Dhs3000.

➡ Medicines (you must be able to produce a prescription).

Discount Cards

Classic student and youth cards are of little use in UAE.

Go Dubai Pass (www.smartdestinations.com/dubai) Savings of up 55% on admission to 39 attractions, including **Burj Khalifa** (p81), **Aquaventure Waterpark** (p114) and **Ski Dubai** (p109). Available from two (adult/child Dhs759/519) to seven days (Dhs1899/1319).

iVenture Card (www.iventurecard.com/uk/dubai) Smart card with up to 60% discount on 30 major attractions. Unlimited access during five days in a seven-day period costs adult/child Dhs1395/1275; a flexipass with three or five attractions over a seven-day period costs Dhs575/875 (child Dhs525/815).

The Entertainer (www.theentertainerme.com) Voucher app for 'buy one, get one free' deals on dining, attractions, bars, spas, health and fitness; valid one calendar year; available on Google Play and App Store; Dhs445.

Groupon (www.groupon.ae/coupons/dubai) Website and app for discounts on everything from seafood buffets to car rentals.

Cobone (www.cobone.com) Home-grown version of Groupon.

Electricity

The electric voltage is 220V AC. British-style three-pin wall sockets are standard, although some can also accommodate two-pin plugs. Ask at your hotel for an adapter or pick one up in supermarkets and electronics stores.

Type G
230V/50Hz

Embassies & Consulates

Embassies usually help in cases of a stolen passport but are not sympathetic to those committing a crime locally, even if the actions are legal back home.

With the exception of the UK, most embassies are in Abu Dhabi, the UAE's capital, but the following can be found in Dubai:

Australian Consulate (☎04 508 7100; www.uae.embassy.gov.au; 25th fl, BurJuman Business Tower, Sheikh Khalifa bin Zayed Rd; ⏲8am-4pm Sun-Thu; Ⓜ BurJuman)

Canadian Consulate (☎04 404 8444; www.canadainternational.gc.ca/uae-eau/consulate_contact-contactez_consulat.aspx?lang=eng; 19th fl, Jumeirah Emirates Towers (Business Tower), Sheikh Zayed Rd; ⏲8am-noon & 1-4pm Sun-Thu; Ⓜ Emirates Towers)

French Consulate (☎04 408 4900; https://dubai.consulfrance.org; 32nd fl, Habtoor Business Tower, King Salman Bin Abdulaziz Al Saud St, Dubai Marina; ⏲8.30am-12.30pm Sun-Thu)

German Consulate (☎04 349 8888; www.dubai.diplo.de; 8A St, Jumeirah 1; ⏲9am-noon Sun-Thu; Ⓜ Financial Centre)

Netherlands Consulate (☎04 440 7600; www.netherlandsworldwide.nl/countries/united-arab-emirates; 30th & 31st fl, Al Habtoor Business Tower, Dubai Marina; ⏲8.30am-4pm Sun-Thu; Ⓜ Damac, 🚊 Dubai Marina)

Omani Consulate (☎04 397 1000; www.ocodubai.com; Consulate Zone, 8th St; ⏲7.30am-2.30pm Sun-Thu; Ⓜ BurJuman) Issues tourist and business visas.

UK Embassy (☎04 309 4444; http://ukinuae.fco.gov.uk/en; Consulate Zone, Al Seef Rd; ⏲7.30am-2.30pm Sun-Thu; Ⓜ Al Fahidi)

US Consulate (☎04 311 6000; http://dubai.usconsulate.gov; cnr Al Seef & Sheikh Khalifa bin Zayed Rds; ⏲8.30am-5pm Sun-Thu; Ⓜ BurJuman)

Emergency

Ambulance	☎999
Fire Department	☎997
Police	☎999 (☎901 non-emergency)
Country Code	☎971

Health

Before You Go

HEALTH INSURANCE

The standard of medical services in Dubai and Abu Dhabi is high.

Travel insurance that includes health coverage is essential as visitors will be charged for health care and fees are steep. Also make sure that your policy covers repatriation.

RECOMMENDED VACCINATIONS

There are no compulsory vaccinations for travel to Dubai and Abu Dhabi, but the Centers for Disease Control (CDC) recommends that your routine vaccinations should be up-to-date. These include: measles-mumps-rubella (MMR), diphtheria-tetanus-pertussis, chickenpox, polio and your annual flu shot.

Medical Services

Doctors are available around the clock with **Health Call** (☎04 363 5343; http://health-call.com). Costs Dhs600 to Dhs800 per visit.

Pharmacies are plentiful around clinics and hospitals and in major shopping malls. Most sell standard medication without a prescription, including antibiotics.

DUBAI

American Hospital Dubai (☎04 336 7777; www.ahdubai.com; Oud Metha Rd; Ⓜ Dubai Healthcare City, Oud Metha) One of the top private hospitals in town with 24/7 emergency room.

Dubai Hospital (☎04 219 5000; www.dha.gov.ae/en/DubaiHospital; Al Khaleej Rd, Deira; ⏲24hr; Ⓜ Abu Baker Al Siddique) One of the region's best government hospitals, with 24/7 ER.

Rashid Hospital (☎04 219 1000; www.dha.gov.ae/en/RashidHospital; off Oud Metha Rd, near Al Maktoum Bridge; Ⓜ Oud Metha) Public hospital for round-the-clock emergencies.

ABU DHABI

The standard of health care in Abu Dhabi is generally high and emergency treatment is free. For locations of 24-hour pharmacies, call 777 929.

Central Al Ahalia Pharmacy (Map p136; ☎02 626 9545; www.dawnpharmacy.com; Hamdan & Liwa Sts, opposite Baroda Bank; ⏲24hr) In Al Markaziyah; one of many open 24 hours.

Sheikh Khalifa Medical City (Map p136; ☎02 819 0000; www.seha.ae; cnr Al Karama St & Al Falah St) One of numerous well-equipped hospitals in the city with 24-hour emergency service.

Gulf Diagnostic Centre (Map p130; ☎02 417 7222; www.gdc-hospital.com; Al Khaleej Al Arabi St; ⏲8am-8.30pm Sat-Wed, to 1pm Thu) A well-regarded private health centre.

Internet Access

Dubai is extremely well wired, and you should have no trouble getting online. Nearly every hotel offers in-room internet access, either broadband or wireless, usually free. Wi-fi is also ubiquitous in cafes and restaurants, although you usually need to request a password.

Through an initiative called Wifi UAE, there's also free public wi-fi in the Dubai Metro, on public beaches, in shopping malls and at hundreds of other locations in the country. Alas, for now you need a UAE mobile phone number to access this service. Consider bringing an old phone and buying a local SIM card, which costs just a few dirhams. For a map with all the hotspots, see www.wifiuae.ae.

SMOKING

Dubai and Abu Dhabi have a comprehensive smoking ban in all public places, with the exception of nightclubs and enclosed bars. In addition:

- Shopping malls, hotels and some restaurants have designated smoking rooms.
- All hotels have non-smoking rooms; some are entirely non-smoking.
- Getting caught lighting up in a nonsmoking area entails a Dhs500 fine; this goes up to Dhs1000 when tossing a cigarette butt into the street.
- Smoking is prohibited in public parks, beaches and recreation areas.
- Electronic cigarettes are illegal and likely to be confiscated on arrival.
- Smoking is not permitted in cars where children are present.

Legal Matters

Abu Dhabi, and Dubai in particular, may seem to be a city where 'anything goes', but this is not really the case. Locals are tolerant of cultural differences – to a point. Go beyond that point, and you could find you are subject to some of the harshest penalties in the region.

As ignorance of Emirati law is no defence, check the Dubai Code of Conduct (www.zu.ac.ae/employment/html/documents/CultureandConductinDubai_000.pdf) to avoid getting into trouble in the first place.

Alcohol-Related Issues

While the drinking of alcohol for non-Muslims is permitted in certain locations, it is against the law to drink in an unlicensed public place. It is also forbidden to buy alcohol from an outlet other than a hotel bar or restaurant without a local liquor licence (exception: the 4L duty-free allowance upon landing). Never offer alcohol to a Muslim, however close your friendship, and drinking and driving is a serious offence.

Cultural Sensitivities

A number of laws and codes of conduct govern personal behaviour.

Displays of affection Married couples holding hands is tolerated, but kissing or fondling is considered an offence to public decency.

Nudity Strictly forbidden.

Insults Avoid vulgar language and rude gestures and don't photograph strangers without permission.

Taboo subjects Don't criticise public figures or the government, or discuss politics.

Religion Do not defame Islam or show disrespect towards any religion. Avoid eating, drinking and smoking in public during daylight hours in Ramadan.

Public nuisance Spitting, issuing a bounced cheque, loud music in public spaces, pet fouling of public areas and littering are all considered public nuisance offences.

Drugs & Illegal Substances

Using illegal drugs is considered a crime and simply a bad, bad idea, even though amendments to the anti-narcotics law in 2016 downgraded drug use from a felony to a misdemeanour. Courts now have the option of punishing first-time offenders with a fine, community service or a stint in rehab instead of a two-year jail sentence. Don't let this change fool you into thinking you can get off easily!

Prescription Medicine

There are import restrictions for prescription medications that are legal in most countries, such as diazepam (Valium), dextromethorphan (Robitussin), fluoxetine (Prozac) and anything containing codeine. This list posted on www.uaeinteract.com/travel/drug.asp provides an overview but may not be current. Check with the UAE embassy in your home country for the latest list. If you need to take such medications, carry the original prescription and a letter from your doctor confirming that you need to take it.

Ignorance No Defence

Penalties for breaching the code of conduct or breaking the law can result in warnings or fines (eg for littering), or jail and deportation (eg for drug possession and criticism of Islam). Ignorance is no defence.

If arrested, call your embassy or consulate and wait until a representative arrives before you sign anything. In a car accident, you should not move the car, even if you're causing a traffic jam, until the police arrive.

The UAE police have established a **Tourist Security Department** (☎800 4438; www.dubaipolice.gov.ae; ⊙24hr) to help visitors with any legal complications they may face on their trip – this may also be helpful if you get into difficulties.

BANNED WEBSITES

In the UAE, web pages are routed through a local proxy that prevents access to certain sites, including pornography, many LGBTIQ+ sites, websites considered critical of Islam or the UAE's leaders, dating and gambling sites, drug-related material and all Israeli domains. These are all officially restricted in the UAE. Some users get around this by setting up a VPN (virtual private network) outside the UAE to access blocked content.

LGBTIQ+ Travellers

Homosexual acts are illegal under UAE law and can incur a jail term and fines. If you see Arab men walking hand in hand, it's a sign of friendship and not an indication of sexual orientation.

Public displays of affection between partners are taboo regardless of sexual orientation.

Many LGBTIQ-related websites, including Grindr

RAMADAN & OTHER ISLAMIC HOLIDAYS

Ramadan falls into the ninth month of the Muslim calendar. It is considered a time of spiritual reflection and involves fasting during daylight hours.

Non-Muslims are not expected to follow suit, but visitors should not smoke, drink or eat (including chewing gum) in public during Ramadan. Hotels make provisions for non-Muslim guests by erecting screens for discreet dining. Opening hours tend to become shorter and more erratic. In 2016 Dubai relaxed restrictions on the daytime sale of alcohol in licensed bars. Some nightclubs are open as well, although live music is a no-no.

Once the sun has set, the fast is broken with something light before prayers. Then comes *iftar*, a big communal meal that non-Muslims are welcome to join in. Many restaurants and hotels set up big festive *iftar* tents. People then rise again before dawn to prepare a meal *(suhoor)* to support them through the day.

Islamic holidays are moveable since they're based on the sighting of the moon. Exact dates are published in newspapers. The main Islamic holidays are:

Eid al Fitr Marks the end of Ramadan.

Eid al Adha Marks the pilgrimage to Mecca.

Islamic New Year (Ras as Sana al Hijria)

Prophet's Birthday (Mawlid)

ISLAMIC YEAR	RAMADAN	EID AL FITR	EID AL ADHA
1437 (2019)	6 May	4 Jun	11 Aug
1438 (2020)	24 Apr	23 May	30 Jul
1439 (2021)	13 Apr	13 May	20 Jul

and other dating apps, are blocked and not officially accessible from inside the UAE.

Sex outside marriage is against the law. Sharing a room is likely to be construed as companionable or cost-cutting, but being discreet about your true relationship is advisable.

A useful read is *Gay Travels in the Muslim World* by Michael Luongo.

LGBT Rights UAE (www.facebook.com/LGBTRights UAE) is a non-governmental organisation that strives to raise awareness about the issues facing the community.

Money

ATMs

ATMs are widely available. Credit cards are accepted in most hotels, restaurants and shops.

Changing Money

Exchange offices tend to offer better rates than banks. Reliable exchanges include Al Rostamani (www.alrostamaniexchange.com) and UAE Exchange (www.uaeexchange.com), with multiple branches in Dubai and Abu Dhabi.

Credit Cards

Visa, MasterCard and American Express are widely accepted and almost everything can be paid for by plastic.

Exchange Rates

Australia	A$1	Dhs2.93
Canada	C$1	Dhs2.91
Eurozone	€1	Dhs4.35
Japan	¥100	Dhs3.32
New Zealand	NZ$1	Dhs2.73
Switzerland	Sfr1	Dhs3.79
UK	UK£1	Dhs4.85
US	US$1	Dhs3.67

For the latest exchange rates, see www.xe.com.

Tipping

Hotels Porters Dhs5 to Dhs10, room cleaners Dhs5 to Dhs10 per day.

Restaurants For decent service 10%, for good service 15% of the bill, in cash to make sure it goes to the servers.

Taxis Dhs5 to Dhs10 or round up to nearest note.

Valets Dhs5 to Dhs10.

Spa staff 10% to 15%.

Opening Hours

Opening hours vary from season to season (especially during Ramadan). The UAE weekend is on Friday and Saturday.

Banks 8am to 1pm (some until 3pm) Sunday to Thursday, 8am to noon Saturday.

Government offices 7.30am to 2pm (or 3pm) Sunday to Thursday.

Private offices 8am to 5pm or 9am to 6pm, or split shifts 8am to 1pm and 3pm to 7pm Sunday to Thursday.

Restaurants noon to 3pm and 7.30pm to midnight.

Shopping malls 10am to 10pm Sunday to Wednesday, 10am to midnight Thursday to Saturday.

Souqs 9am to 1pm and 4pm to 9pm Saturday to Thursday, 4pm to 9pm Friday.

Supermarkets 9am to midnight daily; some open 24 hours.

Public Holidays

New Year's Day 1 January

Commemoration Day 30 November

National Day 2 December

Safe Travel

Crime Dubai and Abu Dhabi have a low crime rate, and violence is rare. Petty crime, such as purse snatching and pickpocketing, occurs, especially in crowds and at the souqs.

Terrorism The US Department of State and British Foreign Office periodically warn travellers of a general threat from terrorism, but this is due to the UAE's geographical location more than any focused threat.

Traffic accidents Dubai has among the highest incidences of accidents and road fatalities in the world. Speeding is common.

Water hazards The Gulf may look innocuous, but rip currents can be very strong and drownings regularly occur.

Taxes

Value-added tax (VAT), a 5% consumer tax on most goods and services, was introduced in January 2018. Hotel rooms, food and petrol are all now subject to VAT. A 'sin' tax was also implemented in October 2017, which doubled the price of tobacco products and energy drinks. Prices of sugary drinks increased by 50%.

In addition to VAT, hotel bills in Dubai are inflated by a 10% city tax, a 10% service charge and a tourism tax of Dhs7 to Dhs20. In Abu Dhabi, the final hotel tab includes a 6% city tax, a 10% service charge and a tourism tax of 4% plus 15 Dhs per night per room.

Telephone

The UAE has a modern, efficient telephone network and three mobile networks: Etisalat, Du and Virgin Mobile. Calls within the same area code are free.

Coin phones have been almost completely superseded by cardphones. Phonecards are available in various denominations from grocery stores, supermarkets and petrol stations.

Calling Dubai from abroad	☎+971 +4 +phone number
Calling Abu Dhabi from abroad	☎+971 +2 +phone number
Calling abroad from UAE	☎00 +country code +area code +phone number
Dubai/Abu Dhabi area codes	☎04/02
Directory Enquiries	☎181
International Directory Assistance	☎151
Mobile numbers	start with ☎050, ☎055 or ☎056
Toll-free numbers	start with ☎800

Mobile Phones

Mobile phones operate on GSM900/1800, the same as Europe, Asia and Australia.

Local SIM cards are easy to find in electronics stores and some grocery stores. A local number is needed to access most public wi-fi.

Time

Dubai and Abu Dhabi are four hours ahead of GMT/UTC. The time does not change during the summer. Not taking daylight saving into account, when it's noon in Dubai or Abu Dhabi, the time elsewhere is as follows:

CITY	TIME
Auckland	8pm
London	8am
Los Angeles	midnight
New York	3am
Paris & Rome	9am
Perth & Hong Kong	4pm
Sydney	6pm

Toilets

Public toilets in shopping centres, museums, restaurants and hotels are Western-style, free and generally clean and well maintained.

Toilets in souqs and bus stations are usually only for men.

The hose next to the toilet is used for rinsing (left hand only if you want to go native); toilet paper is used for drying only and should be thrown in the bin to avoid clogging the toilets.

Tourist Information

Dubai Department of Tourism & Commerce Marketing (☎call centre 600 555 559; www.visitdubai.com; ⏰8am-8pm Sat-Thu) No brick-and-mortar office but a comprehensive website and a call centre for information on hotels, attractions, shopping and other topics.

The Abu Dhabi Tourism Authority maintains

information desks in the **airport arrivals hall – T1** (Map p161; ☎02 599 5135; Terminal 1 Arrivals, Abu Dhabi Airport; ⏰7am-midnight), **Ferrari World** (Map p161; www.visitabudhabi.ae; Ferrari World, Yas Island; ⏰11am-8pm) and **World Trade Center Souk** (Map p136; www.visitabudhabi.ae; World Trade Center Souk; ⏰10am-10pm Sat-Thu, to 11pm Fri). In addition, the following official websites give comprehensive tourist information.

Visit Abu Dhabi (www.visitabudhabi.ae) The city's main tourist-oriented website.

Department of Culture and Tourism – Abu Dhabi (Map p136; ☎800 555, 02 444 0444; www.visitabudhabi.ae; Nation Towers, 4th fl; ⏰8am-4pm Sun-Thu) Useful information online and tourist brochures available.

Yas Island Information (www.yasisland.ae) A good online overview of what's on, when and where on Yas Island.

Visas

- Citizens of 49 countries, including all EU countries, the US, the UK, Canada and Australia, are eligible for free 30-day single-entry visas on arrival in Dubai and Abu Dhabi.
- Entry requirements to the UAE are in constant flux. Always obtain the latest requirements from the UAE embassy in your home country.
- Travellers not eligible for an on-arrival visa (including transit visitors) must have a visitor visa arranged through a sponsor, such as your hotel, a tour operator or a relative or locally based friend before arriving.

Visa Extensions

Visit visas can be extended twice for 60 days for Dhs220 and a fair amount of paperwork by the **General Directorate of Residency and Foreigners Affairs** (☎04 313 9999, 800 5111; www.dnrd.ae; Sheikh Khalifa bin Zayed Rd, near Bur Dubai Police Station; ⏰8am-8pm Sun-Thu; Ⓜ Al Jafiliya). The process usually takes one day, and you may be asked to provide proof of funds. To avoid the hassle, many visitors opt to leave the country for a few hours and obtain a new entry stamp upon returning.

EXPAT LIFE

If you find you like Dubai and Abu Dhabi well enough to stay, consider joining the thousands of expats who call the cities home.

The Rewards

Some expats are drawn to the Gulf in search of tax-free money and the expectation of an easy life. But the days of being paid well for doing little are over, while the realities of extreme temperatures and challenging cultural norms remain. So why consider an expat life? For many it's the excitement of being part of something experimental and optimistic in a region where the pace of change is unparalleled. For others it's the prospect of bringing qualifications and experience to bear in a context where those qualities are useful and appreciated.

In addition to high job satisfaction, many expats enjoy the fact that it's safe to leave houses and cars unlocked, for children to play in the streets and talk to strangers, and where neighbours always make time for a chat. Times are changing, but on the whole the friendly, safe and tolerant environment of Dubai and Abu Dhabi, together with the multicultural nature of the resident population, is a major contributor to the quality of life.

The Challenges

Not everyone is able to cope with the weather. If you're from a cold, wet country, it's hard to imagine getting bored of endless sunshine. But in the summer, the sky is white with heat and the extreme temperatures from April to October (which frequently rise above 45°C) require a complete adjustment as most of daily life takes place in an air-conditioned indoor environment.

The Practicalities

If you have proven skills and preferably qualifications, it's easy to find employment. To secure a three-year residency permit, you need an employer to sponsor you, a spouse with a job, or ownership of freehold property, which comes with a renewable residency permit. Salary packages sometimes include a relocation allowance, annual plane tickets home, housing, health insurance, children's education allowance and generous paid leave.

TOP TIPS FOR WOMEN TRAVELLERS

Dubai and Abu Dhabi are among the safest Middle Eastern destinations for women travellers, but unwanted attention is almost inevitable and solo travellers are sometimes mistaken for 'working women', regardless of age, looks or dress. Although it doesn't officially exist, prostitution catering to both expats and locals is common in clubs, bars and on the backstreets of Deira and Bur Dubai.

Here are some tips to help ward off unwanted attention and generally make travelling as a woman easier:

- Wear a wedding ring – it will make you appear less 'available' (but be ready for awkward questions about abandoning your home and kids).
- If you're unmarried but travelling in male company, say that you're married rather than girlfriend/boyfriend.
- Avoid direct eye contact with men (dark sunglasses help).
- Don't sit in the front seat of taxis unless the driver is a woman.
- On public transport, sit in the women's section towards the front.
- If you need help for any reason (directions etc), ask a woman first.
- If dining alone, ask to be seated in the 'family' section of local eateries.
- If someone follows you in his car, take a picture of his licence plate or just get your mobile phone out.
- Look and be confident. This is the best deterrent for unwanted attention.

Oman Visas

The cost of a 30-day tourist visa for Oman is OR20 (approximately Dhs190). Many nationalities are eligible to apply for a tourist visa online via https://evisa.rop.gov.om. Otherwise, visas are issued on arrival.

Women Travellers

Dispelling the Myths

Many people imagine that for women to travel to Dubai and Abu Dhabi is much more difficult and stressful than it is. First up, let's debunk some of the most common myths:

- You don't have to wear an abaya, burka, headscarf or veil.
- You are allowed to drive a car.
- You won't be constantly harassed.
- It's safe to take taxis, stay alone in hotels (although you may want to avoid the fleabag hotels in Deira and Bur Dubai) and walk around on your own in most areas.

What to Wear

Even though you'll see plenty of female tourists wearing skimpy shorts and tank tops in shopping malls and other public places, you should not assume that it's acceptable to do so. While as hosts they're often too polite to say anything, most Emiratis find this disrespectful. Despite the UAE's relative liberalism, you are in a country that holds its traditions dear and it's prudent not to parade a different set of values. A bit of common sense (such as covering up to and from a beach party or when taking a taxi to a nightclub) helps keep the peace.

Generally speaking, dressing 'modestly' has the following advantages: it attracts less attention to you; you will get a warmer welcome from locals (who greatly appreciate your willingness to respect their customs); and it'll prove more comfortable in the heat. Dressing modestly means covering your shoulders, knees and neckline. Baggy T-shirts and loose cotton trousers or below-the-knee skirts will not only keep you cool but will also protect your skin from the sun. If you travel outside Dubai, keep in mind that social norms are more conservative elsewhere in the UAE.

Language

Arabic is the official language of the United Arab Emirates (UAE), but English is widely understood. Note that there are significant differences between the MSA (Modern Standard Arabic) – the official lingua franca of the Arab world, used in schools, administration and the media – and the colloquial language, ie the everyday spoken version. The Arabic variety spoken in the UAE (and provided in this chapter) is known as Gulf Arabic.

Read our coloured pronunciation guides as if they were English and you'll be understood. Note that a is pronounced as in 'act', aa as the 'a' in 'father', ai as in 'aisle', aw as in 'law', ay as in 'say', ee as in 'see', i as in 'hit', oo as in 'zoo', u as in 'put', gh is a guttural sound (like the Parisian French 'r'), r is rolled, dh is pronounced as the 'th' in 'that', th as in 'thin', ch as in 'cheat' and kh as the 'ch' in the Scottish *loch*. The apostrophe (') indicates the glottal stop (like the pause in the middle of 'uh-oh'). The stressed syllables are indicated with italics, and (m) and (f) refer to the masculine and feminine word forms, respectively.

BASICS

Hello.	اهلا و سهلا.	*ah*·lan was *ah*·lan
Goodbye.	مع السلامة.	ma' sa·*laa*·ma
Yes./No.	نعم./لا.	*na*·'am/la
Please.	من فضلك.	min *fad*·lak (m)
	من فضلِك.	min *fad*·lik (f)
Thank you.	شكران.	*shuk*·ran
Excuse me.	اسمح.	is·*mah* (m)
	اسمحي لي.	is·mah·*ee* lee (f)
Sorry.	مع الاسف.	ma' al·*as*·af

WANT MORE?

For in-depth language information and handy phrases, check out Lonely Planet's *Middle East phrasebook*. You'll find it at **shop.lonelyplanet.com**, or you can buy Lonely Planet's iPhone phrasebooks at the Apple App Store.

How are you?
كيف حالَك/حالِك؟ kayf *haa*·lak/*haa*·lik (m/f)

Fine, thanks. And you?
بخير الحمد الله. bi·*khayr* il·*ham*·du·li·laa
و انتَ/و انتِ؟ *win*·ta/*win*·ti (m/f)

What's your name?
اش اسمَك/اسمِك؟ aash *is*·mak/*is*·mik (m/f)

My name is ...
اسمي ... *is*·mee ...

Do you speak English?
تتكلم انجليزية؟ tit·*kal*·am in·glee·*zee*·ya (m)
تتكلمي انجليزية؟ tit·*ka*·la·mee in·glee·*zee*·ya (f)

I don't understand.
مو فاهم. moo *faa*·him

Can I take a photo?
ممكن اتصور؟ *mum*·kin at·*saw*·ar

ACCOMMODATION

Where's a ...?	وين ...؟	wayn ...
hotel	فندق	*fun*·dug
Do you have a ... room?	عندك/عندك غرفة ...؟	*'and*·ak/*'and*·ik *ghur*·fa ... (m/f)
single	لشخص واحد	li·*shakhs waa*·hid
double	لشخسين	li·shakh·*sayn*
twin	مع سريرين	ma' sa·ree·*rayn*
How much is it per ...?	بكم كل ...؟	bi·*kam* kul ...
night	ليلة	*lay*·la
person	شخص	shakhs

Can I get another (blanket)?
احتاج الى (برنوس) ah·*taaj* i·*la* (bar·*noos*)
الثاني من فضلك؟ i·*thaa*·nee min *fad*·lak

The (air conditioning) doesn't work.
(الكنديشان) (il·kan·*day*·shan)
ما يشتغل. ma yish·*ta*·ghil

Signs

Entrance	مدخل
Exit	خروج
Open	مفتوح
Closed	مقفول
Information	معلومات
Prohibited	ممنوع
Toilets	المرحاض
Men	رجال
Women	نساء

DIRECTIONS

Where's the ...?	من وين ...؟	min wayn ...
bank	البنك	il·*bank*
market	السوق	i·*soog*
post office	مكتب البريد	*mak*·tab il·ba·*reed*

Can you show me (on the map)?
لو سمحت وريني (علخريطة)؟ — law sa·*maht* wa·*ree*·nee ('al·kha·*ree*·ta)

What's the address?
ما العنوان؟ — ma il·'un·*waan*

Could you please write it down?
لو سمحت اكتبه لي؟ — law sa·*maht* ik·ti·*boo* lee (m)
لو سمحت اكتبيه لي؟ — law sa·*maht* ik·ti·*bee* lee (f)

How far is it?
كم بعيد؟ — kam ba·*'eed*

How do I get there?
كيف ممكن اوصل هناكا؟ — kayf *mum*·kin *aw*·sil *hoo*·naak

Turn left/right.
لف يسار/يمين. — lif yee·*saar*/yee·*meen* (m)
لفي يسار/يمين. — *li*·fee yee·*saar*/yee·*meen* (f)

It's ...	... هو	*hoo*·wa ... (m)
	... هي	*hee*·ya ... (f)
behind ...	... ورا	wa·*raa* ...
in front of ...	... قدام	gu·*daam* ...
near to ...	... قريب من	ga·*reeb* min ...
next to ...	... جنب	janb ...
on the corner	علزاوية	'a·*zaa*·wee·ya
opposite ...	... مقابل	moo·*gaa*·bil ...
straight ahead	سيدا	*see*·da

EATING & DRINKING

Can you recommend a ...?	ممكن تنصح/ تنصحي ...؟	*mum*·kin *tan*·sah/ *tan*·sa·hee ... (m/f)
bar	بار	baar
cafe	قهوة	*gah*·wa
restaurant	مطعم	*ma*·ta'm
I'd like a/the ..., please.	... اريد من فضلك.	a·*reed* ... min *fad*·lak
table for (four)	طاولة (اربعة) اشخاص	*taa*·wi·lat (*ar*·ba') ash·*khaas*

What would you recommend?
اش تنصح؟ — aash *tan*·sah (m)
اش تنصحي؟ — aash *tan*·sa·hee (f)

What's the local speciality?
اش الطبق المحلي؟ — aash i·*ta*·bak il·*ma*·ha·lee

Do you have vegetarian food?
عندك طعم نباتي؟ — *'an*·dak *ta*·'am na·*baa*·tee

I'd like (the) ..., please.	عطني/عطيني الـ ... من فضلك.	*'a*·ti·nee/*'a*·*tee*·nee il ... min *fad*·lak (m/f)
bill	قائمة	*kaa*·'i·ma
drink list	قائمة المشروبات	*kaa*·'i·mat il·mash·roo·*baat*
menu	قائمة الطعام	*kaa*·'i·mat i·ta·*'aam*
that dish	الطبق هاذاك	i·*tab*·ak *haa*·dhaa·ka
Could you prepare a meal without ...?	ممكن تطبخها/ تطبخيها بدون ...؟	*mum*·kin *tat*·bakh·ha/ *tat*·bakh·ee·ha bi·*doon* ... (m/f)
butter	زبدة	*zib*·da
eggs	بيض	bayd
meat stock	مرق لهم	ma·*rak la*·ham
I'm allergic to ...	عندي حساسية لـ ...	*'an*·dee ha·saa·*see*·ya li ...
dairy produce	الألبان	il·al·*baan*
gluten	قمح	*ka*·mah
nuts	كرزات	ka·ra·*zaat*
seafood	السمك و المحارات	i·*sa*·mak wa al·ma·haa·*raat*
coffee ...	... نقهوة	*kah*·wa ...
tea ...	... شاي	shay ...
with milk	بالحليب	bil·ha·*leeb*
without sugar	بدون شكر	bi·*doon shi*·ker
bottle/glass of beer	بوتل/قلاس بيرة	*boo*·til/glaas *bee*·ra
(orange) juice	عصير (برتقال)	'a·*seer* (bor·too·*gaal*)
(mineral) water	ماي (معدني)	may (*ma'a*·da·nee)
... wine	... خمر	... *kha*·mar
red	احمر	*ah*·mer
sparkling	فوار	fa·*waar*
white	ابيض	*ab*·yad

EMERGENCIES

Help! | !مساعد moo·*saa*·'id (m) | !مساعدة moo·*saa*·'id·a (f)

Go away! | !ابعد!/ابعدي *ib*·'ad/*ib*·'ad·ee (m/f)

Call ...! | ...! تصل على ti·*sil* 'a·la ... (m) | ...! تصلي على *ti*·*si*·lee 'a·la ... (f)

- **a doctor** | طبيب ta·*beeb*
- **the police** | الشرطة i·*shur*·ta

I'm lost. | .انا ضعت a·na duht

Where are the toilets? | وين المرحاض؟ wayn il·mir·*haad*

I'm sick. | .انا مريض a·na ma·*reed* (m) | .انا مريضة a·na ma·*ree*·da (f)

I'm allergic to (antibiotics). | عندي حساسية (لـ (مضاد حيوي). *'and*·ee ha·saa·*see*·ya li (moo·*daad hay*·a·we)

SHOPPING & SERVICES

Where's a ...? | من وين ...؟ min wayn ...

- **department store** | محل ضخم ma·*hal dukh*·um
- **grocery store** | محل ابقالية ma·*hal* ib·gaa·*lee*·ya
- **newsagency** | محل يبيع جرائد ma·*hal* yi·*bee*·a' ja·*raa*·id
- **souvenir shop** | محل سياحي ma·*hal* say·*aa*·hee
- **supermarket** | سوبرمركت *soo*·ber·mar·ket

I'm looking for ... | ... مدور على moo·*daw*·ir *'a*·la ... (m) | ... مدورة على moo·*daw*·i·ra *'a*·la ... (f)

Can I look at it? | ممكن اشوف؟ *mum*·kin a·*shoof*

Do you have any others? | عندَك اخرين؟ *'and*·ak ukh·*reen* (m) | عندِك اخرين؟ *'and*·ik ukh·*reen* (f)

It's faulty. | .فيه خلل fee *kha*·lal

How much is it? | بكم؟ bi·*kam*

Can you write down the price? | ممكن تكتبلي/ تكتبيلي السعر؟ *mum*·kin tik·*tib*·lee/ tik·*tib*·ee·lee i·*si'r* (m/f)

That's too expensive. | .غالي جدا *ghaa*·lee *jid*·an

What's your lowest price? | اش السعر الاخر؟ aash i·*si'r* il·*aa*·khir

There's a mistake in the bill. | .فيه غلط في الفطورة fee *gha*·lat fil fa·*too*·ra

Where's ...? | من وين ...؟ min wayn ...

- **a foreign exchange office** | صراف si·*raaf*
- **an ATM** | مكينة صرف ma·*kee*·nat sarf

What's the exchange rate? | ما هو السعر؟ maa *hoo*·wa i·*sa'r*

TIME & DATES

What time is it? | الساعة كم؟ i·*saa*·a' kam

It's one o'clock. | .الساعة واحدة i·*saa*·a' *waa*·hi·da

It's (two) o'clock. | .(الساعة (ثنتين i·*saa*·a' (thin·*tayn*)

Half past (two). | .الساعة (ثنتين) و نس i·*saa*·a' (thin·*tayn*) wa nus

At what time ...? | الساعة كم ...؟ i·*saa*·a' kam ...

At ... | ... الساعة i·*saa*·a'...

yesterday ...	... البارح	il·*baa*·rih ...
tomorrow ...	... باكر	*baa*·chir ...
morning	صباح	sa·*baah*
afternoon	بعد الظهر	ba'd a·*thuhr*
evening	مساء	*mi*·saa
Monday	يوم الاثنين	yawm al·ith·*nayn*
Tuesday	يوم الثلاثة	yawm a·tha·*laa*·tha
Wednesday	يوم الاربعة	yawm al·*ar*·ba'
Thursday	يوم الخميس	yawm al·kha·*mees*
Friday	يوم الجمعة	yawm al·*jum*·a'
Saturday	يوم السبت	yawm a·*sibt*
Sunday	يوم الاحد	yawm al·*aa*·had

TRANSPORT

Is this the ... (to Riyadh)? | هاذا ال ... يروح (لرياض؟) *haa*·dha al ... yi·*roh* (li·ree·*yaad*)

boat	سفينة	sa·*fee*·na
bus	باص	baas
plane	طيارة	tay·*aa*·ra
train	قطار	gi·*taar*

Question Words

When?	متى؟	*ma*·ta
Where?	وين؟	wayn
Who?	من؟	man
Why?	لاش؟	laysh

Numbers

1	١	واحد	*waa*·hid
2	٢	اثنين	ith·*nayn*
3	٣	ثلاثة	tha·*laa*·tha
4	٤	اربع	ar·*ba'*
5	٥	خمسة	*kham*·sa
6	٦	ستة	*si*·ta
7	٧	سبعة	*sa*·ba'
8	٨	ثمانية	tha·*maan*·ya
9	٩	تسعة	*tis*·a'
10	١٠	عشرة	*'ash*·ar·a
20	٢٠	عشرين	'ash·*reen*
30	٣٠	ثلاثين	tha·la·*theen*
40	٤٠	اربعين	ar·ba'·*een*
50	٥٠	خمسين	kham·*seen*
60	٦٠	ستين	sit·*een*
70	٧٠	سبعين	sa·ba'·*een*
80	٨٠	ثمانين	tha·ma·*neen*
90	٩٠	تسعين	ti·sa'·*een*
100	١٠٠	مية	*mee*·ya
1000	١٠٠٠	الف	alf

Note that Arabic numerals, unlike letters, are read from left to right.

What time's the ... bus?	الساعة كم الباص ...؟	a·*saa*·a' kam il·*baas* ...
first	الاول	il·*aw*·al
last	الاخر	il·*aa*·khir
next	القادم	il·*gaa*·dim
One ... ticket (to Doha), please.	... تذكرة (الدوحة) من فضلك.	*tadh*·ka·ra ... (a·*do*·ha) min *fad*·lak
one-way	ذهاب بص	dhee·*haab* bas
return	ذهاب و اياب	dhee·*haab* wa ai·*yaab*

How long does the trip take?
كم الرحلة تستغرق؟ kam i·*rah*·la tis·*tagh*·rik

Is it a direct route?
الرحلة متواصلة؟ i·*rah*·la moo·ta·*waa*·si·la

What station/stop is this?
ما هي المحطة هاذي؟ maa *hee*·ya il·ma·*ha*·ta *haa*·dhee

Please tell me when we get to (Al Ain).
لو سمحت خبرني/خبريني وقت ما نوصل (الي (العين). law sa·*maht* kha·*bir*·nee/kha·*bir*·ee·nee wokt ma *noo*·sil i·*la* (al·*'ain*) (m/f)

How much is it to (Sharjah)?
بكم الى (شارقة)؟ bi·*kam* i·*la* (*shaa*·ri·ka)

Please take me to (this address).
من فضلك خذني (علعنوان هاذا). min *fad*·lak *khudh*·nee ('al·'un·*waan haa*·dha)

Please stop here.
لو سمحت وقف هنا. law sa·*maht wa*·gif *hi*·na

Please wait here.
لو سمحت استنا هنا. law sa·*maht* is·*ta*·na *hi*·na

I'd like to hire a ...	اريد استأجر ...	a·*reed* ist·*'aj*·ir ...
4WD	سيارة فيها دبل	say·*aa*·ra *fee*·ha *da*·bal
car	سيارة	say·*aa*·ra

with ...	مع ...	ma' ...
a driver	دريول	*dray*·wil
air conditioning	كنديشان	kan·*day*·shan

How much for ... hire?	كم الإيجار ...؟	kam il·ee·*jaar* ...
daily	كل يوم	kul yawm
weekly	كل اسبوع	kul us·*boo*·a'

Is this the road to (Abu Dhabi)?
هاذا الطريق الى (ابو ظبي)؟ *haa*·dha i·ta·*reeg* i·*la* (a·*boo da*·bee)

I need a mechanic.
احتاج ميكانيك. ah·*taaj* mee·kaa·*neek*

I've run out of petrol.
ينضب البنزين. *yan*·dab al·ban·*zeen*

I have a flat tyre.
عندي بنشار. *'and*·ee *ban*·shar

Behind the Scenes

SEND US YOUR FEEDBACK

We love to hear from travellers – your comments keep us on our toes and help make our books better. Our well-travelled team reads every word on what you loved or loathed about this book. Although we cannot reply individually to your submissions, we always guarantee that your feedback goes straight to the appropriate authors, in time for the next edition. Each person who sends us information is thanked in the next edition – the most useful submissions are rewarded with a selection of digital PDF chapters.

Visit **lonelyplanet.com/contact** to submit your updates and suggestions or to ask for help. Our award-winning website also features inspirational travel stories, news and discussions.

Note: We may edit, reproduce and incorporate your comments in Lonely Planet products such as guidebooks, websites and digital products, so let us know if you don't want your comments reproduced or your name acknowledged. For a copy of our privacy policy visit lonelyplanet.com/privacy.

WRITER THANKS

Andrea Schulte-Peevers

Heartfelt thanks to all the wonderful people who so graciously and generously supplied me with insider tips, background info and insights to make my Dubai research fun and fruitful, including: Rashi, Abhi & Mia Sen, Arva Ahmed, Regine Schneider, Patricia Liebscher, Christian Sanger, Dara Toulch, Janeen Mansour, Paul Matthews, Dominic Ritzer, Sameer Dasouqi, Julia Alvaro and Katie Roberts.

Kevin Raub

Thanks to my wife, Adriana Schmidt Raub, who joined for a few days and fell unexpectedly in love with Abu Dhabi! Lauren Keith, Andrea Schulte-Peevers and all at LP. On the road, Rauda Al Falasi, Alya Al Nuaimi, Paul Oliver, Paula Carreiro, Amer Ghussein, Monique Safayan, Rianne Norbart, Ayan Alieva, Arianna Posenato, Saeed Suleiman, Sam Ioannidis and Hamad Ghanem Shaheen AlGhanem.

ACKNOWLEDGEMENTS

Cover photograph: Al Qasr Hotel with Burj Al Arab view, Jumeirah; Susanne Kremer/4Corners ©

THIS BOOK

This 9th edition of Lonely Planet's *Dubai & Abu Dhabi* guidebook was researched and written by Andrea Schulte-Peevers and Kevin Raub. The previous edition was researched and written by Andrea Schulte-Peevers and Jenny Walker. The 7th edition was written by Josephine Quintero. This guidebook was produced by the following:

Destination Editor Lauren Keith

Senior Product Editor Elizabeth Jones

Product Editor Hannah Cartmel

Senior Cartographer Valentina Kremenchutskaya

Book Designer Lauren Egan

Assisting Editors Imogen Bannister, Peter Cruttenden, Melanie Dankel, Jodie Martire, Kate Morgan, Kellie Langdon

Cover Researcher Wibowo Rusli

Thanks to Lara Brunt, Kate Chapman, Michael Hopfgarten, Anne Mason, Szilvia Nagy, Omo Osagiede, Lindsey Parry, Rachel Rawling

See also separate subindexes for:
EATING P237
DRINKING & NIGHTLIFE P238
ENTERTAINMENT P239
SHOPPING P239
SPORTS & ACTIVITIES P239
SLEEPING P240

Index

ABBREVIATIONS
AA Al Ain
AD Abu Dhabi
EC UAE East Coast
SH Sharjah

Sights 000
Map Pages **000**
Photo Pages **000**

Sights 000
Map Pages **000**
Photo Pages **000**

EATING

DRINKING & NIGHTLIFE

ENTERTAINMENT

SHOPPING

SPORTS & ACTIVITIES

SLEEPING

Dubai Maps

Sights
- Beach
- Bird Sanctuary
- Buddhist
- Castle/Palace
- Christian
- Confucian
- Hindu
- Islamic
- Jain
- Jewish
- Monument
- Museum/Gallery/Historic Building
- Ruin
- Shinto
- Sikh
- Taoist
- Winery/Vineyard
- Zoo/Wildlife Sanctuary
- Other Sight

Activities, Courses & Tours
- Bodysurfing
- Diving
- Canoeing/Kayaking
- Course/Tour
- Sento Hot Baths/Onsen
- Skiing
- Snorkelling
- Surfing
- Swimming/Pool
- Walking
- Windsurfing
- Other Activity

Sleeping
- Sleeping
- Camping
- Hut/Shelter

Eating
- Eating

Drinking & Nightlife
- Drinking & Nightlife
- Cafe

Entertainment
- Entertainment

Shopping
- Shopping

Information
- Bank
- Embassy/Consulate
- Hospital/Medical
- Internet
- Police
- Post Office
- Telephone
- Toilet
- Tourist Information
- Other Information

Geographic
- Beach
- Gate
- Hut/Shelter
- Lighthouse
- Lookout
- Mountain/Volcano
- Oasis
- Park
- Pass
- Picnic Area
- Waterfall

Population
- Capital (National)
- Capital (State/Province)
- City/Large Town
- Town/Village

Transport
- Airport
- Border crossing
- Bus
- Cable car/Funicular
- Cycling
- Ferry
- Metro station
- Monorail
- Parking
- Petrol station
- Subway station
- Taxi
- Train station/Railway
- Tram
- Underground station
- Other Transport

Routes
- Tollway
- Freeway
- Primary
- Secondary
- Tertiary
- Lane
- Unsealed road
- Road under construction
- Plaza/Mall
- Steps
- Tunnel
- Pedestrian overpass
- Walking Tour
- Walking Tour detour
- Path/Walking Trail

Boundaries
- International
- State/Province
- Disputed
- Regional/Suburb
- Marine Park
- Cliff
- Wall

Hydrography
- River, Creek
- Intermittent River
- Canal
- Water
- Dry/Salt/Intermittent Lake
- Reef

Areas
- Airport/Runway
- Beach/Desert
- Cemetery (Christian)
- Cemetery (Other)
- Glacier
- Mudflat
- Park/Forest
- Sight (Building)
- Sportsground
- Swamp/Mangrove

Note: Not all symbols displayed above appear on the maps in this book

MAP INDEX

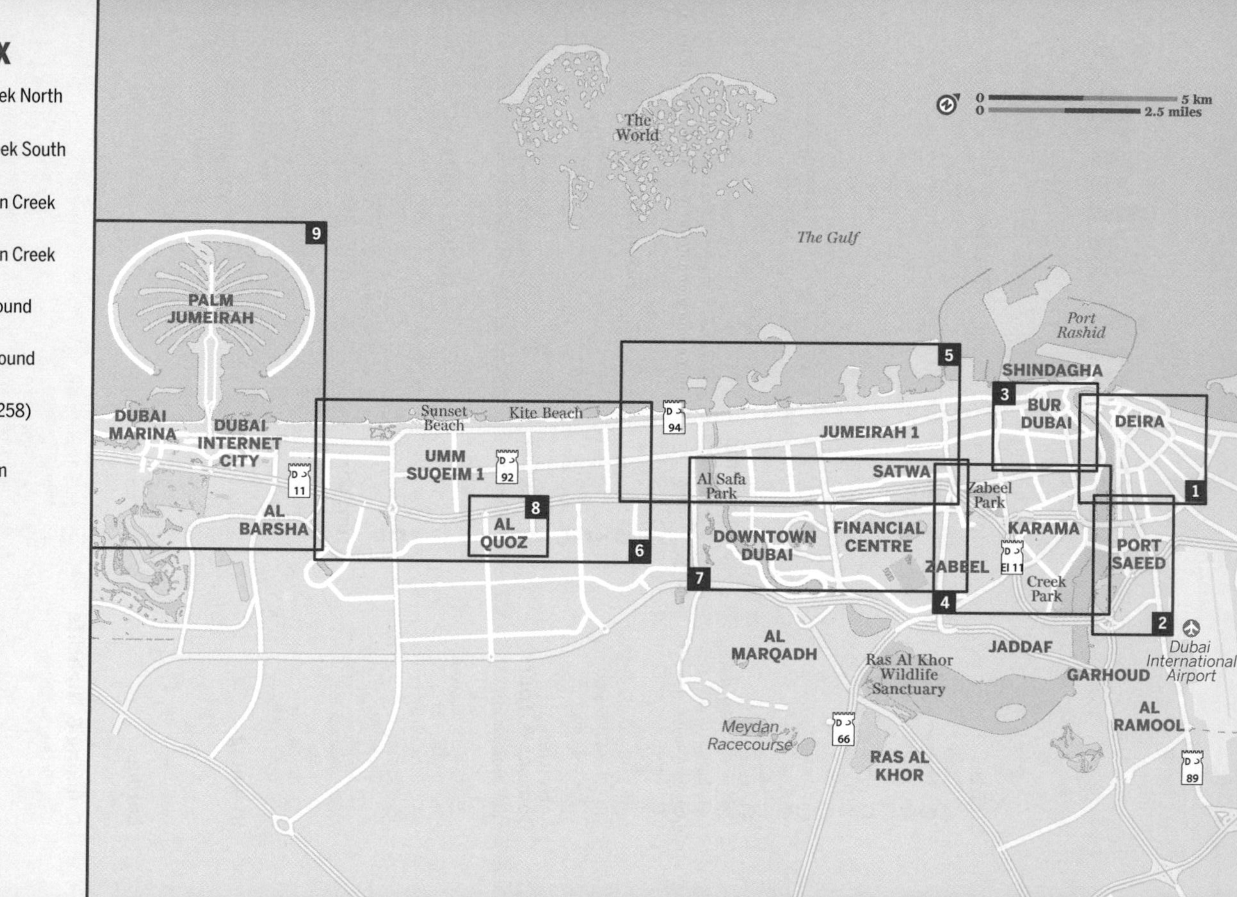

0 5 km
0 2.5 miles
The World
The Gulf
Port Rashid
SHINDAGHA
BUR DUBAI
DEIRA
PORT SAEED
KARAMA
Creek Park
Zabeel Park
ZABEEL
SATWA
JUMEIRAH 1
FINANCIAL CENTRE
DOWNTOWN DUBAI
Al Safa Park
Kite Beach
Sunset Beach
UMM SUQEIM 1
AL QUOZ
AL BARSHA
DUBAI INTERNET CITY
DUBAI MARINA
PALM JUMEIRAH
AL MARQADH
Ras Al Khor Wildlife Sanctuary
Meydan Racecourse
RAS AL KHOR
JADDAF
GARHOUD
AL RAMOOL
Dubai International Airport
94
92
11
66
89
E11
1
2
3
4
5
6
7
8
9

DEIRA & EASTERN CREEK NORTH *Map on p244*

Key on p243

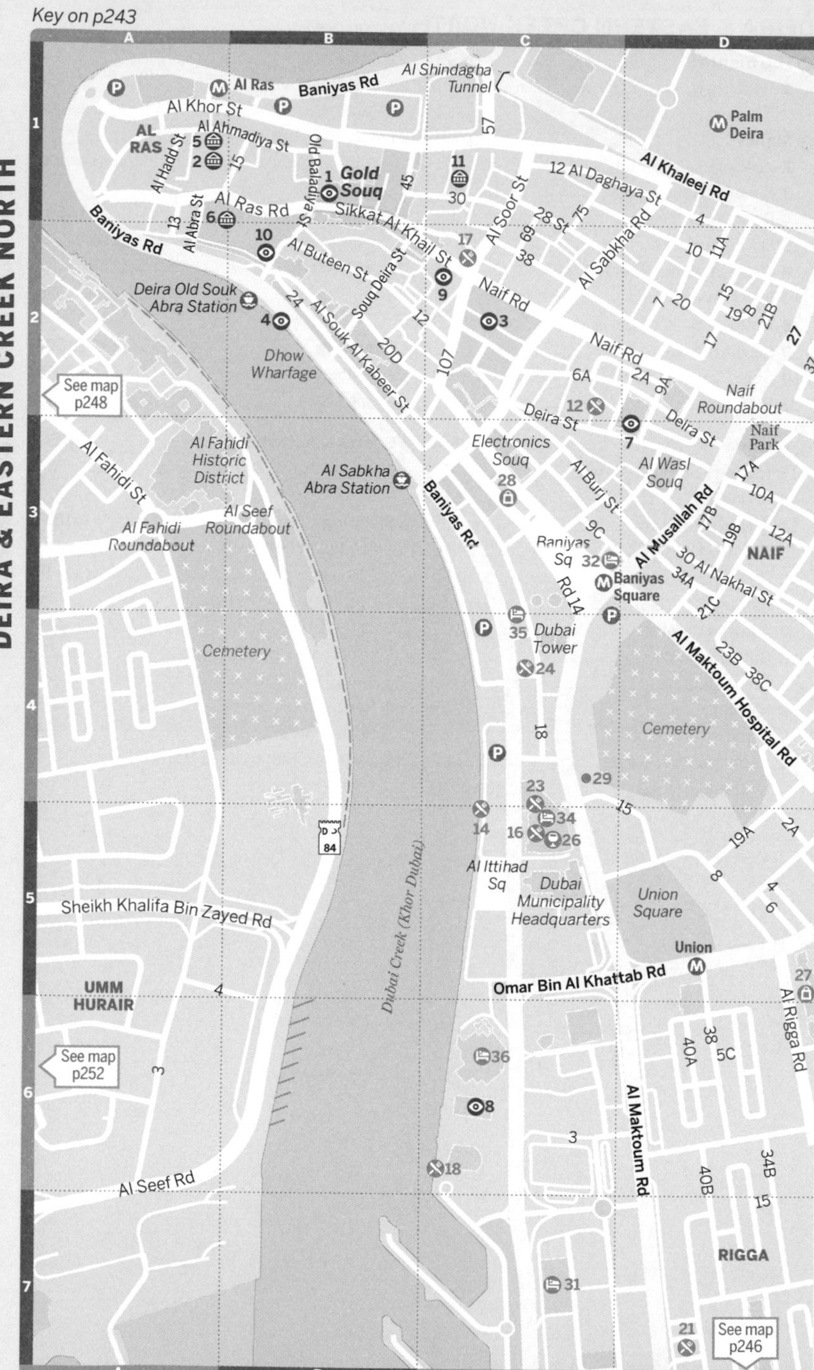

Al Ras
Baniyas Rd
Al Shindagha Tunnel
Al Khor St
Palm Deira
AL RAS
Al Ahmadiya St
Al Hadd St
Old Baladiya St
Gold Souq
Al Khaleej Rd
12 Al Daghaya St
Al Ras Rd
Al Abra St
Sikkat Al Khail St
Al Soor St
28 St
Al Sabkha Rd
Al Buteen St
Souq Deira St
Naif Rd
Deira Old Souk Abra Station
Al Souk Al Kabeer St
Dhow Wharfage
See map p248
Naif Roundabout
Deira St
Naif Park
Al Fahidi St
Al Fahidi Historic District
Electronics Souq
Al Wasl Souq
Al Sabkha Abra Station
Al Buri St
Al Seef Roundabout
Al Fahidi Roundabout
Baniyas Rd
Al Musallah Rd
Baniyas Sq
30 Al Nakhal St
NAIF
Baniyas Square
Rd 14
Dubai Tower
Al Maktoum Hospital Rd
Cemetery
Cemetery
Al Ittihad Sq
Dubai Municipality Headquarters
Union Square
Sheikh Khalifa Bin Zayed Rd
Dubai Creek (Khor Dubai)
Union
Omar Bin Al Khattab Rd
UMM HURAIR
Al Rigga Rd
See map p252
Al Maktoum Rd
Al Seef Rd
RIGGA
See map p246

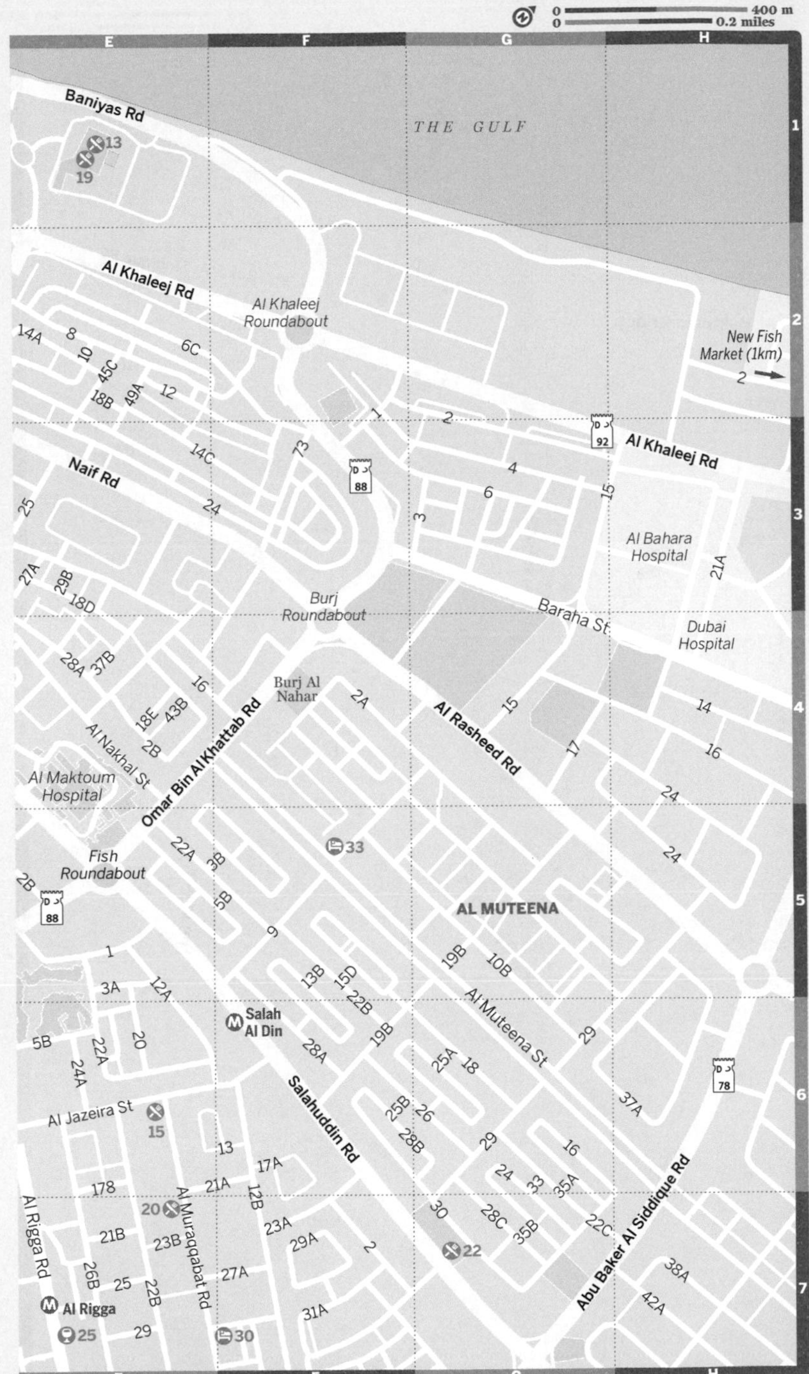

THE GULF
Baniyas Rd
Al Khaleej Rd
Al Khaleej Roundabout
New Fish Market (1km)
Naif Rd
Al Bahara Hospital
Burj Roundabout
Baraha St
Dubai Hospital
Burj Al Nahar
Al Rasheed Rd
Omar Bin Al Khattab Rd
Al Nakhal St
Al Maktoum Hospital
Fish Roundabout
AL MUTEENA
Al Muteena St
Salah Al Din
Salahuddin Rd
Al Jazeira St
Al Muraqqabat Rd
Al Rigga Rd
Al Rigga
Abu Baker Al Siddique Rd

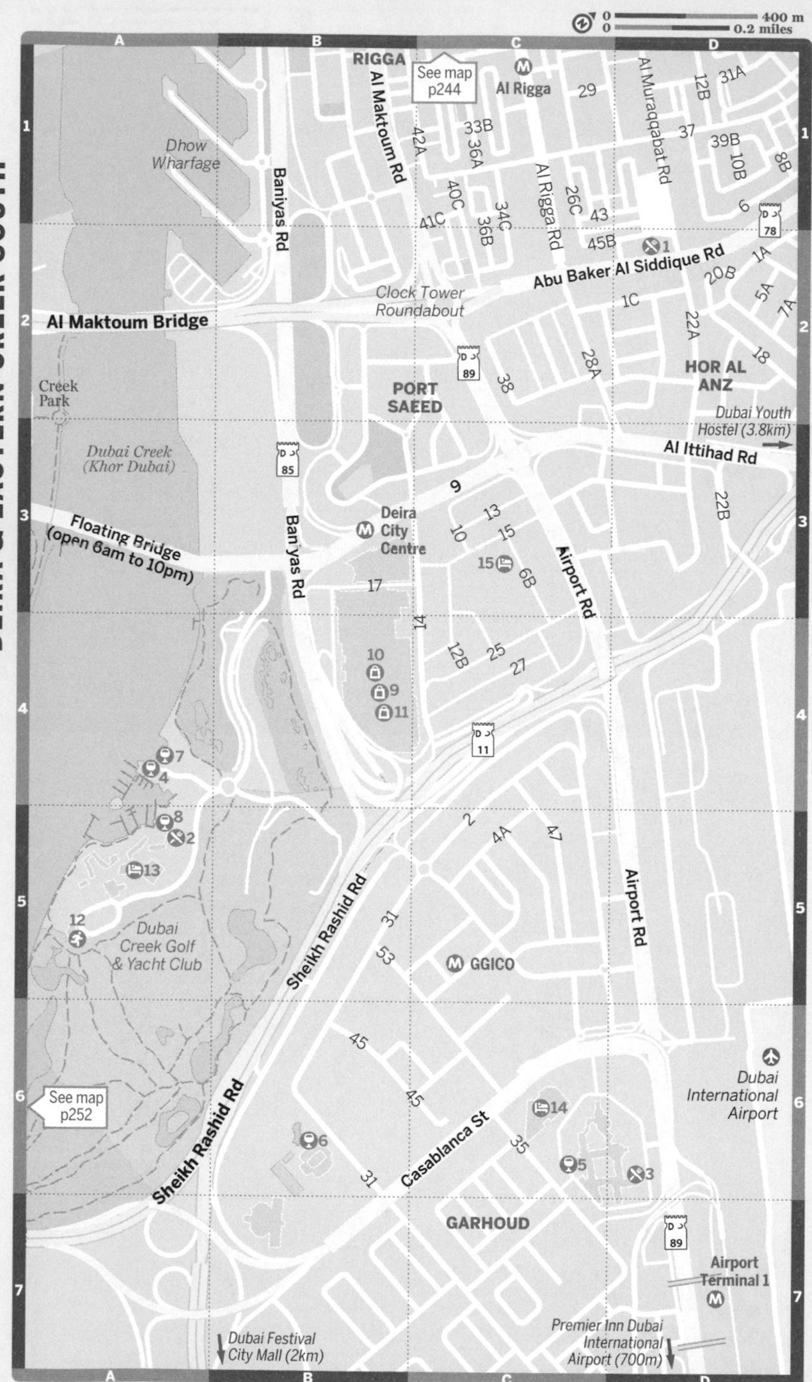

0 400 m
0 0.2 miles
RIGGA
See map p244
Al Rigga
Dhow Wharfage
Baniyas Rd
Al Maktoum Rd
Al Rigga Rd
Al Muraqqabat Rd
Abu Baker Al Siddique Rd
Clock Tower Roundabout
Al Maktoum Bridge
Creek Park
PORT SAEED
HOR AL ANZ
Dubai Youth Hostel (3.8km)
Al Ittihad Rd
Dubai Creek (Khor Dubai)
Floating Bridge (open 6am to 10pm)
Deira City Centre
Airport Rd
Sheikh Rashid Rd
Dubai Creek Golf & Yacht Club
GGICO
See map p252
Casablanca St
Dubai International Airport
GARHOUD
Airport Terminal 1
Dubai Festival City Mall (2km)
Premier Inn Dubai International Airport (700m)

DEIRA & EASTERN CREEK SOUTH

Key on p250

BUR DUBAI & WESTERN CREEK NORTH

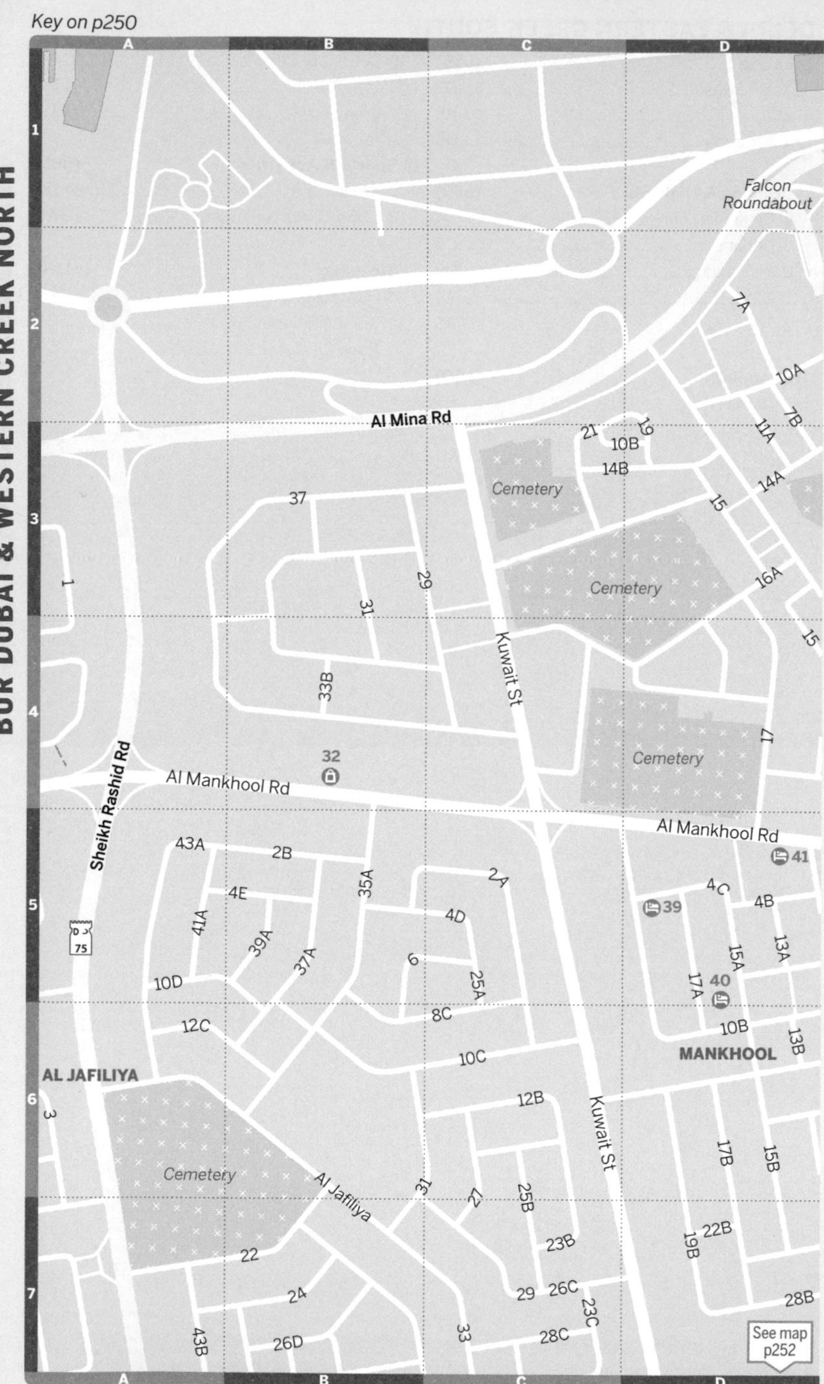

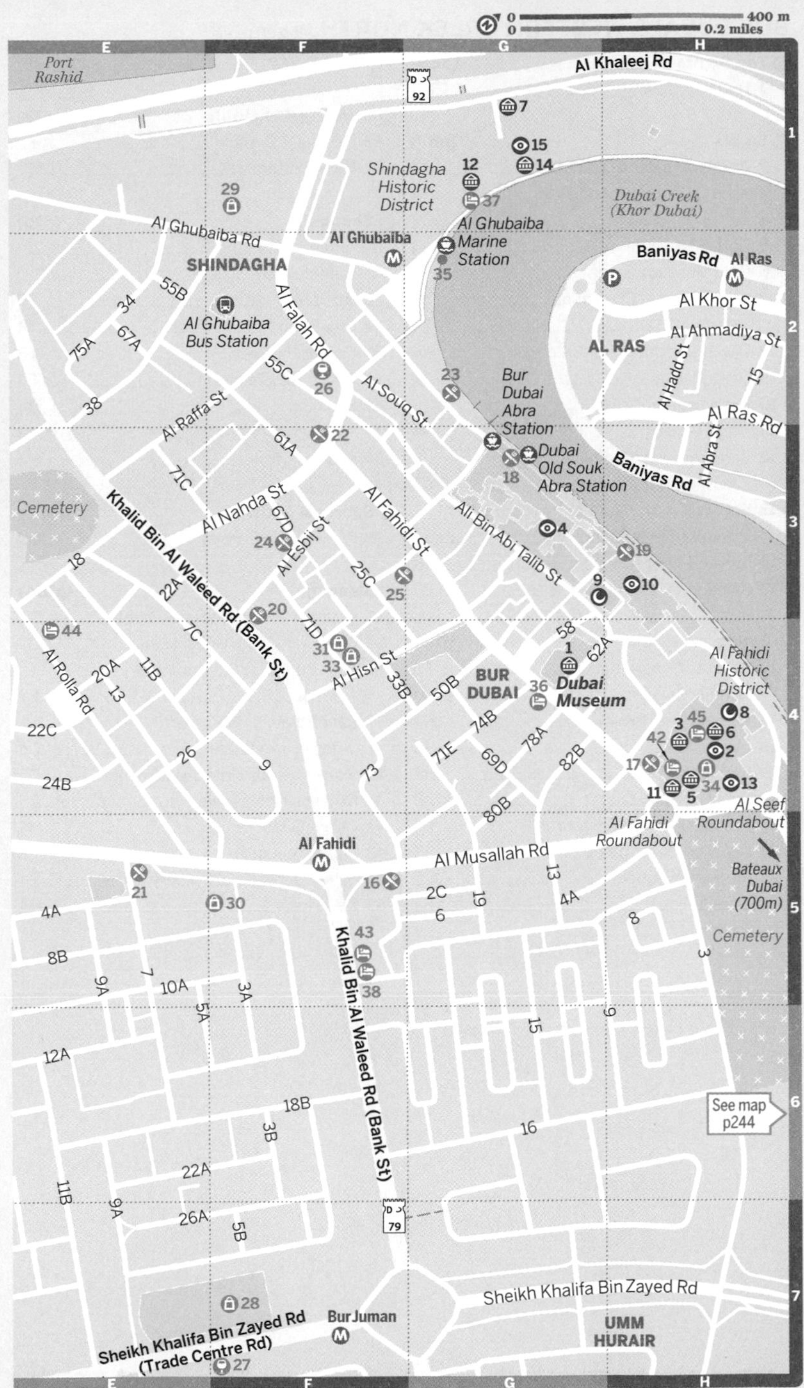

0 400 m
0 0.2 miles
Port Rashid
Al Khaleej Rd
Shindagha Historic District
Dubai Creek (Khor Dubai)
Al Ghubaiba Rd
Al Ghubaiba
SHINDAGHA
Al Ghubaiba Marine Station
Baniyas Rd
Al Ras
Al Khor St
Al Ghubaiba Bus Station
Al Falah Rd
Al Ahmadiya St
AL RAS
Al Hadd St
Al Souq St
Bur Dubai Abra Station
Al Raffa St
Al Ras Rd
Dubai Old Souk Abra Station
Al Abra St
Baniyas Rd
Cemetery
Khalid Bin Al Waleed Rd (Bank St)
Al Nahda St
Al Fahidi St
Al Esbij St
Ali Bin Abi Talib St
Al Rolla Rd
Al Hisn St
BUR DUBAI
Dubai Museum
Al Fahidi Historic District
Al Seef Roundabout
Al Fahidi Roundabout
Al Fahidi
Al Musallah Rd
Bateaux Dubai (700m)
Cemetery
Khalid Bin Al Waleed Rd (Bank St)
See map p244
Sheikh Khalifa Bin Zayed Rd
Burjuman
UMM HURAIR
Sheikh Khalifa Bin Zayed Rd (Trade Centre Rd)
BUR DUBAI & WESTERN CREEK NORTH

BUR DUBAI & WESTERN CREEK NORTH *Map on p248*

Top Sights (p66)
1 Dubai Museum G4

Sights (p67)
2 Al Fahidi Historic District H4
3 Alserkal Cultural Foundation H4
4 Bur Dubai Souq G3
5 Coffee Museum H4
6 Coin Museum H4
7 Crossroads of Civilizations Museum G1
8 Diwan Mosque H4
9 Grand Mosque G3
10 Hindi Lane H3
11 Majlis Gallery H4
12 Saruq Al Hadid Archaeology Museum G1
13 Sheikh Mohammed Centre for Cultural Understanding H4
14 Sheikh Saeed Al Maktoum House G1
15 Shindagha Historic District G1

Eating (p70)
16 Al Ustad Special Kabab F5
Antique Bazaar ..... (see 38)
17 Arabian Tea House H4
18 Bait Al Wakeel G3
19 Creekside Cafe H3
20 Kabul Darbar F3
21 Lebanese Village Restaurant E5
22 Nepaliko Sagarmatha F3
23 Saravana Bhavan G2
24 Sind Punjab F3
25 Vaibhav F3
XVA Café ..... (see 45)

Drinking & Nightlife (p73)
26 George & Dragon F2
27 Rock Bottom Café F7

Shopping (p75)
Ajmal ..... (see 28)
Bateel ..... (see 28)
28 BurJuman F7
29 City Centre Al Shindagha F1
30 Computer Plaza F5
31 Dream Girl Tailors F4
32 Fabindia B4
33 Hollywood Tailors F4
34 Royal Saffron H4

Sports & Activities (p69)
35 Dubai Ferry Cruises G2

Sleeping (p184)
36 Arabian Courtyard Hotel & Spa G4
37 Barjeel Heritage Guest House G1
38 Four Points by Sheraton Bur Dubai F5
39 Four Points by Sheraton Downtown Dubai D5
40 Golden Sands Hotel Apartments D5
41 Majestic Hotel Tower D5
42 Orient Guest House H4
43 Rainbow Hotel F5
44 Savoy Central Hotel Apartments E4
45 XVA Hotel H4

BUR DUBAI & WESTERN CREEK SOUTH *Map on p252*

Sights (p67)

1 Children's City G6
2 Creek Park G6
3 Dubai Frame C3
4 Wafi City D6
5 Zabeel Park C2

Eating (p70)

6 Asha's E6
7 Awtar E7
Chutneys ..... (see 23)
8 Eric's F2
9 Govinda's F1
10 Hot Fish D2
11 Jaffer Bhai's F2
12 Jambo's Grill F2
13 Karachi Darbar E2
14 Khazana E4
15 Lemongrass D4
16 Pars A1
Peppercrab ..... (see 17)
Tomo ..... (see 24)

Drinking & Nightlife (p73)

17 Cooz E7

Entertainment (p75)

18 Movies under the Stars E6

Shopping (p75)

19 Dubai Flea Market C2
20 Karama Market D3
21 Ripe Market C2
The One ..... (see 22)
22 Wafi Mall E6

Sports & Activities (p78)

Pharaohs' Club ..... (see 18)

Sleeping (p184)

23 Mövenpick Hotel & Apartments Bur Dubai E4
24 Raffles Dubai E6

Key on p251

BUR DUBAI & WESTERN CREEK SOUTH

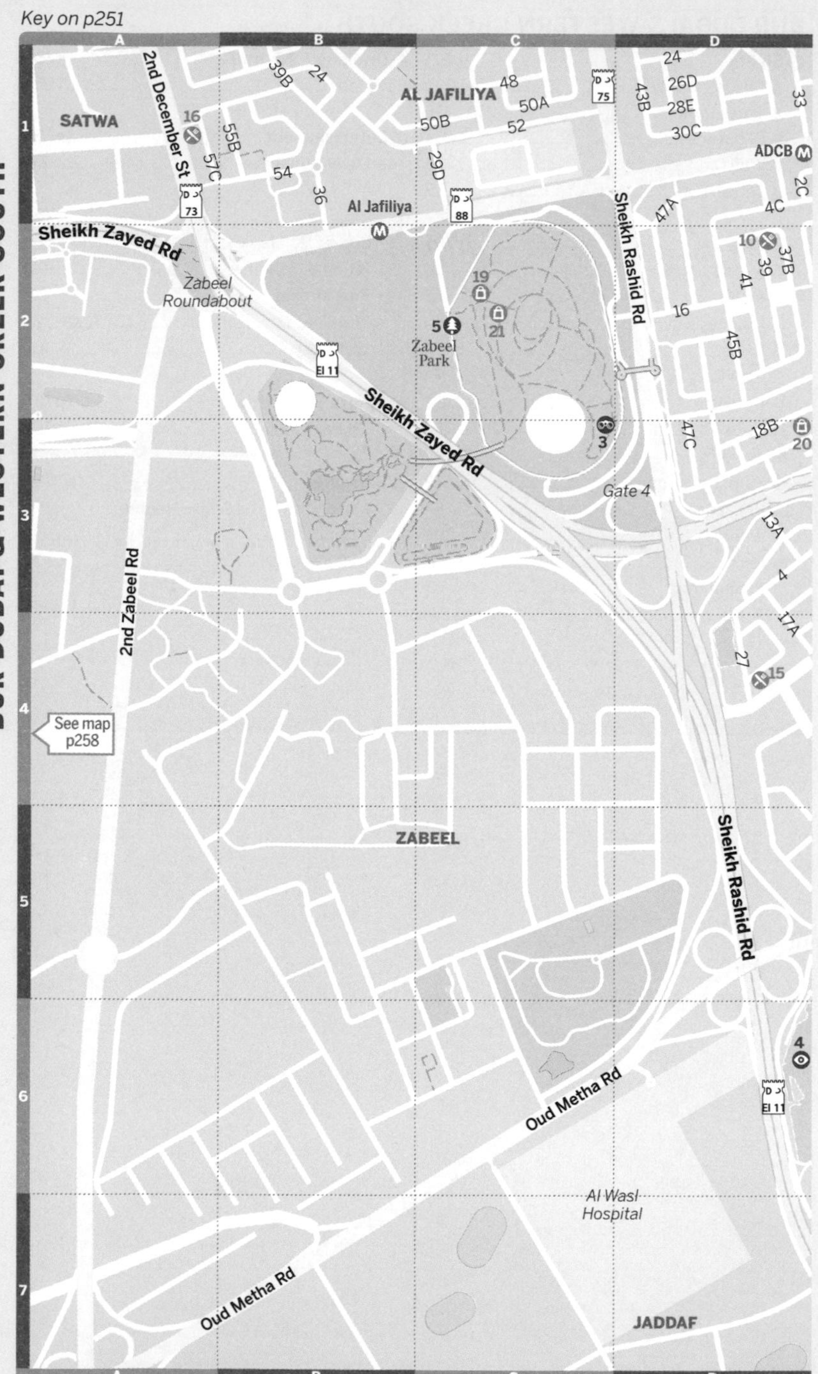

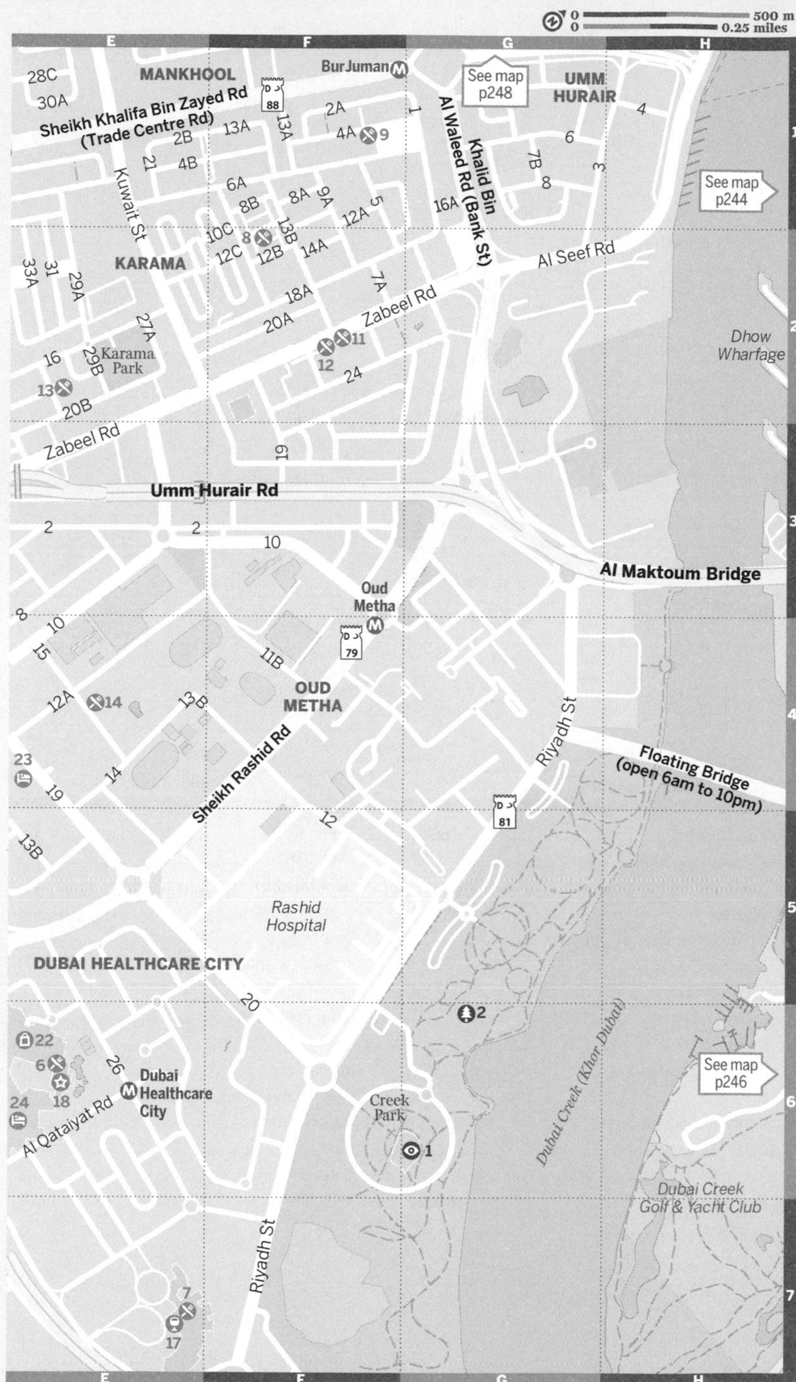

0 500 m
0 0.25 miles
MANKHOOL
UMM HURAIR
KARAMA
OUD METHA
DUBAI HEALTHCARE CITY
BurJuman
Sheikh Khalifa Bin Zayed Rd (Trade Centre Rd)
Khalid Bin Al Waleed Rd (Bank St)
Kuwait St
Al Seef Rd
Zabeel Rd
Umm Hurair Rd
Al Maktoum Bridge
Floating Bridge (open 6am to 10pm)
Riyadh St
Sheikh Rashid Rd
Al Qataiyat Rd
Karama Park
Dhow Wharfage
Oud Metha
Rashid Hospital
Dubai Healthcare City
Creek Park
Dubai Creek (Khor Dubai)
Dubai Creek Golf & Yacht Club
See map p248
See map p244
See map p246

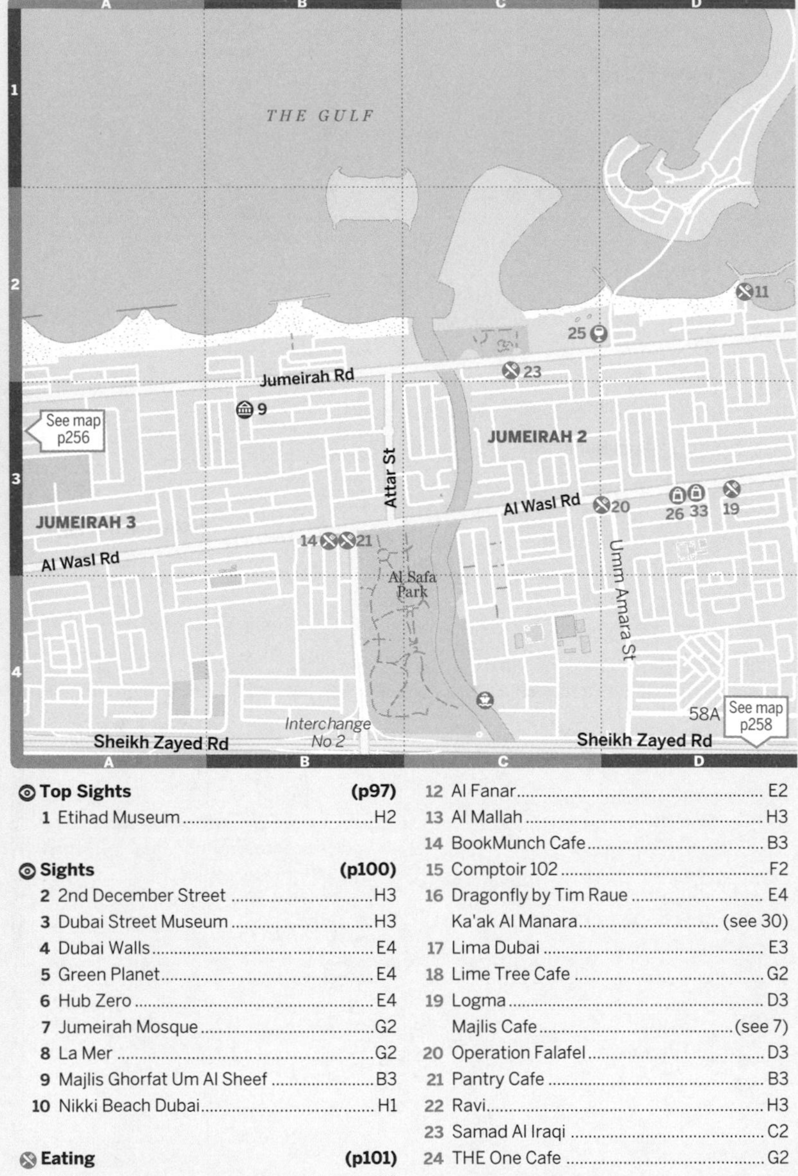

Top Sights (p97)

1 Etihad Museum H2

Sights (p100)

2 2nd December Street H3
3 Dubai Street Museum H3
4 Dubai Walls E4
5 Green Planet E4
6 Hub Zero E4
7 Jumeirah Mosque G2
8 La Mer G2
9 Majlis Ghorfat Um Al Sheef B3
10 Nikki Beach Dubai H1

Eating (p101)

11 3 Fils D2
12 Al Fanar E2
13 Al Mallah H3
14 BookMunch Cafe B3
15 Comptoir 102 F2
16 Dragonfly by Tim Raue E4
Ka'ak Al Manara (see 30)
17 Lima Dubai E3
18 Lime Tree Cafe G2
19 Logma D3
Majlis Cafe (see 7)
20 Operation Falafel D3
21 Pantry Cafe B3
22 Ravi H3
23 Samad Al Iraqi C2
24 THE One Cafe G2

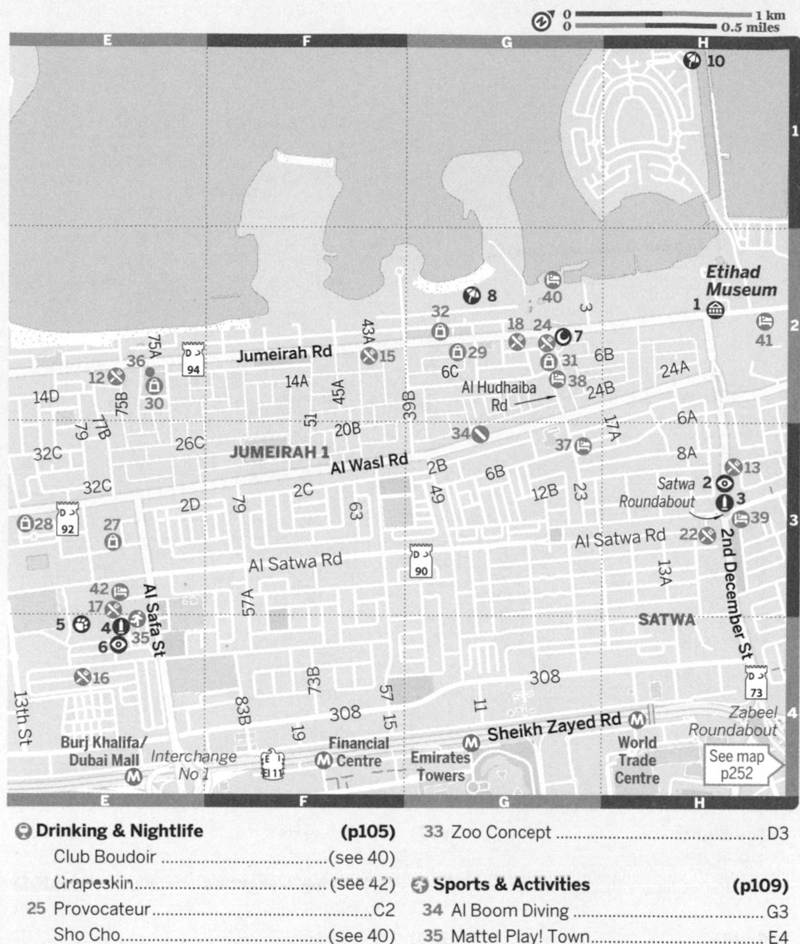

Drinking & Nightlife (p105)

- Club Boudoir ....(see 40)
- Grapeskin ....(see 42)
- 25 Provocateur C2
- Sho Cho ....(see 40)

Shopping (p107)

- 26 BoxPark D3
- 27 City Walk E3
- 28 Galleria Mall E3
- 29 House of Prose G2
- 30 Mercato Shopping Mall E2
- 31 O Concept G2
- 32 S*uce G2
- Typo ....(see 26)
- Urbanist ....(see 26)
- 33 Zoo Concept D3

Sports & Activities (p109)

- 34 Al Boom Diving G3
- 35 Mattel Play! Town E4
- 36 Wonder Bus Tours E2

Sleeping (p188)

- 37 Al Khoory Executive Hotel G3
- 38 Beach Hotel Apartment G2
- 39 Chelsea Plaza Hotel H3
- 40 Dubai Marine Beach Resort & Spa G2
- 41 Holiday Inn Express H2
- 42 La Ville Hotel & Suites E3

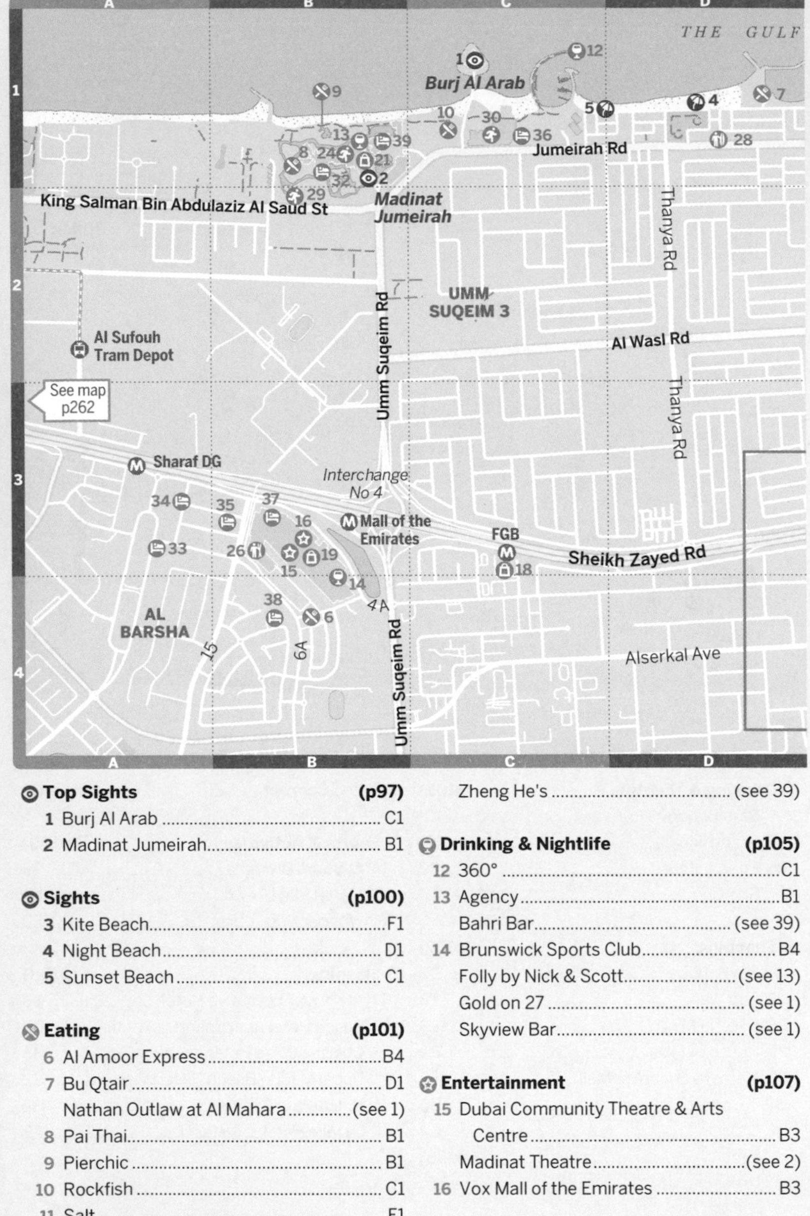

Top Sights (p97)

1 Burj Al Arab ... C1
2 Madinat Jumeirah ... B1

Sights (p100)

3 Kite Beach ... F1
4 Night Beach ... D1
5 Sunset Beach ... C1

Eating (p101)

6 Al Amoor Express ... B4
7 Bu Qtair ... D1
Nathan Outlaw at Al Mahara ... (see 1)
8 Pai Thai ... B1
9 Pierchic ... B1
10 Rockfish ... C1
11 Salt ... F1
Zheng He's ... (see 39)

Drinking & Nightlife (p105)

12 360° ... C1
13 Agency ... B1
Bahri Bar ... (see 39)
14 Brunswick Sports Club ... B4
Folly by Nick & Scott ... (see 13)
Gold on 27 ... (see 1)
Skyview Bar ... (see 1)

Entertainment (p107)

15 Dubai Community Theatre & Arts Centre ... B3
Madinat Theatre ... (see 2)
16 Vox Mall of the Emirates ... B3

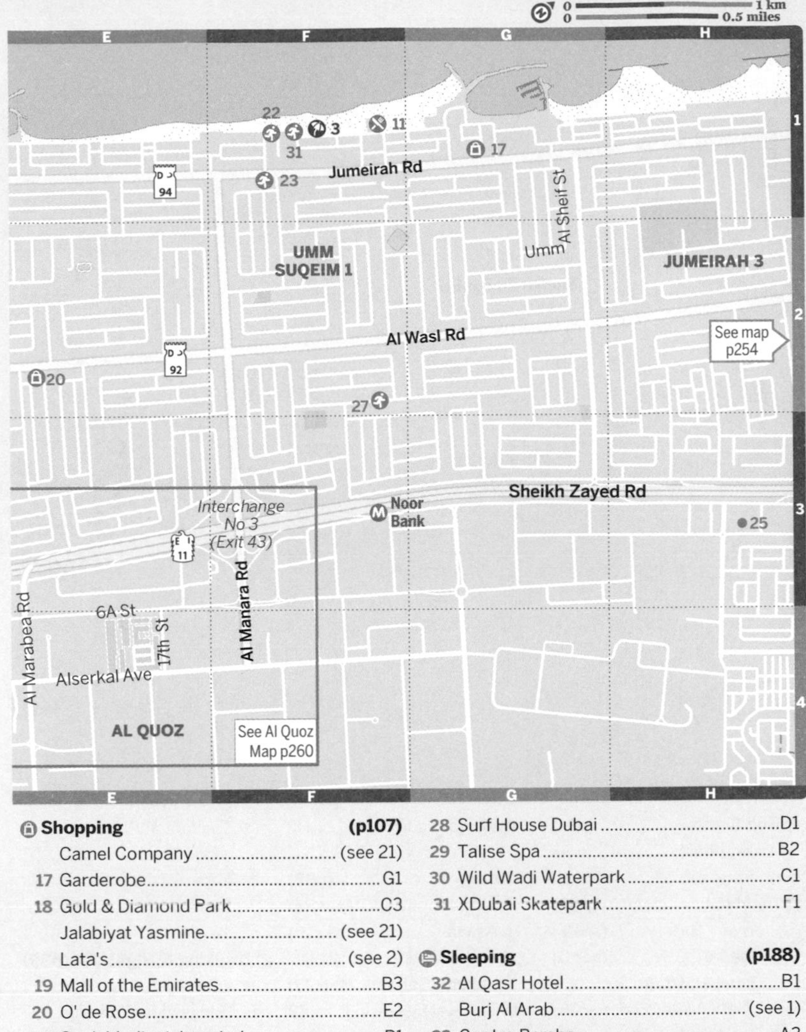

Shopping (p107)

Camel Company .... (see 21)
17 Garderobe G1
18 Gold & Diamond Park C3
Jalabiyat Yasmine .... (see 21)
Lata's .... (see 2)
19 Mall of the Emirates B3
20 O' de Rose E2
21 Souk Madinat Jumeirah B1

Sports & Activities (p109)

22 Dubai Kitesurfing School F1
23 Dukite F1
24 Madinat Jumeirah Abra Rides B1
25 Platinum Heritage Tours H3
26 Ski Dubai B3
27 Splash 'n' Party F2
28 Surf House Dubai D1
29 Talise Spa B2
30 Wild Wadi Waterpark C1
31 XDubai Skatepark F1

Sleeping (p188)

32 Al Qasr Hotel B1
Burj Al Arab .... (see 1)
33 Centro Barsha A3
34 Donatello Hotel A3
35 Ibis Mall of the Emirates B3
36 Jumeirah Beach Hotel C1
37 Kempinski Hotel Mall of the Emirates B3
38 La Villa Najd Hotel Apartments B4
39 Mina A'Salam Hotel B1

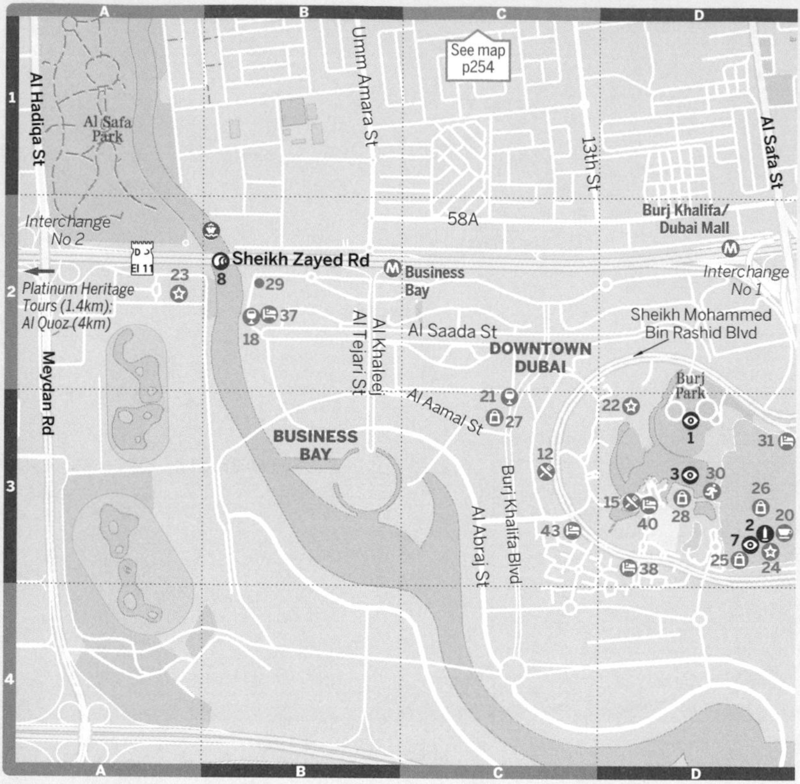

Top Sights (p81)

1 Burj Khalifa D3

Sights (p82)

Ayyam Gallery ....(see 6)
Cuadro ....(see 6)
Dubai Aquarium & Underwater Zoo(see 26)
2 Dubai Dino D3
3 Dubai Fountain.............. D3
4 Dubai International Financial Centre..........F2
5 Empty Quarter F2
6 Gate Village......................F2
7 KidZania D3
8 Sheikh Zayed Bridge Waterfall....................... B2
9 World Trade Centre...... H2

Eating (p85)

Al Nafoorah.......... (see 36)
Asado .... (see 15)
At.mosphere........... (see 1)
Baker & Spice...... (see 28)
10 Carnival by Tresind........F2
Eataly.................... (see 26)
11 Hoi An............................ E1
Karma Kafé.......... (see 28)
12 Leila C3
Milas .... (see 24)
13 Noodle House................F2
14 Sum of Us H1
The Daily .... (see 41)
15 Thiptara at Palace Downtown................... D3
16 Zaroob..............................F2
Zuma ....(see 6)

Drinking & Nightlife (p89)

17 40 Kong...........................H1
18 Bridgewater Tavern...... B2
Cabana .... (see 31)
Cavalli Club.......... (see 34)
Cirque Le Soir...... (see 34)
19 Fibber Magee's...............G1
20 Majlis D3
Nippon Bottle Company........... (see 33)
21 Treehouse....................... C3

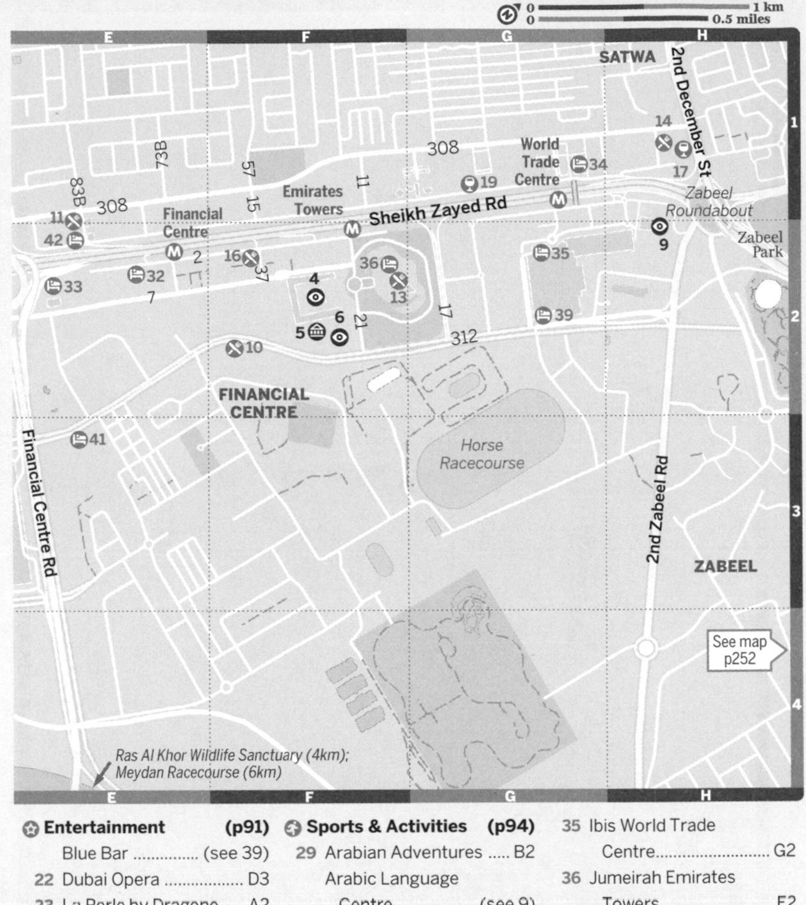

Entertainment **(p91)**

Blue Bar .... (see 39)
22 Dubai Opera D3
23 La Perle by Dragone A2
24 Reel Cinemas D3

Shopping **(p92)**

25 Balqees Honey D3
Candylicious .... (see 26)
26 Dubai Mall D3
27 Farmers Market on the Terrace C3
Kinokuniya .... (see 26)
Nayomi .... (see 26)
28 Souk Al Bahar D3

Sports & Activities **(p94)**

29 Arabian Adventures B2
Arabic Language Centre .... (see 9)
30 Dubai Fountain Lake Ride D3
Dubai Ice Rink...... (see 24)
Spa at Palace Downtown .... (see 15)
Talise Spa .... (see 36)

Sleeping **(p186)**

31 Address Dubai Mall D3
32 Carlton Downtown E2
33 Dusit Thani Dubai E2
34 Fairmont Dubai G1
35 Ibis World Trade Centre G2
36 Jumeirah Emirates Towers F2
37 JW Marriott Marquis Hotel Dubai B2
38 Manzil Downtown D3
39 Novotel World Trade Centre G2
40 Palace Downtown D3
41 Rove Downtown E3
42 Shangri-La E2
43 Vida Downtown Dubai .. C3

AL QUOZ

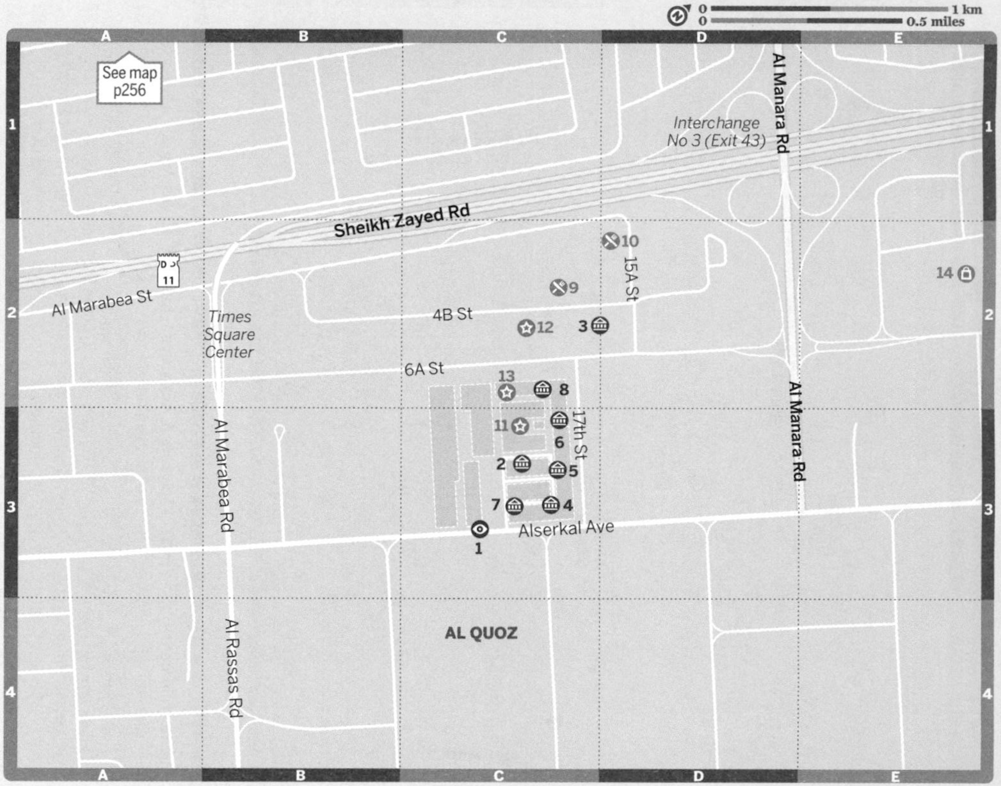

Sights (p84)

1	Alserkal Avenue	C3
2	Carbon 12	C3
3	Cartoon Art Gallery	C2
4	Gallery Isabelle van den Eynde	C3
5	Green Art Gallery	C3
6	Leila Heller Gallery	C3
7	Salsali Private Museum	C3
8	The Third Line	C2

Eating (p89)

9	Lime Tree Cafe	C2
10	Tom & Serg	D2

Entertainment (p91)

11	Cinema Akil	C3
12	Courtyard Playhouse	C2
	Fridge	(see 5)
13	The Junction	C2

Shopping (p92)

	Mirzam Chocolate Makers	(see 13)
14	Raw Coffee Company	E2

DUBAI MARINA & PALM JUMEIRAH *Map on p262*

Sights (p113)

1 Ain Dubai C4
2 Cayan Tower E5
3 Club Mina E5
4 Fairmont The Palm Beach Club F4
5 JBR Beach C5
6 Lost Chambers Aquarium F1
7 Pier 7 .... D5
8 The Beach at JBR C5
9 The Walk at JBR D5

Eating (p114)

101 Lounge & Bar .... (see 60)
Al Khaima .... (see 56)
Al Nafoorah .... (see 54)
Asia Asia .... (see 7)
10 Barracuda D5
11 BiCE D5
Blue Orange .... (see 64)
12 Bouchon Bakery C5
13 Couqley C6
14 Eauzone F5
15 El Chiringuito G4
Fish Beach Taverna .... (see 23)
Fümé .... (see 7)
Indego by Vineet .... (see 53)
Little Miss India .... (see 4)
16 Massaad Barbecue C5
17 Maya Modern Mexican Kitchen D5
18 Mythos Kouzina & Grill D6
Rhodes W1 .... (see 53)
Stay .... (see 60)
Sushi Art .... (see 8)
Tagine .... (see 59)
The Croft .... (see 28)
19 Toro Toro E5
Zafran .... (see 50)
20 Zero Gravity D5

Drinking & Nightlife (p119)

Arabian Courtyard .... (see 30)
Atelier M .... (see 7)
Barasti .... (see 64)
21 Bliss Lounge C5
Buddha Bar .... (see 53)
22 Casa Latina H6
Dek on 8 .... (see 58)
23 Industrial Avenue E5
24 Jetty Lounge F5
Lock, Stock & Barrel .... (see 25)
25 Lucky Voice G6
26 N'Dulge F1
27 Nola Eatery & Social House D6
28 Observatory E5
Pure Sky Lounge .... (see 11)
29 Reem Al Bawadi E5
30 Rooftop Lounge & Terrace F5
Siddharta Lounge .... (see 53)
Smoky Beach .... (see 8)
31 Stereo Arcade C5
32 Tamanya Terrace F5
33 Tap House F3
34 Tribeca C5

Entertainment (p122)

35 Jazz@PizzaExpress C6
36 MusicHall E3

Shopping (p123)

37 Dubai Marina Mall D5
38 Gallery One D5
Ginger & Lace .... (see 39)
39 Ibn Battuta Mall A6

Sports & Activities (p124)

40 Aqua Fun C5
41 Aquaventure Waterpark F1
42 Atlantis Abra Ride F1
43 Beach Gym C5
44 Dhow Cruise D5
Dubai Ferry Cruises .... (see 10)
45 Dubai Marina Water Bus D5
One&Only Spa .... (see 59)
46 Palm Jumeirah Boardwalk G1
47 Skydive Dubai E4
48 Splash Pad C5
49 Yoga by the Sea C5

Sleeping (p190)

50 Address Dubai Marina D5
51 Gloria Hotel G6
52 Grand Midwest Tower G6
53 Grosvenor House D5
54 Jumeirah Zabeel Saray D3
55 Le Meridien Mina Seyahi Beach Resort & Marina E5
56 Le Royal Meridien Beach Resort & Spa D5
57 Marina Dream Hostel C5
58 Media One Hotel E5
59 One&Only Royal Mirage E5
60 One&Only The Palm E4
61 Pearl Marina Hotel Apartments C5
62 Ritz-Carlton Dubai D5
63 Rixos Premium Dubai D5
64 Westin Dubai Mina Seyahi Beach Resort & Marina E5

Key on p261

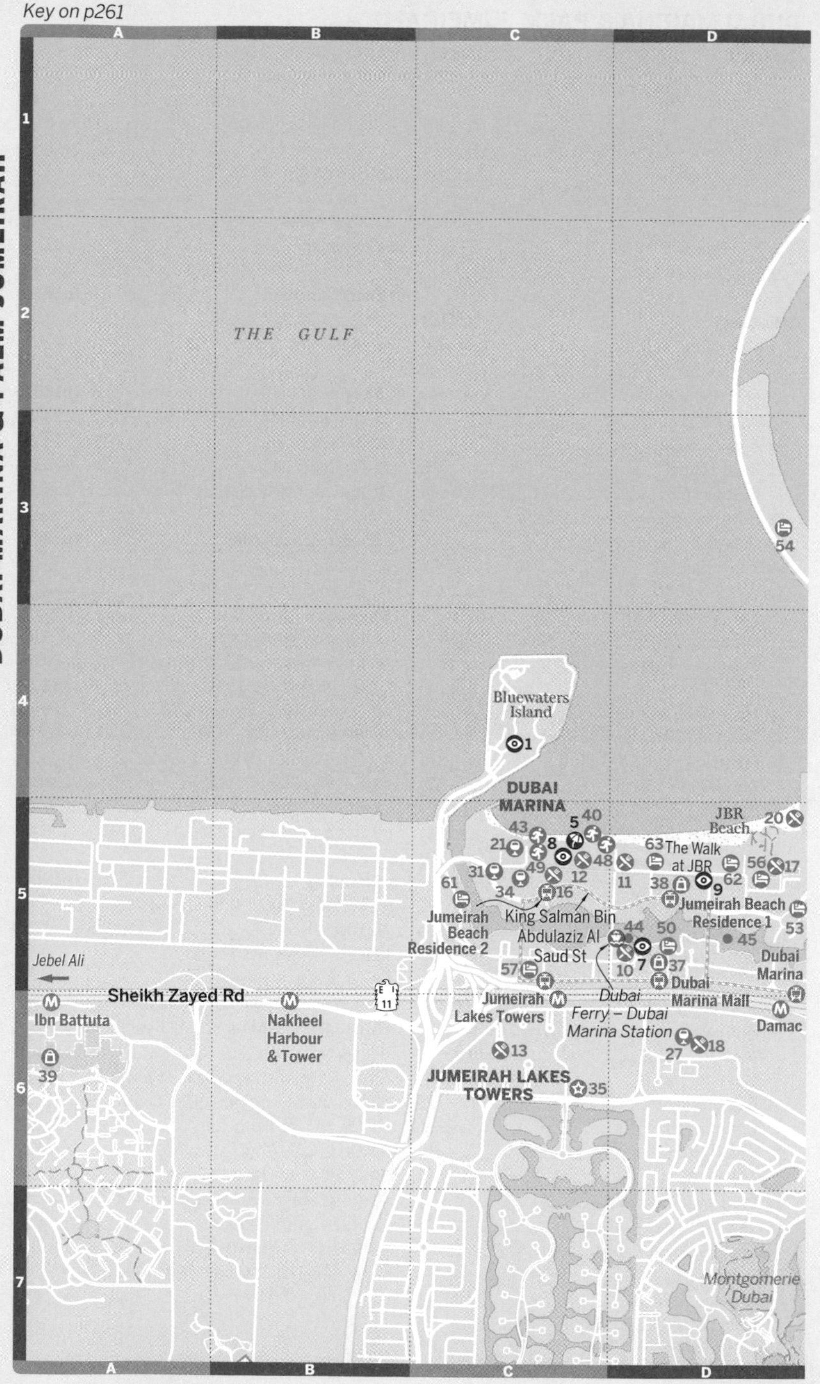
A
B
C
D
1
2
3
4
5
6
7
THE GULF
54
Bluewaters Island
1
DUBAI MARINA
5
40
43
JBR Beach
20
21
8
63
The Walk at JBR
48
56
17
31
49
12
11
38
9
62
61
34
16
Jumeirah Beach Residence 1
Jumeirah Beach Residence 2
King Salman Bin Abdulaziz Al Saud St
44
50
45
53
10
7
37
Dubai Marina
Jebel Ali
57
Dubai Marina Mall
Sheikh Zayed Rd
Jumeirah Lakes Towers
Dubai Ferry – Dubai Marina Station
Damac
Ibn Battuta
Nakheel Harbour & Tower
E 11
27
18
13
39
JUMEIRAH LAKES TOWERS
35
Montgomerie Dubai

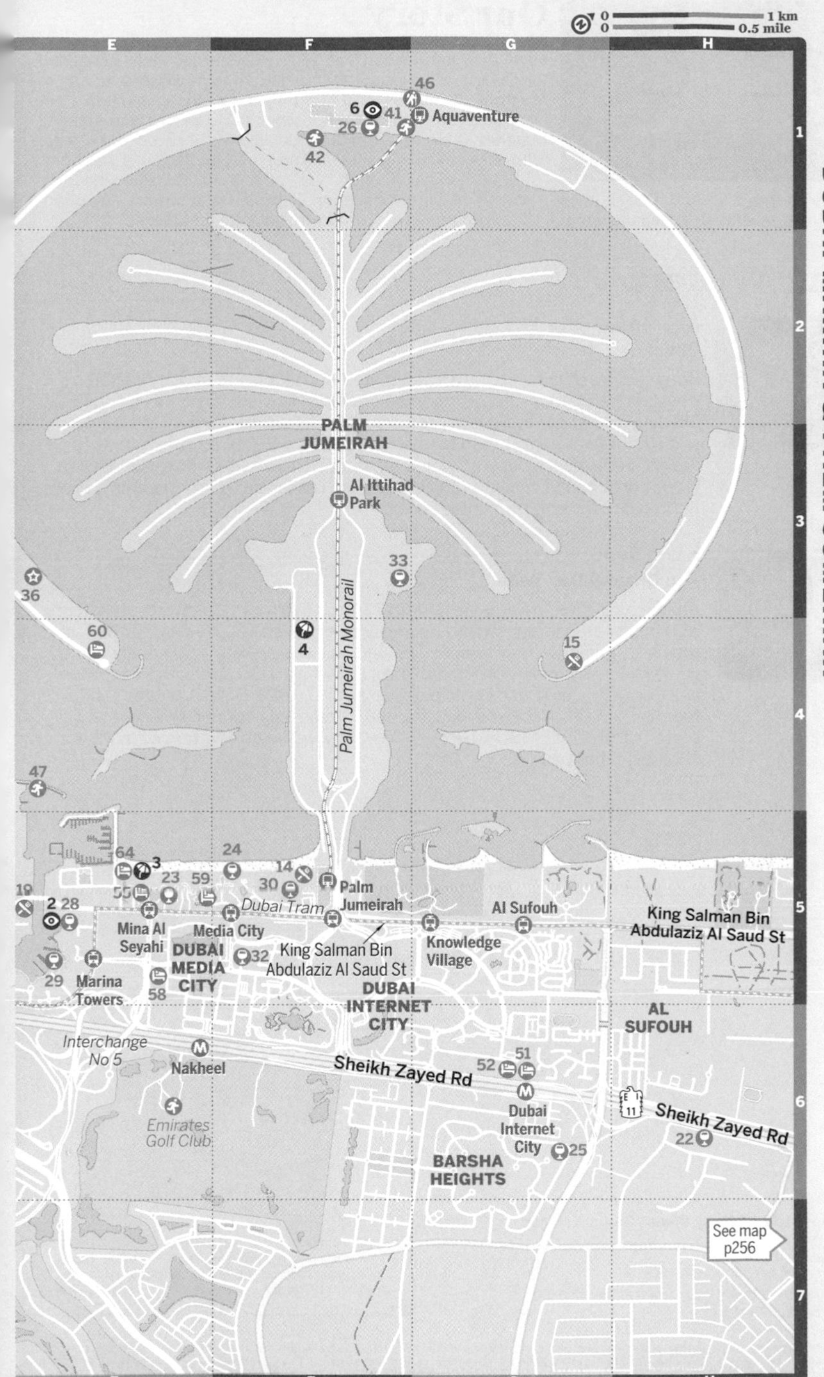

0 1 km
0 0.5 mile
E
F
G
H
1
2
3
4
5
6
7
DUBAI MARINA & PALM JUMEIRAH
46
6
41
Aquaventure
26
42
PALM JUMEIRAH
Al Ittihad Park
33
36
60
4
Palm Jumeirah Monorail
15
47
64
3
24
14
23
59
30
55
Palm Jumeirah
19
2
28
Dubai Tram
Al Sufouh
King Salman Bin Abdulaziz Al Saud St
Mina Al Seyahi
Media City
Knowledge Village
DUBAI MEDIA CITY
32
King Salman Bin Abdulaziz Al Saud St
29
Marina Towers
58
DUBAI INTERNET CITY
AL SUFOUH
Interchange No 5
Nakheel
Sheikh Zayed Rd
51
52
Dubai Internet City
E 11
Sheikh Zayed Rd
22
Emirates Golf Club
25
BARSHA HEIGHTS
See map p256

Our Story

A beat-up old car, a few dollars in the pocket and a sense of adventure. In 1972 that's all Tony and Maureen Wheeler needed for the trip of a lifetime – across Europe and Asia overland to Australia. It took several months, and at the end – broke but inspired – they sat at their kitchen table writing and stapling together their first travel guide, *Across Asia on the Cheap*. Within a week they'd sold 1500 copies. Lonely Planet was born.

Today, Lonely Planet has offices in Franklin, London, Melbourne, Oakland, Dublin, Beijing and Delhi, with more than 600 staff and writers. We share Tony's belief that 'a great guidebook should do three things: inform, educate and amuse'.

Our Writers

Andrea Schulte-Peevers

Dubai

Born and raised in Germany and educated in London and at UCLA, Andrea has travelled the distance to the moon and back in her visits to some 75 countries. She has earned her living as a professional travel writer for over two decades and authored or contributed to nearly 100 Lonely Planet titles as well as to newspapers, magazines and websites around the world. She also works as a travel consultant, translator and editor. She makes her home in Berlin. Follow Andrea on Twitter @ASchultePeevers.

Kevin Raub

Abu Dhabi & Day Trips

Atlanta native Kevin Raub started his career as a music journalist in New York, working for *Men's Journal* and *Rolling Stone* magazines. He ditched the rock 'n' roll lifestyle for travel writing and has written nearly 50 Lonely Planet guides, focused mainly on Brazil, Chile, Colombia, USA, India, the Caribbean and Portugal. Kevin also contributes to a variety of travel magazines in both the USA and UK. Along the way, the self-confessed hophead is in constant search of wildly high IBUs in local beers. Follow him on Twitter and Instagram @RaubOnTheRoad.

Published by Lonely Planet Global Limited
CRN 554153
9th edition – Dec 2018
ISBN 978 1 78657 072 7

10 9 8 7 6 5 4 3 2 1
Printed in China